Five Hundred Years of Printing

Jrit insipiens in corde suo: nõ
est deus, Corrupti sunt et ab-
hominabiles facti sũt i iniqui-
tatibȝ: non est qui fac bonũ,
Deus de celo prspexit sup filios hoïm: ut
videat si est intelligens aut requirens deũ,
Omnes declinauerũt simul inutiles facti
sũt: non est qui faciat bonũ nõ est usqȝ ad
vnũ Donne scient oẽs qui opant iniq̃-
tatem: qui deuorant plebem mea ut cibũ
panis Deũ non inuocaueri illic trepida-
uerũt timore vbi nõ erat timor, Qm̃ ds
dissipauit ossa eoȝ qui hominibȝ placent:
confusi sũt qm̃ ds spreuit eos Quis dabit
ex syon salutare isrl̃: cũ auterit ds captiuita-
tẽ plebis sue exultabit iacob et letabit̃ isrl̃,
Exaudi deus orationẽ meã et ne
despexeris deprecationẽ meã: intende
michi et exaudi me, Contristatus sũ in ex-
ercitacõne mea: et conturbatus sum a voce

The Mainz Psalter; the initials are printed in red. Fust & Schöffer, 1457. Victor Scholderer wrote in his *Fifty-five Essays* (Amsterdam, 1967) that this demonstrates 'typography going all out to show what it could do in rivalry of the copyists'. [G.12216]

Five Hundred Years of Printing

S. H. STEINBERG

NEW EDITION, REVISED BY
JOHN TREVITT

Typographia, ars artium omnium conservatrix

THE BRITISH LIBRARY
& OAK KNOLL PRESS
1996

First published in 1955 by Penguin Books as a Pelican Original

This revised edition published in 1996 jointly by Oak Knoll Press and The British Library

Published in the USA and its possessions and territories, Canada, Central and South America including Mexico by Oak Knoll Press, 414 Delaware Street, New Castle, DE 19720, USA. Distributed in the USA by Lyons & Burford, Publishers, 31 West 21 Street, New York, NY 10010

Published and exclusively distributed throughout the rest of the world by The British Library, Great Russell Street, London WC1B 3DG, UK

British Library Cataloguing in Publication Data is available from The British Library

Library of Congress Cataloging in Publication Data
Steinberg, S. H. (Sigfrid Henry), 1899-1969.
Five hundred years of printing / S. H. Steinberg ; revised by John Trevitt. — 4th ed.
    p.   cm.
This work, first published as a Pelican Original in 1955 and maintained in print in successive editions until 1980, is now available again. It has been completely revised and updated.
Includes bibliographical references and index.
ISBN 1-884718-19-1 (cloth : alk. paper). — ISBN 1-884718-20-5 (pbk. : alk. paper)
1. Printing—History. I. Trevitt, John, 1932- . II. Title.
Z124.S8   1996
686.2'09—dc20   96-12543   CIP

ISBN 1-884718-19-1 (Oak Knoll hardback)
ISBN 1-884718-20-5 (Oak Knoll paperback)
ISBN 0 7123 0414 2 (The British Library hardback)
ISBN 0 7123 0438 X (The British Library paperback)

Designed by John Trevitt
Typeset in Monotype Sabon 10/12 pt by Nene Phototypesetters, Northampton, UK
Printed in the United States of America

Cover illustration: A page from a copy of the Mainz Psalter, printed by Fust and Schöffer in 1457. Not only is this the earliest surviving printed book to carry both the name of the printer and the date of publication, but it is also the first book in which the initials and rubrics were printed in one and two colours together with the text in a single impression. All ten known copies are on vellum. [G.12216]

Contents

Reviser's preface

'These were the five hundred years of the Printer' – so wrote Beatrice Warde in 1955, at the beginning of her foreword to the first Penguin edition of this book – 'the centuries in which there was his way, but no other way, of broadcasting identical messages to a thousand or more people, a thousand or more miles apart.' Note the capital P: for Beatrice Warde printing was a way of life. But despite the characteristic hyperbole, and give or take half a century or so, she was right, for there was no threat to the monopoly of the printed word and picture until the 1920s and the arrival of broadcast radio. Forty more years have passed since 1955 and still there is nothing to suggest that the Printer is about to pass into history.

Sigfrid Henry Steinberg was born in Goslar in 1899. After serving briefly in the German army in 1918 he studied history, art history and German and English language and literature at the universities of Munich and Leipzig. In 1922 he took the degree of Ph.D. at Leipzig; his dissertation was entitled 'Das Urkunden Wesen des Goslarer Rates bis zur Mitte des 14. Jahrhunderts'. Subsequent employment included a spell with the publishing house of Brockhaus, where he worked on the illustration of reference books.

By 1934 Steinberg was beginning to feel uneasy about the direction in which Hitler and the Nazis were taking Germany, and to contemplate moving to England. This he achieved in 1936, when he was offered a research fellowship at the Courtauld Institute of Art in London. This enabled him to bring his family over to settle in England, where he threw himself into as much work as he could find, including giving evening classes in German, which resulted in *A One-Year German Course* (Macmillan). By 1939, when this was published, he had also signed an agreement with Macmillan for his *Historical Tables*. After a brief spell of internment in 1940 Steinberg sent yet another proposal to Macmillan, no less than a plan to modernize their German schoolbook list, and then spent several happy years as a schoolmaster at Sedbergh before ending the war as British liaison officer with the American Office of War Information. Despite being the first passenger in the history of British railways to be shot by a fog detonator, he became a naturalized British citizen and remained in Britain until his death in 1969.

'This was the epoch that we have been calling "modern times"', wrote Warde; and the invention of printing from movable types in Mainz in the early 1450s might well head any synoptic table of world events in the modern period. Steinberg edited the *Historical Tables* from first publication in 1939 up to its eighth edition in 1966, while simultaneously editing *The Statesman's Year-Book* (1946–69) and *Cassell's Encyclo-*

S. H. Steinberg, 1899–1969.

pedia of Literature (1953); writing *A Short History of Germany* (1944), *Five Hundred Years of Printing* (1955, second edition 1961), *Steinberg's Dictionary of British History* (1963) and *The 'Thirty Years War'* (1966); and working as an editor successively for *Chambers's Encyclopaedia* and Cassells. His widow Christine recorded in a note made after his death that 'S.H. never realized till he died that other people were not able or willing to work a 16 hours day as he often did himself'.

Steinberg had a lifelong interest in iconography, and we should love to have today one projected book which never appeared. At the outbreak of the Second World War in 1939 he had nearly finished a study of English portraiture for publication by the Royal Historical Society (of which he was later elected a Fellow). More important pre-occupations then supervened; eventually the typescript was lost. But at least we have *The Shorter Cambridge Medieval History* (1953), which is embellished with nearly three hundred illustrations chosen by him.

'You have a tidy mind,' he was told by the typographer-historian Stanley Morison (a rare compliment from one polymath to another), and so indeed he must have had. The two men knew each other well by 1939, when they collaborated with Bernhard Bischoff on the transcription and translation of *A Fifteenth Century Modus Scribendi from the Abbey of Melk*; better by 1951, when (Nicolas Barker tells us in his *Stanley Morison*) a collection of Morison's papers which had been destroyed in the blitz in 1941 and 'laboriously re-created' by Steinberg disappeared 'in still mysterious circumstances' at Cambridge; and very well indeed by 1963, when Steinberg was one of a distinguished group of scholars under Morison's command who put together the exhibition (and later the book) *Printing and the Mind of Man*. Before Morison's death in 1967 each had written the other's obituary for *The Times*, and Steinberg was later able to offer material help to Barker in the writing of *Stanley Morison*.

In 1940 Morison and Warde, then respectively Typographical Adviser and Publicity Manager to the Monotype Corporation, invited Steinberg to write (or contribute to – accounts differ) a special number of the *Monotype Recorder* devoted to the celebration of the 'fifth centennial of the invention of typography'. Warde wrote in her foreword to *Five Hundred Years* that 'what with the paper famine and the bombing, few copies survive' of this 12-page rarity, which 'contains the 30,000-word gist and promise of this present book' (it actually contains only about 15,000 words). In 1941 Steinberg discussed two ideas with Ellic Howe, himself a historian of 'the trade': one was 'an English counterpart to the *Archiv für Volksbindung*', entitled perhaps 'The Journal of Palaeographic and Typographic Studies', which alas we have never seen. The other idea was a history of printing, which seems also to have foundered at the time and did not re-surface until 1952 when Hans Schmoller, the typographer to Penguin Books, approached Steinberg, probably at Warde's instigation, to write a book about printing for them.

Steinberg's draft list of contents shows a thematic plan ('The title-page', 'The effect on languages', 'Libraries' and so on), each subject to be treated chronologically – very different from the final form of the book. He sent drafts of four of the proposed twelve chapters to Schmoller in 1953. In his response Schmoller advised against harbouring 'too low an opinion of the Pelican public's intelligence' and writing down; and commented on the brevity of the draft material, which amounted to only about 11,000 words, whereas the length of the average Pelican was then about 70–80,000 words. (In the event the book's three chapters made about 65,000 words.)

In 1958 a German edition of *Five Hundred Years* was published under the title *Die Schwarze Kunst* ('The Black Art', a resonant phrase in the cultural history of Europe) by Prestel-Verlag. Steinberg took advantage of this opportunity to correct some details that had been brought to his attention by reviewers and others, and made the same corrections to the English text for a demy 8vo hardback edition published by Faber & Faber in London and Criterion Books in New York in 1959. One criticism of the first edition of *Five Hundred Years* had been the surprising paucity of its illustrations; the German edition had many more, and Prestel made their blocks available to Penguin for the second, fully revised edition published in 1961. After Steinberg's death the late James Moran was asked to revise the text again; this third edition was published in 1974 and twice reprinted.

Altogether Penguin printed seven impressions, or at least 70,000 copies, of *Five Hundred Years* over some 24 years. As an accessible history of the book in the west it had no rival in English (Febvre and Martin's *L'Apparition du Livre* of 1958 was translated only in 1976), and beyond its interest for the 'general reader' it clearly established itself as recommended reading on many courses. On re-reading it after having been invited by The British Library to prepare a new edition I was – no doubt like most of its other readers – struck by its lightly-worn learning both deep and wide, by its early establishment of the invention of printing at the centre of modern history, and by a frequently-recurring feeling that on any and every subject the author knew far more than he had space to tell us.

The task of revision has been triply daunting. There is Steinberg's learning and knowledge (not quite synonymous). There is the fact that it is too soon to write with any certainty about the cultural history of the last 50 years. And there is the complex structure of the book, a generally chronological progression embracing thematic discussions and tempting digressions, which enabled Steinberg to dwell on the cultural implications of the work of publishers and printers at different times and in different places. I owe it to readers to explain how I have tried to deal with these difficulties, which have been simultaneously compounded and eased by my publishers' insistence on limiting the extent of the book to 272 pages.

I have ignored Moran's changes made for the third edition, which were not in any case either numerous or essential, and printed about 95 per cent of Steinberg's final text, the 1969 'revised reprint' of the second edition. Some of the comparison of book prices has lost its force after periods of high inflation and fluctuating currency-exchange rates, and has been omitted; and some discussion of newspapers, periodicals, libraries, censorship and classic reprint series has been shortened.

Despite its title, *Five Hundred Years* was not commissioned as 'merely' a history of printing technique. Nevertheless it has seemed useful to give (in chapter 3) some account of the invention and development of lithography, which Steinberg acknowledged in half a dozen words; and (in chapter 5) of the fundamental technical changes which have convulsed the printing trade since 1955. Authorship and book publishing have not exactly stood still since that date either, and certain developments with, probably, some significance for our cultural life can be summarized.

It would have been impertinent, not to say difficult, to alter the structure of this distillation of a lifetime's study, and in this respect I have limited myself to making three chapters out of Steinberg's third, which he entitled 'The nineteenth century and after', replacing his bibliography and enlarging his index. I have also expanded the discussion of illustration, of the British private presses and of printing in the United States of America.

No doubt the book contains errors, and since Henry Steinberg is regrettably unable to correct them I must claim them as my own. They are there despite the generous help I have received from John Mitchell, Eric Steinberg, Paul Wakeman and David Way, who read the typescript; James Mosley and Nigel Roche of St Bride's Printing Library, who read the bibliography; and Rowley Atterbury, Will Carter, Leonard Chave, Tom Colverson, Peter Foden, Steve Hare, Nick Lee, Paul Luna, Ruari McLean, John Paxton, Colin Randall, John Randle, Antony Rowe, Tanya Schmoller, Lloyd Spencer, Lawrence Wallis and Ella Whitehead, all of whom have been generous with their time and their advice. Above all I must thank my wife Jane (who has entertained Steinberg in her dining room for two years without complaint just as in 1956 Lady Eden reported the Suez Canal flowing through her drawing room) and David Way, Kathy Houghton and their colleagues at The British Library for constant encouragement and help.

All the illustrations are reduced in size and reproduce wherever possible the original margins. With a few exceptions, all are reproduced from books in The British Library, and their shelf-marks are cited in their captions. The unique Wynkyn de Worde *Morte Darthur* in the John Rylands Library, Manchester, is reproduced by kind permission of the Librarian. The Isaiah Thomas title-page is reproduced by courtesy of the American Antiquarian Society. The title-page of *The Whole Booke of Psalmes* is reproduced by courtesy of the Beinecke Rare Book and Manuscript Library, Yale University.

JT

Introduction

Discourse was deemed man's noblest attribute,
And written words the glory of his hand.
Then followed printing with enlarged command
For thought – dominion vast and absolute
For spreading truth and making love expand.
                                        – Wordsworth

The history of printing is an integral part of the general history of civilization. The principal vehicle for the conveyance of ideas during the past five hundred years, printing touches on, and often penetrates, almost every sphere of human activity. Neither political, constitutional, ecclesiastical and economic events, nor sociological, philosophical and literary movements can be fully understood without taking into account the influence which the printing press has exerted on them. As a business proposition the printing trade has its share in the economic development of all other branches of industry and commerce. Being based on a technical process, it is closely linked with the growth of the applied sciences. The history of printing types is but a side-issue. That is to say, the change of typefaces must be traced back to new needs necessitated, or new possibilities opened, by technical improvements; to commercial considerations on the part of printers or publishers; or, lastly, to sociological changes, including those of taste and fashion, on the part of the reading public.

As 'adventure and art' Gutenberg described his epoch-making invention in 1439; and 'adventure and art' have ever since remained the characteristic features of the printed book, from its inception in the mind of the author to the finished product in the bookseller's shop and on the book-lover's shelves.

The history of printing from movable types can roughly be divided into the following periods: (1) 1450–1550, the creative century, which witnessed the invention and beginnings of practically every single feature that characterizes the modern printing piece; (2) 1550–1800, the era of consolidation which developed and refined the achievements of the preceding period in a predominantly conservative spirit; (3) the nineteenth century, the era of mechanization which began with the invention of lithography and ended with Morris's rediscovery of the Middle Ages; (4) 1900–1950, the heyday of the private presses and the inception of paperbacks; and (5) the post-war world, which has seen typesetting, printing and publishing turned upside down, and reading surviving the onslaught of television.

SHS

Nemo cum prophetas versibus viderit esse descriptos me-
tro eos estimet apud he-
breos ligari: et aliquid si-
mile habere de psalmis
uel operibus salomonis. Sed quod in demostene z tullio solet fieri: ut per cola scribant et comata: qui u-
tiq; prosa et non versibus conscripserunt.
Nos quoq; utilitati legentium providentes:
interpretationem nouam nouo scribendi
genere distinximus. Ac primum de ysa-
ia sciendum op in sermone suo diserrus
sit: quippe ut vir nobilis z urbane ele-
gantie: nec habes quicquam in eloquio
rusticitatis ammixtum. Vnde accidit:
ut pre ceteris florem sermonis eius transla-
tio non potuerit conseruare. Deinde etiam
hoc adiciendum: op non tam propheta
dicendus sit op euangelista. Itaq; uni-
uersa xpi ecclesieq; misteria ad liqui-
dum prosecutus est: ut non eum putes de
futuro uaticinari: sed de preteritis historiam texere. Vnde conicio noluisse tunc
temporis septuaginta interpretes fidei
sue sacramenta ethnicis prodere
ne sanctum canibus · et margaritas por-
cis darent: que cum hanc editionem legen-
tis ab illis animaduerteritis abscondita.
Nec ignoro quanti laboris sit prophetas intelligere: nec facile quempiam
posse iudicare de interpretatione: nisi
intellexerit ante que legerit. Nos op pa-
tere morsibus plurimorum: qui stimulan-
te inuidia quod consequi non valent despi-
ciunt. Sciens ergo z prudens in flammam mit-
to manum: et nichilominus hoc a fastidi-
osis lectoribus precor: ut quomodo greci
post septuaginta translatores aquilam et
symachum z theodotione legunt · uel ob stu-
dium doctrine sue · uel ut septuaginta
magis ex collatione eorum intelligant:

sic z isti saltem unum post pores habere
dignentur interpretem. Legant prius · et po-
stea despiciant: ne videatur non ex iudicio · sed ex odii presumptione ignorata
damnare. Prophetauit autem ysaias in
iherusalem et in iudea needum decem tri-
bubus in captiuitatem ductis: ac de
utroq; regno nunc conmixti nunc separa-
tim texit oraculum. Et cum interdum ad
presentem respiciat historiam · z post ba-
bilonie captiuitate reditum populi signifi-
cet in iudeam: tamen omnis eius cura de
uocatione gentium et de aduentu xpi est.
Que quanto plus amatis o paula et
eustochium: tanto magis ab eo petite:
ut per obtrectatione presentium qua me inde-
sinenter emuli laniat: ipse michi merce-
dem restituat in futuro: qui scit me ob
hoc in peregrine lingue eruditione su-
dasse · ne iudei de falsitate scriptura-
rum ecclesiis eius diutius insultarent.

Explicit prologus · incipit ysaias propheta ·

Visio ysaie filii amos: quam
uidit super iudam et iherusalem in diebus ozie ioa-
than achaz z ezechie regum
iuda. Audite celi et auribus percipe tea:
qui dominus locutus est. Filios enutriui et
exaltaui: ipsi autem spreuerunt me. Cognouit bos possessorem suum: z asinus presepe
domini sui. Israel autem me non cognouit:
et populus meus non intellexit. Ve genti
peccatrici: populo graui iniquitate · semi-
ni nequam: filiis sceleratis. Dereliquerunt
dominum: blasphemauerunt sanctum israel: ab-
alienati sunt retrorsum. Super quo percu-
tiam vos ultra: addentes preuaricati-
onem? Omne caput languidum: z omne
cor merens. A planta pedis usq; ad verti-
cem · non est in eo sanitas. Vulnus z
liuor · et plaga tumens: non est circum-
ligata nec curata medicamine: neq;

The 42-line Bible. The headline and initials were inserted by a scribe. Gutenberg, Mainz, 1452–6.
[C.9.d.4]

CHAPTER I

The first century of printing
1450–1550

1. THE INCUNABULA PERIOD

All historical periods are makeshift expedients: people did not go to bed in the Middle Ages and wake up in modern times. Few of these arbitrary breaks, however, can have been more detrimental to a real understanding of an important section of human progress than the restriction of the term *incunabula* to the time from Gutenberg's first production to 31 December 1500. This date cuts right across the most fertile period of the new art, dividing the lives of some of its greatest practitioners such as Anton Koberger (1445–1513), Aldus Manutius (1450–1515), Anthoine Vérard (d. 1512), Johannes Froben (1460–1527), Henry Estienne (1460–1520) and Geofroy Tory (1480–1533).

The word *incunabula* was first used in connection with printing by Bernard von Mallinckrodt, dean of Münster cathedral, in a tract, *De ortu et progressu artis typographicae* (Cologne, 1639), which he contributed to the celebration of the second centenary of Gutenberg's invention. Here he describes the period from Gutenberg to 1500 as 'prima typographiae incunabula', the time when typography was in its swaddling-clothes. The French Jesuit, Philippe Labbé, in his *Nova bibliotheca librorum manuscriptorum* (1653), already equated the word *incunabula* with the 'period of early printing up to 1500'.

The particular interest of the incunabula period long persuaded research workers to concentrate on the fifteenth century to the grievous neglect of the early sixteenth century. Thus the impression was created that the turn of the century signified the end of one and the beginning of another era in the history of printing, publishing and the trade in general. Nothing can be farther from the truth.

The main characteristics which make a unit of the second half of the fifteenth and the first half of the sixteenth centuries are these: the functions of typefounder, printer, publisher, editor and bookseller are little differentiated; the same man or the same firm usually combines all or most of these crafts or professions. Claude Garamond of Paris (d. 1561) and Jacob Sabon of Lyon and (from 1571) Frankfurt were the first to gain fame for specializing in type-designing, punch-cutting and type-founding, while Robert Estienne (d. 1559) consummated the era of the great printer-scholars. Moreover, by 1540 printing and publishing had barely outgrown the restlessness of the early practitioners to whom knowledge of the craft and an adventurous spirit had sufficed to set up shop anywhere and to move about with the ease permitted by a small equipment and a smaller purse. The number of printers was increasing, but the day of the small itinerant man had passed. Printing, publishing and bookselling had become established industries requiring stability and capital and foresight. The

German Diet of 1570 tried (in vain, of course) only to put into a legal straitjacket what had become an economic fact when it limited the setting up of printing presses to the capitals of princely states, university towns and the larger imperial cities, and ordered all other printing establishments to be suppressed. For by this time business concentration had advanced so far that the French book trade can almost be equated to that of Paris, Lyon and Geneva; the Italian to that of Venice, Rome and Florence: that of the Low Countries to Antwerp, Amsterdam and Leiden, while the edict of the German Diet faithfully reflects the anomalous conditions prevailing in the Holy Roman Empire.

From the typographical point of view, too, the first half of the sixteenth century is still part and parcel of the creative 'incunabula' period, with its wealth of different types. The italics of Antonio Blado and the roman letters of Claude Garamond – both cut about 1540 – still show the forceful imagination of the pioneer type-designers. From that time onward, experiments with new types were rather frowned upon; for instance, the excellent cursive gothic which Joachim Louw cut in Hamburg about 1550 came too late to find acceptance, so that every gothic type-face has been confined to one set of letters – a contributory factor for its disappearance in favour of 'Latin' faces with their 'roman' and 'italic' alternatives.

In the middle of the sixteenth century the geography of printing also underwent a change. Both Germany and Italy ceased to be of much importance in the printing and publishing world; France entered upon her heyday of fine printing and publishing; and Christophe Plantin, a Frenchman by birth, inaugurated the golden age of Netherlandish book production. The charter granted to the Stationers' Company in London (1557) may be taken as an outward sign that by then the shades of restrictive planning had fallen across the path of hitherto unfettered expansion.

2. GUTENBERG

The available evidence about the invention of printing with movable types cast from matrices is unfortunately less conclusive than might be wished; but the following facts may be considered well established.

Johann Gensfleisch zum Gutenberg (born between 1394 and 1399), a Mainz goldsmith of a patrician family, began experimenting with printing work towards 1440 when he was a political exile at Strasbourg. At that time other people too were engaged in discovering some method of producing an 'artificial script', as it was called. Avignon, Bruges and Bologna are mentioned as places where such experiments were carried out, and the names of a goldsmith and a book-illuminator who thus tried their hands are extant. The general climate of the age was undoubtedly propitious for Gutenberg's achievement. He returned to Mainz between 1444 and 1448 and by 1450 had perfected his invention far enough to exploit it commercially. For this purpose he borrowed 800 guilders from the Mainz lawyer, Johannes Fust. In 1452 Fust advanced another 800 guilders and at the same time secured for himself a partnership in the 'production of books'. In 1455, however, the financier foreclosed on the inventor. The bulk of Gutenberg's presses and types went to Peter Schöffer of Gernsheim, who was in Fust's service and later married his daughter (and her dowry). Another printer of unknown name obtained a number of inferior types with which he printed calendars, papal bulls, Latin grammars, and similar works. Gutenberg himself seems to have saved very little from the wreck of his fortune – perhaps only one or two presses and the type in which the 42-line and 36-line Bibles and the *Catholicon* were printed – but may have continued in business for a further ten years. However, after 1460 he seems to have abandoned printing – possibly because of blindness. He suffered further loss in the sack of Mainz in 1462 but received a kind of pension from the archbishop in 1465. He died on 3 February 1468 and was buried in the Franciscan church which was pulled down in 1742. A humanist relation later dedicated an epitaph 'to the immortal memory of Johannes Gensfleisch, the inventor of the art of printing, who has deserved well of every nation and language'.

The *Catholicon*, compiled by Johannes Balbus of Genoa in the thirteenth century, deserves mention for three reasons. Its type is about a third smaller than that of the 42-line Bible; it is therefore considerably more economical and thus marks an important step towards varying as well as cheapening book-production by the careful choice of type. Secondly, the *Catholicon* was a popular encyclopedia, and its publication pointed the way towards a main achievement of the art of printing, namely the spread of knowledge. Lastly, the book contains a colophon which it is difficult to believe to have been written by anybody but the inventor of printing himself. It therefore affords the solitary, precious glimpse of his mind; it reads:

Colophon of the *Catholicon*, possibly printed by Gutenberg, Mainz, 1460. [G.11966]

With the help of the Most High at whose will the tongues of infants become eloquent and who often reveals to the lowly what he hides from the wise, this noble book *Catholicon* has been printed and accomplished without the help of reed, stylus or pen but by the wondrous agreement, proportion and harmony of punches and types, in the year of the Lord's incarnation 1460 in the noble city of Mainz of the renowned German nation, which God's grace has deigned to prefer and distinguish above all other nations of the earth with so lofty a genius and liberal gifts. Therefore all praise and honour be offered to thee, holy Father, Son and Holy Spirit, God in three persons; and thou, Catholicon, resound the glory of the church and never cease praising the Holy Virgin. Thanks be to God.

No book or other printed work bearing the name of Gutenberg survives (if indeed any such ever existed), and only one major work can confidently be called a product of his workshop – the 42-line ('Mazarin') Bible which was set up from 1452 and published before August 1456. The oldest European piece printed from movable metal types may be the surviving fragment of a German poem known as the *Sibyllenbuch*, which is set in type similar to that used for the 36-line Bible (which was printed between about 1458 and 1461, and like the 42-line Bible is set in double column). Various dates have been suggested for this fragment, the earliest 1442, the latest perhaps twelve years later. The earliest dated typographical documents are two editions of an indulgence set in type associated with Gutenberg; some copies are dated 1454, others 1455.

There is no doubt that Peter Schöffer was superior to Gutenberg as a typographer and printer; the quality of his work made amends for the equivocal practices which allowed him to reap where he had not sown. What is perhaps Gutenberg's greatest claim to fame is the fact that, after the early experimental stage of which we know nothing, he reached a state of technical efficiency not materially surpassed until the beginning of the nineteenth century. Punch-cutting, matrix-fitting, type-casting, composing and printing remained, in principle, for more than three centuries where they were in Gutenberg's time. Some remarkable technical improvements of the press suggested by Leonardo da Vinci were never put to the test. The only advance of any significance in that period was made about 1620 by the Dutchman, Willem Janszoon Blaeu, who somewhat extended the efficiency and printing area of the screw-and-lever press; but no journeyman of Gutenberg and Schöffer would have found any difficulty in operating Blaeu's press (which, moreover, never became widely known). Until the end of the eighteenth century Gutenberg's original design was still regarded as the 'common' press.

To nine out of every ten readers the sentence that 'Gutenberg invented printing' is a shortened form of 'Gutenberg invented the printing of books'. The inevitable association of Gutenberg's name with the 42-line Bible tends to strengthen this fallacy. For it is not – certainly not primarily – the mechanical production of books which has made Gutenberg's invention a turning point in the history of civilization.

Books were printed before Gutenberg, and there is no reason why printing from wood-blocks, engraved metal plates, drawings or photographs on stone, and other media should not have gone on with ever greater refinement – as it has actually done. The books 'printed' by William Blake, and now phototypesetting, come readily to mind as examples of printing without movable type. What was epoch-making in Gutenberg's process was the possibility of editing and correcting a text which was then (at least in theory) identical in every copy: in other words, mass production preceded by critical proof-reading.

Moreover, it was not the production of books that was revolutionized by the use of movable types or its application to the machine-made edition. In fact, printed books were at first hardly distinguishable from manuscripts, and the title-page is virtually the one feature which printers have added to the products of the scribes – and one which scribes, too, would sooner or later have hit upon, as did the Florentine bookseller Vespasiano da Bisticci. It is in two vastly different spheres that Gutenberg has changed the aspect of reading matter in its widest sense. When he and Fust preceded and accompanied their great adventure of book-printing with the issue of indulgences, calendars and pamphlets on ephemeral topics, the proto-typographers created what came to be known as job-printing. With it they laid the foundations of modern publicity through the printed word, which is dependent on the identical mass production of freely combinable letter-units in almost infinite variety of composition – the very characteristics of Gutenberg's invention.

At the same time, when Gutenberg made it feasible to put on the market a large number of identical copies at any given time, he thereby foreshadowed the possibility of ever increasing the number of copies and ever reducing the length of time needed for their issue. The principle once established, it was a matter of technical progress to develop the turning out of ten thousand identical indulgences within a month into the turning out of a million identical newspapers within a few hours. Thus Gutenberg can be acclaimed also as the progenitor of the periodical press.

Again, while it is easy to say that 'Gutenberg invented printing', it requires a long treatise to say what actually constituted Gutenberg's 'invention'. Down to Moxon's *Mechanick Exercises*, that is to say, for 250 years, the literary allusions to the 'mystery' are vague or ambiguous, and illustrations of printers at work are rarely accurate about technical details. The only tangible sources therefore are the products of Gutenberg's press, from which the process by which he achieved them must be inferred.

In order to remove popular misunderstandings, we may perhaps proceed by a series of negative propositions.

Gutenberg was not the first to grasp the need for, and the potentialities of, large-scale production of literature. On the contrary, his invention was prompted largely by the fact that the multiplication of texts was not only a general want but had also, by the middle of the fifteenth century, become a recognized and lucrative trade. Professional scribes catered for the wealthy collector of classical manuscripts as well as for the poor student who needed his legal and theological handbooks. Vespasiano da Bisticci employed up to fifty scribes at a time; literacy was spreading and universities were flourishing, and in the university towns, of which Paris was the most important, the copyists of learned texts were numerous enough to form themselves into guilds. The religious congregation of the Brethren of the Common Life in Deventer specialized in copying philosophical and theological books for which they established a market all over northern Europe. Diebold Lauber ran a veritable book factory in the Alsatian town of Hagenau; he, like any later publisher, produced books for the open market; 'light reading' was Lauber's speciality, and illustrations, also produced by rote, added to the popular appeal.

Nor was 'printing' from a negative relief surface a new invention. The Chinese had practised it for about a thousand years (the legendary date of its inception is A.D. 594), and their method of hammering or rubbing off impressions from a wood-block had spread along the caravan routes to the west, where block-prints and block-books expressive of popular piety were well known at the time of Gutenberg. The oldest known block-prints ('xylographica') bear the dates of 1418 and 1423. Block-books were made up from single sheets, and block-printing survived well into the age of letterpress, until about 1480. The *Biblia pauperum* in which related scenes from the Old and New Testaments are accompanied by brief expository verses in Latin and the vernacular, is perhaps the best-known example of the block-book.

From China, too, had come the invention of paper, which was to prove the ideal surface for printing. Vellum, it is true, was (and still is) occasionally used for luxury printing; but paper has the advantage over vellum of being available in virtually unlimited quantities and thus allows mass production, the distinguishing feature of printing.

Again, Gutenberg followed precedent when he replaced wood by metal, and the block by the individual letter. In this respect he stood in the tradition of his own trade of goldsmith, for goldsmiths and kindred artisans had always cut punches for their trade-marks or the lettering with which they struck inscriptions on cups, bells, seals and other metalware.

Gutenberg also found at hand an instrument suitable for compressing and flatten-ing a moist and pliable substance (such as printing paper), namely the wine-press which the Romans had introduced in his native Rhineland a thousand years earlier. The principles of textile printing, which had been practised in the Rhineland for centuries, suggested new methods of reproducing words and pictures. Letterpress printing was in the air, else Gutenberg's invention would not have spread with such lightning speed through the Rhine towns.

Gutenberg's achievement, then, lies first in the scientific synthesis of all these different trends and trials. He fulfilled the need of the age for more and cheaper read-ing matter by substituting machinery for handicraft. Drawing on the technical ex-perience of the writing-master, the wood-engraver and the metal-worker, he produced movable types which could be combined at will. Here at last comes the point where we can speak of at least two genuine inventions made by Gutenberg. Types had to be available in large numbers even for the setting of a single sheet; they would be re-quired by the thousand for the composition of a whole book. How could they be multiplied from the one model produced by the letter-designer and punch-cutter? Gutenberg overcame this difficulty by applying the principle of replica-casting. A single letter, engraved in relief and struck or sunk into a slab of brass would provide the intaglio or 'matrix' (female die) of that letter in reverse; from this matrix any number of mechanical replicas of that letter could be cast by pouring molten lead into it. The replica-letters, the types, had to be cast with a long enough shank to permit finger and thumb to grasp them securely while they were being fitted together into words and lines. Whatever character was being cast, this shank or 'body' had to be of precisely the same length, so that the composed lines and columns of type, stand-ing on the level bed of the press, would present a uniformly flat printing surface. It is not certain how far Gutenberg himself developed the principle of the typecaster's 'mould' – the instrument of which the two interlocking parts provide an orifice roughly an inch deep, sealed at one end by the intaglio matrix, open at the other end for the molten metal, and adjustable to any specific width of letter from broad W to narrow I. Tradition assigns its invention to Schöffer. But Gutenberg, before he arrived in Mainz and joined forces with Fust and Schöffer, must have worked out some prac-ticable method of replica-casting from matrices unlimited quantities of metal types that would combine in optical alignment to create a level composite printing surface. In doing so he had not only established the main principle of letterpress printing and, in T. L. de Vinne's words, 'invented typography', but also introduced to Europe, more than three centuries ahead of its general adoption by industry, the 'theory of inter-changeable parts' which is the basis of all modern mass-manufacturing technique.

Gutenberg's second invention, without which printing as we understand it would have been impossible, was the preparation of an ink which had to adhere to the metal types and therefore would have chemical properties very different from those of the ink with which impressions were taken from wood-blocks.

The process by which the Rhenish vintners' wine-press was transformed into a printing-press cannot be reconstructed with certainty. The first circumstantial report on the art of printing, which Koelhoff embodied in his *Chronicle of Cologne* (1499), pays scant attention to technicalities. Dürer's drawing of 1511, one of the earliest views, is not considered by technical experts to be quite accurate; it was probably drawn from memory after a visit to the office of his godfather Anton Koberger. In any case, while the productions of the early presses are still living objects of pleasure and instruction, the wooden screw-and-lever press has become a museum piece. To modern eyes, accustomed to the sight of power-driven printing machines, it seems a slow and cumbersome instrument. Its working required a great amount of muscular force; the pull and weight of the machine made presswork toilsome; the area of the forme was very small and so necessitated repeated readjustments of the sheets. But it sufficed for its day, and for the then limited section of the public that could read its product; and presses of Gutenberg's kind remained in use without any very radical improvement for more than three centuries.

However, as these very products continuously enlarged the number of literate people, the old press eventually became incapable of coping with the demand it had created. It was thus the principal agent in superseding itself.

3. TYPE-DESIGN

After the sacking of Mainz in 1462 printers followed the trade-routes of Europe, particularly those leading south, and within fifteen years after Gutenberg's death in 1468 printing-presses had been set up in every country of western Christendom from Sweden to Sicily and from Spain to Poland and Hungary. Less than a century later, in the middle of the sixteenth century, the western comity of nations had made up their minds as to the outward form in which they wanted to have printing matter presented to them. Whereas it is possible to examine country by country the intellectual contributions made to European civilization by the printers of each nation, the development of type-design was intrinsically a supra-national affair; it is therefore surveyed briefly in chronological order.

It was the penetration of western Europe by the spirit of humanism that brought about the victory of 'roman' and 'italic' types; and it was the resistance to the spirit of humanism that made the Germans, Russians and Turks cling to the isolationism of the Fraktur, Cyrillic and Arabic types. The transition to the 'Latin' alphabet by the Germans and Turks is a major step towards the unity of world civilization; just as the refusal of post-Lenin Russia to abandon the Cyrillic letter is a significant omen of the deep cleavage between East and West.

In outward appearance books printed between 1450 and 1480 are almost indistinguishable from contemporary manuscripts. Just as the early printers printed mainly those texts which were already favourite medieval reading material (Bibles and commentaries, liturgical and devotional works, classics, fables and chivalric romances) and made their printed products resemble handwritten books as closely as possible, so they took over virtually the whole range of scripts used in mid-fifteenth-century Europe: the *textura* of liturgical works, the *bastarda* of legal texts, the *rotunda* and *gothico-antiqua*, both Italian compromises between Carolingian and late-medieval scripts, the formal *lettera anticha* and the cursive *cancelleresca* favoured by Italian humanists, and so on. Neither manuscript nor printed book had a title-page or page numbers; when coloured initials and other illustrations were wanted, they had to be inserted by a specialist other than the scribe or printer. The same material, from the roughest to the finest paper and from the coarsest to the smoothest parchment, was used for the same sizes which had become fairly settled, with quarto and folio easily leading.

Why did the printers thus follow so closely the scribes? It is sometimes said that they wished to deceive the public by making their 'substitute' look as near as possible like the 'real' thing. The true explanation, however, is to be found in the attitude of the consumer rather than the producer. Extreme conservatism as to the presentation of reading matter has always been the outstanding characteristic of the reading public. 'The typography of books requires an obedience to convention which is almost absolute'; and 'for a new fount to be successful, it has to be so good that only very few recognize its novelty' – these are among the 'first principles of typography' as abstracted by Stanley Morison from the study of five centuries of printing. The same rules apply to the shape of individual letters and to the look of a whole page or an opening. William Morris would have been deeply mortified, had he but known it, that a contemporary of Gutenberg or Caxton would hardly have recognized a product of the Kelmscott Press as a 'book' but more likely have marvelled at it as a kind of purposeless curio. A book which, in some way or other, is 'different', ceases to be a book and becomes a collector's piece or museum exhibit, to be looked at, perhaps admired, but certainly left unread; the fate of most productions of private presses.

The incunabula printers were artisans and craftsmen, without any of the arty-crafty ambitions or illusions that haunted English, French and German 'reformers' from 1880 to 1910. In other words, while they were proud – and justifiably proud – of the quality of their handiwork, they had to make their living by it and therefore sell goods which their customers would be willing to buy. The regularity of each letter, the compactness of each line, the closely woven pattern of each page, comparable to a latticed gothic window or an oriental carpet – these rather than clarity and legibility were the effects which a well-trained scribe sought to produce. The printer unhesitatingly accepted this convention. The lawyer who needed a copy of the Decretals knew exactly what the Decretals ought to look like because he had handled it all his life. Schöffer's, Richel's, Wenssler's, Koberger's or Grüninger's editions, with the commentary printed on the margins round the text, without spacing or leading, teeming with ligatures and abbreviations, without title-page, table of contents, or index – these a fifteenth-century lawyer would instantly have been familiar with, whereas any modern annotated *Codex juris canonici*, with footnotes and appendices, would have left him completely bewildered. The wish to make a printed book look like a handwritten one has by no means become extinct, but it must now be regarded as a romantic aberration rather than a legitimate variety of the printer's craft.

It was the recognition of the basic difference between the effects created by the metal-worker and those produced by the quill-driver which brought about the victory of the punch-cutter over the scribe and with it the supersession of the imitation-manuscript by the authentic book. By 1480 the second generation of printers had become conscious of the intrinsic autonomy of their craft.

It is precisely in the lucid arrangement of a given text that the printers have achieved the greatest advantage over the scribes. The value of an accurate and uniform text made possible by the printing press has already been alluded to. This gain is enhanced further by the skilful use of graduated types, running heads at the top and footnotes at the bottom of a page, tables of contents at the beginning and indexes at the end of a tract, superior figures, cross-references, and other devices available to the compositor – all identical and therefore quotable by any reader. They are so many aids to the easier understanding not only of scholarly treatises but even more of time-tables, dictionaries, travel guides, manuals of every description, and much else.

An important by-product of this development was the gradual reduction of the contents of the compositor's case. Gutenberg used nearly three hundred different letters, ligatures and abbreviations. These have now been brought down to about forty in the 'lower case' and even fewer in the 'upper case': the surviving ligatures are restricted to ff, fi, fl, ffi, ffl, æ, œ (and, as is evident here, not always all of these); and the ampersand & is the sole existent abbreviation.

Handwriting, type-founding and printing were discussed together in the *Dialogues pour les jeunes enfans* which Plantin published in 1567. The author, Jacques Grévin, first talks about penmanship with the writing-master Pierre Hamon, and then about the tools and procedure of the printing shop with a second interlocutor, 'E.', who may be Robert Estienne or the Dutch type-founder Laurens van Everbroeck. Although the usefulness of the booklet for 'young children' of any period may be doubted, it still makes pleasant reading for any printer who wants to sample the flavour of sixteenth-century craftsmanship.

Within about 50 years after Gutenberg's death the original profusion of types had sorted itself out into two streams: on the one hand, the 'antiqua' founts of 'roman' and 'italics'; on the other, the 'gothic' founts of 'Fraktur' and 'Schwabacher'. All these names are fanciful inventions of later writers. In fact, roman types were cut first in Strasbourg in 1467 and brought to perfection in Venice by the Frenchman Nicolas Jenson, in 1470. The origin of italics is the cursive humanist script which was made serviceable for printing by the punch-cutter Francesco Griffo, who worked for Aldus Manutius in Venice about 1500, and the script of the Papal chancery which was adjusted to printing by the Roman writing-master Ludovico Arrighi and the Roman printer Antonio Blado in about 1520. Fraktur grew out of the various types used all over Europe during the fifteenth century. Its English name 'gothic' still points to this origin, whereas the French term *caractères allemands* alludes to the fact that it received its final form in Augsburg and Nürnberg about 1510–20. Schwabacher, also one of the many gothic types then in use, appears from about 1480 in Nürnberg, Mainz and elsewhere; it certainly did not originate in the little Franconian town of Schwabach.

Roman type

The victory of the 'antiqua' type over its 'gothic' rival was mainly due to the business genius of the printer Aldus Manutius. He was backed, it is true, by the powerful tradition in which his most influential customers had been brought up since the days of the Florentine humanists, Coluccio Salutati, Poggio and Niccolò Niccoli. They had established the principle that the 'littera antiqua' was the proper medium for the transmission of ancient texts.

It was therefore quite natural that the very first book printed in Italy should appear in a type which more nearly approximated the 'round hand' of the Renaissance scribes than the gothic textura of the Mainz printers: for it was a classical text, Cicero's *De oratore*, printed by Sweynheym and Pannartz in Subiaco, 1465. ('The printers of [this] Cicero intended it to correspond with the style that readers of Cicero had then for twenty years at least been … securing from their scribes. The Cicero type … is one of the most noble of that or any other day' – Morison.) Similarly, the first printers in

uolunt dicere.Res eñi hoc poſtulat.ut eoɼ expectationi qui
audiũt q̃ celerrime occuratur: cui ſi ɩ́nitio ſatiſfactũ non ſit:
multo plus ſit ɩ́n reliqua cauſa laboradũ. Male eñi ſe res
habet quę non ſtatim ut dici cepta eſt: melior fieri uidetur.
Ego ut ɩ́n oratore optimus quiſq̃ eſt: ſic ɩ́n oratone firmiſſimũ
qdq̃ ſit p̃mum: dum illud tamẽ ɩ́n utroq̃ teneatur ut ea quę
excellunt ſeruẽtur etiã ad porandum ſi quę erũt mediocria:
Nam uitioſis nuſq̃ eſſe oportet locũ: ɩ́n mediam turbã atq̃ ɩ̃
gregem coniciũtur.Hiſce omnidus rebus conſideratis.tum
deniq̃ id quod p̃mũ eſt dicendum: poſtremo ſoleo cogitare
quo utar exordio: Nam ſi quãdo id p̃mum ɩ́nuenire uolui
nullũ mihi occurrit.niſi aut exile aut nugatoriũ: aut uulga-
re: aut cõe.Principia aũt dicẽdi ſemp cum accurata et acuta
et ɩ́nſtructa ſententiis apta uerbis: tum uero cauſarũ ‚ppria
eſſe debẽt.Prima eſt ei quaſi cognitio & cõmendatio orationis
ɩ́n principio.quęq̃ continuo eum qui audit permulcere atq̃
allicere debet: ɩ́n qua admirari ſoleo non ęquidem iſtos qui
nullam huic rei operã dederũt: ſed hoiem ɩ́n p̃mis diſertum
atq̃ eruditum philippum: qui ita ſolet ad dicendũ ſurgere:
ut quod p̃mũ uerbum habiturus ſit neſciat: et ait idem cum
brachiũ concalefecerit: tũ ſe ſolere pugnare: Neq̃ attendit
eos ipſos.unde hoc ſimile ducat: illas p̃mas iactare haſtas
ita leniter ut & uenuſtati uel maxie ſeruiant et reliq̃s uiri-
bus ſuis conſulant: nec eſt dubiũ quin exordium dicẽdi ue-
hemẽs & pugnax nõ ſepe eſſe debeat.Sed ſi ɩ́n ipo illo gla-
diatorio uitę certamine: quo ferro decernitur: tamen ante
congreſſum multa fiunt: quę non ad uulnus: ſed ad ſpeciem
ualere uideãtur: q̃to hoc magis ɩ́n oratone ſpectandũ: ɩ́n qua
non uis potius: ſed delectano poſtulatur: Nihil eſt deniq̃ ɩ̃
natura rerũ oïum quod ſe uniuerſum ‚pfundat.et qd totum

Cicero, *De oratore*. Sweynheym & Pannartz, Subiaco, 1465. [C.19.d.10]

Eusebius, *De evangelica praeparatione*. Nicolas Jenson, Venice, 1470. [C.14.c.2]

France used an antiqua fount, for their employers, two dons of the Sorbonne, wanted to utilize the printing press for the spread of humanism, and an instruction in the art of elegant Latin composition, Gasparinus Barzizius's *Epistolarum libri*, was the first text printed in Paris (1470). Sweynheym and Pannartz's round type, in the slightly varied form it was given by the Roman printer Ulrich Han, remained popular with Roman presses for a long time, until this roman of a German typographer was ousted by the Venetian roman of the Frenchman, Nicolas Jenson. (It was, however, pleasant enough to cause St John Hornby, a fastidious typographer, to revive it for his Ashendene Press in 1902.)

Jenson, one of the greatest type-designers of all time, cut his roman fount for the printing of a Roman text, Cicero's *Epistolae ad Brutum* (1470). Born about 1420 at Sommevoire near Troyes, Jenson was a die-cutter by profession, and is said to have been sent by Charles VII to Mainz to spy out the new mystery of printing – an early instance of industrial espionage. It seems certain that he actually learned printing in Germany, perhaps in Mainz, before he settled in Venice shortly before 1470; he was in any case the first non-German printer of whom we know. We may no longer share the exaggerated enthusiasm of William Morris, who maintained that 'Jenson carried the development of roman type as far as it can go', but the strength and nobility of this first true roman at once set the highest standard for every subsequent roman face. However, Jenson himself later reverted to the use of gothic types (and very fine they are) in, for example, *Gratianum decretum* (1474); and vernacular printing matter continued for a while even in Italy and France to be composed in non-antiqua founts. The gothic cursive, called *lettre bâtarde*, designed in Paris in 1476, remained for some decades the type normally used for French texts.

The turn of the tide came with the publications of Aldus Manutius. He was extremely fortunate in his choice of type-designer, Francesco Griffo of Bologna. Above all, Griffo supplied a novel fount which Jenson had not thought of. It was based on the 'cancelleresca corsiva' of the papal chancery, which humanists had taken over for their informal writing, and later received the name of 'italics'. (It is pleasant to find that the Spaniards call it *letra grifa*.) It proved to be the ideal companion, in print as it had been in handwriting, to the formal roman type. Griffo also cut several founts of the latter; these are particularly important in that Griffo went for his models beyond the hands of humanist scribes (who had mistaken the Carolingian script for a product of the classical era) to the inscriptional lettering of imperial Rome. Griffo's most satisfactory roman founts are his first – used initially for Pietro Bembo's *De Aetna*, 1495 – and third – used for the curious *Hypnerotomachia Poliphili* in 1499. Both these types exerted their fascination on successive generations of typographers from Simon de Colines and Robert Estienne in the sixteenth century to van Dyck and Grandjean in the seventeenth, Caslon in the eighteenth, and Stanley Morison in the twentieth century. Morison indeed identified the *De Aetna* type as marking 'a new era in typography' and the book itself as 'in important respects ... the first "modern" book'.

But the typographical qualities of Griffo's founts would hardly have had the effect of finally ousting black-letter as well as Jenson's roman types, had they not been sponsored by the greatest publisher of the time. Aldus Manutius chose Griffo's italic for his popular series of classical authors, not because it was beautiful but because it suited his commercial intentions in that it was condensed and narrow and therefore made the most economic use of the type area.

Backed by the international prestige of the printer-publisher Aldus, there was henceforth no doubt that antiqua was to be the common European type. As in the sixteenth century France took over from Italy the leading role in typography, it was of importance that French printers should presently adopt the Aldine pattern even for the printing of Books of Hours and other liturgical works for which the medieval textura had been customary longest. Thielmann Kerver, tentatively, and Geofroy Tory, as a matter of principle, took this decisive step.

Tory (1480–1533) crowned his work as a practising printer by writing the first theoretical treatise on the designing of types, *Champ-fleury* (1529). He was rewarded by François I with the title of *Imprimeur du roi* (1530). Tory also advocated the use of the accent, apostrophe and cedilla in French printing, and was a poet in his own right and an able translator from the Greek. He effected very quickly the change from gothic type and decoration to the roman type which took almost 200 years in England. An additional claim to glory has now been disproved; it was not Tory, but the Parisian printer Antoine Augereau (d. 1534), to whom Claude Garamond was apprenticed in 1510 and who thus became the teacher of one of the greatest type-founders. Augereau, who cut his own roman types, and also romans for Simon de Colines, must be given great credit for the leading role taken by Paris in the assimilation and export of Aldine typographic design.

LA MVLTITVDINE DEGLI AMANTI GIOVENI, ET
DILLE DIVE AMOROSE PVELLE LA NYMPHA APOLI
PHILO FACVNDAMENTE DECHIARA, CHI FVRO-
NO ET COME DAGLI DII AMATE. ET GLI CHORI DE
GLI DIVI VATI CANTANTI VIDE.

LCVNO MAI DI TANTO INDEFESSO ELO
quio aptamente se accommodarebbe, che gli diuini ar
chani disertando copioso & pienamente potesse euade
re & uscire. Et expressamente narrare, & cum quanto di
ua pompa, indesinenti Triumphi, perenne gloria, festi
ua lætitia, & fœlice tripudio, circa a queste quatro iuisi
tate seiuge de memorando spectamine cum parole sufficientemente ex-
primere ualesse. Oltra gli inclyti adolescentuli & stipante agmine di inu-
mere & periucunde Nymphe, piu che la tenerecia degli anni sui elle pru-
dente & graue & astutule cum gli acceptissimi amanti de pubescente
& depile gene. Ad alcuni la primula lanugine splendescéte le male in-
serpiua delitiose alacremente festigiauano. Molte hauendo le facole sue
accense & ardente. Alcune uidi Pastophore. . Altre cum drite haste
adornate de prische spolie. Et tali di uarii Trophæi optimaméte ordinate

Francesco Colonna (?), *Hypnerotomachia Poliphili*. Aldus Manutius, Venice, 1499. [86.k.9]

Garamond (1480–1561) was the first to confine himself to the designing, cutting and casting of types, which hitherto had formed part of the printer's training and profession. Garamond was not himself a printer, but from 1531 onward he created a series of roman founts (commissioned and first used by the publishing firm of Estienne) which influenced the style of French printing down to the end of the eighteenth century. He was probably also the designer of the later italic types used by Simon de Colines: these owed their origins to Arrighi in place of Colines's earlier Aldine italics. Garamond's influence throughout Europe was immense.

Robert Granjon was the son of a Paris printer and himself combined the professions of punch-cutter, founder, printer and publisher. From 1556 to 1562 he lived in Lyon, having previously supplied the Lyonese printer de Tournes with various founts. For his own firm in 1557 he designed a special fount, called *Civilité*, which he intended to become the French national type. This was an adaptation of gothic cursive handwriting and received its name from its frequent use in children's books such as Louveau's translation from Erasmus, *La Civilité puérile distribuée par petitz Chapîtres et Sommaires*. But by this time Griffo's italic had established itself too firmly in the favour of printers and readers to admit any rival as the subsidiary antiqua fount. Moreover, the idea of a 'national' type ran counter to the whole development of printing as a vehicle of international understanding. Although *Civilité* kept its place in the specimen sheets of French, Dutch and German printers for more than two hundred years, it was never used as an everyday type. For, unbeknown to himself, Granjon had created in his *Civilité* the first display fount, admirably suited for a diversity of jobbing matter, such as business circulars, high-class advertisements and the like – not a rival but a valuable supplement to the ordinary book types.

Gothic type

By the time of Aldus's death in 1515 Germany had set out on the way towards a typographical style of her own. About 1510 the Augsburg printer Johann Schönsperger had cut some founts for which the clerks of the imperial chancellery had supplied the designs. Ten years later, about 1520–2, this proto-Fraktur was disciplined and given its final shape by the Nürnberg writing-master Johann Neudörffer (1497–1563) and the Nürnberg punch-cutter Hieronymus Andreae. 'Fraktur' was to remain the typical German letter for four hundred years.

The Neudörffer-Andreae type of Fraktur owes its ascendancy as the dominant German type largely to the favour it found with the Frankfurt publisher Sigmund Feyerabend (1528–90). He began as a type-cutter and designer of book ornaments and worked in Augsburg, Mainz and Venice before settling in Frankfurt in 1560. Here he soon became the head of a rapidly expanding publishing company which eventually employed nearly every Frankfurt printer for its numerous and variegated production. Faithful to his artistic upbringing, Feyerabend secured for his firm the services of some of the best book-illustrators, such as Virgil Solis (1514–62) and Jost Ammann (1539–91), whose popularity in turn increased the familiarity of the public with the Fraktur letterpress accompanying their woodcuts.

Neudörffer's Fraktur superseded the 'Schwabacher' type which from 1480 to 1530 was the most popular face of German presses. Or rather should it be said, Fraktur relegated Schwabacher to a subsidiary place as a kind of italic beside the dominant fount. But Schwabacher, although more rounded and open than Fraktur, is on the whole so little distinguished from Fraktur that it cannot be considered an independent second face. This shortcoming is one of the reasons which render Fraktur so inferior to antiqua. In addition, Fraktur has no small capitals, and its own capitals cannot be combined to make a legible word.

The original reason for the prevalence of the black-letter in Germany and the Scandinavian and Slavonic countries in cultural dependence on her may be found in the preponderance of theological over humanistic writings in Germany. This was backed first by the strictly Thomist teachings of Cologne and later by the Lutheran theology of Wittenberg, two university towns which at the same time were busy centres of printing.

However, it seems that non-German texts – classical as well as modern – were always set up in antiqua type; and down to the end of the eighteenth century 'foreign words' (*Fremdwörter*) were frequently printed thus even in an otherwise black-letter text.

4. THE SPREAD OF PRINTING

In view of the fact that printing from movable type was a German invention and first practised in the German city of Mainz, it is not surprising that the first practitioners of the new art in every country of Europe and even in parts of the New World should have been German nationals. It is no exaggeration to describe Gutenberg's invention as Germany's most important single contribution to civilization. However, the printers who, from about 1460 onward, went on their travels from Mainz were little concerned with German culture. They were craftsmen and businessmen; they wanted to make a living; and they readily adapted themselves and their art to the conditions of international trade. Until printing had firmly established itself as an everyday commodity – that is to say, until well into the beginning of the sixteenth century – a map showing the places where printers had settled down is virtually identical with a map showing the places where any commercial firm would have set up an agency.

It is quite purposeless to enumerate the dozens of one-horse towns in the Abruzzi or Savoy which can boast of one or perhaps even two early presses or to trace the steps of these wandering printers in their quest for patrons and customers. Fascinating though the study of some of these men and their productions is for the student of incunabula, the history of printing is too much bound up with the history of big business to mention here more than one of these small fry. Except for the high quality of his work, the career of Johann Neumeister of Mainz is typical of that of many of his fellow craftsmen. Perhaps a direct pupil of Gutenberg, Neumeister was invited to Foligno by a humanist scholar and there produced the first edition of Dante's *Divina Commedia* in 1472; he then returned to Mainz, and later set up a press at Albi in Languedoc. In both places he drew on his familiarity with Italian art when he produced Turrecremata's *Meditationes* (1479, 1481) with illustrations cut after the mural paintings in S. Maria sopra Minerva in Rome. Finally Neumeister was called by the cardinal d'Amboise to Lyon where he printed the magnificent *Missale secundum usum Lugduni* (1487).

Individual patrons, however, were not enough to guarantee the printer a livelihood and to secure the sale of his books. Right from the beginning, the printer (who, be it remembered, was his own publisher and retailer) was faced by the alternative, unchanged ever since, of basing his business on the support of organized institutions or of relying on the fairly stable market of a literate, book-loving and book-buying clientele of sizable dimensions. Official backing was (and is) provided mainly by governments, churches and schools; private patronage, by the educated middle class.

The aristocracy, which in the following centuries was to build up those magnificent libraries, most of which have eventually found their last refuge in public libraries, greeted the new invention with little enthusiasm if they did not condemn it outright. The attitude of the Duke Federigo of Urbino as reported by Vespasiano da Bisticci was at the time, about 1490, shared by most connoisseurs. In his splendid library 'all books were superlatively good and written with the pen; had there been one printed book, it would have been ashamed in such company'. It is in keeping with this contempt of the mechanically produced book that Cardinal Giuliano della Rovere (later Pope Julius II) had Appian's *Civil Wars* copied by a superb scribe in 1479 from the text printed by Wendelin of Speier in 1472. The calligrapher even adopted the printer's colophon; he only changed 'impressit Vindelinus' to 'scripsit Franciscus Tianus'. As late as the second half of the eighteenth century a voluptuary aesthete, Cardinal Rohan, used only handwritten service books when he celebrated mass.

It was, then, people of moderate means, who could not afford to be squeamish about the outward appearance of the tools of their profession, to whom the early printers had to look for custom. It was the binders rather than the printers who overcame the reluctance of highbrow connoisseurs in admitting printed books to their stately shelves; and down to the present the sumptuousness of choice bindings frequently contrasts oddly with the shoddiness of printing and the worthlessness of contents thus bound.

It is quite in keeping with the well-organized and world-wide net of international trade at the end of the Middle Ages that printing by no means spread in ever-widening circles from Mainz over southern Germany, central Europe, and to the fringes of the then known world. On the contrary, the ease of firmly established communications all over the Continent permitted the printers to reach out at once to those places which offered the brightest prospects, that is to say the flourishing centres of international trade. So it came about that printing presses were established in quick succession in Cologne (1464), Basel (1466), Rome (1467), Venice (1469), Paris, Nürnberg, Utrecht (1470), Milan, Naples, Florence (1471), Augsburg (1472), Lyon, Valencia, Budapest (1473), Cracow, Bruges (1474), Lübeck, Breslau (1475), Westminster, Rostock (1476), Geneva, Palermo, Messina (1478), London (1480), Antwerp, Leipzig (1481), Odense (1482), Stockholm (1483). University towns as such had no attraction for printers: learning and diligence is no substitute for ready cash. Cologne, Basel, Paris, Valencia, Seville and Naples acted as magnets because they were thriving centres of trading, banking and shipping, and seats of secular and ecclesiastical courts.

The only university town which seems to be an exception was Wittenberg; but there it was one professor only who made printing a success, and before and after Martin Luther's connection with Wittenberg University the place does not occur in the annals of printing. In fact, Wittenberg can be said to owe its fame partly to the one blunder the shrewd Nürnberg printer, Anton Koberger, ever committed when he turned down Luther's invitation to become his publisher.

The church, and especially the monastic orders and congregations with their far-flung connections, too, provided easy ways of transmitting the art regardless of political frontiers. When in 1463 the two printers, Conrad Sweynheym and Arnold Pannartz, went to the Benedictine abbey of Subiaco near Rome to set up the first press

Die offinbarung

Das zweintzigst Capitel.

Vnd ich sahe eynen Engel vom hymel steygen / der hatte den schlüssel zum abgrund vnd eyne grosse keten ynn seyner hand / vnd er greyff den drachen die allte schlange / wilche ist der teuffel vnd der Satanas / vnd band yhn tausent iar / vnd warff yhn ynn den abgrund / vñ band yhn / vñ versiegelet oben drauff / das er nicht mehr verfuren solt die heyden / bis das vollendet wurden tausent iar / vnd dar nach mus er los werden eyn kleyne zeyt.

Vnd ich sahe stuele / vnd sie satzten sich drauff / vnd yhn ward gebē das vrteyl / vnd die seelen der enthewpter vmb des zeugnis Jhesu vnd vmb das wort Gottis willen / vñ die nicht anbettet hatten das thier / noch seyn bild / vnnd nicht genomen hatten seyn maltzeychen an yhre styrn vnd auff yhre hand / dise lebten vnd regnierten mit Christo tausent iar / Die andern todten aber wurden nicht widder lebendig / bis das tausent iar vollendet wurden / Dis ist die erste aufferstehung / Selig ist der vñ heylig / der teyl hat an der ersten aufferstehung / vber solche hat der ander todt keyne macht / Sondern sie werden priester Gottis vnd Christi seyn vnd mit yhm regniern tausent iar.

Vnd wenn tausent iar vollendet sind / wirt der Satanas los werden aus seynem gefencknis / vnd wirt ausgehen zuverfuren die heyden ynn den vier orten der erden / den Gog vnd Magog / sie zuversamlen ynn eynen streyt / wilcher zal ist / wie der sand am meer / Vnnd sie tratten auff die breytte der erden / vnd vmbringeten das heerlager der heyligen vnd die geliebte stad / vñ es fiel das fewr von Gott aus dem hymel vnd vertzeret sie / Vñ der teuffel der sie verfuret / ward geworffen ynn den fewrigen teych vnd schwefel / da das thier vnnd der falsche Prophet war / vnd wurden gequellet tag vnd nacht von ewicket zu ewicket.

Vnd ich sahe eynen grossen weyssen stuel / vnd den der drauff sas / fur wilchs angesicht floch die erden vñ der hymel / vnd yhn ward keyne stete erfunden / vnd ich sahe die todten beyde gros vnd kleyn stehen fur Gott / vnd die bucher wurden auffgethan / vnnd eyn ander buch ward auffthan / wilchs ist des lebens / vnd die todten wurden gericht nach der schrifft ynn den buchern / nach yhren wercken / vnd das meer gab die todten die drynnen waren / vnd der tod vñ die helle gaben die todten die drynnen waren / vñ sie wurden gericht eyn iglicher nach seynnen wercken / vñ der tod vñ die helle wurden geworffen ynn den fewrigen teych / Dis ist der ander tod / Vnd so yemand nicht ward erfunden geschrieben ynn dem buch des lebens / der ward geworffen ynn den fewrigen teych.

Die eyn vnd zweintzigste figur.

Johannis. XCIII.

Das Neue Testament Deutzsch, translated by Martin Luther, woodcuts by Lucas Cranach. M. Lotter, Wittenberg, 1522.
[1562/285]

outside Germany, they most probably travelled via Augsburg (the Augsburg abbey of SS. Ulric and Afra maintained the closest relations with Subiaco). Both abbeys excelled in the zeal and quality of their scriptoria, and it was in SS. Ulric and Afra that a few years later the first Augsburg press was established. As Subiaco abbey was under the supervision of the great Spanish cardinal, Torquemada, it was a natural step for the two printers to move to Rome very soon, after they had printed four books. Later their literary adviser, Giovanni Andrea dei Bussi, was rewarded with a bishopric in Corsica; and Sweynheym received a canonry at St Victor's in Mainz (1474).

However, the shelter of a monastery and the patronage of a prince of the church were not sufficient to maintain a steady output and sale. Intellectual impetus and economic power had long since become the property of the laity. It was the big towns and the world of industry and commerce which became the mainstay of book production.

In northern Europe the net of international trade which the Hanse towns had spun from Russia to England and from Norway to Flanders now provided easy openings for the printer's craft. The trade routes which the south German merchants had established to Milan and Venice, Lyon and Paris, Budapest and Cracow were now

19

trodden by printers and booksellers. The very first printer next to Gutenberg, Johann Fust, died in 1466 in Paris where he had gone on business. The 'Great Trading Company' of Ravensburg, which had a virtual monopoly in the trade with Spain, was instrumental in establishing presses in Valencia, Seville, Barcelona, Burgos and elsewhere; and one of their emissaries, Juan Cromberger of Seville, introduced printing in the New World, when in 1539 he dispatched a printer and a press to the capital of the then Spanish colony of Mexico.

Germany

By the end of the fifteenth century printing presses had been established in about sixty German towns. Only a dozen of these towns rose to eminence in this field, and their attraction to printers was entirely based on their position in the economic life of the empire. Mainz and Bamberg, which had seen the glory of the earliest presses, soon dropped out of the race; although no mean episcopal sees, they were economically unimportant. Their place was taken in south Germany by Basel, Augsburg, Strasbourg and, above all, Nürnberg, the wealthiest German centres of international banking and trade; and in north Germany by the towns which were members of, or affiliated to, the German Hanse, with Cologne, Lübeck and Bruges in the forefront.

STRASBOURG. Strasbourg seems to have profited by the presence of the earliest workmen with whom Gutenberg had conducted his first experiments before he returned to Mainz about 1445. That would explain certain primitive features of the productions brought out by the first Strasbourg printer, Johann Mentelin. He was a careless printer but obviously a smart businessman. His first publication was a Bible, issued in 1460–1 in direct competition with Mainz; but whereas the 42-line Bible occupied 1286 pages, Mentelin succeeded in squeezing the work into 850 pages (slightly shorter than Gutenberg's 36-line Bible), thus saving almost a third of the paper. His next book again shows his sound commercial instinct: it was the first Bible printed in German or in any vernacular and, although full of schoolboy howlers, it nevertheless remained the standard text of all German Bibles before Luther.

Mentelin was the first professor of the new art to cater deliberately for the laity, and other Strasbourg printers followed his lead. He published Wolfram von Eschenbach's *Parzival* and *Titurel* epics (both in 1477), probably at the instigation of his patron, Bishop Rupert, who earlier on had ordered similar romances of chivalry from the writing establishment of Diebold Lauber in Hagenau. But both these epics proved a flop; no reprint was called for until the nineteenth century when they were relegated to university seminars. After Mentelin's death (1478) other medieval and contemporary poetry, folk legends, Bible translations, sermons, and similar popular books and pamphlets continued to leave the Strasbourg presses. Adolf Rusch, one of Mentelin's sons-in-law – who were all printers – introduced roman types into Germany. The early Strasbourg firms flourished until the middle of the sixteenth century: Johann Prüss, who printed from 1482 to 1510, was succeeded by his son of the same name who carried on until 1546. Most of their books were meant for popular consumption, but Martin Flach, who printed from 1487 to 1500, preferred theological works in Latin. His widow brought the business to her second husband, Johann Knoblauch, who by the time of his death in 1528 had printed some three hundred books; their son, Johann the younger, carried the press on until 1558. Martin Schott, another son-in-law of Mentelin, who printed from 1481 to 1499, was followed by his son, Johann, who continued the firm until 1548. The second quarter of the sixteenth century was a heyday for the Strasbourg printers as they threw themselves vigorously into the religious warfare on the side of the Lutheran Reformation. Johann Schott published also two English tracts by the ex-Franciscan William Roy, 'A lytle treatous or dialoge between a Christian father and his stubborn son' (1527) and 'The burying of the Mass' (1528), each in an edition of 1000 copies as Schott testified on oath. The one printer who remained faithful to the old church, Johann Grüninger, brought out the one great scoop of the Catholic camp, Thomas Murner's *Exorcism of the Great Lutheran Fool* (1522).

BASEL. Whereas Strasbourg was from the very beginning in the forefront of popular publishing, Basel earned its fame as a centre of printing through the high quality of its scholarly output. Here, the art was introduced by an immediate pupil of Gutenberg, one Berthold Ruppel, who in 1467 completed the *editio princeps* of St Gregory's *Moralia super Job*, the most popular commentary on any book of the Bible, and in about 1468 a *Biblia Latina* in a gothic-roman similar to Schöffer's. Within a few years printing became a recognized part of Basel industry, so that a strike of the printers' journeymen in 1471 – the first recorded in the trade – caused a minor sensation. The names of seventy printers and journeymen are recorded between 1470 and 1500. The growth of printing was assisted by the establishment of papermaking mills.

The glory of Basel started when Johann Amerbach (1443–1513) set up his press in 1477. A pupil of Johann Heynlin at the Sorbonne, where he obtained his degree as Master of Arts, Amerbach made the press the vehicle of the Christian humanism of his teacher. A scholar and aesthete himself, he saw to it that his editions were not only printed with fastidious taste but also edited with care and accuracy. His main adviser was Heynlin who had left Paris for Basel. Heynlin's relation with Amerbach was very much that of the editorial director of a modern firm, advising the policy of the house and seeing its major publications through the press. Other professors of Basel university served Amerbach as editors and proof-readers.

The tradition of the Amerbach press was maintained by Johann Froben (1460–1527), who had learned the trade in Amerbach's shop and from 1491 to 1513 worked in partnership with Amerbach and Johann Petri (a native of Mainz, who appears first as a printer in Florence in 1472). Johann Froben and, after him, his son Hieronymus (d. 1563) were the standard-bearers of humanism in Germany. Their chief literary adviser was Erasmus of Rotterdam, and they printed his *Institutio principis Christiani, Epigrammata* and New Testament. Whereas Heynlin inclined towards supporting the *via antiqua* of the schoolmen, Erasmus was the leader of the *via moderna* of the new learning; but as both men avoided narrow partisanship, the firm of Amerbach and Froben was able to produce over a period of sixty years books which, in their judicious selection, careful editing, and fine workmanship, satisfied the needs and desires of scholars all over Europe.

Amerbach's 11-volume edition of St Augustine (1506), Froben's 9-volume edition of St Jerome (1516) and Erasmus's Greek New Testament (1516) are the outstanding monuments of Basel printing. The last-named paved the way for biblical criticism, although Erasmus's text was amazingly bad even in the light of contemporary philological knowledge. Its fame is chiefly based on the fact that Erasmus was the first to treat critically the text of the Vulgate and that his Greek version was the source of Luther's translation (which thus perpetuated some of Erasmus's errors). Froben was the first publisher to launch a collected edition of Luther's Latin tracts (four editions between October 1518 and July 1520), which he sold in France, Spain, Italy, Brabant

QVO PACTO POSSIS ADVLATOREM
AB AMICO DIGNOSCERE, PLVTAR
CHI, ERASMO INTERPRETE.

(Latin text of Erasmus facsimile page)

Erasmus, *Institutio Principis Christiani*. Johannes Froben, Basel, 1516. [526.k.2]

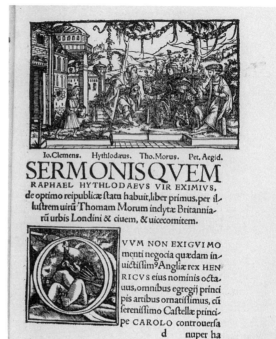

Io.Clemens.   Hythlodæus.   Tho.Morus.   Pet. Aegid.

SERMONISQVEM
RAPHAEL HYTHLODAEVS VIR EXIMIVS,
de optimo reipublicæ ftatu habuit,liber primus,per illuftrem uirū Thomam Morum inclytæ Britanniarū urbis Londini & ciuem, & uicecomitem.

VVM NON EXIGVI MOmenti negocia quædam inuictiffimꝰAngliæ rex HENRICVS eius nominis octauus,omnibus egregij principis artibus ornatiffimus, cū fereniffimo Caftellæ principe CAROLO controuerfa
d   nuper ha

Thomas More, *Utopia*. Johannes Froben, Basel, 1518. [713.f.1(1)]

and England. But he stood by Erasmus when the two reformers parted company over the problem of free will (1524).

The learned disposition of the Basel printers was carried on by Johannes Oporinus, who in 1541 began setting up a Latin translation of the Koran, and in 1543 printed that landmark in the history of medicine, Andreas Vesalius's *De humani corporis fabrica*, a masterpiece of typographical harmony. It took the personal intervention of Luther to overcome the prejudices of the Basel city council against the Koran – only a few years earlier the Pope had ordered a Venice edition of the Arab original to be burned. Luther, on the other hand, emphasized that actual acquaintance with the Koran could only resound to 'the glory of Christ, the best of Christianity, the disadvantage of the Moslems, and the vexation of the Devil'. So the Latin Koran eventually came out in 1542 with prefaces by Luther and Melanchthon – without justifying either the fears of its opponents or the hopes of its sponsors.

ZÜRICH. As long as the houses of Froben, Petri and Oporinus flourished, that is to say, until about 1560, the European importance of Basel as a centre of printing and publishing could not be challenged by any other Swiss town. However, from 1521 to the end of the century the Swiss market, or at least that of the Protestant cantons, became the domain of the Zürich printers Christoph Froschauer, uncle (d. 1564) and nephew (d. 1590). The elder Froschauer was a keen partisan of Zwingli, all of whose writings appeared under his punning imprint of the 'frog on the meadow'. He also

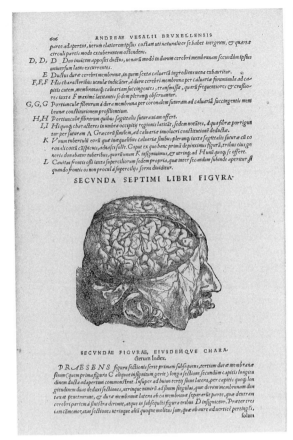

Andrea Vesalius, *De humani corporis fabrica*. Johannes Oporinus, Basel, 1543. [C.54.k.12]

Nicolas Copernicus, *De revolutionibus orbium coelestium*. Ioh. Petreius, Nürnberg, 1543. [C.112.g.4]

brought out the first complete Protestant Bible (6 vols, 1524–9) and a monumental Latin Bible annotated by the Reformed scholar Conrad Pellikan (7 vols, 1532–7). Among the 900 titles issued by the Froschauers some 500 were of a religious character; these include 28 German, 10 Latin and one English Bibles, and 26 German, 18 Latin, 4 Greek and one English New Testaments. With Johannes Stumpf's *History of the Swiss Confederation* with 4000 illustrations (1548) Froschauer scored a deserved popular success in a different field. The younger Froschauer is noteworthy for his gothic cursive type, not dissimilar to Granjon's *Civilité*; but it failed to gain a permanent place in the range of gothic founts.

In 1760, the firm was bought up by Conrad Orell, the publisher of J. J. Bodmer, J. J. Breitinger and Wieland, and thus lives on in the present-day house of Orell, Füssli & Co. of European reputation.

AUGSBURG. A characteristic feature of the Augsburg presses was their early and successful attempt to amalgamate letterpress and illustration, or rather to continue the tradition of the illuminated manuscript in the novel medium of print. It is not without significance that the first printer – Günther Zainer, probably trained in Mentelin's shop in Strasbourg – was called to Augsburg by the abbot of SS. Ulric and Afra. By the side of its famous scriptorium the abbey now set up a press which produced three large-scale books of moral instruction in 1472–6. From 1475 Anton Sorg, originally a *Briefmaler* who had learned printing in Zainer's shop, worked on the abbey premises. He soon turned to the publication of vernacular texts, first biblical and theological, but from 1480 to his death in 1493 mainly historical and travel books. These include Marco Polo's and Breydenbach's realistic descriptions of the Near and Far East as well as the fabulous exploits of St Brendan and John de Mandeville, and above all the history of the Council of Constance by Ulrich von Richental, magnificently illustrated with 44 woodcuts.

Zainer himself (d. 1478) produced the first illustrated book on a large scale, Jacobus de Vorgaline's *Legenda aurea* in 2 volumes with 131 woodcuts (1471–2), and, together with Jodocus Pflanzmann, the first illustrated Bible (1475). It is characteristic of the popular trend of Augsburg publishing that both these books were German translations. Zainer was also the first printer (after the magnificent but solitary trial by Schöffer in the Mainz *Psalter* of 1457) to use a specially designed set of initials instead of leaving blanks which illuminators were later to fill in by hand. The ornamentation of books by means of initials, borders and woodcuts reached an aesthetic height, rarely surpassed, in the prints of Erhard Ratdolt (1447–1527 or 28). When he returned to his birthplace in 1486 he had already gained renown as a printer in Venice where, among other books, the first edition of Euclid's *Elementa geometriae* (1482) stands to his credit. Ratdolt printed also a handsome black-letter edition of Euclid, which featured a not unsuccessful attempt at printing in gold. He introduced in Augsburg an italianate style of printing skilfully adapted to mathematical and astronomical works as well as to missals and other liturgical books, in which he specialized. Ratdolt was, moreover, the first to produce a real title-page and the first to issue a type-specimen; about these achievements something will be said elsewhere.

Johann Schönsperger the Elder (1481–1523) was the first printer to receive official recognition as imperial court printer by appointment to the Emperor Maximilian I. The emperor was the earliest monarch to realize the potential value of the printing press for political propaganda. He was the first ruler to issue a 'White Book' in 1509 which published a number of state papers to vindicate his aggressive war against Venice. He drew up an ambitious programme of 130 books which were to broadcast the glories of the house of Habsburg and especially of Maximilian himself. For the sumptuous illustrations of these tomes Maximilian employed the foremost artists of the time, including Hans Burgkmair and Albrecht Dürer, and special types were cut for each volume. But by the time of Maximilian's death only two volumes (and a 'picture-book' with captions only) were finished, both printed by Schönsperger. The Emperor's Prayer-Book, begun in 1513, was never completed; only ten specimens were pulled, all on parchment; the *Theuerdank*, a fantastic *roman à clef*, describing Maximilian's wooing of Mary of Burgundy in the style of medieval romances, was accomplished at Nürnberg in 1517. For Augsburg did not maintain its original impetus as a centre of printing. Both Erhard Ratdolt's and Johann Schönsperger's sons, who carried on the paternal businesses, were of no importance.

However, pleasing ornaments and a wealth of illustrations remained characteristic of Augsburg publishers, such as the German Petrarch which Heinrich Steiner printed in 1532 with 261 woodcuts. Steiner had begun as a printer of religious tracts in the interest of the Reformers; but from about 1530 he specialized in making foreign literature, chiefly Italian, accessible to the German public. His greatest hit was the publication of Andrea Alciati's *Emblemata*. The first edition came out in 1531, containing 104 Latin 'emblems' with 98 woodcuts. It was frequently reprinted and augmented, and soon translated, with further additions, into French, Italian and Spanish.

In the emblem books, word and picture were mutually interdependent, in that a motto in prose or verse with a moral lesson interpreted a symbolic picture and was in turn interpreted by it. During the next 150 years such an emblem book was to enter the library of every man of fashion and thought all over western Europe.

ULM. Although politically and economically Augsburg's near-equal among the imperial towns of Swabia, Ulm as a printing place reflects only dimly the splendour of Augsburg achievements. The combination of letterpress and illustrations is characteristic of Ulm book production as well. The Ulm proto-typographer (from 1472), Johann Zainer, seems to have been a brother of Günther Zainer in Augsburg. His editions of Boccaccio (1473) and Aesop (1476), translated by the humanist and town-physician Heinrich Steinhöwel, were adorned with tasteful woodcuts and borders. More important is Ptolemy's *Cosmographia* which Leonhard Holle published in 1482; its 32 woodcut maps and the pleasing roman type (resuscitated by St John Hornby for his Ashendene Press under the name of 'Ptolemy') have a permanent appeal to the book-lover. However, both Zainer and Holle went bankrupt, and that was the end of notable printing in Ulm.

NÜRNBERG. The leading role in the first century of German printing fell to the imperial city of Nürnberg. Here the connection between printing and commerce is particularly striking. Not a producer of raw materials, but the home of many finishing industries, Nürnberg reached its position as the commercial hub of central Europe through the liberal policy of its ruling families who favoured the free exchange of goods. Thus Nürnberg attracted merchants and bankers from every part of Europe who found it advantageous to transact business in and from this town. This was the very place to give scope to the capitalistic enterprise of the biggest European printer of the fifteenth and sixteenth centuries, Anton Koberger (1445–1513). He set up shop in 1470 and for a time combined printing, publishing and bookselling. All these things he did on a grand scale, on the lines of the international cartels and trusts of the era of 'early capitalism'. At the height of his activities, Koberger ran 24 presses served by over 100 compositors, proof-readers, pressmen, illuminators and binders. The catalogue of his firm over the years 1473–1513 enumerates more than two hundred titles, most of them large folio volumes. Hartmann Schedel's *Liber chronicarum* ('Nürnberg chronicle') (1493) was perhaps the most sumptuous of Koberger's publications; it contained some 1800 woodcuts by Michael Wolgemut (the outstanding German illustrator before the advent of his pupil Dürer) – and a limited edition had them coloured by hand – which make the book a mine of iconographic, geographic and cartographic information. Amazingly, the original layouts and sketches for the illustrations survive.

Koberger went into partnership with printer-publishers in Basel, Strasbourg and Lyon, partly because his own presses could not cope with the output, partly because he wished to facilitate the sale of his books abroad. In Paris he maintained an agency of his own; elsewhere he shared his agents with other importers, not necessarily booksellers. The final account in 1509 of the *Liber chronicarum* showed unsold stock in Paris, Lyon, Strasbourg, Milan, Como, Florence, Venice, Augsburg, Leipzig, Prague, Graz and Budapest. The narrow-mindedness and jealousy of the guilds eventually forced Koberger to concentrate on one trade only: abandoning printing, binding and retail selling, he chose to remain a publisher. Koberger, though by no means unlettered, was above all a businessman – but of the type which has remained prevalent among publishers: a businessman with ideals and a sense of responsibility towards

Giovanni Boccaccio, *De claris mulieribus*. Johann Zainer, Ulm, 1473. According to May Morris, William Morris thought that the woodcuts 'could not be excelled for romantic and dramatic force'. [I.B.9110]

Hartmann Schedel, *Das Buch der Croniken*, woodcuts by Michael Wolgemut and others. Anton Koberger, Nürnberg, 1493. The spread shows the Church of the Templars, Jerusalem, St Bernard, and various marvels. [I.C.7458]

Geoffrey Chaucer, *The Canterbury Tales*. William Caxton, Westminster, 1483(?). [G.11586]

Bernhard von Breydenbach, *Peregrinationes ad Terram Sanctam*. Peter Schöffer, Mainz, 1486. [C.20.e.3]

his authors and his public. As happens so often, the genius of the founder of the firm did not pass on to his heirs; having rested on their laurels, the Kobergers had to close down in 1526.

The extent to which the international trade of places such as Nürnberg and Augsburg facilitated the acquisition of books can be gathered from the library of the Nürnberg physician Hieronymus Münzer (d. 1508) who ordered books from Venice, Lyon, Bologna, Florence, Milan, and at the same time bought in Nürnberg books published in Venice, Reutlingen, Padua, Treviso, Louvain, Strasbourg. On 9 August 1516 Ulrich von Hutten wrote from Bologna to the Englishman Richard Croke, at the time Greek lecturer at Leipzig university, and asked him for a copy of the *Epistolae obscurorum virorum*: on the 22nd he acknowledged receipt of the book – a feat made possible through the excellent courier service of the trading companies.

MAINZ. In glaring contrast with those bustling centres of every kind of business activity, Mainz, the birthplace of printing, was kept from utter oblivion in the annals of printing by one man only, Johann Schöffer, Peter's son. He took over the business on his father's death in 1503 and until his death in 1531 was a kind of unofficial printer to the university. Most of his productions are in the realm of classical scholarship. In his first year he commissioned the first German translation of Livy; it came out in 1505 with 214 woodcuts, and was reprinted seven times before the firm closed down in 1559. The 1505 edition deserves mention also because of its preface. This clearly sets out the origins of the invention which later scholars have done their worst to obscure: 'In Mainz', it says, 'the ingenious Johann Gutenberg invented the wonderful art of printing in the year of Our Lord 1450, after which it was improved and finished by the industry, expenses and labour of Johann Fust and Peter Schöffer in Mainz.'

In addition to the German Livy, Johann Schöffer brought out a complete Latin edition (1518–19), which was textually and typographically a great advance on the two previous editions published in Rome (1469) and Venice (1498). His friend Ulrich von Hutten, some of whose anti-papal pamphlets he printed, may have inspired or strengthened Schöffer's interest in the national aspects of medieval history. Their common friend Sebastian von Rotenhan planned a collection of German chronicles, of which, however, only one volume was completed as Rotenhan was called away on diplomatic missions. Archaeology seems to have been Schöffer's great love. He printed an enlarged edition of the *Inscriptiones vetustae Romanae* which Konrad Peutinger had collected in and near Augsburg (1520); the *Collectanea antiquitatum Maguntinensium* (1520), a description of Roman monuments in and near Mainz; and the *Liber imperatorum Romanorum* (1526) which was illustrated, not by the fancy pictures of Renaissance knights which spread themselves in other books of the time, but by reproductions adapted from genuine Roman coins and other ancient monuments.

COLOGNE. Cologne, the most populous town of medieval Germany, became for some decades the centre of north-west German printing. Between 1464, when Ulrich Zell established the first press, and the end of the century more than 1300 titles went forth from Cologne; but two-thirds of them were pamphlets of twelve leaves or less. Nearly all books published in Cologne were in Latin; more than half were theological writings and of them more than half were treatises in the Albertist and Thomist tradition. This one-sidedness of Cologne book production finds its explanation in the strictly orthodox Thomistic attitude of the university teachers, whose hostility to humanist learning was soon to draw upon them the satire of the *Epistolae obscurorum virorum*.

Ulrich Zell, who died in 1507, produced more than two hundred titles; Heinrich Quentell, a native of Strasbourg who, after some years in Antwerp, printed in Cologne from 1486 to his death in 1501, surpassed him with about four hundred items; he supplied the greater part of the philosophical texts read at the universities of Cologne and Trier. Johann Koelhoff, a pupil of Wendelin of Speier in Venice, started his career in Cologne (1472–93) with the edition of a dozen tracts by Thomas Aquinas; Peter Quentell, Heinrich's grandson, finally became the leading anti-Lutheran printer after 1520, although this did not prevent him from printing for William Tyndale the Protestant English translation of the New Testament in 1524–5.

The two outstanding productions of early Cologne printing, however, are two German books, Heinrich Quentell's Low German Bible (1479) and Johann Koelhoff the younger's *Chronicle of Cologne* (1499). Quentell's Bible came out in two editions, one in the Rhenish-Westphalian dialect and the other in that of Lower Saxony. Its numerous illustrations exerted considerable influence on later Bibles, as the woodblocks were bought by Koberger and used for his popular Nürnberg Bible of 1483.

Even Albrecht Dürer (1471–1528) drew some of the inspiration for the famous gothic woodcut illustrations to his *Apocalypse* (1498) from Quentell's cuts. The influence of Dürer's engravings accompanied the new rebellious wave of religious awakening that spread across Europe. Dürer's engraved title-pages for his religious books, says John Harthan, 'exhibit the greatest poignancy, and contributed to the evolution of the title-page as a gateway to the book's contents. Like the Angel of the Apocalypse, Dürer is a towering figure, and stands with one foot in the medieval, the other in the modern world.' The first book to be illustrated throughout with copperplate engravings was Colard Mansion's edition in French of Boccaccio's *De casibus viriorum illustrium* (Bruges, 1476); but it was not until late in the sixteenth century that copperplate was to oust woodcut.

Koelhoff's *Chronicle of Cologne*, invaluable for us because of its notes on the origin of printing, however, ruined the printer: the book was confiscated and banned, and Koelhoff was exiled (d. 1502). For England, Cologne has a special significance in that William Caxton learned printing there in 1471–2 and Theodore Rood and John Siberch, the first Oxford and Cambridge printers, were natives, Rood of Cologne city, Siberch of the neighbouring town of Siegburg.

LÜBECK. Lübeck, the head of the Hanseatic League, was of signal importance for the spread of printing to north-east and eastern Europe. Its greatest printer was Stephen Arndes, a native of Hamburg. He had learned type-founding, composing and printing at Mainz and spent the years 1470–81 in Italy, where he first collaborated with Johann Neumeister in Foligno. He was then called to Schleswig, probably through a high Danish official whose son he had met in Italy, and in 1486 settled in Lübeck. Besides a number of liturgical books commissioned by various Danish chapters and monastic orders, Arndes's main production is the Low German Bible of 1494, a masterpiece of presswork as well as illustration. Like so many of the early printers, Arndes does not seem to have made a financial success out of his work: although he continued printing until his death in 1519, he was obliged to supplement his earnings by a clerkship to the Lübeck courts.

Through the old-established Hanseatic trade channels even south German publishers sold their books to northern customers. In 1467 a Riga bookseller had in stock two Bibles, fifteen Psalters and twenty Missals printed by Schöffer in Mainz.

From Lübeck set sail the printers who introduced the new craft to the Baltic towns among which Rostock and Danzig were the most important. Johann Snell, who printed in Lübeck from 1480 to about 1520, set up the first presses in Denmark and Sweden, although for some time the bulk of Danish and Swedish books were still printed in Lübeck. Lübeck was also the starting point of the first abortive attempt to introduce printing in Russia. Emissaries of the Tsar Ivan III, who in 1488–93 went to Germany in order to obtain the services of German technicians, invited the Lübeck printer, Bartholomaeus Gothan, to set up a press in Moscow. Gothan, who had recently (1486–7) worked in Stockholm and printed the first book for use in Finland (*Missale Aboense*, 1488), went in 1493 to Novgorod (and perhaps Moscow). He was dead before September 1496, probably murdered by the Russians, before he had produced any books in Russian. However, a curious survival of Gothan's stay in Russia did come to light. Russian manuscript translations of a Dialogue between Death and Life, the History of Troy, the Tyrant Dracolewyda, the Lucidarius, and other German texts circulated in Novgorod in the early sixteenth century: all of them can be traced to books printed in Lübeck between 1478 and 1485; they may well have formed part of Gothan's luggage.

It was the great Ivan IV the Awesome (usually mistranslated 'the Terrible') who eventually established Russian printing. At his request, Christian III of Denmark in 1552 dispatched a Copenhagen printer, Hans Missenheim, to Moscow where he initiated Ivan Feodorov, the Russian proto-typographer, into the art of printing.

Italy

Italy was the first foreign country to which German printers took the new invention in 1465. It was also the first country where the German printers lost their monopoly. In 1470 the first book, a Quintilian, was completed at a press owned by an Italian, Johannes Philippus de Lignamine, a native of Messina resident in Rome: in 1471 the first book appeared, actually printed by an Italian, the priest Clement of Padua working in Venice; and by 1475 the native genius had asserted itself and henceforth dispensed with trans-alpine tutelage. The motherland of the new learning, the centre of Christian civilization, the country of origin of modern banking and accounting offered opportunities to adventurous publishers and printers for which there was little room in the still predominantly medieval structure of German society. Thus it was Italy where there originated the two kinds of type which have ever since been the basic elements of western printing, roman and italic; which produced the first Greek and Hebrew founts; where the title-page and pagination, music print and pocket edition were launched upon the world of letters.

ROME. It was inevitable that the first printers in Italy, Sweynheym and Pannartz, should within a short space of time transfer their activities from the tranquil monastery of Subiaco to Rome. The seat of the Curia was naturally also a hub of big business, ecclesiastical as well as worldly. Much work hitherto done by the efficient scribes of the papal administration gave permanent occupation to the printing press. Indulgences and papal bulls had been among the earliest productions at Mainz, and official forms, decrees, circular notes and the like have kept Roman printers busy every since. In addition, Rome had, from the times of Cicero and Horace, been the central book market of the Mediterranean world and beyond; and people who used to buy manuscripts in Rome now purchased printed books there.

The number of titles available in Rome at this time was, indeed, quite remarkable. In an application to Pope Sixtus IV in 1472, Sweynheym and Pannartz stated that they had printed 28 works in 46 volumes, some of them in several editions, usually 275 copies each. The list includes the two editions (1468, 1470) of the two-volume collection of St Jerome's letters, which is chiefly remarkable, at least to English readers, for containing a treatise erroneously ascribed to the doctor of the church but actually written by a very unsaintly Englishman. It is the 'Dissuasio Valerii ad Rufinum ne uxorem ducat', an amusing diatribe against the dangers of matrimony – the very book which, 80 years earlier, the fifth husband of the Wife of Bath used to read 'gladly night and day for his desport' and at which 'he lough alwey ful faste'. The sometime clerk of Oxford's copy was bound up with other tracts on 'wykked wyves', including one by St Jerome, and it owed its immense popularity not least to the mistaken identification of its author. In reality, it is culled from the 'Entertainments of Civil Servants' (De nugis curialium) by the twelfth-century wit Walter Map, who thus became the first Englishman to appear in print.

At the same time Ulrich Han, another Roman printer of German birth, issued some eighty books, mostly editions of Latin authors, but including also a *Missale Romanum* (1476), in which for the first time the lines and notes of the music were printed with the letterpress.

On the whole, however, the productions of the Roman presses are less remarkable for their typography, which is generally mediocre, than for their contents, which reflect the international position of the city. The *Mirabilia urbis Romae*, the medieval Baedeker for the guidance of pilgrims and sightseers, which from about 1140 had been copied innumerable times, was now printed and reprinted with frequent amendments which often supplanted medieval folklore by flights of Renaissance pseudo-scholarship. Ptolemy's *Cosmographia*, planned by Conrad Sweynheym and published after his death by Arnold Buckinck in 1478 and reprinted in 1490, showed on 27 engraved maps the picture of the world as it had been known to the West for a thousand years. It was the Roman printer Stephan Planck from whose press the first print of Columbus's letter went out, from which Europe learned of the revolution of its geographical conception; this pamphlet, too, kept Roman printers busy for many years.

Only two Roman printers deserve special mention: Ludovico degli Arrighi and Antonio Blado. Arrighi, a writing-master, professional copyist and minor official in the Cancelleria Apostolica, published in 1522 the first printed specimen book which taught laymen the use of the *littera cancelleresca* of papal briefs. These cursive letters were cut by the goldsmith Lautizio Perugino, with whom Arrighi in 1524 started a printing and publishing partnership. The most distinguished among their many distinguished patrons was the humanist poet, Giangiorgio Trissino, remembered for his introduction of blank verse into drama and as a keen spelling reformer, one of whose innovations – the differentiation of *u* and *v* and *i* and *j* – was adopted by Arrighi and has thus survived. Trissino recommended Arrighi to Pope Clement VII as a man 'who, as in calligraphy he has surpassed all other men of our age, so, having recently invented this most beautiful method of doing in print almost all that he formerly did with the pen, has in beautiful types gone beyond every other printer'. Arrighi probably perished in the Sack of Rome in 1527. Antonio Blado worked from about 1515 to 1567 and was in 1549 awarded the title of Tipografo Camerale or printer to the Holy See; in this capacity he printed the first *Index librorum prohibitorum* in 1559. Blado is famous in the history of literature as the publisher of two first editions of a very different character: Machiavelli's *Il Principe* (1532) and Loyola's *Exercitia spiritualia* (1548), the epitomes of worldly statecraft and religious devotion. The type in which these books were printed was an improvement on Arrighi's design; the Blado type recreated by Stanley Morison in 1923 is a happy blend of the best features of Arrighi's and Blado's scripts.

VENICE. As has already been observed in Germany, intellectual and spiritual forces were insufficient to attract the businessmen of the printing trade. They followed the high roads of commerce, and in Italy these led to Venice, the queen of the Adriatic and in the fifteenth century the mistress of trade all over the then known world. Two brothers from Speier in the Rhenish Palatinate, John and Wendelin, opened the first press in Venice in 1467. In the following year John brought out the first book printed there. It was Cicero's *Epistolae ad familiares*; the first edition of 300 copies was sold out at once, and a second 300 were struck off within four months. After John's death in 1470 Wendelin successfully carried on. He turned out ten books in 1470 and fifteen each in the two following years. The publications of the brothers were well produced and show discrimination in their choice of authors. Apart from Latin classics, the stock-in-trade of every printer in Italy, they issued the first books in the Italian language, including Petrarch's *Canzoniere* (1470) and a Bible translation (1471).

The monopoly granted to John of Speier lapsed with his death, and the printing

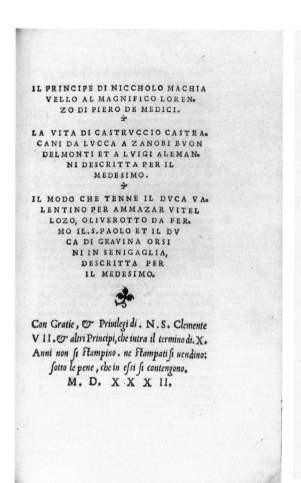

IL PRINCIPE DI NICCHOLO MACHIA
VELLO AL MAGNIFICO LOREN.
ZO DI PIERO DE MEDICI.

LA VITA DI CASTRVCCIO CASTRA.
CANI DA LVCCA A ZANOBI BVON
DELMONTI ET A LVIGI ALEMAN.
NI DESCRITTA PER IL
MEDESIMO.

IL MODO CHE TENNE IL DVCA VA.
LENTINO PER AMMAZAR VITEL
LOZO, OLIVEROTTO DA FER.
MO IL.S.PAOLO ET IL DV
CA DI GRAVINA ORSI
NI IN SENIGAGLIA,
DESCRITTA PER
IL MEDESIMO.

Con Gratie, & Priuilegi di . N.S. Clemente
VII. & altri Principi, che intra il termino di. X.
Anni non ſi Stampino. ne Stampati ſi uendino:
ſotto le pene, che in eſsi ſi contengono.
M. D. X.X X II.

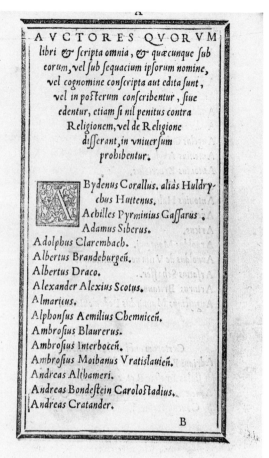

AVCTORES QVORVM
libri & ſcripta omnia, & quæcunque ſub
eorum, vel ſub ſequacium ipſorum nomine,
vel cognomine conſcripta aut edita ſunt,
vel in poſterum conſcribentur, ſiue
edentur, etiam ſi nil penitus contra
Religionem, vel de Religione
diſſerant, in vniuerſum
prohibentur.

A Bydenus Corallus, aliàs Huldry-
chus Huttenus.
Achilles Pyrminius Gaſſarus.
Adamus Siberus.
Adolphus Clarembach.
Albertus Brandeburgeñ.
Albertus Draco.
Alexander Alexius Scotus.
Almaricus.
Alphonſus Aemilius Chemniceñ.
Ambroſius Blaurerus.
Ambroſius Interboceñ.
Ambroſius Moibanus Vratislauieñ.
Andreas Althameri.
Andreas Bondeſtein Caroloſtadius.
Andreas Cratander.

B

Niccholo Machiavelli, *Il Principe*. Antonio Blado, Rome, 1532. [C.55.f.2(2)]

Index librorum prohibitorum. Antonio Blado, Rome, 1559. [11900.aaa.53]

trade was thrown open to competition, for the Signoria of Venice firmly believed in free enterprise, the pillar of Venetian commerce. The first rival of Wendelin was another foreigner, a Frenchman, Nicolas Jenson. His first production was an edition of Cicero's *Epistolae ad Atticum* (1470), and within ten years he produced about 150 books, which is the same average as that of the Speier presses, and may therefore be taken as a testimony to the capability of editors, compositors and printers during the 1470s. Jenson cultivated a variety of subjects, with the fathers of the church and Latin classics in evidence: Justin, Eusebius (both 1470) and Augustine (1475) among the former, and Caesar, Suetonius, Quintilian, Nepos (all 1471) and Pliny's *Natural History* (1472) among the latter. Several further writings of Cicero were inevitably included in his programme; but a Vulgate (printed in gothic letters in 1476) was still something rare on the Italian market. Jenson's expanding business made him take into partnership financiers whom he found chiefly among the German merchants of the Fondaco dei Tedeschi; but he never became dependent on them. He was patronized by Pope Sixtus IV, who in 1475 made him a papal count; but it was as the pope's honoured guest and not his indigent retainer that he died at Rome in 1480. Stanley Morison praised 'the quality of the engraving, casting, composition and impression of his types' as combining 'to produce the perfect book of the period'.

32

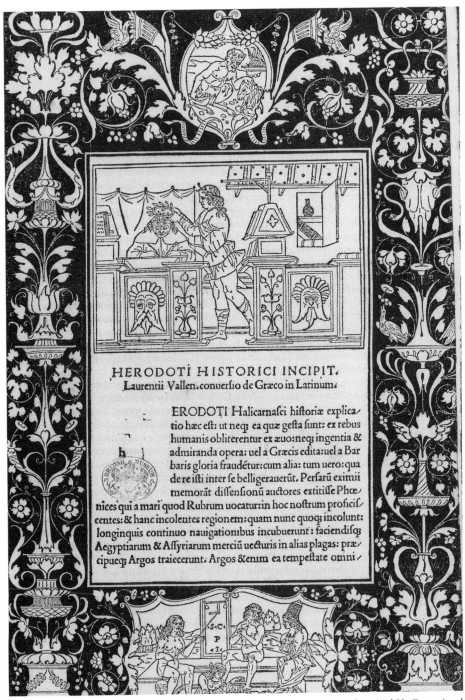

HERODOTI HISTORICI INCIPIT.
Laurentii Vallen.conuersio de Græco in Latinum.

ERODOTI Halicarnafei hiftoriæ explica-
tio hæc eft: ut neq; ea quæ gefta funt: ex rebus
humanis obliterentur ex æuo:neq; ingentia &
admiranda opera: uel a Græcis edita:uel a Bar
baris gloria fraudêtur:cum alia: tum uero:qua
de re ifti inter fe belligerauerût. Perfarû eximii
memorât diffenfionû auctores extitiffe Phœ-
nices qui a mari quod Rubrum uocatur:in hoc noftrum proficif-
centes:& hanc incolentes regionem:quam nunc quoq; incolunt:
longinquis continuo nauigationibus incubuerunt : faciendifq;
Aegyptiarum & Affyriarum merciû uecturis in alias plagas: præ-
cipueq; Argos traiecerunt. Argos &enim ea tempeftate omni-

Herodotus, *Historia*. Space was left in the letterpress for a scribe to write in the initial H. Gregorius de Gregoriis, Venice, 1494. [I.B.21057]

The importance of Venice as a centre of the book market appears in the enormous number of about 150 presses which were at work there around the turn of the century, by which time as many as four thousand texts or editions had been printed there. Their quality, however, was inverse to their numbers. Erhard Ratdolt, after Jenson's death the best printer in Venice, returned to his native Augsburg in 1486; the general standard remained low, and a firm like that of the Florentine, Lucantonio Giunta, is remarkable only for its shoddy mass-production.

All the more brightly shines the star of the greatest printer of sixteenth-century Venice, Aldus Manutius. Like all Venetian printers of any consequence, Aldus was a foreigner. He was born about 1450 in Bassiano on the northern fringe of the Pontine Marshes, and early came into personal contact with Pico della Mirandola, the brilliant champion of Florentine Platonism. From him Aldus imbibed his love for the Greek language and literature which was to impress itself on his activities as a publisher. Two princes of Carpi, nephews of Pico and his former pupils, supplied the capital for the press which Aldus set up in Venice about 1490; to one of them Aldus dedicated the first edition of his Latin grammar (1493). However, the editing of Greek authors was Aldus's principal aim and interest.

The signal success of these Greek editions (about which more will be said later on) encouraged Aldus to apply his scholarship and business acumen to a new venture in the production of Latin texts. Here he struck out a line for himself. By this time new generations of book-readers had grown up to whom the stately tomes of liturgical books or collected editions of ancient writers and fathers of the church had little appeal. The *conoscenti* and *dilettanti*, the gentlemen of leisure who had imbibed the taste and a little of the scholarship of the humanists, and the schoolmasters, parsons, lawyers and doctors who had passed through their university courses of *litterae humaniores*, wanted books which they could carry about on their walks and travels and read at leisure in front of their fireplaces, and which would incidentally be within the financial reach of the poorer of these potential book-buyers. Aldus had one of those brainwaves which distinguish the truly great publisher. He embarked on the production of a series of books which would at the same time be scholarly, compact, handy and cheap. In order to be commercially successful, it was necessary not only to raise the number of copies of each edition – Aldus printed 1000 instead of the 100, 250, or at most 500 hitherto considered the rule – but also to cram as much text as possible on the octavo page which he allowed for his pocket editions. Here his liking for cursive letters stood him in good stead; and Francesco Griffo's italic fount fulfilled this condition.

From April 1501, when Virgil's *Opera* came out in Griffo's cursive, Aldus issued every two months over the next five years one of the 'Aldine' editions over the imprint of the dolphin and anchor, which, in addition to the excellence of the texts supplied by eminent scholars, was accepted all over Europe as a sure guarantee of an impeccable, handsome and reasonably priced edition of ancient authors.

An interesting sidelight on Aldus's international reputation is seen in the fact that reprints of his editions, purporting to come from Aldus's press, were at once rushed out by unscrupulous rivals. The printers of Lyon published no fewer than 59 'Aldines' between 1501 and 1526; they were aided and abetted in this sordid trade by Griffo, who cut several sets of punches for Lyonese firms. Even the first edition of the *Epistolae obscurorum virorum* appeared in 1515 with the colophon *In Venetia in impressoria Aldi Minutii*; it was, in fact, printed by Heinrich Gran of Hagenau in

Alsace. In view of the prevalent laxity towards what we now call plagiarism, it is therefore a rare example of scholarly honesty that Johannes Sturm, the founder of the Strasbourg *Gymnasium* (1538), handsomely acknowledged his debt to Aldus. From 1540 Sturm brought out reprints of Aldine editions for the use of his students, and he mentioned his source in these words: 'We have followed Aldus throughout, partly because of his personal authority and partly because of the annotations of the Italian scholars.'

Aldus very nearly became also the pioneer in the field of polyglot Bible editions – an honour which was to fall to Cardinal Ximenes, the originator of the Complutensian Bible. In 1497 or 1498 Aldus projected a Hebrew-Greek-Latin Bible; but for unknown reasons the plan was abandoned and a single specimen page (the only known copy is in the Bibliothèque Nationale, Paris) is the sole witness to this bold scheme.

For over a century the firm of Manutius maintained its honoured place. After Aldus's death in 1515 his father-in-law, Andrea Asolano, himself the owner of the late Nicolas Jenson's press, acted as faithful steward for his nephew Paulus (b. 1511) until the latter came to maturity. More a scholar than a man of business, Paulus increased the fame of the firm through his excellent editions, especially that of Cicero, but failed to expand or even maintain its commercial success. His son Aldus the younger, who inherited the firm after Paulus's death in 1574, was as good a philologist and as bad a businessman as his father. Having handed the press over to a manager in 1585, he closed it in 1590 when he was appointed head of the Vatican press.

Its geographical position and historic associations made Venice also the natural avenue through which the southern Slavs came into contact with the art of printing. Of all the incunabula preserved in Yugoslav libraries about 75 per cent came from Venetian presses. Croats – not always easily recognizable as such – occur as printers in Venice from 1476. Boninus de Boninis (Dobric Dobričević), who printed in Verona, Brescia and Lyon, is perhaps the most important. In Venice also originated the first books printed in the Croatian language and with Glagolitic letters: a Missal (1483), a Breviary (1493) and an Evangelistary (1495).

The first books printed east of the Adriatic are a Serb-Cyrillic 'Oktoih' (1493) and Psalter (1495) and a Croat-Glagolitic Missal (1494), all published in Cetinje by Hieromonachos Makarios, who later (1507–12) also became the first printer in Walachia. But the first great secular Dalmatian book, Peter Zoranić's novel *Planine*, again appeared from a Venetian press (1569).

Alone among the Italian cities, Venice preserved its printing tradition throughout the sixteenth century. While the house of Manutius continued to specialize in ancient authors, two other great Venetian publishers applied themselves whole-heartedly to the cultivation of Italian letters. Francesco Marcolini, a native of Forlì, came to Venice in 1534. He was the publisher of Pietro Aretino, perhaps the most gifted satirist, pornographer and literary blackmailer of any age, but made up for it – if the thought ever occurred to him that he had to make up for it – by his graceful edition of Dante. His elegant presswork did much to popularize the Roman cursive as developed by Arrighi, Blado and Tagliente.

Even more important for the propagation of the national literature was Gabriele Giolito de Ferrari, a Piedmontese who settled in Venice together with his father in 1538 but made himself independent three years later. He became not only the publisher of Ariosto, of whose works he brought out almost 30 editions, but also

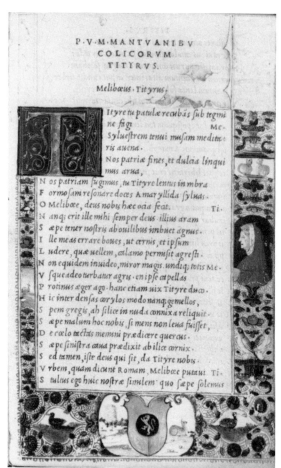

Virgil, *Opera*. Aldus Manutius, Venice, 1501. [C.19.f.7]

Compositor, printers and bookseller at work: woodcut from the *Dance of Death* printed by Matthias Huss at Lyon in 1499. [I.B.41735]

reprinted older Italian masters, especially Petrarch and Boccaccio. When the church began to frown on the semi-paganism of these writers, Giolito adapted himself to the change of climate and from 1568 published a series of edifying books called *Ghirlanda spirituale* (spiritual garland). By the time he died in 1578 he had published some 850 books, but under his sons the firm rapidly declined and in 1606 was dissolved.

PADUA. Printing began in Padua in 1471; the first printers there were natives of Italy, Prussia, Haarlem, Basel and Stendal. In 1474 they were joined by the Frenchman Pierre Maufer of Rouen (who italianized his name as Piero Fransoso). His ambitious publishing programme involved him in constant litigation with his numerous creditors, and enough of the court decisions and other legal documents involved have survived for us to learn a mass of details unavailable elsewhere and gain a unique insight into the running of a printer's workshop. Giovanni Mardersteig has described the production in 1477 of Maufer's most important book, Gentile da Foligno's commentary on the third book of Avicenna's *Canone di medicina*. The printing of this was financed by Johann Rauchfass, a Frankfurt bookseller who lived in Padua and acted as agent for German firms in Venice and also for the export of Italian books to the Frankfurt book fair. He commissioned two new gothic typefaces (one for the text, the other for the glossary) for the book from Francesco Griffo; these were modelled on a gothic type used by Nicolas Jenson (and Rauchfass and Jenson later formed a partnership in Padua). Like other early printers, Maufer was restless: he left Padua in 1479, and then worked successively in Verona, Venice, Modena and Mantua.

France

The history of the printed book in France is from the very beginning marked by two features which one is inclined to ascribe to the French national character: centralization of the trade and elegance of the production. Lyon is the only place besides Paris that held its own as an independent centre of printing and publishing, until the Inquisition stifled and killed this seat of Protestantism. Geneva, it is true, achieved for Calvinist literature the importance Wittenberg had in the Lutheran world, but Genevan printing was more influential outside than inside France. Places such as Rouen and Orléans lived only on the crumbs that fell from the table of the Paris printers. Since the decline of Lyon Paris has been the sole French centre of typography, printing and publishing.

This trend was strengthened by the fact that printing was introduced in France as the official concern of the Sorbonne, the intellectual centre of the country, and soon enjoyed the special attention of royalty. Charles VII's patronage of Nicolas Jenson may be spurious – in any case, Jenson did not return to Paris but went to Venice; but Louis XII and particularly François I displayed a genuine interest in the art of printing, though not untinged by the desire to make it serve the political aims of the monarchy.

The first printing venture in France derives its main interest from the fact that it was the first enterprise in which the publisher held the whip-hand over the printer. It is not surprising that the printer's exclusive dominion was first challenged by the university dons: they have, understandably, definite ideas about the kind of book they consider worth promulgating for the sake of learning as well as teaching. The Sorbonne, the oldest university north of the Alps, led the way. As early as 1470 its rector and librarian invited three German printers to set up a press on the premises of the university; the rector and librarian selected the books and supervised the printing, even to specifying the type; their insistence on a roman fount was decisive in preparing the speedy overthrow of gothic lettering in the western world. The books were mostly textbooks for students, chosen with an eye on their suitability as models of elegant Latin style; among them Leonardo Bruni's translation of Plato's letters (1472) is worth mentioning as the only print of this work ever done, as well as the only Platonic text printed in France in the fifteenth century. When in 1473 the two academic dignitaries who had sponsored the press left Paris – Johann Heynlin for Basel where he became the adviser of Johann Amerbach, and Guillaume Fichet for Rome – the three German printers carried on for five more years as a private company, and from 1478 to his death in 1510 only one of them, Ulrich Gering of Constance, remained in business.

By this time, although a number of other Germans were at work in Paris, French-born printers had established themselves. Among them, Pasquier Bonhomme brought out the first printed book in the French language, the *Croniques de France*, in three volumes in 1476. But the men who set the pace for the development of the specifically French book were Jean Dupré and Antoine Vérard. Both of them specialized in illustrated and ornamented *éditions de luxe*. Dupré, who opened shop at the sign of the

Two Swans in 1481, is perhaps more remarkable for his business capacity. The counterpart of Koberger and Manutius, for a time he controlled the French book market through his association with wealthy financiers and the foundation of branches and agencies throughout the provinces, including a flourishing establishment in Lyon. Vérard, on the other hand, who began printing in 1485 and died in 1512, was the first Frenchman to print the Books of Hours – of which he himself produced nearly 200 different editions – which in their harmonious blend of neat lettering, elegant borders and delicate illustrations set a target for fine bookwork by which French printing has profited ever since. Philippe Pigouchet (*fl.* 1488–1515), Thielmann Kerver (*fl.* 1497–1522), and others vied with Vérard in the charm and care bestowed on their productions, which, beside the Books of Hours, included chronicles, courtly romances and the famous *Dance of Death* which Guy Marchant published in 1485. At this time in France the monarchy was held in almost mystical veneration, and *La mer des histoires* (Pierre le Rouge, Paris, 1488) celebrates the achievements of the French kings in over 2000 woodcuts cut with great skill in a style reminiscent of manuscript illustration.

'Few books demonstrate more clearly than *Les loups ravissans* by Robert Gobin (Vérard, Paris, about 1505) the conservative role of printing in preserving and disseminating the religious attitudes of the later medieval period' – Harthan. But about the turn of the century the taste for these fundamentally medieval categories of reading matter abated, and the spirit of the Renaissance began to permeate French thought. Vérard was a pioneer in introducing Renaissance forms in his book-ornaments; but it was of greater importance for the growth of the specifically French brand of classicism that he was followed by a galaxy of scholar-printer-publishers who, throughout the sixteenth century, gave France the lead in European book production.

The line opens with the Fleming Josse Bade (1462–1535), who latinized his name to Jodocus Badius Ascensius, from Aasche near Brussels (although his birthplace was Ghent). He studied in Italy and then learned the printing trade in Lyon at the press of Johann Trechsel, whose daughter Thalia he married. Lyon is an exception to the general rule in that the first printer there was a Frenchman, or rather a Walloon, called Guillaume le Roy (*fl.* 1473–88), who had been trained in the press of the Speier brothers in Venice, and that he was followed by German nationals, among whom Trechsel, a graduate of Erfurt university, takes pride of place. Compared with the sixty-odd printers traceable in Paris during the last decades of the fifteenth century, Lyon numbered some forty presses during the same time – sufficient evidence to show the economic importance of the city whose world-famous fairs attracted merchants from Germany, Italy and Spain, and which enjoyed the special patronage of Louis XI (1461–83). Moreover, the Lyon printers had the advantage of being far removed from the censorship exercized by the theologians of the Sorbonne and were therefore, in contrast to their brethren in Paris, free to follow the humanist trend, of which Trechsel's illustrated Terence (1493) is a good specimen.

Bade left Lyon for Paris in 1499 and there continued his father-in-law's work with a series of ancient and modern Latin authors; among the latter were most of the early writings of Erasmus. In addition, he was the first publisher of Guillaume Budé, one of the greatest Greek scholars of all times. The Praelum Ascensianum, as Bade called his firm, used as its device a printing press, which is incidentally the earliest representation of the instrument. After Bade's death his firm merged with another which

Collige ab exemplo qui tranſis,perlege,differ,
In ſpeculo ſpeculare meo lacbrymabile carmen,
Qui ſim,qui fuerim licet,qui marmore claudor.
Sanguine claruseram Vicecomes ſtirpe Ioannes.
Præful eram,paſtórque ſui,baculúmque gerebam,
Nomine,nullas opes poſſidebat latius orbe:
Imperio titulóque meo mibi Mediolani
Vrbs ſubiecta fuit,Laudenſe ſolum,Placentia grata,
Aurea Parma,bona Bononia,pulchra Cremona,
Bergoma magna ſatis lapidoſis montibus altis,
Brixia magnipotens,Bobienſis terra,tribúſque
Eximijs dotata bonis Derthona vocata,
Cumarum tellus,nouáque Alexandria pinguis,
Et Vercellarum tellus,atque Nouaria,& Alba,
Aſt quoque cum caſtris Pedemontis iuſſa ſubibant,
Ianuáque ab antiquo quondam iam condita Iano
Dicitur,& vaſti narratur Ianua mundi,
Et Sauonenſis Rax,& loca plurima quæ nunc
Difficile eſt narrare mibi,mea iuſſa ſubibant,
Triſtia tota meum metuebant languida nomen.
Per me obſeſſa fuit populo Florentia plena,
Belláque ſuſtinuit tellus Peruſina ſuperba,
Et Piſæ & Senæ timidum reuerenter honorem
Præſtabant:me me metuebat Marchia tota.
Italiæ partes omnes timuere Ioannem.
Nunc me petra tenet,ſaxóque includor in iſto,
Et lacerant vermes,laniant mibi denique corpus.
Quid mibi diuitiæ,quid & alta palatia proſunt,
Quum mibi ſufficiat quòd paruo marmore claudor?

MATTHAEVS SECVNDVS.

EX teſtamento Ioannis vniuerſum imperium æquiſſima ratione trifariam diuiſum,tribus Stephani liberis ceſſit,ea conditione vt Mediolanum & Genua communis eſſent ditionis, ab vnóque tantùm prætore regerentur, quem pari iudicio delegiſſent : reliquæ porrò vrbes nobilioráque oppida à grauiſſimis Iureconſultis amicíſque communibus fideliter æſtimata,digeſtáque in tres portiones,ſortem ex vrna ſequerentur.Matthæo Bononia obuenit,quæ ex ipſa ſolenni tranſactione quatuor vrbes tanquam ſua membra ſecum trahebat, Laudem ſcilicet Pompeiam,Placentiam,Parmam,& Bobium in Apennini vallibus ſitum:item Lucam & Maſſam togatæ Galliæ, Pontémque tremulum ſupra Macram amnè, Apuanorum Ligurum caput, & Sancti Donini oppidum, quod in Aemilia via à Tarro amne ſeptè milibus paſſuum diſtat. Sed Matthæus nequaquam diu Bononia potitus eſt,Olegiano eius vrbis imperium occupante. Is enim ſub id tempus quo Ioannes Archiepiſcopus ſuprema tentatus valetudine decumbebat, rebellantibus Patritiis atque arma capiétibus,in foro proſperè conflixerat,coniurationíſque principes captos,ſecuri percuſſerat,in quibus nonnulli ex Blanchis,Gozadinis,Bentiuolíſque & Sabadinis fuerant.Poſt id factum quum ædificatam à Ioanne Antiſtite veterem arcem egregiè permuniſſet , inuaſit iuſto ſibi arripiendi imperii,cuius ipſe præcipuus defenſor extitiſſet. Itaque fortuna nefariis cœptis aſpirante,Prætorè

P. Giovio, *Vitae duodecim vicecomitum mediolani principum*. Robert Estienne, Paris, 1549. [C.97.c.5]

gained even greater fame as a fountain diffusing classical literature, namely that founded in or shortly before 1502 by Henri Estienne (Henricus Stephanus). His outstanding adviser and author was Jacques Lefèvre d'Étaples (Faber Stapulensis), the leading French Greek scholar, whose *Psalterium quintuplex* (1509) and commentaries on the Psalms (1507) and the Pauline Epistles (1512) first subjected biblical studies to philological methods. For his Latin editions Stephanus enjoyed the editorial assistance of Geofroy Tory (1480–1533), who afterwards set up a printing press of his own.

Henry Estienne's widow married a partner of her late husband, Simon de Colines, who worthily continued the tradition of the firm until Robert Estienne (1503–59) entered the business in 1525. Robert was married to Perette Badius and after his father-in-law's death in 1535 amalgamated the presses of Badius and Stephanus. At the same time there flourished another son-in-law of Badius, Michel Vascosan; and it is to Colines, Tory, Robert Estienne and Vascosan that the reign of François I (1515–47) owes its appellation as the Golden Age of French typography. These printers introduced to France the principles of the Aldine press – the exclusive use of roman and italic founts of Aldine design, handy sizes and cheap prices. Influenced by Tory's principles, Colines and Estienne acquired entirely new sets of types. Colines himself is credited with the design of italic and Greek founts and especially the roman 'St Augustin Sylvius' of 1531, the ancestor of all 'Garamond' types. The firm was

LE TIERS LIVRE,

QVant le E.est droict assis en ligne equilibree, & que le A.luy est adherent en summit, le dict A.se treuue hors de la dicte ligne equilibree, en la facon que voyez icy pres en deseing.

DOncques si vous voules bien escripre, & faire icelle Diphtongue de le A.& de le E.faictes les en la forme et facon quil sensuit, & vous trouueres la raison estre bonne sans doubte aucune. Et si on vous replique que les aultres lettres veulent estre ainsi assises & situees lune ioignant a lautre, dites que non veulent, mais requerêt estre en grande liberte loing a loing lune de laultre, lespace dũg I.por le moigns entre les deux, & le A, estant en diphtongue auec le E.ne veult aucune espace intermi-

se par la pointe de son pied, au quel le E.veult, comme iay dict, estre adherent. IE reuiens a noz lettres, & les vois designer, escripre, & figurer toutes lune apres laultre, auec la bonne grace de nostre seigneur Dieu,

Le signe de la Croix,

NOus ferons doncques en la bonne heure, & au nom de Dieu, tout premierement vne Croix, qui sera, comme iay cy deuant dict, de deux lignes. Lune perpédiculaire, & lautre ligne diametrale & trauersante equilibree, pour nous donner bon heur & commancement a entrer en noz lettres, & pour aider a les designer côme y leur est requis selon Reigle & Côpas. Icelle Croix veult estre aussi haulte que large, & aussi large que haulte, pour la loger en vng Quarre equilateral, dedans le quel ferons & designerons vne chascune lettre en son

Diuision du Quarre equilateral,

renc luy estant diuise iustement & precisement en vnze lignes perpédiculaires, et aultres vnze lignes trauersantes & equilibrees en Croix, qui rêdront en nombre cent petits Quarreaulx equilateraulx, & dune grandeur, desquelz la largeur de lung, & du quel quon vouldra, sera le modele & la certaine mesure de la largeur de la iambe en la lettre que vouldrons faire entre deux

Bône reigle pour faire lres,

lignes equidistantes & equilibrees selon le-space entremise que nous y vouldrons, Car en gardât nostre proportion & nombre des vnze lignes, nous pouuons faire lre Attique tant grâde & tant petite quil nous plaira . La dicte croix et le dict Quarre veulent estre en la forme qui sensuyt,

Geofroy Tory, *Champ-Fleury*. Paris, 1529. [60.e.14]

fortunate in obtaining the services of Claude Garamond as their punch-cutter and 'typographical adviser', as we should now describe his functions.

Simon de Colines, although not a scholar himself, fully maintained and even extended the range of learned and scientific works, including the natural sciences (Jean Ruel's *De natura stirpium*), cosmology and astrology (Jean Fernel and Sacrobosco), in addition to pleasant Aldine-type editions of Horace and Martial.

Robert Estienne and, after him, his son Henry II (1528–98) are the two most eminent scholar-printers of their century. Robert was both a sound classical student and a devout Christian, and these inclinations combined happily in his critical editions of the Vulgate (1527–8) and the Old Testament in Hebrew (1539–41, revised 1544–6). In his Greek New Testament of 1551 he divided the chapters into numbered verses, an innovation which quickly became generally accepted. His folio Bible of 1532 gave an early showing to Garamond's Gros Canon types. Robert's greatest achievement in the field of pure scholarship was his *Thesaurus linguae latinae* (1531 and frequent revised editions); it is still not entirely superseded. His *Dictionarium latino-gallicum* (1538), *Dictionaire francoislatin* (1539–40), and concise school editions of both – all frequently reissued – made Robert also the father of French lexicography.

Robert Estienne enjoyed the patronage, amounting to personal friendship, of François I, except the twentieth-century exiled Manuel of Portugal the only sovereign of all ages who bestowed on printing that loving care that Charles I displayed for his picture gallery and George V for his stamps, and most monarchs reserved for grandiose buildings and the jewellery of their mistresses. Like Maximilian I, François shrewdly recognized the immense power which might result from an appeal to what later became known as public opinion, through the medium of the printed word. In 1527 his government publicly explained and justified their policy in a pamphlet *Lettres de François Ier au Pape* which, in its studious *suppressio veri* and *suggestio falsi*, set the standard for many a subsequent official publication. Later, Estienne lent his pen and press to several such documentary publications which 'properly informed everyman' why the alliances of the Most Christian King with the German Protestants and the Turkish Sultan served the cause of European peace and religious concord.

A more honourable posterity issued from two other measures taken by François. In 1538 he ordered Estienne to give one copy of every Greek book printed by him to the royal library, which, from this modest beginning, became the first copyright library. In the following year the king promulgated a code of rules for printers, the most important of which is the clause banning the use of any printer's mark which might be confused with that of another press – an order which safeguarded equally the interests of the producers and buyers of books.

François I's death in 1547 deprived the Calvinist Robert Estienne of the protection he needed against the hostile theologians of the Sorbonne. He therefore left Paris for Geneva in 1550, while the firm continued in both Paris and Geneva. In Paris, Robert's brother Charles (1504–64) brought out a complete edition of Cicero (1555) as well as a *Guide des chemins de France* which is enlivened by comments on 'bad roads', 'infested by brigands', 'good wine', 'plentiful oysters'. Charles died in the debtors' prison, however, leaving a sorely encumbered business to his nephew Robert II (1530–71) who had remained faithful to the church of Rome. Meanwhile Robert's sons Henri II (1528–98) and François (1537–82) maintained the splendour of the paternal press in Geneva. Henri has to his credit a long series of pagan and early Christian classics including the *editiones principes* of Anacreon, Plutarch and

Diodorus Siculus; but his outstanding achievement is the *Thesaurus linguae graecae* (1572), the worthy counterpart and companion of his father's work. Henri II's son, Paul (1567–1627), co-operated with the great Genevan philologist, Isaac Casaubon, his brother-in-law, in maintaining the scholarly standard of the Geneva branch. But he fell foul of the authorities and fled to Paris. Here his son, Antoine, returned to the old faith and was rewarded with the title of *imprimeur du roi* and *gardien des matrices grecques*. His death in 1674 ended the uninterrupted tradition through nearly two centuries of the most brilliant family of scholar-printers that ever existed.

The Estiennes thus bridged the period between the incunabula and the Imprimerie Royale of Louis XIII, showing the unique stability as well as the almost uniform excellence of French printing through the centuries. But the ultimate return of the family to Paris also indicates the unrivalled role of the metropolis in the world of French letters. Only Lyon, the greatest – virtually the only – competitor of Paris, brilliantly maintained its position for almost a century. In Lyon, printing proper remained in the hands of German immigrants longer than anywhere else, and the influence of neighbouring Basel is very much in evidence. The branch which Anton Koberger opened in Lyon not only sold the products of the Nürnberg firm on the French market but also made independent arrangements with many Lyonese printers in order to cope with the demands for Koberger books.

The Lyon press of Johann Trechsel was carried on by Johann Klein, who married the founder's widow, and printed from 1498 to 1528, and afterwards by Trechsel's sons, Melchior and Caspar. The brothers' most famous productions are the two series of woodcuts which they commissioned from Hans Holbein in Basel and published as *Historiarum veteris instrumenti icones* and *Les Simulachres et historiees faces de la mort*, both in 1538, supplemented by Old Testament passages and Dance of Death verses respectively. The Trechsels were also the first publishers of the Spanish doctor Michael Servet, who edited for them among other books Ptolemy's *Geography* (1535). The book which caused Servet's death at the stake in Geneva in 1553, his *Restitutio Christianismi* (1552–3), was published in Vienne by Balthasar Arnoullet – both printer and place probably chosen for their obscurity. In this book Servet described the pulmonary circulation; but this discovery remained unknown as all copies of the book were burned, only three secretly surviving. William Harvey was unaware of it when he laid before his contemporaries the *Exercitatio anatomica de motu cordis et sanguinis in animalibus* (Frankfurt, 1628).

Besides the Trechsels, Sebastian Greyff, latinized Gryphius (1491–1556), a native of the Swabian imperial city of Reutlingen, is one of the eminent printers of Lyon, where he worked from 1520. His editions of ancient authors rivalled those of the Aldus and Stephanus presses. For his critical editions of the classical physicians, Hippocrates and Galen, Gryphius obtained no less an editor than François Rabelais. A Lyon printer, who unfortunately does not give his name, also produced Rabelais's *Gargantua* (2nd edition, the oldest extant, 1532) of which, so the author proclaimed, more copies were sold in two months than Bibles in nine years – perhaps a somewhat Gargantuan statement. Only two copies survive, though. Gryphius was also the first publisher of the free-thinking humanist Étienne Dolet, who in 1538 opened a press of his own from which he issued Clément Marot's Calvinist satire *L'Enfer* (1542) and his own heretical tracts which eventually led him and his books to the stake in Paris (1546).

Lyon's fame in the history of printing rests as much with its type-designers as with

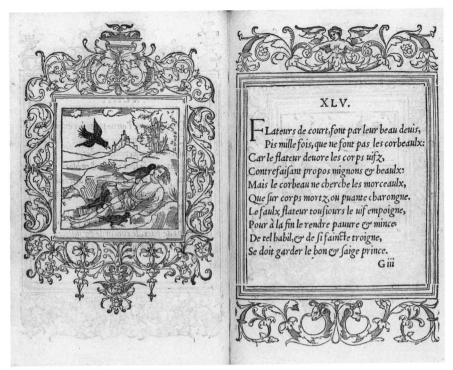

Guillaume de la Perrière, *Théâtre des bons Engins*. Denys Janot, Paris, 1539. [98.a.19]

Jacques Focard, *Paraphrases de l'Astrolabe*, woodcuts by Bernard Salomon. Jean de Tournes, Lyon, 1546. [717.d.6]

its printers. The greatest of them was Robert Granjon. He moved to Lyon in about 1556, having been in close contact with that town for some ten years. In 1546 he had supplied a set of italics to the Lyonese printer Jean de Tournes I, who printed with it a book on the astrolabe illustrated by the wood-engraver Bernard Salomon (whose daughter, Antoinette, Granjon subsequently married). Salomon also cut the arabesques 'which gave his editions such notable originality and distinction. ... Thus there first appeared in typography the beautiful large floating fleurons such as those in the *Marguerites*' – Morison. In Lyon, Granjon continued to furnish de Tournes with punches and matrices; but at the same time he published books under his own imprint. Granjon's types, Salomon's illustrations and ornaments and the presswork of Jean de Tournes, father (1504–64) and son (1539–1605), shed a final lustre on the Lyon book production of the second half of the sixteenth century, in books such as *La Vita et Metamorfosa d'Ovidio* (1584). Jean I was connected with the literary *salons* of Lyon of which Louise Labé, *la belle cordière*, was the uncrowned queen. Her only book, immortal through the sonnets it includes, was published by de Tournes in 1555. Jean II, because of his Protestant faith, had to emigrate to Switzerland in 1585 and died there.

Lyon was outdone by the overpowering competition of Paris when it was still at its height, instead of petering out in penury and incompetence as did most of the German and Italian cradles of early printing.

Spain and Portugal

Spanish civilization, in all its aspects, has throughout the centuries been marked by distinctive peculiarities which, though difficult to pin down in detail, keep Spanish art, Spanish literature, Spanish music, Spanish religiosity separate from the general development of the rest of Europe. The same specific flavour can also be found in the history of the printed book in Spain.

All the early printers were Germans – but they became at once acclimatized to a far greater degree than any German or French printer in Italy ever became italianized. They began printing in the most up-to-date roman types – but at once reverted to gothic founts which were lineal descendants of Spanish manuscript lettering. More than anywhere else they depended on ecclesiastical patronage – but right from the start books in the vernacular outnumbered those in Latin. Liberal leading, white initials on a black background, woodcut title-pages frequently decorated with armorial designs, are some of the typographical characteristics which put early Spanish books in a class by themselves.

The Great Trading Company of Ravensburg in southern Swabia, the biggest export-import firm of fifteenth-century Europe, was the agency which provided Spain with her first printers. Their main factory in the Iberian peninsula was Valencia in Aragon, and here in 1473 the German manager set up a press serviced by three of his compatriots, Lambert Palmart of Cologne, John of Salzburg, and Paul Hurus of Constance. Of these, Palmart remained in Valencia while John and Hurus went to Barcelona in 1475, Hurus later to Zaragoza. Castile, at the time lagging far behind Aragon in economic and cultural importance, received its first presses from Aragon. Burgos, the original capital and still a political and ecclesiastical centre of the kingdom, Salamanca and Alcalá, the two university towns, and Seville, the great emporium for the trade with the New World, became the seats of flourishing presses before the end of the century. Madrid, raised to the status of royal residence in 1561, first appears in printing history in 1566, but thereafter outstripped the older places.

In 1495 a Spanish princess, Queen Eleanor of Portugal, called the printers, Valentin of Moravia and Nicholas of Saxony, to Lisbon, where in 1489 the first book had been produced by a Hebrew printer. The first vernacular book published in Lisbon in 1495 was a Portuguese translation of Ludolf of Saxony's *Life of Christ* in four volumes.

In addition to the usual Latin indulgences, missals, grammars and dictionaries, Spanish literature made an early entry in print. Diego de San Pedro's novel *Cárcel de amor* was published by Johann Rosenbach in Barcelona in 1493 and by Frederick Biel of Basel in Burgos in 1496; Juan de Lucena's *Repetición de amores* by Hutz and Sanz in Salamanca in 1496; Vagad's *Crónica de Aragón* by Hurus in Zaragoza in 1499. Religious and secular poetry, edifying and entertaining prose, collections of laws and statutes, in Spanish and Hebrew (which up to 1492 was almost the second literary language of Spain), comprise about two-thirds of all Iberian book production.

In 1490 Queen Isabel put printing in Seville on a permanent footing by commissioning four *Compañeros alemanes* to print a Spanish dictionary, the first of a dignified line of officially sponsored national dictionaries of which those of the Académie Française, the Spanish Academy, and Oxford University Press were to become the most famous.

The most noteworthy press in Seville was that founded by Jacob Cromberger in 1502. He was the main publisher of the great humanist Elio Antonio de Nebrija (or Lebrixa) whose editions of Persius and Prudentius were famous for their scholarship and are still attractive for their presswork. The text was set in roman and was surrounded by the commentary in gothic. King Manuel I of Portugal commissioned Cromberger to print the *Ordonançes do reino* in 1507 and summoned him to Lisbon for the second edition in 1520; the third was done in 1539, again in Seville, by Jacob's son Juan, who had taken over the press in 1527. As Seville was the port in which the whole commerce with the Americas was concentrated, Juan Cromberger's attention was drawn to the prospects which the New World might offer to the printing trade. He obtained an exclusive privilege for printing in Mexico and sent over one Juan Pablos (= Johannes Pauli?) who in 1539 published the first American book, *Doctrina christiana en la lengua mexicana e castellana*, a fitting epitome of the Spanish combination of missionary zeal and imperialist expansion.

The printers at Salamanca specialized in the publication of classical authors for which they used roman types, which after the turn of the century were gradually introduced also in Spanish texts. Salamanca's fame as a seat of learning was rivalled, and as a seat of printing outdistanced, by the new foundation of Alcalá (1508). Cardinal Francesco Ximenes, its founder and generous patron, appointed as university printer Arnão Guillén de Brocar of Pamplona, the first native Spanish printer of significance. He began his career at Pamplona in 1492 with theological books of which he had issued not more than sixteen by 1500, all printed with great care in noble round gothic letters. They were followed by 76 more before he died in or shortly after 1523; and his reputation is well attested by the fact that Charles I (better known as the Emperor Charles V) appointed him typographer royal, a dignity which Charles later conferred also on his son, Juan.

However, Arnão's reputation as the greatest printer of sixteenth-century Spain derives from his magnificent production of the Complutensian Polyglot (Complutum being the Latin name of Alcalá de Henares), a multilingual Bible in Hebrew, Chaldee, Greek and Latin. Cardinal Ximenes, who died in 1517, did not see the completion

'Complutensian' polyglot Bible. Arnão Guillén de Brocar, Alcalá de Henares, 1514–17. [G.11951]

of this monument of scholarship and craftsmanship which, in his words, was 'to re-vive the hitherto dormant study of the Scriptures' and in fact marks the beginning of the Catholic Reformation. Ximenes spent the princely sum of 50,000 gold ducats on it. The editorial work began in 1502, the printing of the six volumes stretched from 1514 to 1517, but the book was issued only in 1522. Brocar's trial-run, as it were, of the beautiful Greek type was an edition of Musaeus's *Hero and Leander*. It is a fitting tribute to the great cardinal that one of the last books of typographical merit printed in Alcalá – or, for that matter, in Spain – should have been his biography written by Alvar Gómez de Castro and published by Andres de Angulo in 1569.

A number of the punches and matrices used by Spanish printers in the sixteenth century have come down to our time as part of the stock of the Spanish branch of the Bauer Foundry of Frankfurt. This foundry was originally owned by the monastery of San José in Barcelona and appears as a business concern from 1745. As Barcelona was one of the earliest printing places in the peninsula, it is quite possible that here some genuine 'incunabula' matrices may have survived.

England

England is the only country in Europe which owes the introduction of printing to a native, to a man, moreover, who was a gentleman rather than a professional, a dilettante rather than a scholar, supported by, but not dependent on, the nobility and gentry of the realm – William Caxton. 'His services to literature in general, and particularly to English literature, as a translator and publisher, would have made him a commanding figure if he had never printed a single page. In the history of English printing he would be a commanding figure if he had never translated or published a single book. He was a great Englishman, and among his many activities, was a printer. But he was not, from a technical point of view, a great printer' – Updike.

Born in the Weald of Kent in 1420/4, he became a businessman and spent about 30 years in Bruges, the central market of northern European commerce, where he eventually rose to the position of a modern Consul-General in charge of the interests of the English mercantile community. After relinquishing his office (perhaps not of his own free will), he found leisure for an English translation of Raoul Lefèvre's chivalrous romance *Recueil des histoires de Troye* which he dedicated to his patroness, Margaret of York, sister of Edward IV and duchess of Charles the Bold of Burgundy, in whose territories Bruges was situated. The (very early) copper-engraved frontispiece shows Caxton bending his knee to present his book to Margaret.

In order to publish the book according to his own taste, Caxton, like William Morris four centuries after him, set himself to learn the craft of printing. This he did in 1471–2 in Cologne with one of the many printers active in that teeming city. After his return to Bruges, demands for copies from 'dyuerce gentilmen and frendes' caused him to set up a press of his own in 1473, and as its first fruit the *Recuyell of the Histories of Troye* came out in 1474. This was quickly followed by the popular *Game and Playe of the Chesse*, translated by Caxton from the Latin of Jacobus de Cessolis; a second edition of the *Recuyell*; *Les Faits de Jason*; *Méditations sur les sept psaumes* and *Les quatre dernières choses*. All these books were once ascribed to the Bruges calligrapher, bookseller and printer Colard Mansion; but it has now been established that they came from Caxton's press, where Mansion learned printing before setting up independently in 1474.

Caxton returned to England in 1476 and established his press in the abbey precincts at Westminster, first near the Chapter House and later in the Almonry, at the sign of the Red Pale. At the same time he imported books from abroad on a fairly large scale, and perhaps also exported some to France; the latter, 'printed in French', may have been copies of Caxton's Bruges publications or simply unsold remainders of the imported stock. Thus, Caxton was not only the first English printer-publisher but also the first English retailer of printed books, all his London contemporaries in this trade being Dutch, German and French.

Up to his death in 1491 Caxton enjoyed the patronage, custom and friendship – it is difficult to make clear-cut distinctions – of the Yorkist kings Edward IV and Richard III and their Tudor successor, Henry VII. The second Earl Rivers, Edward IV's brother-in-law, was his first author: his *Dictes or Sayengis of the Philosophres*, the first book to be published on English soil, left Caxton's press on 18 November 1477. In the same year he brought out an *Ordinale Sarum* which is worth mentioning because it was accompanied by the first advertisement in the history of English publishing – a handbill addressed to 'ony man spirituel or temporel' who might be interested in acquiring 'good chepe' a 'well and truly correct' edition of the festival calendar according to the use of Salisbury.

Caxton's real importance lies in the fact that among the 90-odd books printed by him, 74 were in English. Some 20 of them were in his own translations which, together with the prologues and epilogues which he contributed to his other publications, secure for Caxton a lasting place in the history of English prose writing. Caxton's selection of titles shows him to have been a good businessman. They comprise chivalrous romances such as the heroic deeds of the 'good crysten man' Eracles and the conquest of the Holy Land by Godfrey of Boloyne (1481), handbooks of social and moral education such as the *Fables of Esope* (1484) and *The Doctrinal of Sapience* (1489), classical authors such as Cicero and Virgil's *Eneydos* (from a French paraphrase), a popular encyclopedia, *The Myrrour of the Worlde* (1481, reprinted 1490), English and universal histories, *Brut* (1480) and Higden's *Polychronicon* (1482) – in short, books that strongly appealed to the English upper classes at the end of the fifteenth century. However, while all these contemporary favourites have been forgotten, it is to the immortal credit of this public and its publisher that Caxton also printed, and English society bought, the *editiones principes* of the greatest glories of English medieval literature: Chaucer's *Canterbury Tales* (the first edition of 1478 was soon followed by a second in 1484, and Caxton's immediate successors had to satisfy further demands in 1492, 1495, and 1498), *Parliament of Foules, House of Fame, Boece, Troilus and Cryseide*; John Gower's *Confessio Amantis* (1483); several poems of John Lydgate's, and Sir Thomas Malory's *Le Morte Darthur* (1485). 'In appearance and in spirit Caxton's books belong to the age of chivalry and to the closing years of the Middle Ages. ... As far as England went, books were still a Gothic production' – Lewis.

After Caxton's death in 1491, his business went to his assistant Wynkyn de Worde, a native of Wörth in Alsace. He excelled in quantity rather than quality, for by 1535, the year of his death, he had published about eight hundred items. His two best books owe everything to Caxton – the English translation of the *Golden Legend*, which came out in 1493, and two reissues of the *Canterbury Tales*. However, about two-fifths of Wynkyn's output was intended for the use of grammar-school boys. These books include not only the well-worn grammars by and after Donatus and John Garland but also the then most up-to-date reformers of the school curriculum, such as Colet, Erasmus and William Lily. Wynkyn de Worde may justly be called the first publisher who actually made the schoolbook department the financial basis of his business.

In 1500 Wynkyn moved from Westminster to the City of London, where other printers were already at work. One of them, Guillaume Faques, who overcame the disadvantage of French origin by changing his name to William Fawkes, was appointed *regius impressor* to Henry VII in 1503. By royal command he printed 'in celeberrima urbe London, 1504' a beautiful *Psalterium*, a devotional book which, however, could not compete with the immensely popular *Horae ad usum Sarum*. Some 250 issues of the latter are recorded between Caxton's edition of *c.* 1477 and 1558, after which it was superseded by the *Book of Common Prayer*. Fawkes was succeeded as royal printer in 1508 by Richard Pynson, a Norman by birth. He had started printing in London in 1490 and remained in business until his death in 1530. During these years Pynson published some 400 books, technically and typographically the best of the English incunabula. They include the *Canterbury Tales* and much popular reading matter in English as well as his finest efforts – a *Horae* (1495) and three Missals (1501, 1504, 1512) *ad usum Sarum*. But Pynson's main publishing interest lay in the legal sphere. He obtained a virtual monopoly of law codes and legal handbooks for the use of professional lawyers as well as laymen such as justices of the peace and lords of the manor.

Pynson was printer to Henry VIII from 1509 to 1530, and printed Henry's learned *Assertio septem sacramentorum adversus Martinum Lutherum* (1521) which Leo X honoured with the bestowal of the title of Defender of the Faith on the royal author and his successors *in perpetuum*. Between them, Wynkyn de Worde and Richard Pynson published about two-thirds of all books for the English market from 1500 to 1530; of the remainder, local rivals and foreign presses had an almost equal share, but from 1520 onwards English printers began to make headway against both the London giants and foreign competitors.

Before the humanists and reformers got their hands on the printing press it had already been used to produce a great proliferation of prayer books in both Latin and the vernacular. In Britain the Church authorities did not permit vernacular translations of the Scriptures as a whole. Thus it came about that all the earliest English Bibles were printed abroad. When Cuthbert Tunstall, Bishop of London, refused permission for William Tyndale to translate the New Testament into English, Tyndale fled to the Netherlands and Germany; his New Testament appeared in Cologne, Worms and Mainz (incidentally from the presses of the stout Catholics, Quentell and Schöffer), his hexateuch in Antwerp. He was betrayed to the authorities there and executed before he could complete the Old Testament. The first complete Bible in English, by Miles Coverdale, came out in Antwerp (1536); its revised edition (Southwark, 1537) would have been published in Paris, had not the French Inquisition intervened and forced the printer to flee across the Channel. Matthew's Bible of 1537, the first to bear the King's authorization, was probably printed in Antwerp also. The Great Bible, as it came to be called, was finished in London under the patronage of Thomas Cranmer in 1539 after Thomas Cromwell had succeeded in acquiring the Paris press and matrices. Seven editions were called for within two years. Owing to the King's vacillating policy, its printer, Richard Grafton, was thus actually commissioned by Henry to publish a work for which, only two and a half years earlier, Tyndale had died. ('Wyclif's Bible' translation was printed only in 1850.)

In 1543 Richard Grafton and Edward Whitchurch were given the royal privilege to print all service books for use in the King's realm. Two years earlier and again in 1543 Whitchurch had produced the first Anglican breviary, *Portiforium secundum usum Sarum ... in quo nomen romano pontifici falso ascriptum omittitur*. Henry's privilege is of special interest in that it mentions for the first time the importance of the book trade for the 'balance of payment' of the country in addition to its potential political use which other sovereigns had already recognized. The first English Act of Parliament to concern itself with printed books had in 1484 expressly exempted the printer, bookseller, illuminator etc. 'of what nation or country he be' from the restrictions imposed on foreign labour; this enlightened view was very likely due to the personal interest of Richard III and the men of his court and council. This Act was repealed in 1534 when foreign 'prynters and bynders of bokes' were excluded from selling books in England. Now, in 1543, the official draftsman of the royal privilege made Henry say: 'In tymes past it has been usually accustomed that theis bookes of divine service ... have been printed by strangiers in other and strange countreys, partly to the great loss and hindrance of our subjects who both have the sufficient arte, feate and treade of printing and by imprinting such bookes myght profitably and to thuse of the commonwealth be set on worke.'

This privilege obliged the printers, whatever their personal opinions may have been, to print all the divergent and mutually exclusive service books which the changing

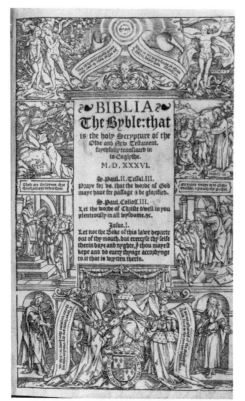

Three English Bibles printed abroad. William Tyndale's translation, 1536 [C.18.b.8]; Matthew's Bible, 1537 [C.18.c.5]; Cranmer's Great Bible, 1539 [C.18.d.1].

policies of successive governments required them to publish. The names of Grafton (d. 1572) and Whitchurch (d. 1562) appear indifferently on Henry VIII's catholic *Primer* and Edward VI's compromising *Order of Communion* and on the English translation of Calvin's radical *Forme of common praiers*, on the two Edwardian as well as the Elizabethan *Booke of common prayer*. They would probably have printed also for Mary I had not Grafton published the proclamation of accession for Lady Jane Grey in July 1553. Mary showed herself not at all 'bloody' on this occasion: Grafton escaped with a few weeks' imprisonment, a fine and the deprivation of his title as the Queen's Printer. He even entered Parliament, first for the City of London and later for Coventry.

In the next century one Henry Hills managed to be successively printer to the army, the Anabaptists, the Lord Protector, the Rump Parliament, Charles II and James II, and nearly succeeded in gobbling the Oxford University Press.

Mary's reign marks a turning point in the history of the English book trade. In 1557 the printer-publishers, organized since 1403 in the Stationers' Company, received a royal charter, partly for the better tracking down and punishing of the producers and purveyors of heretical or seditious writings. The Company was soon to become an all-powerful executive organ which, while it lasted, effectively stifled the free development of the English book-trade.

In 1586 Star Chamber issued a decree prohibiting printing outside London, though the universities of Oxford and Cambridge were allowed one press each, and in 1662 printing was permitted at York for the convenience of Charles I in his conduct of the Civil War. This restriction remained until the Licensing Act expired in 1695.

In view of the unique role which the two great English university presses have come to play in academic life in Britain and beyond, it is rather surprising to see how slowly Oxford and Cambridge grasped the potentialities inherent in Gutenberg's invention. It is characteristic that, in contrast with London, the first presses in both towns were established by Germans. In Oxford, Dietrich Rode (Theoderich Rood) of Cologne between 1478 and 1486 printed seventeen undistinguished books, mostly writings of the schoolmen, with Cicero's *Pro Milone* (1486) as the first classical author published in England – and this in the place which had enjoyed the humanist patronage of 'good Duke Humphrey'. Considering the meticulous care which the publishers at Oxford University Press now bestow on its productions, the 'imp who supplies the misprints' – the *Druckfehlerteufel* in German printers' parlance – must have enjoyed himself when he dropped an x out of the date of the colophon in Rood's first book: the reading MCCCClxviii instead of the correct MCCCClxxviii has provoked some learned controversy among bibliographers.

Cambridge even lagged 40 years behind Oxford. John Lair, or John Siberch as he called himself after his place of birth, Siegburg near Cologne, arrived in Cambridge in 1519, and by the time he left early in 1523 he had produced only ten small books and an indulgence. His modest importance rests on his being the first to have Greek types in England, although the *primus utriusque linguae in Anglia impressor*, as he styled himself, printed no books in Greek. In 1534 Cambridge secured a charter from Henry VIII which authorized the Chancellor or his deputies to appoint three 'stationers and printers' who might produce and sell books approved by the university. But it was not until 1584 (Cambridge) and 1585 (Oxford) that these licensees issued books approved by the universities and became university printers in the proper sense.

Greek and Hebrew printing

When Aldus Manutius in about 1490 decided upon making the editing of Greek authors the mainstay of his business, his first problem was the creation of a fount of Greek letters. The frequent occurrence of Greek words in Cicero's correspondence had right from the beginning caused printers to add Greek letters to their founts, as did Peter Schöffer and Sweynheym and Pannartz as early as 1465. They usually employed Latin letters for those which are identical in appearance in both languages, such as A, B, E, H, O, P, C, T, X, Y, and had special punches made only for specifically Greek letters such as Δ, Θ, Φ. Jenson in 1471 used a Greek type as noble as his roman fount. The first book printed entirely in Greek was Constantine Lascaris's ΕΡΩΤΗ-ΜΑΤΑ, a Greek grammar which came out in Milan in 1476, and Milan remained for some time the main centre of Greek printing. Demetrius Chalcondylas of Crete, who had written the (Latin) preface to Lascaris's book, himself edited the first printed Greek text of Homer; dedicated to Lorenzo de' Medici, it was published in two folio volumes in Florence in 1488–9. Before that date Erhard Ratdolt had already included a full set of Greek letters in his specimen sheet of 1486. All these early designers tried to evolve a Greek type that would match the Latin founts and therefore aimed at reproducing calligraphic forms which, in both cases, ultimately derived from epigraphic lettering. The beautiful, stately and clear Alcalá type in which Arnão Guillén de Brocar in 1514 printed the Greek portions of Cardinal Ximenes's Polyglot Bible is the greatest achievement of this school of type-design. It was modelled on a manuscript which Pope Leo X had put at the cardinal's disposal expressly for this purpose.

Unfortunately, Aldus's predilection for cursive letters, which made him a pioneer in the printing of Latin texts, led him to commission Greek founts which made the fine printing of Greek texts a virtual impossibility. Instead of adopting or adapting the serviceable Greek fount cut by the Venetian printer, Giovanni Rosso, in 1492, Aldus chose as the model for his Greek type the informal everyday hand of his contemporary Greek scholar-friends, a careless and ugly script, made even less legible through its numberless contractions and ligatures (the only feature of the Aldine Greek which was later abandoned). It was, it is true, convenient for the pen-man, but for that very reason lacked the clearness, discipline and impersonality which are the hall-marks of any type that aspires to be generally applicable. From Aldus's press there were issued the *editiones principes* of Musaeus, Theocritus, Hesiod (1495), Aristotle (1495–8), Aristophanes (1498), Thucydides, Herodotus, Sophocles (1502), Plato (1513) and some twenty more which have kept alive Aldus's fame among scholars, if not typographers.

The unfortunate precedent set by Aldus was made a permanent feature of Greek printing when Claude Garamond accepted Aldus's principles for the founts which he cut at the behest of François I of France. For the Complutensian Greek face found no favour elsewhere, probably because its width was too large for economic commercial productions. Thus the field was left to Garamond's *grecs du roi* until quite recently Robert Proctor, Victor Scholderer, Jan van Krimpen, W. A. Dwiggins and Hermann Zapf produced Greek sets which are equal to the best Latin founts.

The three sets of *grecs du roi* remained the property of the crown and after some vicissitudes eventually found their place in the Imprimerie Nationale; but matrices were put at the disposal of printers on condition that the books thus printed bore the note '*typis regis*'. Typographically – that is, 'for evenness of colour, for precision of

casting, and for the exactness of alignment and justification' – the *grecs du roi* consti-
tute a huge advance over Aldus's types, but Robert Proctor's praise as 'by far the best
type of its kind that has ever been cut' seems extravagant. For Garamond, too, used
as his model a contemporary Greek hand which, if anything, contained even more
contractions and ligatures than the one that served the Venetian cutter. The calligrapher who drew the designs, Angelos Vergetios of Crete, received the title of professor
from the king. Robert Estienne was the first printer to be permitted the use of the
grecs du roi. Four books by Eusebius (1544–6) and three editions of the New Testament (1546–50) propagated the three founts, all of which were used together in
Estienne's edition of Appian (1551). Curiously, Estienne was appointed *imprimeur
& libraire ès lettres hebraiques & latines* (1539), whereas the title of royal printer for
Greek was bestowed, together with his naturalization, on one Conrad Neobar of
Cologne. After Neobar's death in 1540, Robert Estienne called himself *typographus
regius* without further qualification.

Italy was also the birthplace of Hebrew typography. It is most likely that Jewish
scholars, craftsmen, and financiers were at once alive to the intellectual and commercial possibilities inherent in the new invention. As German printers turned up for
shorter or longer periods in dozens of Italian towns and townlets, Jews, who were to
be found all over the peninsula, must have had ample opportunities of closely watching them at work. The first books in Hebrew characters appeared from 1475 onward
in a number of places. Abraham ben Garton of Reggio di Calabria and Meshullam
of Pieve di Sacco were the Hebrew proto-typographers; in 1475 the former printed
a commentary on the Pentateuch, and the latter a Jewish law code. Mantua, Ferrara,
Bologna and Soncino were the next places from which Hebrew books emanated.
Among them the village of Soncino near Cremona has gained special fame thanks
to the printers' dynasty which took their family name from it. The Soncino family
originally came from Germany (Speier in the Palatinate or Fürth near Nürnberg).
Israel (d. 1489) took to printing after his banking business had failed. His son Joshua
set up a press in Naples but died as early as 1492. His younger son, Gerson, was to
become 'the greatest Jewish printer the world has ever known'. As restless as the
majority of the early printers, he moved to Brescia, Barco, Fano, Pesaro, Ortona,
Rimini, spent some time in France, and finally left for Turkey in 1527. There he
printed at Constantinople and eventually Salonika where he died in 1534. Gerson's
descendants continued to print in the Ottoman empire and are last heard of in Cairo
in 1562–6.

The Soncinos issued some 130 books in Hebrew founts. In addition Gerson also
printed in the vernacular; for his edition of Petrarch's poems (1503) he used types cut
by Francesco Griffo of Venice. Gerson was driven out of business in Italy by the
competition of a Venetian printer. This man, Daniel Bomberg, a Christian business
man of German descent, obtained from the Senate a privilege for printing Hebrew
books (1515–49), and to the end of the sixteenth century Hebrew printing in Venice
remained in Christian hands.

'The most prolific cutter of Hebrew types' was also a gentile. Guillaume Le Bé
(1525–98), a Frenchman from Troyes, learned the trade in Robert Estienne's type-
foundry. In 1545 he went to Venice and there he cut no fewer than eight Hebrew
founts for two Christian printers during the next four years, in addition to Greek and
roman punches. Back in France, he supplied more Hebrew founts to Garamond and
Plantin.

Thereafter, Hebrew typography went from bad to worse, with the exception of the founts designed by Christoffel van Dyck and those used by the Jewish printer, Joseph Athias of Amsterdam (d. 1691), who bought the amalgamated foundry of van Dyck and Daniel Elzevir after the latter's death (1680).

5. PRINTING IN THE VERNACULAR

The effect of the spread of printing on the intellectual conditions of the European nations resulted in the simultaneous strengthening of two diametrically opposed trends of thought. On the one hand, the ties which linked the individual members of the European commonwealth of nations were strengthened. The thoughts of philosophers, the discoveries of scientists, the writings of poets, and many other products of the human mind now swiftly became common property and were soon to be the precious heritage of all nations regardless of their national and personal origin. The medieval conception of the *Respublica Christiana* was dying when Gutenberg made his invention; the printer's craft resuscitated it in the form of the *Respublica Litterarum* in which every nation exerts its proportionate influence.

On the other hand, the spread of printing tended to deepen, and even created, national frontiers in the sphere of intellectual activities. For the more the circle of readers widened, the less authors and publishers could rely on their mastering Latin, the common vehicle of communication in the Middle Ages. The public who were now given easy access to literature wished it to be made easier still and preferred books printed in their mother tongue to those in the idiom of scholars.

'Scholars' here includes schoolboys. It was not only Cicero, Livy, Virgil, Horace and the rest of the present-day school authors who were read in sixteenth-century grammar schools. Italian masters, it is true, believed in the superior virtue of a strictly 'classical' curriculum, but in Spain, France, the Low Countries and Germany there were teachers who preferred medieval Christian authors whose style could pass muster to the ancient pagans whose morals could not. The versification in hexameters of the Gospel according to St Matthew by the fourth-century Spaniard Juvencus was printed ten times before 1519. Of the poems of his greater contemporary and compatriot Prudentius some twenty editions appeared between 1497 and 1540. Their places of publication were the main seats of a decidedly Christian humanism: Deventer, Zwolle, Leipzig, Salamanca, Paris, Antwerp, Vienna; but centres of a more secular outlook, such as Nürnberg, Lyon and Rouen, are also represented. Erasmus's insistence on Cicero's latinity as the sole standard of purity eventually eliminated these and similar authors from the school curricula. This, however, did not damp the enthusiasm of the Holoferneses for the imitations of Virgil's *Eclogues* by the Carmelite general Battista Mantovano; 'Ah, good old Mantuan! Who understandeth thee not, loves thee not.' Knowledge – perhaps not invariably matched by love – of Mantovano's poems is sufficiently attested by more than three hundred editions published between their first appearance in 1488 and Shakespeare's schooldays.

The numbers of titles printed in Latin and the vernaculars is in itself no absolute yardstick as, at least from the beginning of the sixteenth century onward, editions of Latin texts tended to become proportionally smaller. Even so, the change of the ratio of books tells its own story. Before 1500, about three-quarters of all printed matter was in Latin, about one-twelfth each in Italian and German. Only in England and Spain did vernacular books outnumber Latin ones from the beginning. The proportion of Latin and German titles sold at the Frankfurt and Leipzig book fairs was

71:29 in 1650, 38:62 in 1700, 28:72 in 1740 and 4:96 in 1800. Publishers in university towns held out longer: in 1700 Jena still produced 58 per cent of books in Latin and Tübingen even 80 per cent; whereas, at the same date, the mercantile town of Hamburg listed only 37 per cent of books in Latin.

The first books printed in the vernacular are therefore of special interest, as they permit an estimate of the taste of the class which had no Latin but was capable of reading and affluent enough to buy reading matter. The list of vernacular books in German is headed by Ulrich Boner's *Edelstein* and Johann von Tepl's *Ackermann aus Böhmen*, the first letterpress books to contain illustrations, both published by Albrecht Pfister in Bamberg in 1461 who produced also an illustrated *Biblia pauperum* in German and Latin. Both are moralizing fables of considerable literary merit, the former written in 1349, the latter in 1405; they have continued to appeal, the one to rationalist, the other to pious readers of later ages. These were followed in 1466 by the first Bible in German translation, published by Johann Mentelin in Strasbourg.

A Bible translation heads the list of books in Italian – or rather two, both of which appeared in Venice in 1471. This incidentally shows how quickly competition was growing. Two years later a printer in Parma apologized for the careless printing of a book: because other printers were bringing out the same text, he says, he had to rush his book through the press 'more quickly than asparagus could be cooked'. The *editio princeps* of Dante's *Divine Comedy*, published by Johann Neumeister in Foligno in 1472, has already been mentioned. An Italian-German dictionary, printed by Adam of Rottweil at Venice in 1477, is remarkable as the first dictionary of two living languages. The Latin-German editions of Aesop by Johann Zainer in Ulm (1476–7) and of Cato by Johann Bämler in Augsburg (1492) are among the earliest bilingual texts.

The French and Danish languages appeared first in print in national chronicles, the *Croniques de France* (Paris, 1477) and the *Danske Rym-Kronicke* (Copenhagen, 1495) and the first book in modern Greek was appropriately the immortal Greek epic, a translation of Homer's *Iliad* (Venice, 1526).

Geneva, otherwise of little importance in the early history of printing, is remarkable for the high percentage – about one-third – of vernacular books among its incunabula. The first four books, printed in the same year, 1478, by the Genevan proto-typographer Adam Steinschaber, a graduate of Erfurt university, are all in French: two theological books translated from the Catalan and Latin, and two French romances. Romances remained popular with Genevan printers and, no doubt, their customers; they probably included the first appearance in print of the *Roman de la Rose* (about 1480).

In the development of vernacular printing England again occupied a unique position in European letters, as had been its happy lot in Anglo-Saxon times. Just as from the seventh to the twelfth centuries England was the only country in western Christendom which kept its language alive in poetry and prose while the Continent was submerged by Latin, so England entered the era of printing with a wealth of books in the English tongue. The mantle of King Alfred fell on William Caxton's shoulders. More than four-fifths of Caxton's books were in the English tongue, either original works or translations. The next generation of English printers continued in this vein, with the result that the victory of English over Latin as the most popular medium of printed literature was assured from the very beginning.

In Britain, as everywhere else, the printing press has preserved and codified, sometimes even created, the vernacular; with numerically small and economically weak peoples its absence has demonstrably led to its disappearance or, at least, its exclusion from the realm of literature. The survival of Welsh is largely due to the fact that from 1546 books were printed in Cymric. The first Welsh book, a collection of prayers known by its incipit as *Yny Lhyvyr hwnn* ('in this book'), was printed in London by Edward Whitchurch, probably commissioned by the Welsh antiquary, Sir John Price. The first Welsh text printed in the Principality was a Roman Catholic tract, *Y Drych Cristianogawl* (The Christian Mirror), printed clandestinely in Rhiwledyn near Llandudno in 1586–7. But the fact that Welsh has to this day remained the only Celtic language with a living literature equal to that of any other nation is largely due to the magnificent Bible translation of Bishop William Morgan (1588). Combining the rich and flexible vocabulary of bardic poetry with the majestic rhythms of Jerome's Vulgate and the Geneva Bible, Morgan set a standard which determined the course of Welsh prose as Luther's Bible and the Authorized Version did for German and English literatures.

At the same period, and also in connection with the Elizabethan settlement of the national church, the Irish language was drawn into the orbit of the printing press. In or before 1567 Elizabeth I ordered the cutting of a special fount of Irish types for editions of the New Testament and the Anglican catechism; but it was used first for the printing of an 'irishe balade' on the Day of Doom by a contemporary Irish bard of the Roman faith (1571). As has not infrequently happened with the English government's activities in the affairs of Ireland, the result was very different from the intention. Far from converting the Irish to the English church, the Gaelic characters became a powerful weapon against the English church and state. Irish literature (and Irish tourism) would probably be better off without the encumbrance of a script which, though most decorative on postage stamps, raises an additional bar to its understanding; but there can be little doubt that here again type-founders and printers have done a permanent job in sustaining a national civilization. The opposite fate overcame Cornish, the next-of-kin of Welsh and Irish; it became extinct for the lack of a printed literature.

The same applies to the Basque language; that relic of Old Iberian has been fixed in print since 1545 and thus has a fair chance of surviving. The survival of the Catalan language too owes much to the fact that the first printing presses in the Iberian peninsula were set up in Catalonia. A collection of poems in honour of the Blessed Virgin (1474) and a Bible translation (1478) were the first books in the Catalan language. The Valencia Bible (i.e. translated into Valencian Catalan) has suffered a tragic fate; it was burnt for dogmatic rather than nationalistic reasons by the Inquisition. Not only was it prohibited as a vernacular version; additionally, it had been made by Jewish converts (*conversos*), and the Inquisition were looking for evidence of judaizing practices among *conversos*. The one copy saved from the holocaust perished in 1697 when the royal library in Stockholm was damaged by fire. The Inquisition also suppressed the most beautiful Book of Hours from the press of Thielmann Kerver in Paris (1517) because the prayers to the Holy Virgin were printed in Spanish; only one copy is known to have survived.

Even in the Baltic and Balkan countries, where the economic and cultural foothold of Germany was strongest, the main effect of printing was a national revival, first of the languages and later of the literatures of those peoples. The Lithuanian, Latvian, Estonian and Finnish languages might in the course of the sixteenth century have been absorbed by German, Polish and Swedish, as were the languages of the Prussians,

Pomeranians, Courlanders, and other tribes before them, had they not been preserved in print. Estonian, Latvian and Livonian translations of Lutheran writings, printed in Wittenberg, were shipped to Riga and Reval as early as 1525; a Lithuanian translation of Luther's Catechism was printed in Königsberg in 1547; Bishop Agricola's Finnish Primer, in Stockholm in 1542 – these were the first printed books in the respective languages. Although they were printed abroad – and printing in Finland, for instance, did not begin until 1642 – their very existence sufficed to form the basis of vernacular literatures in the Baltic languages, reaching international recognition in, for example, the award of the Nobel prize to the Finnish writer, Sillanpää (1939).

The fate of the languages spoken by the Germans in what used to be the fringes of the Holy Roman Empire was also conditioned to a great extent by the printing press. The Netherlands, which formally seceded from the empire only in 1648, had established their Low Frankish dialect as a distinct 'Dutch' language when, after the early publication of an Old Testament in Dutch (Delft, 1477), in 1523 Luther's New Testament was translated and printed in Antwerp. Switzerland – until 1648, too, a nominal member state of the German empire – took a different road. The Zürich edition of the New Testament which came out in 1524 kept closely to Luther's text, only sparingly introducing a few Alemannic words and phrases. The great bulk of Swiss literature has followed this method ever since, so that attempts made from time to time to elevate 'Swiss German' to the rank of a literary language have met with no lasting success. The farthest outposts of German settlements in Europe – in Transylvania and the Baltic countries – which might have developed their own languages as easily as the Netherlands, remained entirely within the orbit of the German language as they accepted Luther's Bible together with the Lutheran creed.

The foregoing examples have already shown the strong impact on the spread of vernacular printing exercised by the Reformation. Bible translations, mostly following the Lutheran version, therefore play a conspicuous part in sixteenth-century vernacular book production. In Germany, up to 1517 – the year when Luther published his 95 theses – the yearly output of books in the German language averaged 40; in 1519, it was 111; in 1521, it reached 211; in 1522, 347; in 1525, 498. Of the last, 183 were publications by Luther himself, 215 by other reformers, and 20 by opponents of the new faith, leaving about 80 vernacular books on secular subjects.

By 1500, 30 Bible translations had already been printed in vernacular versions (mostly in German), compared with 94 Latin editions of the Vulgate. After 1522 every European nation received the Scriptures in its mother tongue: the Netherlands in 1523 (N.T.) and 1525 (O.T.); England in 1524 (Tyndale's N.T.), 1535 (Coverdale's Bible), 1537 (the Matthew Bible), 1539 (the Great Bible) – all of which had to be printed abroad; Denmark in 1524 (N.T.) and 1550; Sweden in 1526 (N.T.) and 1540–1; Iceland in 1540 (N.T.) and 1584; Hungary in 1541 (N.T.); Spain and Croatia in 1543; Finland in 1548–52; Poland in 1552–3; the Slovenes in 1557–82; the Rumanians, in 1561–3; the Lithuanians in 1579–90; the Czechs in 1579–93.

Having fortified the 'language walls' between one nation and another, the printers proceeded to break down the minor differences of speech – most noticeably of vocabulary, grammatical forms, and syntax – within any given language group. If today the 'Queen's English' has become the standard idiom of millions of writers and readers, beside which the dialects of Kent, Lancashire, Northumberland and all the rest have dwindled into local insignificance, Caxton and his brothers-in-art may justly claim the credit for it. It was Caxton who overcame the perplexing confusion of

Middle-English dialects, and, by adopting that of the Home Counties and London, fixed a standard which has never been abandoned and is now the common medium of expression and thought of millions of people all over the world.

Caxton was very conscious of his service to a unified English language. He reinforced his argument by the charming anecdote of the Kentish woman off North Foreland whom a London merchant asked for some 'eggys'. 'And the good wyfe answerde that she coude speke no frenshe.' It was only when another man asked for 'eyren' (cp. German 'Eier') that she 'sayd she vnderstod hym wel'. Wynkyn de Worde continued this process. For his edition of Bartholomaeus Anglicus (1495) he used a manuscript written about fifty years earlier, but he changed all those words which did not conform to the standard speech Caxton had adopted. A comparison between the manuscript and the print shows that every one of Wynkyn's alterations has come to stay: *call* and *name* for *clepe*, *go* for *wend*, *two* for *twey*, *third* for *þridde*, etc. Wynkyn thus can put forward a modest claim to having inaugurated what we now call the house-style of a printing or publishing firm, which overrides the inconsistencies of individual authors.

The standardization of the English language through the effect of printing has led to a tremendous expansion of the vocabulary, a virtual ban on the development of accidence and syntax, and an ever-widening gulf between the spoken and the written word. As soon as a printed grammar of sorts became available to every schoolboy – and Latin grammars and English primers were among the first books to pour forth from the presses – people got hold of the idea that there are fixed standards of 'right' and 'wrong'. The rules laid down by the author of a grammar or dictionary became binding and stopped the free development of the language – at least so far as its appearance in print is concerned. Thus the most remarkable, or at least the most visible, expression of the standardization of the English language through the egalitarianism of the press is to be seen in our modern spelling. Up to the invention of printing, spelling was largely phonetic; that is to say, every scribe rendered the words on parchment or paper more or less as he heard them (although monastic scriptoria and princely and municipal chancelleries strove after a certain uniformity within their orbits): the modern keyboard operator sets them up as Oxford and Chicago, Webster and Hart, decree. Milton was one of the last authors who dared to force on his printers the idiosyncrasies of his spelling, such as the distinction between emphatic *hee* and lightly spoken *he*.

The mighty influence of the printed word may be observed in the development of the German and Italian languages. Whereas throughout the Middle Ages Low German and High German were two independent literary languages, the Wittenberg printers of Luther's translation of the Bible secured for 'Lutheran German' (a skilful blend of the two with Central German) the undisputed ascendancy which soon reduced all other forms to the status of dialects. Similarly in Italy the Tuscan tongue, as used in Annibale Caro's *Lettere familiari* (1572–5), was adopted by all Italian printers and thus superseded the rival claims of the Roman, Neapolitan, Lombard and other dialects. In France the use of the acute and grave accents and the apostrophe was established by Robert Estienne in the 1530s.

The central figure of the early book trade was the printer. He procured the services of an engraver to cut punches specially for him and had them cast at a local foundry; he chose the manuscripts he wished to print and edited them; he determined the number of copies to be printed; he sold them to his customers; and all the accounts went through his ledgers – if he kept any. If he did not perform all these functions himself, it was he who had to raise the capital, commission an editor, and organize the distribution through his own agents.

It is only the paper-makers and bookbinders who from the beginning to the present have kept their independence: their crafts went back to the times of the handwritten book, and their technical skill and experience were at the printers' disposal, saving these newcomers the need for capital outlay and costly experiments.

The situation has gradually changed, until today the publisher is the life-force of the book trade. He selects the author and the book – frequently originating and commissioning a particular subject; he chooses the printer and mostly the type and paper; he fixes the price of the books; and he organizes the channels of distribution. The printer, in fact, has, in the public eye, become a mere appendage of the publisher; not one in ten thousand readers has probably ever looked at the printer's imprint.

The difficulty of combining the functions of printer, editor, publisher and book-seller was in itself formidable enough to cause a gradual separation – all the more as, even at the beginning, the personal inclinations of the individual must have made him concentrate on one or the other aspect of the business. Already Peter Schöffer, whose main interest was typographical, employed proof-readers, and one of them gratefully mentions their liberal remuneration. The three German printers who were invited to the Sorbonne in 1470 brought with them three German correctors, and a few years later the first British proof-reader, David Laux of Edinburgh, appears among these specialists in Paris. Johannes Froben neatly expressed the good publisher's concern for his public in the words: '*Qui librum mendis undique scatentem habet, certe non habet librum sed molestiam*' – the buyer of a book full of misprints does not really acquire a book but a nuisance. Froben's star author Erasmus's solicitude for faultless texts made him issue, in 1529, the first *Errata et Addenda* appendix. Aldus Manutius preceded him with the insertion of a slip in his Aristotle edition where a whole line had dropped out; but Erasmus filled 26 pages with about 180 corrections 'so that owners of his writings might rectify their books and printers of future editions could avail themselves of his emendations'.

Very early the idea must have recommended itself to form publishing companies in which authors or editors, businessmen and printers would pool their knowledge, money and practical experience. The first two ventures of this kind are even more remarkable in that the partners envisaged a definite programme of publications. In Milan in 1472 a priest, a schoolmaster, a professor, a lawyer, a doctor and a printer formed such a publishing company. The participants were not just financing the printer: they constituted a policy-making board which decided the selection of the books to be issued and fixed their prices.

An ambitious undertaking on similar lines was started in Perugia in 1475. Jacob Langenbeck, son of the burgomaster of the Hanse town of Buxtehude and a professor of theology at the Sapienza Vecchia, conceived the idea of publishing the *editio princeps* of the *Corpus juris civilis*. For this purpose Langenbeck combined with a representative of the Baglioni, the ruling family of Perugia – and the reign of terror they exercised must have made such a re-insurance most desirable – a punch-cutter from Ulm, the printer Stephen Arndes from Hamburg and the university bedel, a native of the Rhineland, who was to sell the firm's books to the professors and students. Langenbeck's brother Hermann, professor of civil law and vice-chancellor of Greifswald university, was to join the firm as editor. But when he arrived in Perugia Jacob had died and the ambitious enterprise petered out in bankruptcy and lawsuits, the *Digestum vetus* and the first part of the *Pandects* being the only tangible result. Two of the partners, however, were to get on very far: Hermann Langenbeck became burgomaster of Hamburg (1482–1517) and, through his maritime law code (1497) and commentary on the Hamburg town law, the creator of Hanseatic jurisprudence; and Stephen Arndes became the leading printer of the Low German and Danish world centred on Lübeck.

As the majority of the early printers were of humble station and small account, there is a scarcity of biographical information which hardly permits generalizations concerning their individual fortunes: but it would seem that only a few succeeded in making the book trade a paying proposition. These few, however, who rose to an assured place in the commercial world, owed their prosperity – if not always their reputation with posterity – to their publishing activities rather than their typographical achievements.

The first man to make publishing (and bookselling) his exclusive occupation seems to have been Johann Rynmann, who died at Augsburg in 1522. Of the nearly 200 books which appeared over his imprint, not one was produced by Rynmann himself; he had them printed in Augsburg, Basel, Hagenau, Nürnberg, Venice and elsewhere, and 'the most famous and leading archibibliopola of the German nation' – according to his own valuation – confined himself to their stocking and selling.

Most of the early printers, including Gutenberg himself, seem to have been better printers than businessmen. Their lack of commercial success can be attributed to the fact that they did not realize the dominant dilemma of the publishing trade, namely the outlay of considerable capital in advance of each publication coupled with the slowness of the turnover, if any. And if they realized it, most of them, again including Gutenberg himself, were unable to supply the necessary capital. The few printer-publishers who were in a position to invest large sums, and to tide themselves over the waiting period, made good; as is borne out by the firms of Schöffer, Amerbach-Froben, Manutius and Koberger. But as a rule the printers had to secure their capital from outsiders, and this co-operation of artisan and financier easily led to the subsequent separation of printer and publisher. This development is reflected in the way in which the one and the other have been introducing themselves to the purchaser of their products.

The colophon (literally the end-part or tail-piece of the book) was the first means by which the printer-publisher proclaimed his part in the technical process, secured his moral and legal rights – such as his rivals were prepared to acknowledge – in the commercial exploitation of the finished article, and vouchsafed any further information that might stimulate its sales. Owing to the parting of the ways of printer and publisher, the present-day colophon in the true sense of the word has been reduced to a bare statement, and might have disappeared altogether from English books if it were not enforced by law.

The early colophon fulfilled to some extent the function of a modern title-page. It also contained material which would nowadays be restricted to the blurb or left to the discretion of the reviewers. A laudatory reference to the quality of the printer's work is very common, and the novelty and marvel of the art of printing is often stressed. Thus Gutenberg says of the *Catholicon* of 1460 that 'it was printed and put together not with the aid of reed, stylus or quill but by the marvellous harmony, symmetry and regularity of punches and matrices'.

In 1471, in the preface of one of the first books printed in France, the Paris professor Guillaume Fichet refers to 'Johann, surnamed Gutenberg, who was the first to devise the art of printing by which books are formed not by the reed (as did the ancients) or by the quill (as we do) but by letters of bronze, and in an elegant and beautiful fashion'.

The colophon which Arnold Pannartz added to his edition of Lorenzo Valla's *De elegantia linguae latinae* (1475) comprehends an advertisement in terms so modest that *The Times Educational Supplement* would not refuse it: 'Anyone who wants to master spoken Latin should buy this book for he will rapidly become efficient if he applies himself carefully and zealously to the task.' Other publishers tried to stimulate the sale of their publications by running down those of rival firms. Ulrich Han, in the colophon to his *Decretals* (1474), told the prospective buyer to 'acquire this book with a light heart' as he would find it so excellent that, by comparison, other editions 'are not worth a straw' (*floccipendes*).

Some, perhaps most, printers had the colophons composed by professional writers. Wendelin of Speier, for instance, employed the poet Rafael Zovenzoni of Trieste during the years 1471–3 who, with pride entirely unjustified, appended his name to these 'carmina'.

The spurious *Letters of Phalaris*, which in the last years of the seventeenth century created the famous controversy out of which Richard Bentley emerged as the greatest classical scholar of the age, had long before gained notoriety in the history of English books. Its first edition, brought out by Theodore Rood of Cologne in Oxford in 1485, contains a colophon in verse for which the Oxford don who composed it may well claim the invention of the 'Buy British' slogan. With a fine disregard for truth, he boasts:

> Quam Ienson Venetos docuit vir Gallicus artem
> Ingenio didicit terra Britanna suo.
> Celatos Veneti nobis transmittere libros
> Cedite: nos aliis vendimus, O Veneti.

(The art which the Venetians had to be taught by the Frenchman Jenson, Britain has learned by its native genius. Cease, ye Venetians, sending us any more books for now we sell them to others.)

Caxton's colophons are in a class by themselves. They often combine a genuine colophon with a dedication and all that a modern editor would put into a preface or postscript. They are in fact brilliant little essays on the text they follow, and as much part of English literature as of English printing.

Usually printed after the colophon, devices or printers' marks have also been used from the very beginning of printing. The identity of printer and publisher soon turned them also into publishers' devices. The purpose was the same: to serve as a hall-mark of quality, and to safeguard what later became known as copyright.

Heraldic propriety, artistic design or striking inventiveness make many of the early printers' devices precious specimens of graphic art. Their importance is heightened when they appear together with, or in place of, a famous firm. Fust and Schöffer's well-known double-shield is in the tradition of the trade-marks of medieval crafts-men, such as goldsmiths and masons. The heraldic devices of Spanish printers are among the most impressive. The serpent coiled round the cross (Melchior Lotter of Wittenberg) or a flowering branch (Robert Granjon of Lyon) were popular. Aldus Manutius's dolphin and anchor is perhaps most famous of all. The devices of the later sixteenth and the seventeenth century suffer from the baroque exuberance of the designers. That of the Stephanus press, for instance, which represents the tree of knowledge as interpreted by humanist philosophy, is an illustrated motto (and has actually been used as such in emblem books); it fails in the main purpose of a trade-mark, namely to be recognized at first glance.

Within two decades of the invention of printing, the printers had evolved the main forms of publicity which publishers have used ever since to advertise their production: the leaflet containing details about a book or a number of books published; the prospectus announcing intended publications; the poster to attract casual passers-by; and the list showing the stock of a publisher or bookseller. Again and again the historian is struck by the fact that all these various offshoots of Gutenberg's art sprang into existence full-grown and fully armed, like Athena from Zeus's forehead.

When referring to the 'first' prospectus, catalogue, etc., we must keep in mind the parlous state of preservation of these ephemeral by-products of the printing press. The fact that most of these early specimens have survived in one copy only is eloquent in itself. Mentioning the first item means only the first extant piece, so that the date of its actual 'invention' may be even earlier.

Heinrich Eggestein of Strasbourg, otherwise known as the printer of the second German Bible translation, issued the earliest known advertisement in 1466. He was speedily followed by Peter Schöffer, Bertold Ruppel, Sweynheym and Pannartz, and by Mentelin about 1470, Caxton in 1477, Koberger, Ratdolt and others from about 1480 onwards. Schöffer's first advertisement already included 21 titles. Sweynheym and Pannartz, who showed 19 titles in 1470 and 28 in 1472, introduced the useful features of adding the prices of each book and the number of copies of each edition. The prices ranged from 16 groschen for Cicero's *De oratore* to 10 ducats for Thomas Aquinas's *Catena aurea* and 20 ducats for their 2-volume Bible; the editions comprised normally 275 and occasionally 300 copies.

7. EARLY BESTSELLERS

The criterion of popularity of medieval books is the number of manuscripts that have survived or are known to have existed. Wolfram von Eschenbach's *Parzival*, with more than eighty manuscripts, and Chaucer's *Canterbury Tales*, with more than sixty, rank among the favourites of entertaining narrative literature.

From Gutenberg onward the number of editions and the size of each edition have to be combined in assessing the success of a book. Care must be taken, however, to distinguish between the visible, and usually instantaneous, success of some books, which can be expressed in figures, and the imponderable, and usually slow, effect of others, which defies arithmetical analysis. There have always been books which, despite their modest circulation, have exerted a tremendous influence on the general climate of opinion. Neither Jacob Burckhardt's *Civilization of the Renaissance in Italy* nor Karl Marx's *Das Kapital* was a publisher's success, but the study of history, art history, sociology, economic theory, political science and the state of the world would be very different from what they are today but for these two books.

On the other hand, the 'bestseller' provides the historian with a fairly reliable yardstick of the prevalent mode of thought and taste of a period. There are, of course, certain categories of printed matter which give no clue to the real interests of the public. When, for instance, Johann Luschner printed at Barcelona 18,000 letters of indulgence for the abbey of Montserrat in May 1498, this can be compared only with the printing of income-tax forms, which hardly respond to a genuine demand on the part of a public thirsting for information or entertainment.

For similar reasons schoolbooks must be excluded from the consideration of bestsellers, although their publication has, from the incunabula period onwards, always been the most profitable branch of the publishing trade. Gutenberg's press issued no fewer than 24 editions of Donatus's grammar. Some 20 Latin grammars and dictionaries were published by one Cologne printer within only four years. Between 1518 and 1533, Robert Wittington published 13 Latin grammars, all of which had to be reprinted several times. Ten thousand copies of the popular *ABC and Little Catechism* were sold within eight months in 1585. Lily's Latin grammar, first published by Wynkyn de Worde in 1527, remained in use at Eton until 1860. And so the tale goes down to Noah Webster's *The American Spelling Book* (1783) of which about 65 million copies were sold within a hundred years, and to Hall and Stevens's *School Geometry* (1903) and Kennedy's *Latin Primer*, probably the best-selling schoolbooks in Great Britain.

The greatest difficulty in assessing bestsellers is our ignorance of the numbers of copies printed or sold of any given book. On the whole, publishers have been rather secretive on the subject unless they want to use such figures for advertising purposes. A statement such as 'third edition' or 'fifth reprint' may mean much or little, according to the size of each impression. It may, of course, be prudent not to reveal the fact that only 1000 copies have been printed of a book which the blurb asserts 'no intelligent reader can afford to miss'; but it may be suggested that publishers would do themselves and the public a service if they would openly state '2nd edition (11th–20th thousand)' or whatever the case may be. At best, it would be splendid publicity, free of cost; at worst, it would show the solicitude of a publisher for a book which he considers worth keeping alive even if of limited appeal.

The average edition of a book printed in the fifteenth century was probably not more than about 200 – which, it must be kept in mind, was a 200-fold increase on a scribe's work. Exceptions can usually be explained by special circumstances. Thus, the 800 copies on paper and 16 on vellum of the *Revelations of St Bridget*, which Gothan printed in Lübeck in 1492, were commissioned by the convent of Vadstena in Sweden. Aldus Manutius of Venice seems to have been the first publisher who habitually printed editions of 1000 copies. He was also the first publisher to make the imprint of his firm a determining factor in the sale of his books. Book-buyers in 1500, just as book-collectors in 1950, asked for an 'Aldine' Horace because of the general reputation of the house rather than the particular quality of the edition.

The first printed book that deserves the appellation of bestseller (and quickly also became a steady seller) was Thomas à Kempis's *De imitatione Christi*. Two years after the author's death (1471), Günther Zainer of Augsburg printed the *editio princeps*, and before the close of the century 99 editions had left the presses, including translations of which a French one, printed by Heinrich Mayer in Toulouse in 1488, and an Italian one, printed by Miscomini in Florence in 1491, were the earliest. The collected edition of Thomas's writings which Hochfeder published in Nürnberg in 1494 was less successful, but the *Imitation* remained the most widely read book in the world, next to the Bible. More than 3000 editions have been listed, and it was considered worthy to be the first publication of the Imprimerie Royale (Paris, 1640) as well as to be included in the popular Penguin Classics.

The next supplier of bestsellers of European format was another Dutchman, Erasmus of Rotterdam. Between 1500 and 1520, 34 editions of 1000 copies each were sold of his *Adagia*; 25 editions of his *Colloquia familiaria* were printed between 1518 and 1522 and enlarged and revised editions followed year after year; and the *Encomium Moriae* surpassed both of them.

Erasmus is a pioneer in the history of letters as much by his personality (which can still be enjoyed in his correspondence) as his writings. Both the *Moria* and the *Colloquia* were later put on the *Index librorum prohibitorum*, which contributed no little to keeping them in circulation. He was the first author deliberately to seek out a suitable publisher and to try to mould the publishing policy of a firm, as well as to make agreements which stipulated author's fees – an innovation which was not taken up again by either publishers or authors for about 200 years. But then Erasmus had an international reputation which permitted him to impose conditions on publishers who, conversely, could be sure to get their money's worth. In Venice, 1507–8, he worked in Aldus's establishment, in Paris he co-operated with the Ascensian Press of his compatriot, Josse Badius, and in 1513 he came – through the mistake or deception of his literary agent in Cologne – into contact with the Basel firm of Johannes Froben, with which his name has ever since been linked. In his last will he made the directors of the firm his heirs and executors.

Erasmus had the failing of many a zealous partisan in that he saw the country going to the dogs when his faction suffered a set-back. Only thus can it be understood that in 1529 he seriously maintained that 'everywhere where Lutheranism prevails learning is languishing. For what other reason should Luther and Melanchthon recall people so emphatically to the love of studies? The printers assert that, before this gospel spread, they had sold three thousand copies more easily than six hundred now.'

The truth, of course, is that by this time Erasmus's theological and moral treatises, commentaries on the Scriptures, editions of the Fathers, and philological controversies had been ousted – never to be resuscitated – by the writings of the Reformers. Erasmus's epitaph on his lifelong friend Thomas More: 'If only More had not meddled in these dangerous matters and left theological questions to the theologians' is sufficient to explain his dethronement by an age which took very seriously theology and other 'dangerous matters'. (The first edition of More's *Utopia* (1517) was printed in Louvain for want of an English printer brave enough to print it.) Both Luther and Loyola rejected Erasmus.

The great publishing successes of the sixteenth century were achieved in the realm of theology. With the publication in 1517 of the 95 theses (those '95 sledgehammer blows directed against [the sale of indulgences], the most flagrant ecclesiastical abuse of the age'), which he had nailed to the door of the university church, the unknown young professor of Wittenberg university became at one stroke a figure of national fame, and the small Wittenberg press of Hans Lufft suddenly gained a place among the biggest firms. Thirty editions of Luther's *Sermon on Indulgences* and 21 editions of his *Sermon on the Right Preparation of the Heart* – authorized and pirated – poured from the presses within two years (1518–20). Over 4000 copies of his address *To the Christian Nobility* were sold within five days in 1520.

The popular appeal of these pamphlets was far outstripped by the sales of Luther's translation of the Bible. In all about 150 Bibles were produced before 1500, and there had appeared in print nearly 20 German Bibles before Luther, all of which had found a market, above all the splendid Low German version of 1494, printed by Stephen Arndes in Lübeck; but Luther's translation was the first to become a bestseller in the strict meaning of the term.

The first edition of his New Testament was printed in September 1522 by Melchior Lotter, with woodcuts by Lucas Cranach. Despite the high price (1½ fl.) 5000 copies were sold within a few weeks, and in December a second edition was called for. Fourteen authorized and 66 pirated editions came out within the next two years. The Old Testament began to appear in parts from 1523, and the first whole Bible came out in 1534. The number of copies printed is not known; that of the edition of 1541 was 1500. All in all, about 400 editions of the whole Bible or parts of it appeared during Luther's lifetime. Of these, only a quarter were genuine Wittenberg editions; the others were pirated reprints. It is quite impossible to give even an approximate estimate of the number of copies printed, especially as there would have to be added numerous unauthorized editions with major or minor variants.

Luther's fierce opponent, Hieronymus Emser, not only used Luther's text almost verbatim for his 'translation', but also incorporated Cranach's woodcuts including the one depicting papal Rome as the Babylonian woman of the Revelation – plagiarists cannot be too careful!

Apart from the writings of Erasmus and Luther only two books of the sixteenth century can be acclaimed as bestsellers. One is Ludovico Ariosto's *Orlando furioso*, 'the culminating point in the development of the Italian romantic epic' (Barbara Reynolds), which came out in its final version in 1532, shortly before the poet's death. Within the next ten years it was reprinted 36 times and down to the present more editions of it have been published than of any other Italian book. It is, however, worth noticing that *Orlando furioso* is a typical 'national' bestseller. This superb epitome of Renaissance civilization has never captured the imagination of non-Italians, even to the extent of the distant respect accorded to Tasso's unreadable *Gerusalemme liberta*. It is significant that no translation of even moderate distinction has ever appeared in any European language.

The other is *Das Narrenschiff* ('The ship of fools') by Sebastian Brant (Basel, 1494, and often reprinted elsewhere): a satirical work containing knowing references to classical writers, intended to entertain a new sophisticated reading public. In the book is one of the first references to Columbus's discovery of America.

8. THE TITLE-PAGE

'The history of printing', Stanley Morison says in his *First Principles of Typography*, 'is in large measure the history of the title-page.' It might even be true to say that the introduction of the title-page constituted one of the most visible and distinct advances from script to print. For neither ancient nor medieval authors, scribes and librarians seem to have felt a need for what has become that part of the book which is the beginning, and often the end, of reading it.

The Ptolemaic library of Alexandria (probably following the usages of Assyrian

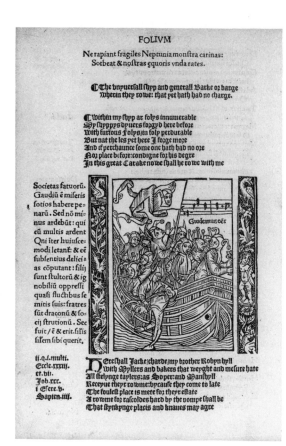

Sebastian Brant, *The Ship of Fools*, showing the use of both gothic and roman type. Richard Pynson, London, 1509. [G.11593]

Sebastian Brant, *Das Narrenschiff*. Peter Wagner, Nürnberg, 1494. [I.A.7997]

and Egyptian libraries) was catalogued according to incipits, i.e. the first word or words of a text. Where the modern librarian will look up the press-mark of Homer's *Iliad*, his Alexandrian colleague would have searched for that of Μῆνιν ἄειδε. The fact that we call the books containing the 'good tidings' of Our Lord by the name of evangel (Anglo-Saxon, *gospel*) is a survival of this custom, as the oldest report – and therefore *the* report, at least in Rome, its place of origin – was only known under the 'title' of Ἀρχὴ τοῦ εὐαγγελίου, 'the beginning of the gospel'.

Throughout the Middle Ages there remained this indifference to the proper naming of books and, even less understandable from the modern viewpoint, to that of their authors – both the sources of innumerable wrong or doubtful ascriptions as well as of hopeful and often rewarding searches among composite codices of miscellaneous tracts by various unnamed authors.

'The invention of printing did away with many of the technical causes of anonymity, while at the same time the movement of the Renaissance created new ideas of literary fame and intellectual property' – with this conclusion E. P. Goldschmidt aptly sums up his penetrating and incidentally very entertaining study of the age of untitled books.

It was, however, neither the name of the author nor that of the book which was first given prominence on what was to evolve into our title-page; nor was this 'title-page' placed where we are accustomed to find it, namely on the first, or more usually on the second, leaf of the made-up book. Continuing and expanding the habit of medieval scribes who liked to put their names, the date of the completion of their labour, a prayer or other brief notes at the end of a codex, the very first printers instituted the colophon. Of the features of a modern title-page and verso, the earliest colophons contain one or more of these items: the place and date of printing, the printer's name and device, the title (but not yet the author) of the book. The earliest known colophon is fuller than some later ones: the title (*Psalmorum codex*), the names of the printers (Johannes Fust and Peter Schöffer) and, by implication, the place of printing (Mainz) and the exact date of completion (14 August 1457). The next extant colophon gives the title (*Catholicon*) – omitting characteristically the author, viz. Johannes Balbus – the place (Mainz) and year (1460) of printing; it is most regrettable that the printer left out his own name, for it probably came from the press of Gutenberg himself. The third colophon again mentions Fust and Schöffer as printers, Mainz as the place, and 14 August 1462 as the date of publication; the book – a two-volume Bible – needed no author's name; but its description in the colophon, '*hoc opusculum*', is distinctly odd.

The inventor of the 'real' title-page was Peter Schöffer, but, like so many inventors in every field of science, he did not fully realize the importance of his invention, and thus gave it up after only one trial. His failure to grasp the inherent potentiality of this device is even clear from the object to which Schöffer applied it: not to one of his Bible, Psalter, or Rationale books with their unlimited possibilities, as the future was to show, but to a papal bull (of 1463), that is to say, a kind of broadsheet for which a modern printer would rightly regard a line of display letters as quite sufficient.

Equally sporadic was the next attempt at bringing in a title-page. This was made in 1470 by Arnold Therhoernen, a printer of Cologne, in his edition of Werner Rolevinck's *Sermo de praesentatione beatae Mariae*. This booklet is of importance also in another respect in that it is one of the first publications with the foliation inserted. The numbering of the pages seems to us an obvious and indispensable aid to the reader, yet it became fully established only at the beginning of the sixteenth century. Pagination was preceded by the insertion of catchwords, i.e. the repetition of the first word (or syllable) of a page at the foot of the preceding page. Such catchwords occur for the first time in the Tacitus printed by John of Speier at Venice in 1469. The catchword was first abandoned by the Foulis Press of Glasgow from 1747 onward. It survives in the rationalized form of the 'signature', i.e. the letter or figure appearing on the first page of a sheet which acts as guide in gathering the sheets before binding and in collating the sequence of folded sections. However, this practice, too, was not immediately followed up, although, like foliation and pagination, it was not altogether unknown to scribes of manuscripts. It has largely disappeared from modern books, having been superseded by numbers or stepped marks on the back edges of the folded sections.

All these early title-pages, and quite a number of later ones, took in fact the place of a modern 'half-title' and probably served the same purpose, namely, to prevent the first printed leaf from becoming dirty while lying about in the printing shop before passing into the hands of the binder. However, the astute businessmen who still combined the functions of printer, publisher and bookseller very soon realized the inherent potentiality of the full title. Erhard Ratdolt, of Augsburg and Venice, was the first to take this step. His edition of Johannes Regiomontanus's astronomical and astrological calendar of 1476 was preceded by a page which supplied all the details we expect to find on a title-page, including a laudatory poem which is rather the equivalent of an introductory preface by the author's friend or of a gratifying review. The whole page is set in a beautiful woodcut frame and is thus clearly distinguished from the text itself.

Regiomontanus's calendar sold so well that Ratdolt was able to reissue it in the original Latin as well as in vernacular translations. It therefore must have played its part in conditioning its readers to the appearance of this new feature. From the producer's point of view, the title-page offered more than the technical advantage of a protective cover: it was at the same time an effective and cheap means of advertising the book. This aspect emerges from a scrutiny of the books which were first adorned with a title-page: they were all new publications which needed some introduction to the public. The first 'reprint' bearing a title-page is Giorgio Arrivabene's edition of the Vulgate, printed in Venice in 1487, and preceded by a leaf with the single word 'Biblia' on it. By 1500 the title-page had established itself; and in any book of the sixteenth century or later it is its absence rather than its presence that requires comment and explanation.

Another device which had come to stay was the insertion of running heads. They appear for the first time in the Brescia edition of 1490 of Albertus Magnus's *Philosophia pauperum*. Their use incidentally suggests that imposition, that is the printing of multiple pages from the same forme, had by this time become the practice.

More than any other single part of the book, the title-page has ever since been a true reflection of the general taste of the reading public – not only with regard to typography. Baroque, rococo, classicism, Art Nouveau, expressionism, surrealism – each art period has produced title-pages in its own image.

The decorative woodcut border, introduced by Ratdolt, dominated the first half of the sixteenth century, and artists such as Dürer, Holbein and Cranach added lustre and distinction to it – as did William Morris and his followers at the end of the nineteenth century when they revived the style of the early printers in a spirit, as we now see, as remote as possible from their alleged ancestors. The earliest surviving example of Holbein's book-illustration is Erasmus's *Encomium Moriae* (Paris, 1511). He later spent eight years in Basel and worked closely with Froben. Although he subsequently settled in England he illustrated no English books.

Very soon, however, printers were groping for a principle which has eventually come to be accepted as basic to true typography – namely, that every page of a book, apart from additional illustrations, should be composed solely out of the compositor's case. That is to say, ornaments should be type-ornaments, consisting either of common letters arranged in decorative patterns or of decorative patterns cut and moulded as supplements of a type-fount: the latter becoming known as printers' flowers.

Type-ornaments were sporadically used by Wynkyn de Worde and Antonio Blado; their real popularity dates from Robert Granjon who, from about 1560, cut a wealth of complicated but always pleasing arabesques. These were copies of binders' tools, but Granjon transformed them into combinable and elegant units. The Netherlands, at the time the leading European book market, and England greatly appreciated these patterns down to about 1640. Pierre-Simon Fournier (in his *Modèles des Caractères* of 1742, in which he showed a vast range of fleurons and other rococo type-ornaments) revived and enlarged this fashion, which, from about 1760 to 1780, found imitators and copyists all over Europe – the German Johann Michael Fleischmann and the Dutch firm of J. Enschedé (for which Fleischmann worked from 1743 to 1768) excelling through inventiveness.

While the engravers had to watch some of their decorative work disappear with the growing popularity of type-ornaments, which could be printed with the text, they profited from the new fashion for baroque engraved title-pages. The first example, already as fully repulsive as this aberration was ever to be, appeared in London in 1545. The artist is likely to have been a Dutchman, for the best engravers at this time were found in the Netherlands, and it was the Antwerp printer Christophe Plantin who soon afterwards made the engraved title-page a European epidemic spreading from the pocket editions of the Elzevirs to the stately folios with which the Imprimerie Royale accompanied the reign of Louis XIV. They usually took the form either of architectural porticoes or of portraits of patrons. It was the violation of typographical honesty and good taste, inherent in the combination of an engraved border with the proper title set in ordinary type, which eventually opened the eyes of the printers and led to the abandoning of this device.

With the growth of the 'classical' school of typographers, for which may stand the names of Baskerville, Didot and Bodoni, the purely typographical title-page carried the day, relegating woodcuts and engravings to freak productions mostly of a sham-archaic character which lingered into the twentieth century.

All through these centuries the wording of the title itself reflects the prevalent mood and taste of each successive period. Throughout the sixteenth and seventeenth centuries there can be observed the gradual change from the matter-of-fact purity of the Renaissance, through the wordy didacticism of the mannerist period, to the verbosity of the baroque, hand in hand with an increasing artificiality of the layout, culminating in the tomfooleries of titles arranged in the shape of triangles, hexagons, hour-glasses and other fantastic patterns.

The present title-page of the *Book of Common Prayer* faithfully preserves, under the statutory force of an Act of Parliament, the exhaustive and exhausting wordiness of its seventeenth-century origin – twice as long as the Edwardian and Elizabethan title and twenty times as long as a modern author and publisher would allow: 'The Book of Common Prayer' would no doubt be considered sufficient. This title is even preserved in the Book of Common Prayer of the Episcopal Church of the United States of America.

Geofroy Tory, the Paris printer of *c.* 1530, was the first to practise the natural lay-out, and French printers even in the worst periods have evinced a more sensitive as well as sensible attitude than any other nation towards the need for clarity and simplicity. In one respect the older printers were luckier than their successors from the eighteenth century onward: they were not bound by the schoolbook regulations concerning the division of syllables nor by grammatical considerations regarding the comparative weight of nouns, articles, prepositions, etc.

The divergent opinions of sixteenth- and twentieth-century printers as to the proper layout of a title-page can best be illustrated by contrasting the edition of Sir Thomas Elyot's famous treatise on education brought out in 1534 by the King's Printer, Thomas Berthelet, with the shape a modern editor and designer might give it. THE/BOKE/NA-/med the Gouernour, de-/vysed by Sir Tho-/mas Elyot/knight/1534/ would probably now appear as THE/GOVERNOR/THOMAS ELYOT/ [name and location of publisher/date]. In Oliver Simon's words, 'besides fulfilling its function of announcing the subject or name of the work and its author, [the title-page] gives to the book the general tone of its typographical treatment'. The same applies to sub-titles, such as in the second, 1687 edition of Thomas Stanley's *History of Philosophy*, 'containing the lives, opinions, actions and discourses of the philosophers of every sect', which only elaborate the obvious implications of the main title. Making the title short and self-explanatory and making the typography of the title-page conform with the typography – and, to a certain extent, the subject-matter – of the text are, in fact, two aspects of the general tendency of modern typography towards sense and sensibility.

9. BOOK ILLUSTRATION

The picture-book may lay some claim to paternity of the book printed with movable types. Block-books with each page printed from a solid block of wood containing the picture and the caption, both cut together on the same piece of wood, preceded Gutenberg's invention by about 30 years. Woodcuts were first printed on single sheets; of these the Virgin with four Saints of 1418 in the Royal Library in Brussels and the St Christopher of 1423 in the John Rylands Library in Manchester are the oldest surviving dated specimens. From about 1430 onward (no block-book is dated before 1470, though a Dutch *Apocalypse* may have been published in 1451–2) they were printed together in book form. Nearly all of them originated in western Germany, Switzerland and the Netherlands.

One of these xylographers, Laurens Janszoon Coster of Haarlem (1405–84), has even been credited with the invention of printing with movable types in or about 1440. This 'Coster legend', fabricated by a Dutchman in 1568, has been proved to be a fable by modern Dutch scholars; but the monuments erected in Coster's honour by his townsmen will no doubt keep the myth alive among such people as will believe that Bacon wrote Shakespeare.

By about 1480 the block-books had outlived their usefulness and were no longer produced. An interesting late-comer, however, appeared in 1593 in Manila. The first book printed in the Philippine Islands, a bilingual *Doctrina Christiana* in Spanish and Tagalog, is a block-book. The type was probably designed by one of the Dominican missionaries; but the execution lay in the hands of Chinese craftsmen to whom the block-book had for centuries been the only known medium of printing. Here, then, East and West met bodily, 150 years after their amalgamation in Gutenberg's office.

Measured by the technical production of the block-books, Gutenberg's invention signalled an advance in two directions: the break-up of the compact text into individual letters and the supersession of wood by metal, thereby increasing the durability as well as the precision of these individual letters.

The older technique, however, lived on for some time. Playing cards, illustrated broadsheets and other ephemeral matter were until the end of the eighteenth century produced and hawked by numerous *Briefmaler* (illuminators of documents – *Briefe* – playing cards, broadsheets, etc.). A Strasbourg by-law as early as 1502 carefully distinguished them from 'honest printers'. In fact, many of the productions of these *Briefmaler* – who flourished especially in Nürnberg, Augsburg and Regensburg – were as disreputable as any modern horror comic.

The great majority of the block-books were cheap tracts for the half-literate to whom the picture was more important than the caption, which anyway had to be very brief because of the laborious process of cutting the letters. Books of religious edification, such as the *Biblia pauperum*, treatises on the Last Things, the *Mirabilia urbis Romae* and legends of popular saints, lent themselves most easily to this kind of mass production.

In this way readers were quite used to combining the concepts of 'book' and 'illustration'; and printers were quite ready to embellish their novel productions in one or other of the customary ways. Ornamented initials and woodcuts therefore make their appearances simultaneously with books printed from movable type. It has been computed that about one-third of all books printed before 1500 were illustrated. Albrecht Pfister of Bamberg in the 1460s inserted woodcuts in his popular books: they were drawn in outline only, presumably for hand-colouring. From about 1470 onward Augsburg specialized in illustrated books, and nearly two hundred were printed there before 1500. When Bernhard von Breydenbach went on a pilgrimage to the Holy Land, he was accompanied by an artist, Erhard Reuwich, whose sketches, including a valuable map of Palestine, were duly incorporated in the traveller's *Peregrinationes in Terram Sanctam* (Mainz, 1486). Reuwich himself cut his drawings in wood and supervised the printing of the book which, thanks to its combination of pilgrims' guide, travelogue and geographical textbook, had a tremendous success and was soon translated into German, Dutch, French and Spanish.

This early collaboration of author and illustrator is all the more remarkable as normally the correspondence between text and picture was very slight indeed. In the most lavishly illustrated book of the fifteenth century, Hartmann Schedel's *Liber chronicarum*, which Koberger published in 1493, the 1809 illustrations were supplied by only 645 wood-blocks. The 596 portraits of emperors, popes, and other celebrities were made up from 72 wood-blocks, so that the same effigy was used, with a different caption, for eight or nine different personalities, and the same view of a walled city was named Rome, Jerusalem, Paris or whatever the context required. Most printers used the blocks they had in stock without much discrimination whenever sales considerations demanded a book with illustrations (a practice that was repeated in the early nineteenth century by the printers of cheap broadsides). The so-called Leda-Bible of 1572 is a notorious late example of this indifference. In it the New Testament was illustrated with woodcuts taken from an edition of Ovid's *Metamorphoses*; an initial depicting Jupiter visiting Leda in the guise of a swan introduced the Epistle to the Hebrews.

As regards the quality of the illustrations, Italy, for a while, outclassed every other country. Here Ulrich Han produced in 1467 the first book illustrated by as many as 30 woodcuts, namely Johannes de Turrecremata's *Meditationes*. The second edition published in 1473 contained three more illustrations. Johannes of Verona printed in 1472 the first illustrated book on a technical subject, Roberto Valturio's *De re militari*. This treatise on military engineering reflects the obsession with warfare which seems so at odds with the civilized splendours of Renaissance Italy. In Venice Erhard Ratdolt perfected his charming borders and ornaments designed by Bernard Maler, and Aldus produced 'the most famous and the most beautiful woodcut book ever published', as Francesco de Colonna's *Hypnerotomachia Poliphili* (1499) has been called. The weight of line of the 170 woodcuts by an otherwise unknown artist is scrupulously matched to the colour of the type. Nicolaus Laurentii, a German printer working in Florence, brought out the first book illustrated with metal engravings in 1477; but this process did not catch on before the middle of the sixteenth century, when the *Speculum romanae magnificentiae* (Antonio Lafreri, Rome, 1548–68) supplied on more than 130 engraved plates a conspectus of the surviving monuments of ancient Rome and thus constituted the earliest topographical work of permanent value. The first illustrated editions of Dante's *Commedia* (1481), also by Nicolaus Laurentii, and Boccaccio's *Decameron* (1492) testify further to the good taste as well as the capability of Italian printers.

The .xxi. boke

ladyes vanyſſhed. And anone the kyn
ge callyd vpon his knyghtes/ ſquyres.
& comey. and chargyd them lyȝgly to
fetche his noble loȝds & wyſe byſſhops
vnto him. And whan they were come
the kynge tolde to them his aduyſyoy
what ſyr Gawayne had tolde hym &
warnyd him/ that yf he faughte oy þ
moȝy. he ſhold be ſlayne. Thenne the
kynge comaunded ſyr Lucay the but:
ler & his brother ſyr Bedwere / wyth
two biſſhops wyth them. and charged
them iy ony wyſe and they myght/ ta
ke a treatyſe foȝ a moneth daye wyth
ſyre Moȝdȝed . And ſpaȝe not/ pȝoffȝe
hym londes & goodes/ as moche as ye
thynke beſte. So thenne they depaȝtid
& came to ſyr Moȝdȝed/ where he had
a grymme hoſte of ay hundȝd thou/
ſande mey. And there they entreatyd
ſyr Moȝdȝed longe tyme/ And at the
laſte ſyr Moȝdȝed was agreed. foȝ to
haue Coȝnewayle and Kent by kyng
Arthurs dayes. and after the dayes of
kynge Arthur/ to haue all Englonde
to his obeyſſaunce.

¶ How by myſauenture of ay adder/ the batayll begay. where ſyr Moȝdȝed
was ſlayne/ & Arthur huȝt to deth. ¶ Capȝm .iiij.

Theñe were they condeſcended
that kyng Arthur & ſyr Moȝ
dȝed ſholde mete betwyx both ther hoſ
tes/ and eueryche of them ſholde bryn
ge .xiiij. perſones. And they came with
this woȝde vnto Arthur. ¶ Thenne
ſayd he I am gladde that this is doñ
And ſoo he went iy to the felde . And

Thomas Malory, *Morte Darthur*. Wynkyn de Worde, London, 1498. 'To the modern eye, both the drawing and the cutting [of the woodcuts] ... are wild and wonderful' – Hodnett.

In France, the illustration of printed books continued the high standard of French illuminated manuscripts. Martin Huss of Lyon, it is true, bought the 259 woodcuts for his *Miroir de la redemption humaine* from the Basel printer Bernhard Richel (1478; 2nd edn 1479; 3rd edn by Matthias Huss, 1482). But the next illustrated book, a French version of Breydenbach's *Peregrinationes* (Lyon, 1488), already shows a remarkable degree of independence. The text was thoroughly revised by the editor, Nicolas de Huen, who drew on his own experiences in the Holy Land; and the wood-cuts of the original were replaced by free adaptations, some of which were executed in the new technique of copper-engraving. The Books of Hours produced by Vérard, Kerver, Tory and others vie with one another in the excellence of the draughtsman-ship and presswork of their graceful ornaments and borders. Most of them were after-wards coloured by hand, and these illuminators, too, were craftsmen of the highest order.

Two English books of the early period contain woodcut illustrations of particular interest: Caxton's translation of Aesop's *Fables* (1484) and Wynkyn de Worde's edition of Malory's *Morte Darthur* (1498). Just as most of the books printed by Caxton were translations of established French and Latin texts, so, says Hodnett, 'the best woodcut illustrations in English books of the first period' were copied from imported books. The 186 cuts in the Aesop were no exception, being copied (at one remove) from those used by Johann Zainer of Ulm in about 1476. They show, says Hodnett, 'the northern European impulse to … retell the story in naturalistic pictures – a deviation from the medieval, oriental and Italian urge to celebrate through decoration'.

Wynkyn inherited Caxton's blocks and made as much use of them as he could, without fussing too much about their appropriateness; but the Malory illustrations are original and interpretative, creating for the reader 'a true world of imagination' (Hodnett).

Peter Schöffer tried at a remarkably early date to simplify production by making the printer do the work of the rubrisher as well as the scribe of hand-written books. There the scribe always left blank spaces in which the rubrisher afterwards painted large coloured initials. Schöffer now printed his *Psalter* – one of the world's most beautiful books, its pages closely similar to those of an illuminated manuscript – of 1457 with black, red and blue letters so that the book could go straight from the press to the binder. But the process of colour-printing presumably proved to be too labori-ous and expensive. Although bold attempts continued to be made to print initials, headings, and other portions of the text in colour, colouring by hand remained the rule into the eighteenth century.

François Rabelais, *Gargantua*. Juste, Lyon, 1537.
[C.57.a.2]

CHAPTER II

The era of consolidation
1550–1800

The main characteristics of the 250 years following the 'heroic century' of the printed book may be summarized as follows.

Virtually no technical progress took place in the composing and printing rooms. New typefaces represented refined imitations of the achievements of Jenson, Griffo, and Garamond rather than fresh conceptions. Printers lost their independence as the producers of their own types, obtaining their founts ready-made from the type-founder, with the result that a few prominent foundries gained an immense influence on the kind of type that printers had at their disposal, not only in their respective native lands but also, through a brisk export trade, all over western Europe.

The book trade evolved towards its present shape as booksellers began to function as publishers, contracting with authors and placing manufacture with printers, and sold their books direct to the public and wholesale through pamphlet dealers or chapmen. Tradesmen in the provinces and colonies undertook all these activities and more besides, such as newspaper publishing and a wider range of retail selling than simply books.

The professional author entered the arena as an independent force between the publisher and the public. The reading public widened considerably and in the process changed its character. Publishers and authors had to cater for new readers with new tastes, different from the fairly homogeneous public of churchmen, academics and sophisticated gentry whom a Gutenberg, Aldus, Stephanus or Caxton supplied with reading matter. The spread of literacy gradually induced new sections of the population to adopt the habit of reading. Women and children, in particular, presented the publisher with the potentiality of doubling or trebling his output. The periodical and newspaper press became the chief vehicles of spreading knowledge among this new public.

1. TYPE DESIGN

Roman type

During the period from the middle of the sixteenth to the end of the eighteenth century, a number of brilliant French, Dutch and English type-designers and punch-cutters perfected the achievements of Griffo and Garamond. Each of the typefaces which Granjon created in the sixteenth century, van Dyck and Grandjean in the seventeenth, Caslon, Baskerville, the Fourniers and Bodoni in the eighteenth, is in its kind beautiful and serviceable and has left a permanent mark on the art of typography. Held against the pioneer efforts of the first century of printing, the chief merit of these new founts lay precisely in the fact that their designers did not attempt to replace the accepted Aldus pattern by any startling innovation. They introduced, it is true, a good many refinements of detail, and succeeded in giving each of their various founts a greater consistency in itself; but this was mainly due to improvements in the mathematical precision of design and in the technical manufacture of punches and matrices. On the whole, however, the unity underlying all 'antiqua' faces outweighs their differences and stresses the fact that the literary civilization of the West was now firmly based on the one Latin alphabet.

At the same time, the profession of punch-cutter and founder was no longer commonly bound up with that of printer and publisher. In fact, it seems that type-founding became a specialized profession at a very early date. One Nicolas Wolf, a native of Brunswick, for instance, appears as a *fondeur de lettres* in Lyon in 1493, and supplied the local printers with types before he eventually set up as a printer in 1498; and there were 18 type-founders active in Lyon between 1500 and 1550. Garamond, however, was the first to concentrate on the large-scale production of punches and matrices for general sale. Granjon followed his example. He was the first to trade on an international scale. He delivered matrices to Italy, France, Germany, Switzerland and especially the Netherlands. From the middle of the sixteenth to the end of the seventeenth century leadership of type-design and type-founding went to the Low Countries. But the types which became known to every printer and reader in Europe through the agency of the dominant publishers, Plantin and Elzevir, were those cut by Garamond and Granjon, and thus lastly modelled on the founts cut by Griffo for Aldus. French designers, such as Jacob Sabon (who completed a set of punches begun by Garamond), father and son Le Bé and Granjon himself, were mainly responsible for the work done for the house of Plantin. The Dutchman Christoffel van Dyck (1601–1669/70), a goldsmith by profession, was the chief supplier of punches for the Elzevirs, as far as they did not buy their material from the Luther foundry in Frankfurt.

The quick entry of 'Dutch' founts into every moderately well-equipped printing shop throughout Europe is largely due to the business ascendancy exercized by some big type-foundries of European reputation. Only a few printing houses could afford to order and produce types for their exclusive use, and the majority of printers now bought types off the shelf. The foundry established by Christian Egenolf in Frankfurt in 1531, and from 1629 known by the name of Luther, was perhaps the most influential firm in the seventeenth century; even in the eighteenth century they sold their produce as far afield as Philadelphia, where the first American foundry was established as late as 1772 by Christopher Sauer, a customer of the Luther firm. By that time the first place had been taken by the Leipzig firm of Ehrhardt, which had their best founts cut by Nicholas Kis in Amsterdam, 1683–9. The Frankfurt and Leipzig foundries described their types generally as 'Dutch' (*holländische Schriften*). This may be taken as an acknowledgement of the superior achievements of Dutch letter-design, dating back to Henric of Delft (who called himself Henric de Lettersnider) in the fifteenth century and now represented by Van Dyck, Bartholomaeus and Dirk Voskens and others who worked for the great printer-publishers of Antwerp, Amsterdam, Leiden, Haarlem; not to forget the 'Sieur Zonen' (Mister Son) whom Fournier made inherit Dirk Voskens's business. The term 'Dutch types' was therefore a useful trade-mark. Imitating – and often vulgarizing – French types stemming from Garamond and Granjon, exchanging material with the Plantins and Elzevirs, the Luther and Ehrhardt foundries could therefore compete successfully in the Dutch market, which throughout and beyond the seventeenth century dominated the European publishing trade. The famous collections of types which Dr Fell bought in the Netherlands for the Oxford University Press in 1675 were exhaustively catalogued and described by Stanley Morison in *John Fell* (1967), that noble monument to both a fine scholar and the great tradition of Oxford printing. They included some French sets of Granjon provenance and some supplied by van Dyck.

The supersession of the Netherlands by the France of Louis XIV as the principal economic and political power of the Continent aptly found its typographical expression in the execution of a completely new set of type. Commissioned by the king himself in 1692 for the exclusive use of the Imprimerie Royale, the *romain du roi* exhibited the cold brilliance distinctive equally of the absolute monarchy and the logical mind of France. A committee of the Academy of Sciences, of which the Abbé Nicolas Jaugeon was the most active member, was charged with the theoretical preparation of the design, and they deliberately turned away from the principles of calligraphy and epigraphy which had so far guided every type design. The academicians drew up the design of each letter on a strictly analytical and mathematical basis, using as their norm a rectangle subdivided into 2304 (i.e. 64 × 36) squares. The artist, in William Morris's words, was ousted by the engineer. The resultant aridity of the design was fortunately mellowed by the eminent type-cutter Philippe Grandjean (1666–1714), who from 1694 to 1702 gave his whole time to the work, supported by some able assistants. Although the 21 sizes cut between 1697 and 1745 by Grandjean, Alexandre and Luce remained the exclusive property of the Imprimerie Royale, the *romain du roi* epitomized the aesthetic ideals of the age of reason to such an extent that every French typographer imitated it as far as the royal privilege would permit him to do. The royal monopoly of the *roman du roi* was protected by penalties against its unauthorized reproduction.

The *Modèles de Caractères* (1742), in which Pierre-Simon Fournier (1712–68) presented the whole range of his typefaces, show to perfection that the *romain du roi* could, in the hands of a sensitive cutter, be adapted to suit the taste of a new age. This tradition was continued by the Didot family, François (1689–1758), François-Ambrose (1730–1804) and Firmin (1764–1836), the last French *imprimeur du roi* (1829). Their typefaces took the contrast between thick and thin strokes to such an extreme that there was a constant risk of their breaking up under pressure. Yet by the turn of the century they were supreme in France, and Garamond had vanished into the pot. The three volumes of Racine printed at the Louvre by Pierre Didot l'Aîné, which were illustrated by great neo-classical artists, were adjudged 'the most perfect printing of all ages' at the 1801 exhibition of French industrial products.

For the first 320 years of printing both the height-to-paper and the sizes of types varied from one printer to another. A French decree of 1723 to regulate these matters was largely ignored, but in 1737 Fournier le Jeune adopted the decreed height-to-paper as standard; however, he cut his punches according to a scale of units of his own devising, which provided 72 points to the French inch. It was not until 1775 that François-Ambroise Didot perfected Fournier's system: he based his new measuring system for punch-cutting and mould-making on the official French foot, the *pied du roi*, which comprised 12 French inches, but preserved Fournier's subdivisions and made 72 Didot points (or 6 Ciceros) to the French inch, in the process abandoning the use of the traditional names (e.g. Parisienne, nonpareile, gaillarde, petit romain)

Martin Dominique Fertel, *La Science pratique de l'Imprimerie*. S. Omer, 1723. [60.e.24]

Fournier-le-Jeune, *De l'Origine et des Productions de l'Imprimerie*. Barbou, Paris, 1759. [687.d.33(2)]

to identify his type-sizes and instead calling them by their body-size in points, e.g. 12 pt. The Didot point is still the accepted unit of measurement in continental Europe for letterpress printing. (It was not until 1880 that Marder, Luse & Co., type-founders of Chicago, adopted what is now known as the Anglo-American point system, in which one point is defined as one-twelfth of the pica, and in so doing rendered obsolescent such traditional type-sizes as diamond, minion and brevier.)

The hegemony of English commerce and industry in the eighteenth century could not fail to stimulate the English printing trade to make itself independent of foreign supply. England was the last western nation to admit roman type as the standard for vernacular printing. The turning point came as late as 1611 when Robert Barker, then King's Printer, issued the Authorized Version in both roman and black-letter editions. By this time the English and Scottish public had become conditioned to reading their Bible in roman characters. The 'Geneva Bible' of 1560 was the first Bible in English thus printed. It was translated by Protestant exiles of whom John Knox was one, and financed by John Bodley, father of the future founder of the library at Oxford. The New Testament portion was printed by Conrad Badius, Josse's son and Robert Estienne's brother-in-law, and Calvin contributed an introductory epistle. Although the English government championed the black-letter 'Bishops' Bible' of 1568, Cecil winked at the importation of copies of the Geneva Bible and Walsingham encouraged its reprinting in London. The General Assembly of the Kirk authorized it in 1579 for

Scotland. By 1611 about 150 editions had made every literate English and Scottish home accustomed to read the family Bible in roman type.

For another century English printers remained dependent on the importation of continental matrices, chiefly from Holland. The majority of type-founders in Britain were French Huguenots and Protestant refugees from the Spanish Netherlands; the first Englishman who carried on type-founding as his sole occupation and not as a side-line of printing was Benjamin Sympson (1579). It was William Caslon (1692–1766), a Worcestershire man, who freed England from this servitude. He set up in London as a type-cutter and type-founder in 1716, thanks in no small measure to the patronage of the printer William Bowyer, who lent him £500 to set up shop. His first specimen sheet (1734) established his fame once and for all and brought England to the van of European typography. His types became especially popular in America, where they were championed by Benjamin Franklin, who caused the authenticated copies of the Declaration of Independence to be printed in Caslon types by Mary Katharine Goddard in Baltimore.

Caslon's types represent (in Updike's words) a 'thoroughly English' variety, 'legible and common-sense', of the tradition which, through the Dutch designers of the seventeenth century, goes back to Garamond and Granjon in the sixteenth and eventually Griffo in the fifteenth century. William Caslon II joined his father as a partner in 1742, and the firm of 'William Caslon & Son' remained in the family until the death of the last male Caslon in 1873.

For some unknown reason Caslon chose for the display of his types the beginning of Cicero's first Catiline oration, and *Quousque tandem* for long remained the stock-in-trade of typographical specimens. This was unfortunate, as a capital Q is of the rarest occurrence in English and, because of its tail, requires a special treatment quite uncharacteristic of other capital letters. The letter which, in upper and lower case, affords the widest facilities of judging any given set of letters is M and m; it has therefore by general agreement been made the yardstick by which students of incunabula unravel the intricacies of early types and identify them.

Caslon was followed by John Baskerville (1707–75), another Worcestershire man and the greatest type-designer of the post-incunabula age. Like many of the earliest printers, Baskerville came to typography through calligraphy, which he taught from 1733 to 1737 – Fournier le Jeune thought Baskerville's italic 'the best to be found in any type-foundry in Europe', and Fournier's italic, like Baskerville's, has its origin in the copperplate hand. Like the early printers he applied his versatile genius to type-design as well as to type-founding, to composing as well as to printing, to paper as well as to ink. His attention to the right kind of paper and his improvement of printers' ink were hardly less important than his creation of a new kind of type.

His first book began in 1757 the series of some 50 Baskerville productions which, as Philip Gaskell has said, 'has few rivals in the whole history of printing'. This was the quarto *Virgil* about which F. E. Pardoe remarks that 'what marks it out from its contemporaries, certainly from all the products of the English presses of the times, is the astonishing presswork and inking'. John Dreyfus tells us that 'to obtain an edition of 1500 copies he would print 2000; and from these sort out 1500 of even colour'. He used his type once only.

Baskerville's masterpiece, the folio Bible of 1763, which he printed under the licence of Cambridge University, 'achieved a particularly happy liaison between type, layout, paper, and ink. It is [Gaskell continues] one of the finest books of the whole eighteenth

ESSAI

DE

FABLES NOUVELLES.

AU ROI.

FABLE PREMIERE.

LE COQ.

Le lion, plein de courage,
L'aigle, au vol audacieux,
D'un roi ne m'offrent point l'image:
Tous deux ils vivent de carnage,
Et leur regne m'est odieux.
Des sujets innocents, soumis et sans reproche,
Comme des criminels, tremblent à leur approche:
Je ne vois pour eux nul recours;
Vainement de la fuite ils cherchent le secours:
Ces cruels ont bientôt immolé leurs victimes;
Par le meurtre et le sang ils soutiennent leurs droits,
Droits affreux, droits illégitimes:
Ce sont des tyrans, non des rois.

THE

PSALTER,

OR

PSALMS of DAVID,

Pointed as they are to be sung or said in Churches.

THE FIRST DAY.

MORNING PRAYER.

PSAL. i. *Beatus vir, qui non abiit.*

BLESSED is the man that hath not walk-
ed in the counsel of the ungodly, nor
stood in the way of sinners: and hath not sat
in the seat of the scornful;

2 But his delight is in the law of the Lord:
and in his law will he exercise himself day and
night.

3 And he shall be like a tree planted by the
water-side: that will bring forth his fruit in
due season.

4 His leaf also shall not wither: and look,
whatsoever he doeth, it shall prosper.

5 As for the ungodly, it is not so with them:
but they are like the chaff which the wind
scattereth away from the face of the earth.

X   6 Therefore

Pierre Didot, *Essai de Fables Nouvelles*. Didot, Paris, 1786. [637.c.1]

The Book of Common Prayer. John Baskerville, Printer to the University, Cambridge, 1760. [3407.d.17]

century'. As a Bible it must rank with the Doves Bible and the Oxford Lectern Bible. (It cost twice as much as a comparable contemporary Bible.) One of Baskerville's outstanding contributions to modern printing is his insistence on typography pure and simple as the means of achieving a fine book. This idea, which has now become commonplace, was revolutionary in an age when a book was judged by the contribution of the illustrator and engraver rather than the groundwork of the compositor and printer.

Benjamin Franklin bought six copies of the *Virgil*, and thought it 'the most curiously printed of any Book hitherto done in the World'. Baskerville's style 'immensely interested foreign connoisseurs' (Morison), the 'brilliancy' of his presswork drew praise from Fournier, and as a true prophet he was not without honour – save in his own country. Impoverished and derided, he repeatedly tried to sell his whole equipment to some continental printing firm, and failed only because of the 'excessive' price of £8000 he demanded. His widow eventually, in 1779, sold his punches, matrices and presses to Beaumarchais for his Kehl edition of Voltaire. Thereafter Baskerville

Virgil, *Bucolica, Georgica, et Aeneis*. John Baskerville, Birmingham, 1757. [687.k.1]

types were sold and resold to various French foundries, and their origin had been completely forgotten when, in 1917, Bruce Rogers, then typographical adviser to Cambridge University Press, rediscovered them. In 1953 Charles Peignot, of Deberny & Peignot, made a princely gift of all the surviving original punches to Cambridge University Press (they are now kept at the Cambridge University Library) – except the (very undistinguished) Greek type which Baskerville made in 1758 for Oxford University Press.

Between them Caslon and Baskerville not only reformed the English printing of their day but have exercized a lasting influence on the typography of every nation that uses the Latin alphabet. Their types owed their success to the aesthetic satisfaction of the graceful shape of each letter as well as to their adaptability to printing matter of every description, from the stately tomes of a lectern Bible to the charming presentation of lyrical poetry. They possess the great virtue of unobtrusiveness combined with graceful readability. They never seem to come between reader and author and can be read for long periods with less eye-strain than most faces.

'Baskerville's example inspired William Martin, John Bell, Thomas Bensley, William Bulmer and others. The 60 years from after 1757 represent the finest period of native English design using new material backed with high technical craftsmanship and rational spacing' – Morison. Fournier and particularly Baskerville were the chief inspiration of the only great Italian typographer of the eighteenth century, Giambattista Bodoni (1740–1813). After his apprenticeship at the Vatican Press he spent his whole life in the service of the dukes of Parma as the head of their Stampa

THE

CONTAINING THE

OLD TESTAMENT

AND

THE NEW:

Tranflated out of the

AND

With the former TRANSLATIONS

Diligently Compared and Revifed,

By His MAJESTY's Special Command.

❖❖❖❖❖❖❖❖❖❖❖❖❖❖❖❖❖❖❖❖❖❖❖❖❖❖❖❖❖❖❖❖❖❖❖❖❖❖

APPOINTED TO BE READ IN CHURCHES.

❖❖❖❖❖❖❖❖❖❖❖❖❖❖❖❖❖❖❖❖❖❖❖❖❖❖❖❖❖❖❖❖❖❖❖❖❖❖

C A M B R I D G E,

Printed by *JOHN BASKERVILLE*, Printer to the UNIVERSITY.

M DCC LXIII.

CUM PRIVILEGIO.

Holy Bible. John Baskerville, Cambridge, 1763. [687.l.1]

Reale, which was housed in the old ducal palace, nicknamed La Pilotta. Here Bodoni was in a position to work according to his maxim: '*Je ne veux que du magnifique et je ne travaille pas pour le vulgaire.*' Soon after seeing Baskerville's *Orlando furioso* (1773), Bodoni is to be found widely – even magniloquently – spacing his types and his pages in his first book in the grand manner, an *Epithalamium* set in various exotic languages. Like Baskerville, he aimed for typographical purity and brilliant press-work, while in his type-forms he remained faithful to the narrow-bodied letters of Grandjean, Fournier and the Didots.

He sought to remove everything from books that was not printing, while simultaneously exercizing considerable ingenuity in perfecting his types. A single fount of Bodoni's type comprised nearly four hundred punches, so it is not surprising that when Arthur Young, the English traveller and writer, visited Parma in 1789 he found that the Stamperia Reale held over thirty thousand matrices. Bodoni's *Manuale tipografico* (1788; second and final edition, seen through the press by his widow, 1818) shows the reasons for his immense popularity during his lifetime and the comparative neglect after his death. The solemnity, even pomposity, of his designs made them unfit to serve the objectives to which the typographers and printers of the nineteenth century were to apply themselves – mass-instruction and mass-entertainment.

Gothic type

After the defection of England in the first half of the seventeenth century, black-letter type had become an anomaly. No new design of Fraktur faces could therefore have any repercussions in European typography. There were, anyway, very few new designs, and of these only the ones cut by the Leipzig type-founder, Bernard Christoph Breitkopf (1695–1777), are of some merit. The Berlin founder Johann Friedrich Unger (1750–1804) was deeply impressed by the work of Didot and Bodoni, but his attempt to adapt Fraktur to the canons of classicist taste was a complete failure. His 'Neue Deutsche Lettern' of 1791 (some of which were engraved by Firmin Didot) abandoned the only meritorious features of Fraktur, namely robustness and colour. Thus, as Updike succinctly sums up the development of black-letter, 'by the year 1800 the boldest and noblest typography in Europe had degenerated to the weakest and poorest'.

Judicious men had by this time come to see that the stubborn adherence to gothic types was a main obstacle to Germany's full share in the life of the civilized world. In 1765 the grammarian, encyclopedist and translator Adelung stated that the use of gothic letters 'is undoubtedly the reason that prevents other nations from learning our language and thus deprives them of the use of many good books produced in Germany'. Some years earlier the first non-academic German book had appeared in roman print, Ewald von Kleist's nature poem, *Der Frühling* (1749); but this bold venture of an officer of Frederick the Great found hardly any followers for 200 years. Among them, however, was the best-produced German book of the eighteenth century, Wieland's collected works, which Göschen printed in a fashionable roman type specially commissioned from Justus Erich Walbaum (1768–1837) 'after Didot' (42 vols, 1794–1802).

For there were those (and their number was to increase during the next century) who treated as a matter of national prestige what at first had been not more than a matter of taste and accident. Common sense as well as aversion to the nationalistic associations of the 'German' script combined to bring about the eventual defection

QVINTI
HORATII FLACCI
CARMINVM
LIBER QVARTVS.

~~~~~~

ODE I.

AD VENEREM.

Intermissa, Venus, diu,
   Rursus bella moves. Parce, precor, precor!
Non sum qualis eram bonae
   Sub regno Cinarae. Desine, dulcium
Mater saeva Cupidinum,
   Circa lustra decem flectere mollibus
Iam durum imperiis: abi,
   Quo blandae iuvenum te revocant preces.
Tempestivius in domo
   Paulli, purpureis ales oloribus,
Comissabere Maximi,
   Si torrere iecur quaeris idoneum.

Horace, *Opera*. Giambattista Bodoni, Parma, 1791. [11385.k.9]

of the Scandinavian countries. The first Danish book printed in roman appeared in 1723; and in 1739 the Swedish Academy, under the chairmanship of Linnaeus, recommended the use of roman in Swedish books and decreed that its own proceedings were forthwith to be printed thus. Although some Scandinavian books continued to be printed in gothic type for another 150 years, it was obvious by the end of the eighteenth century that black-letter had become a German provincialism.

Irish and Anglo-Saxon types

Religious propaganda, which was responsible for the cutting of oriental types destined originally for polyglot Bibles and later of considerable assistance in the study of oriental languages, was also the mainspring of two curious bypaths of western typography. The creation of both Irish and Anglo-Saxon founts was a by-product of the Elizabethan church policy. The Irish characters, however, were speedily used for spreading Irish nationalism rather than Anglican theology; they have therefore been referred to in the chapter dealing with the bearing of printing on the growth of vernacular literature.

Anglo-Saxon founts, on the other hand, were introduced into the composing room with no view to reviving Anglo-Saxon speech, but in order to enable Archbishop Parker to publish from 1566 a series of Anglo-Saxon texts. Although Parker and his assistants were considerable scholars, their purpose in collecting and printing pre-Conquest books in Anglo-Saxon (and Latin) was mainly conditioned by their wishful belief that those writers would furnish material with which to underpin the tenets of the Elizabethan church settlement.

However, these artificial founts – German, Irish, Anglo-Saxon – are outside the main stream of western letters. It is rather one of the most wholesome consequences of the world-wide expansion of the printing press that the one Latin alphabet should have become the one medium in which every human thought can find adequate expression.

2. BOOK PRODUCTION

The Netherlands

The Dutch publishing trade of the seventeenth century owed its pre-eminence to the speculative spirit of a venturesome mercantile community, ever on the look-out for fresh markets and not greatly hampered by respect for traditional authority (other than its own, be it said). The two leading firms were Plantin, dominating the southern, Roman Catholic part of the country, and Elzevir, reigning supreme in the Protestant north. The pivotal position of the Low Countries in European affairs in the second half of the sixteenth and throughout the seventeenth centuries extended the market of both these firms far beyond the confines of their countries. Plantin's agents went as far as north Africa, where they sold his Hebrew Bibles to the numerous Jewish congregations.

Christophe Plantin (c. 1520–89) was a Frenchman by birth, and learned to print in Paris. He settled in 1549 in Antwerp, where printing was already prosperous and distinguished, and soon became the foremost publisher of the leading emporium of northern European trade. Considerably more than half of all books printed in the Low Countries before the middle of the sixteenth century had come from

Polyglot Bible. Christophe Plantin, Antwerp, 1564. [6.h.4]

Antwerp Presses. Plantin's first important book was the *Vivae imagines partium corporis humani* (1566), in which he used a considerable part of the text of Vesalius's *De fabrica corporis humani*, but with the difference that for his illustrations he preferred to commission copperplate engravings rather than copies of the original woodcuts.

In 1576 Plantin employed 22 presses, thus equalling Koberger's establishment three generations earlier; no other firm, including Aldus and Stephanus, ran more than from two to six. He took great care with the production of his publications, employing the best French type-cutters and setting much store by good and copious illustrations. In his lifetime he printed nearly 2000 books.

Plantin's main interest, however, lay in publishing rather than printing, and the diversity of his publications is as imposing as their number. Liturgical and edifying religious books (he enjoyed a near-monopoly in the printing of missals and breviaries), Greek and Latin authors, scientific and medical works as well as modern French writers are represented in his list. The greatest work that came out under Plantin's imprint was the Polyglot Bible in eight volumes (1568–73). It was to be subsidized by Philip II of Spain, who in 1570 appointed Plantin his court printer and made him the supervizor of all Dutch printing: but Philip never paid up. In Philip's honour, the Bible was called *Biblia regia*. It was meant to take the place of the Complutensian Bible, which by this time had gone out of stock; 1212 copies were printed, twelve of them on parchment for the king, the others on paper of varying quality with corresponding differences of price.

For ten years, however, the fate of the *Biblia regia* was in suspense as the theologians of Salamanca tried to have it placed on the *Index librorum prohibitorum*. In fact, while the Bible was irreproachable from the strictest Roman point of view, its printer-publisher was secretly an adherent of a Protestant sect which set no store by denominational differences and institutional worship. After the sack of Antwerp by the Spanish soldiery (1576) Plantin left the town and from 1583 to 1585 worked in Leiden as printer to the university. The Antwerp press he left in charge of his two sons-in-law, Francis van Ravelingen (Raphelengius) and Jan Moerentorff (Moretus, 1543–1610). After Plantin's return to Antwerp in 1585 Raphelengius, another Protestant, took over the press in Leiden (where he later became a professor at the university), while Moretus remained Plantin's chief assistant and after his father-in-law's death (1589) became the sole proprietor of the Antwerp branch. Through eight generations Moretus's descendants kept the firm in business in the same premises until 1875 when Hyacinth Moretus sold it to the city, which established the Musée Plantin-Moretus, the premier museum of the history of printing.

Moretus's son, Balthasar (d. 1641), was a friend of Peter Paul Rubens (1577–1640) who made a large number of designs, especially title-pages, which were engraved on copper-plates and further enhanced the splendour of Plantin's books. Flemish book illustration was almost synonymous with Rubens, who mastered the allegorical function of the title-page, and learnt to use it to introduce the contents of the book in a decorative as well as a symbolic manner.

The liberation of the northern Netherlands from their Spanish overlords was speedily followed by a flowering of literature, science and learning, the stage and the arts, which, against the background of an unbroken economic prosperity, justifies the appellation of the Golden Age which the Dutch have given to their seventeenth century. It was also the Golden Age of the Dutch book trade, and this coincided with the fortunes of the house of Elzevir. The founder of the firm, Louis, a native of Louvain, entered the trade in Plantin's shop in Antwerp. As a Calvinist he fled from Alba's persecution and in 1580 settled in Leiden as a bookseller. His connection with the university (of which he was a beadle) may have encouraged him to venture into publishing. His first book was an edition of Eutropius (1593), and editions of classical authors remained the chief concern of the firm. Its activities coincided with the great age of Dutch classical scholarship, thus securing a deserved reputation for accuracy which only the subtler methods and fresh discoveries of the later nineteenth century superseded. Of the 38,000 students whom the Leiden professors attracted between 1575 and 1700 nearly 17,000 were foreigners, some of them from as far afield as Norway and Ireland, Spain and Poland, Turkey and Persia. Every one of them can be assumed to have graduated with some textbooks bought in Leiden and thus become a propagandist of Elzevir editions.

For his trade-mark Louis chose an eagle holding seven arrows and the motto of the seven United Provinces '*Concordia parvae res crescunt*': the spirit of enterprise that animated the Republic also pervaded the house of Elzevir. Louis and his descendants deliberately concentrated on the business aspects of the trade. They were content to leave the editing to their editors and the printing to their pressmen. Contrary to the belief held by some dealers and collectors, the typography of Elzevir books is almost uniformly mediocre. The need to obtain capital made Louis buy up and subsequently auction whole libraries. He thus struck out in a new line of business which has since proved to be the most lucrative branch of the book trade, that of the second-hand book-dealer. Wholesale, retail and second-hand bookselling remained to all subsequent generations of the family as important as printing and publishing. Their close contact with the book-buying public conversely benefited their publications for, better than any preceding printer-publisher, they knew their market, that is, the intellectual requirements as well as the length of the purses of their actual and potential customers.

By the time of his death (1617) Louis had established the firm on a broad international basis. Two of his seven sons had settled as booksellers in The Hague and Utrecht, while Matthias, the eldest, and Bonaventura, the youngest, together carried on the paternal house in Leiden. Matthias retired from business as early as 1622; so it came that the peak period of the firm was managed by Bonaventura (1583–1652) and Matthias's sons, Abraham (1592–1652) and Izaak (1596–1651). They inaugurated in 1629 the duodecimo series of classical authors, which carried the name of Elzevir all over France, Germany, Italy, England and Scandinavia. Aldus Manutius had been the pioneer of such editions, well-produced and cheap; but the Elzevirs did better in scholarship and price – though perhaps not in the make-up. The uniform price of one guilder for the 500-page volume was an additional asset as it took count of the psychology of book-buyers who like to associate a series with its outward appearance as well as its price. They also sponsored the series of 'Little Republics', 35 monographs in sextodecimo which dealt each with the geographical, political, economic, etc., structure of a European or overseas country. A director of the Dutch East India Company acted as advisory editor of these useful little handbooks.

Izaak, however, had as early as 1616 established a press on his own account and in 1620 become printer to the university of Leiden. He specialized in oriental books, but a few years later sold out to Bonaventura and Abraham, who in turn were appointed university printers – an honour which henceforth remained vested in the family. The first contemporary author published by the Elzevirs was Hugo Grotius, whose *Mare liberum* appeared in 1609. This side gained special importance in the Amsterdam branch of the firm, opened by Louis III, the son of the Utrecht bookseller, in 1638. Bonaventura's son Daniel (1626–80) went with him into partnership and, while the Leiden branch was slowly declining, gave a new lease of life and prosperity to the old name. Descartes, Bacon, Comenius, Pascal, Molière, Milton, Hobbes are among the eminent authors published by the Amsterdam Elzevirs. With Daniel's death the Amsterdam firm became extinct; but the survival of its fame is attested by the duodecimo edition of 1794 of John Locke's *Conduct of Understanding* which, though published in London, purported to be 'printed for Daniel Elsevier junior'. The Leiden branch survived somewhat longer, but under Abraham's son, Jan (1622–61), and grandson, Abraham II (1653–1712), the business declined steadily and disappeared unhonoured and unsung on the latter's demise.

A branch of printing in which the Dutch – then the leading seafaring nation – excelled was the design and publication of maps and atlases. The very term 'atlas' was first used by Rumold Mercator, who in 1595 published the maps of his greater father, Gerhard (1512–94), under this title. In 1604 the Mercator plates were sold to

Joost de Hondt, an Amsterdam engraver and map-dealer; he had worked for some years in London and there married the sister of Pieter van de Keere, another Dutch map-engraver who was to become more famous as the printer of the first English newsbook. From 1606 to the end of the eighteenth century, atlases published by the firm of Hondt were to be found all over Europe. Their most eminent rivals were the atlases published by another Amsterdam firm, that founded by Willem Blaeu (1571–1638) and continued by his sons Jan and Cornelis. Their *Atlas novus* (6 vols, 1634–62) and *Atlas major* (11 vols, 1650–62), which also appeared in German, French and Spanish editions, were masterpieces alike of geographical science, typographical skill and the engraver's art – a combination never surpassed by the more utilitarian products of modern cartographical institutes. Jan Blaeu's shop is said to have comprised nine letterpress machines, six copperplate presses and a type-foundry.

Another article of primary importance for the Dutch export trade in books was the 'emblem book' which, from about 1580, reached the height of its international vogue. It was the superiority of Dutch engravers and printers in the production of illustrated books which made them paramount in this field. The *Sinnepoppen*, literally 'Dolls for the Spirit', which Roemer Visscher published in Amsterdam in 1614, is an attractive example; the 180 pictures by Claes Janszoon Visscher show objects from the everyday life of contemporary Dutch burghers and farmers. The first English emblem book, Geoffrey Whitney's *A Choice of Emblems and other Devices*, was therefore appropriately printed in the Low Countries; Plantin published it in Leiden in 1586. Even a generation later it was a Fleming by descent (though already a Londoner by birth), Martin Droeshout, who engraved the portrait of Shakespeare which formed the frontispiece of the First Folio of 1623.

It was again the Plantin press with its excellent craftsmanship which inaugurated the second wave of fashion of the emblem books. When their appeal to courtiers and nobles began to pall, their mottoes and pictures were adapted to devotional and educational purposes. Both the Jesuits and the Puritans quickly realized the good use they could make of the still prevailing mode of allegorical interpretation of spiritual and moral truths. Moretus's volume commemorating the first centenary of the Society of Jesus, *Imago primi saeculi Societatis Jesu* (1640), is the most sumptuous of these publications.

One Dutch firm whose origins go back to the 'golden age' has not only survived to this day but, in the fields of type-designing and printing, regained for the Netherlands of the twentieth century the position of international eminence the country occupied in the seventeenth century: Johann Enschedé & Zonen of Haarlem. Its founder, Izaak Enschedé (1682–1762), started a printing shop in 1703. His firm printed the Book of Psalms for the Dutch Reformed Churches from 1713, and from 1737 the *Haarlemsche Courant*, the town's newspaper (founded in 1656) where Izaak had learned the trade; until 1869, members of the Enschedé family even edited the paper. Izaak's son, Johannes (d. 1780), entered the business in 1719 and soon added to it a retail bookshop and the marketing of paper. However, father and son branched out in what was to become the backbone of the firm when, in 1743, they bought up the type-foundry of Hendrik Floris Wetstein of Amsterdam. This contained among other types several sets of roman and italic cut by J. M. Fleischmann, then the most popular and saleable letters in the international market. To them were later added hundreds of founts, nearly all produced by the best eighteenth-century punch-cutters such as Dirk Voskens, J. F. Unger and Firmin Didot. In the nineteenth century, Johann Enschedé & Zonen (as the firm had been renamed in 1771) bought up the founts of Ploos van Amstel, which included the valuable Hebrew types once belonging to Joseph Athias, and the superb collection of matrices brought together by Pierre Didot. Their quality as printers was recognized when the Bank of the Netherlands entrusted them with the production of its banknotes in 1814 and the Dutch government with the printing of its postage stamps in 1866. New life and energy was infused into the business with the employment from 1923 to his untimely death in 1958 of Jan van Krimpen as type-designer and typographical adviser.

France

In contrast with the businesslike and comparatively liberal attitude of the Dutch authorities, France maintained her lead thanks to the continuance of the conservative, centralized and classicistic tradition going back to the patronage of François I, the scholarship of the Stephanus family and the typographical canons established by Garamond and Granjon.

Louis XIII (1608–43) was as great a patron of the art of printing as François I had been a century earlier, but he lacked the easy-going ways and the intellectual curiosity of his ancestor, and generous support of printers and binders was to him exclusively a means of enhancing and glorifying royal absolutism. In 1620 Louis established a private press in the Louvre. In 1640 Richelieu made it a state-controlled office under the name of Imprimerie Royale and appointed as its first director the Paris printer-publisher Sebastien Cramoisy. Through all the vicissitudes of French history, changing its appellative to 'de la République' and 'Impériale', again to 'Royale', 'Nationale', 'Impériale', and finally back to 'Nationale', this foundation has remained to the present day the centre of French printing. *Éditions de luxe* of Thomas à Kempis's *Imitatio Christi* (1640, a supremely well-printed folio in Garamond types with copperplate vignettes by Nicolas Poussin) and of the complete works of Bernard of Clairvaux (1642) were the first fruits of the new enterprise.

They were followed in the reign of Louis XIV (1638–1715), the 'Sun King', by collections of the Church Councils (37 vols), Byzantine authors (29 vols) and ancient writers expurgated 'in usum delphini' (64 vols), the *Médailles sur les principaux événements du règne de Louis le Grand* (1702, 'a magnificent folio which reaches the very highest pitch of craftsmanship ... undoubtedly the most splendid example of the ornate and sophisticated book' – Morison), and other books exalting French history, as well as mathematical and scientific works – all characterized by the strict classicism of their contents and the austere beauty of their appearance.

Louis's patronage also extended to the folio edition of the Greek Fathers which the Société de la Grand' Navire, a syndicate of Paris booksellers, printed with the *grecs du roi* in 1624 and to the Polyglot Bible which was to outrival Plantin's *Biblia regia*. The political connection which France had maintained with the Turkish empire since François I's time facilitated the importation of oriental types as well as oriental scholars. Antoine Vitré was appointed *Imprimeur du roi pour les langues orientales* (1622), and the ten volumes of the French Polyglot Bible displayed Armenian, Chaldee, Coptic, Samaritan, Syrian and other early translations of the Scriptures, most of which had hitherto been unavailable in the West. A member of the Paris Parlement, Guy-Michel Le Jay, paid for the whole editorial and typographic work out of his own pocket. After Vitré's and Le Jay's death (both died in 1674) the precious oriental matrices went to the Imprimerie Royale in 1692.

The tendency of the absolute monarchy towards directing every aspect of the life of the subject did not overlook the book trade. Louis XIII's ordinance of 6 July 1618 attempted a comprehensive regulation of the whole trade. The Chambre des Syndicats which it set up was to exercise functions very similar to those entrusted to the Stationers' Company sixty years earlier. But there was a telling difference: the French booksellers were obliged to meet and deliberate in the presence of two crown officials, and for all practical purposes became an organ of the royal administration rather than a self-governing body. In order to facilitate the control, the number of licensed printers was finally restricted to 36 in Paris, 18 in Lyon and Rouen, 12 in Bordeaux. Censorship remained in the hands of the Sorbonne until the combination of absolutist and Gallican tendencies eventually led to its transfer to royal officials.

The stifling restrictions to which French publishing was subjected under the *ancien régime* resulted not unnaturally in the publishers' choosing the easy way of preferring fiction, poetry and plays of recognized authors to the hazards of books which might bring upon their heads the wrath of the temporal or spiritual powers. But these French books played an important part in conditioning the rest of Europe to French taste and civilization, especially when, from the middle of the seventeenth century, French book-illustrators broke the hegemony of the Dutch engravers. Henri Estienne's treatise on *L'Art de faire les devises* (Paris, 1645), which epitomized and regularized the tradition of emblem books, at once gained European fame; an English translation, Thomas Blunt's *The Art of Making Devises*, appeared within a twelvemonth.

Soon French publishers were lucky to obtain the co-operation of the best artists of the time. Claude Gillot designed the ornaments for Houdar de la Motte's *Fables* (1719); François Boucher illustrated an edition of Molière (1734); Gravelot an Italian and a French *Decamerone* (1757); Joseph Eisen and Pierre-Philippe Choffard contributed the vignettes and miniatures to La Fontaine's *Contes* (1762) and Ovid's *Metamorphoses* (1767–71); Jean-Baptiste Oudry, the animal painter, drew nearly 300 charming illustrations for La Fontaine's *Fables* (1755–9); Cochin *fils* illustrated Ariosto's *Roland furieux* (1775–83); Charles Percier contributed fine neo-classical illustrations and headpieces to the *Works* of Horace (1799); and the great Jean-Michel Moreau (Moreau-le-Jeune) illustrated Voltaire, Molière and Rousseau – to mention only some outstanding achievements of rococo fine-book production in France which are still the delight of every connoisseur. Gravelot worked in London for 13 influential and highly profitable years, and was employed by Baskerville. John Bell gave work to Moreau-le-Jeune.

The first collected edition of Voltaire's works, which came out in 1785–9 in 70 volumes octavo or 92 volumes duodecimo, is one of the epics of printing and publishing. It was planned and carried out by Pierre-Augustin Caron de Beaumarchais (1732–99), the author of *The Barber of Seville* and *The Marriage of Figaro*. For 160,000 francs he bought the copyright of all Voltaire's manuscripts from the Paris publisher Pancoucke, to whom Voltaire had bequeathed the task of producing his collected works. For 150,000 francs he bought the entire equipment of Baskerville's press from the latter's widow, thus securing the best type of the eighteenth century for the century's greatest writer. From the Margrave of Baden he secured premises in the little fortress town of Kehl opposite Strasbourg, with privileges which made him all but the ruler of an independent principality. Beaumarchais then founded a *Société*

DE
IMITATIONE
CHRISTI
LIBER QVARTVS.

De Sacramento.

Deuota exhortatio, ad sacram
Communionem.

Vox Christi.

 ENITE ad me omnes,
qui laboratis, & one-
rati estis, & ego refi-
ciam vos, dicit Do-
minus. Panis, quem ego dabo,

Kkk iij

Thomas à Kempis, *De Imitatione Christi*. Imprimerie Royale, Paris, 1640. [13.f.11]

tous affemblés au Palais du Comte , prefts à fe
mettre à table , elle paffa entre les gens , fans
changer d'habit , avec fes deux fils entre fes
bras. Quand elle fut montée en la falle , jufques
au milieu où elle vit le Comte , elle fe jettant
à fes pieds , lui dit en pleurant : Monfeigneur ,
je fuis ta pauvre & infortunée femme , qui
pour te laiffer retourner & demeurer en ta mai-
fon , fuis allée long temps coquinant par le monde , je te requiers pour l'honneur de Dieu , que
tu me tiennes les conditions que les deux Che-
valiers que je t'envoyai me rapporterent de ta
part : car voici entre mes bras , non-feulement
un fils de toi , mais deux , & pareillement ton
anneau : il eft donc temps que , fuivant ta pro-
meffe , je doive eftre reçue de toi comme ta
propre femme. Le Comte oyant ceci fut tout
étonné , & reconnut l'anneau , & pareillement
les enfans qui lui reffembloient , & toutefois il
dit : Comment cela peut-il eftre arrivé ? La
Comteffe avec grande admiration du Comte &
de tous les autres qui eftoient préfens , conta par
ordre tout le fait , & comme il eftoit advenu ,
pour laquelle chofe le Comte connoiffant qu'elle
difoit vrai , & voyant fa perféverance , & fon bon
fens , & deux fi beaux petits garçons , auffi pour
garder ce qu'il avoit promis , & complaire à tous
fes Sujets , relâcha fon obftinée rigueur , & la fit
lever , puis l'embraffa & la baifa , & la reconnut
pour fa légitime époufe , & les deux garçons pour

fes enfans. Et après l'avoir fait veftir d'habits con-
venables à elle , avec grand plaifir de tous ceux
qui y eftoient , & de tous fes autres vaffaux qui
le fçurent , il fit non feulement tout ce jour-là ,
mais plufieurs autres , très-grandes cheres , &
de ce jour en avant l'aima & l'honora comme fa
femme & époufe , & elle lui fut très-grande-
ment chere.

Giovanni Boccaccio, *Le Decamerone*, illustrations by H. Gravelot engraved by N. S. Mire. London, 1757. [K.T.C.36.a.5]

La Fontaine, *Fables*, illustrations by J.-B. Oudry engraved by C. N. Cochin. C.-A. Jombert, Paris, 1755. [76.k.1]

16   FABLES CHOISIES.

Il nous faudroit mille perfonnes
Pour éplucher tout ce canton.
La chanvre étant tout-à-fait crûe,
L'Hirondelle ajoûta : ceci ne va pas bien,
Mauvaife graine eft tôt venue.
Mais puifque jufqu'ici l'on ne m'a crue en rien,
Dès que vous verrez que la terre
Sera couverte, & qu'à leurs bleds
Les gens n'étant plus occupés,
Feront aux Oifillons la guerre,
Quand reginglettes & réfeaux
Attraperont petits Oifeaux,
Ne volez plus de place en place ;
Demeurez au logis, ou changez de climat :
Imitez le canard, la grue & la bécaffe.
Mais vous n'êtes pas en état
De paffer, comme nous, les déferts & les ondes,
Ni d'aller chercher d'autres mondes :
C'eft pourquoi vous n'avez qu'un parti qui foit fûr,
C'eft de vous renfermer aux trous de quelque mur.
Les Oifillons, las de l'entendre,
Se mirent à jafer auffi confufément,
Que faifoient les Troyens, quand la pauvre Caffandre
Ouvroit la bouche feulement.
Il en prit aux uns comme aux autres.
Maint Oifillon fe vit efclave retenu.

Nous n'écoutons d'inftincts que ceux qui font les nôtres,
Et ne croyons le mal que quand il eft venu.

littéraire et typographique of which he was the sole member. This society acted as the publicity agency of the Kehl publishing house, and a lottery with a first prize of 24,000 francs was one of its baits for attracting subscribers. The Empress Catherine II of Russia was to be the patron of the undertaking, and a set of Voltaire's works printed on parchment at the cost of 40,000 francs was dedicated to her. But Catherine objected to the inclusion of her correspondence with Voltaire, and her political dislike of Beaumarchais, the stormy petrel of the Revolution, turned her also against his 'Voltaire figaroisé'. This taunt was without foundation for, considering the absence of modern bibliographical criteria, Beaumarchais's edition was a masterpiece of editorial skill as well as typographical achievement.

Robert Darnton's pioneering study of the publishing history of Diderot and d'Alembert's great *Encyclopédie*, *The Business of Enlightenment*, has told us much in general about the influence of the printing and publishing processes on the substance and transmission of ideas in the second half of the eighteenth century; and even more in particular about the century's most important publishing enterprise. Reason, memory and imagination: these faculties, said the Encyclopedists, are all man needs to know the world and live in it intelligently. So, asks Darnton, where did the Encyclopedists who dared to publish this dangerous book come from?

Twenty-five thousand sets of the six editions published between 1751 and 1782 (variously running to 23–36 volumes of text and 3–12 volumes of plates containing 2885 copperplate engravings) in eight French, Swiss and Italian cities were sold, over 50 per cent of them outside France. That is Darnton's other question: who bought them?

Germany

The Lutheran Reformation had spent its impetus by the middle of the sixteenth century; but Protestantism, and consequently the Protestant book trade, maintained its ascendancy over the intellectual life of Germany well into the beginning of the nineteenth century. This incidentally meant the shift of the centre of gravity from the south to central and north Germany. The barriers erected by the Habsburg and Wittelsbach rulers against the danger of heretical writings, it is true, gave the publishers of Vienna and Munich a monopoly within these dominions; but their influence on German life and letters was nil. It was not until Bartholomä Herder (1774–1839) sailed with the animating breeze of the 'catholic *Aufklärung*' that a catholic publisher took his place in the front rank of German publishing: the 14 editions of Carl von Rotteck's *Allgemeine Geschichte* (9 vols), which he published between 1812 and 1840, contributed more than any other single book to the political awakening of German liberalism and democracy.

But this belongs to a later period. From 1550 to 1800 type-founding, printing, publishing and bookselling were almost Protestant preserves. This applies also to Frankfurt. Even when its book fair was ruined by the Jesuit censorship, Frankfurt retained a leading role in the production and marketing of types and in the design and printing of illustrated books. The reputation gained by the woodcuts published by Egenolff and Feyerabend was increased by the copper-engravings in which Theodor de Bry (1528–98) and his sons Johann Theodor and Johann Israel excelled. Frankfurt craftsmanship was fed from the Low Countries and Switzerland. Theodor was a native of Liège; Johann Theodor's son-in-law, who was to outrival the de Bry firm, was Matthäus Merian from Basel (1593–1650). Far into the eighteenth century his descendants, especially his grandson Johann Matthäus (1659–1716), carried on the tradition established by Matthäus in the fields of sumptuously illustrated folios. Two series gained special and well-deserved fame; both covered, or aimed to cover, the whole of Europe. The *Theatrum europaeum* (1633–1738) gave a chronicle of contemporary events, comparable with Edmund Burke's *Annual Register* (1759 to date); while the 29 volumes of the first edition (1642–72) of the *Topographia* is a priceless pictorial record of seventeenth-century towns, famous for the realistic as well as the artistic perfection of its 92 maps and 2142 prospects. The *Grands voyages* (1590–1640) publicized the exploration of the world beyond Europe, with texts in German, French, English and Latin.

As in the days of Anton Koberger, Nürnberg became once more the seat of a gigantic firm of printer-publishers. Georg Endter (1562–1630) founded it; his son Wolfgang (1593-1659) led it to its apex: it came to an end in 1717. The greatest production of the Endters was the 'Electors' Bible' of 1641, commissioned by Duke Ernest the Pious of Gotha and illustrated by Joachim von Sandrart, whose *Teutsche Akademie* (1675–9) made him the father of German art history.

Two more books of general importance which appeared over Endter's imprint are the Nürnberg poet Georg Philipp Harsdörffer's *Frauenzimmer-Gesprächspiele* (8 parts, 1641–9) which provided suitable material for polite conversation, and the same author's *Poetischer Trichter* (3 parts, 1647–53) which epitomized, as it were, the rule of reason in the sphere of poetry.

Duke Ernest originally intended to have the 'Elector's Bible' printed and published by the firm of Stern in Lüneberg, which was the greatest rival of the Endters in the German book trade of the seventeenth century. The house of Stern had the unique distinction of having been owned and run for nearly 400 years by the direct descendants of the founder, Hans Stern, who set up shop in 1580 and died in 1614. Bibles, theological tracts, hymn books, calendars and almanacs were the backbone of the business; the Scheits Bible, named after the Hamburg engraver Matthias Scheits who contributed the 150 illustrations, was their most ambitious undertaking (1672). Their business extended as far as Amsterdam, Copenhagen, Stockholm, Danzig, Königsberg, Reval, Vilna – and even Nürnberg.

None of these places, however, could bear comparison with Leipzig, which from the middle of the seventeenth century became the centre of German book production and distribution.

Leipzig was favoured by its geographical position in the heart of central Europe, the privileges with which the Saxon government had endowed its trade fairs and the liberality with which the town council interpreted them, the importance of its university where the professors Gottsched and Gellert from 1730 to 1770 exercized a virtual dictatorship over the literary life of Germany, and last but not least the business acumen of its printers, publishers and booksellers. The firm which Johann Friedrich Gleditsch (1653–1716) founded in 1694 continued until 1830, when Brockhaus bought it up. The firm founded by Moritz Georg Weidmann in 1682 owed its survival to the present day to Gleditsch's younger brother, Johann Ludwig (1663–1741), who married Weidmann's widow; he was also very active in persuading the leading Dutch booksellers to transfer their business with central and eastern Europe from Frankfurt to Leipzig. It was a partner of the house of Weidmann who gave the *coup de grâce* to the Frankfurt book fair when he dissolved his Frankfurt warehouse in 1764 and made other Leipzig firms follow suit. This man, Philipp Eras-

ENCYCLOPÉDIE,

OU

DICTIONNAIRE RAISONNÉ

DES SCIENCES,

DES ARTS ET DES MÉTIERS.

A

 a & *a*, f. m. (*ordre Encyclopéd. Entend. Science de l'homme, Logique, Art de communiquer, Gramm.*) caractere ou figure de la premiere lettre de l'Alphabet, en latin, en françois, & en presque toutes les Langues de l'Europe.

On peut considérer ce caractere, ou comme lettre, ou comme mot.

I. A, en tant que lettre, est le signe du son *a*, qui de tous les sons de la voix est le plus facile à prononcer. Il ne faut qu'ouvrir la bouche & pousser l'air des poumons.

On dit que l'*a* vient de l'*aleph* des Hébreux : mais l'*a* en tant que son ne vient que de la conformation des organes de la parole ; & le caractere ou figure dont nous nous servons pour représenter ce son, nous vient de l'*alpha* des Grecs. Les Latins & les autres peuples de l'Europe ont imité les Grecs dans la forme qu'ils ont donnée à cette lettre. Selon les Grammaires Hébraïques, & la Grammaire générale de P. R. p. 12. l'*aleph ne sert* (aujourd'hui) *que pour l'écriture*, & *n'a aucun son que celui de la voyelle qui lui est jointe*. Cela fait voir que la prononciation des lettres est sujette à variation dans les Langues mortes, comme elle l'est dans les Langues vivantes. Car il est constant, selon M. Masclef & le P. Houbignan, que l'*aleph* se prononçoit autrefois comme notre *a* ; ce qu'ils prouvent surtout par le passage d'Eusebe, *Prép. Ev.* liv. X. c. vj. où ce P. soutient que les Grecs ont pris leurs lettres des Hébreux : *Id ex Græcâ singulorum elementorum appellatione quivis intelligit. Quid enim aleph ab alpha magnopere differt ? Quid autem vel betha a beth ?* &c.

Quelques Auteurs (Covaruvias) disent, que lorsque les enfans viennent au monde, les mâles font entendre le son de l'*a*, qui est la premiere voyelle de

Tome I.

mas, & les filles le son de l'*e*, premiere voyelle de *femina* : mais c'est une imagination sans fondement. Quand les enfans viennent au monde, & que pour la premiere fois il poussent l'air des poumons, on entend le son de différentes voyelles, selon qu'ils ouvrent plus ou moins la bouche.

On dit *un grand A, un petit a* : ainsi *a* est du genre masculin, comme les autres voyelles de notre alphabet.

Le son de l'*a*, aussi bien que celui de l'*e*, est long en certains mots, & bref en d'autres : *a* est long dans *grace*, & bref dans *place*. Il est long dans *tâche* quand ce mot signifie un ouvrage qu'on donne à faire ; & il est bref dans *tache, macula*, souillure. Il est long dans *mâtin*, gros chien ; & bref dans *matin*, premiere partie du jour. *Voyez l'excellent Traité de la Prosodie de M. l'Abbé d'Olivet.*

Les Romains, pour marquer l'*a* long, l'écrivirent d'abord double, *Aala* pour *Ala* ; c'est ainsi qu'on trouve dans nos anciens Auteurs François *aage*, &c. Ensuite ils insérerent un *h* entre les deux *a*, *Ahala*. Enfin ils mettoient quelquefois le signe de la syllabe longue, *âla*.

On met aujourd'hui un accent circonflexe sur l'*a* long, au lieu de l'*s* qu'on écrivoit autrefois après cet *a* : ainsi au lieu d'écrire *mastin, blasme, asne*, &c. on écrit *mâtin, blâme, âne*. Mais il ne faut pas croire avec la plûpart des Grammairiens, que nos peres n'écrivoient cette *s* après l'*a*, ou après toute autre voyelle, que pour marquer que cette voyelle étoit longue : ils écrivoient cette *s*, parce qu'ils la prononçoient ; & cette prononciation est encore en usage dans nos Provinces méridionales, où l'on prononce *mastin, testo, besti*, &c.

On ne met point d'accent sur l'*a* bref ou commun.

L'*a* chez les Romains étoit appellé *lettre salutaire* : *littera salutaris*. Cic. Attic. jx 7. parce que lorsqu'il s'agissoit d'absoudre ou de condamner un accusé, les

A

mus Reich (1717–87), known in his days as 'the prince of the German book trade', has left his name in the annals of the trade as the inventor, one might say, of the 'net price' principle, as the indefatigable fighter against the pirate printers, and as the originator of the idea of a booksellers' association (1765) which eventually materialized in the Börsenverein of 1825. With Wieland's *Musarion* (1768) and *Agathon* (1773) and Lavater's *Physiognomische Fragmente* (1775–8), Weidmann crossed the threshold of the 'classical' era of German literature. But the 'age of Goethe' is represented in print chiefly by the three publishers, Göschen, Cotta and Ungar.

Georg Joachim Göschen (1725–1828) of Bremen opened his publishing house in Leipzig in 1785; Schiller's *Don Carlos* (1787), Goethe's *Iphigenie* (1787), *Egmont* (1788), *Tasso* (1790), the *Faust* fragment (1790) and the first collected edition of his writings (1786) appeared over his imprint. When Goethe and Schiller went over to Cotta, Göschen enticed Wieland from Weidmann, and between 1794 and 1802 brought out two editions (in quarto and octavo) of his works.

Johann Friedrich Cotta (1764–1832) was a descendant of Johann Georg Cotta (1631–92), a native of Saxony, who after his apprenticeship with Wolfgang Endter in Nürnberg set up in the Swabian university town of Tübingen in 1659, from where the firm moved to Stuttgart in 1810. Cotta met Schiller in 1793 and thereafter published most of his work, from *Die Horen* (1795) to *Wilhelm Tell* (1804). Goethe, introduced to Cotta by Schiller, made Cotta the principal publisher of his later works, from *Faust I* (1808) to *Faust II* (1832), and several collected editions (1806–8 etc.), culminating in the complete edition (60 vols) of 1827–42. On Schiller's recommendation Cotta also published Hölderlin's *Hyperion* (1797–9) and, later, the first edition of his *Gedichte* (1826). He also launched the *Musenalmanach für 1802*, in which A. W. Schlegel and Tieck presented the poets of the Romantic school. But this venture proved a dismal failure, as did Kleist's *Penthesilia* (1808), and Cotta henceforth fought shy of romantics and Romantics.

Georg Friedrich Unger (1753–1804) was too much engaged in his printing (1780), type-founding (1790) and newspaper (*Vossische Zeitung*, 1802) businesses to give much time to the publishing side. However, he has to his credit Goethe's *Neue Schriften* (7 vols, 1792–1800) – including *Reineke Fuchs* and *Wilhelm Meisters Lehrjahre* – Schiller's *Jungfrau von Orleans* (1802) – printed in roman at the express wish of the poet, who objected to 'Ungers altdeutscher Eiche' – and, above all, A. W. Schlegel's translation of Shakespeare (9 vols, 1797–1802, 1810). Unger's untimely death caused the bankruptcy of his far-flung enterprises. It also deprived him of the honour of becoming one of the foundation members of the Börsenverein der deutschen Buchhändler (1825), in which all the other publishers and booksellers mentioned here took an active part.

The English-speaking countries

ENGLAND. From the time of Caxton to the middle of the sixteenth century and again from about 1560 to the beginning of the Civil War the book-buying public twice enjoyed 80 years of remarkable stability as regards the price of printed matter charged by the retail trade. The dividing line is the debasement of the coinage in the early 1540s, or rather its aftermath, for book prices have always lagged behind the rise of prices of other commodities. Chaucer's *Canterbury Tales*, for instance, was sold at 3s. unbound and 5s. bound from 1492 to 1545. The average level was 1d. for 3 sheets until 1550, and for 2 or 1½ sheets from 1560 to 1635, after which date book prices

Theodor de Bry, *Der ander Theyl, der Newlich erfunden Landtschafft Americae*. Gothic and roman types used together. J. Wecheli, Frankfurt, 1591. [10003.e.16]

William Cunningham, *The Cosmographical Glasse*. John Day, London, 1559. [59.i.28]

rose by about 40 per cent. Illustrated books were twice as expensive (per sheet) as unillustrated ones, and poetry was dearer than prose.

Some famous Elizabethan books were retailed as follows: Ascham's *The Scholemaster* (1573; 6*d*.); Camden's *Britannia* (1594; 5*s*); Castiglione's *The Courtyer* (1577; 2*s*. 4*d*.); Hakluyt's *Voyages* (1589; 11*s*. 11*d*.); Holinshed's *Chronicles* (1577; 26*s*.); Hooker's *Ecclesiasticall Politie* (1597; 6*s*. 6*d*. unbound); North's translation of *Plutarch's Lives* (1579; 14*s*.); Spenser's *Shepherdes Calendar* (1591; 1*s*. unbound); Shakespeare's *Venus and Adonis* (1573: 1*s*.).

In the history of the English book-trade the turn of the seventeenth to the eighteenth century was epoch-making. The lapse of the Licensing Act in 1695 and the passing of the Copyright Act in 1709 (with effect from 1 April 1710) were the two decisive events.

English literature, it is true, had not had to wait for the relaxation of the fetters imposed upon it by the Star Chamber or the Stationers' Company, or for the legal protection secured to authors and publishers by act of Parliament. The Authorized Version of 'King James's Bible', all the Quartos and the four Folios of Shakespeare, Bacon's *Essays*, Milton's *Paradise Lost*, Bunyan's *Pilgrim's Progress*, Herrick's *Hesperides*, Sir Thomas Browne's *Religio Medici* and Izaak Walton's *Compleat Angler* are only a few of the highlights of English seventeenth-century writing. But

97

their interest is literary and historical; as achievements of the printer's art these books deserve little respect. The London Polyglot Bible printed by Thomas Roycroft, which began publication in 1654 was, said Morison, 'admirable as a technical achievement', presenting as many as ten versions of the same text in parallel columns, 'but cannot be said to be a fine performance'.

All these works of national literature were also satisfactory from the publishers' bread-and-butter point of view. Shakespeare was a success from the beginning, taking into account the limiting effect on sales of the then high price of £1 for the First Folio; Bunyan at once started as a bestseller. In between these two, however, the 'Catalogue of the most vendible books in England' (1657) acclaimed two writers who are now known only to the specialist of seventeenth-century literature, Francis Quarles and George Wither. Their most popular books appeared both in the same year, 1635, and each of them was a shining representative of a particular category of emblem books. Wither, the Puritan Parliamentarian, compiled *A Collection of Emblemes Ancient and Modern* which modified the moral tenets of chivalrous Elizabethans to suit the outlook of middle-class Roundheads. Quarles, the Anglican Royalist, brought up to Caroline standards the sentiments of Spenser and Sidney in his *Emblemes* and, 1638, *Hieroglyphikes of the Life of Man*. These were combined in a single volume in 1639, which was reprinted in 1643 and, after the interval of the Commonwealth when Wither proved more acceptable to the ruling taste, fifteen times up to 1777 – an illuminating commentary on the persistence of a literary fashion long after it has lost its intellectual and social impetus.

It is characteristic of the low quality of English book-work in this period that even the text of the Scriptures was affected by the prevailing carelessness. Notorious examples are the Judas Bible of 1611, in which Matt. 26:36 has Judas instead of Jesus; the Wicked Bible of 1632 ('Thou shalt commit adultery'); the Printers' Bible of 1702 ('Printers have persecuted me', Psalm 119:161); and the Vinegar Bible of 1717 ('Parable of the Vinegar', Luke 20). The Reims Bible of 1582, a good specimen of Elizabethan prose, was treated with almost incredible levity by successive revisors, publishers and printers. There is hardly an edition down to the present century in which single words, groups of words, or whole lines have not been omitted through sheer carelessness.

Dr John Fell (1625–86), dean of Christ Church, vice-chancellor of the university of Oxford, and bishop of Oxford, started the reformation of English printing. His acquisition of Dutch and French matrices has already been referred to. He also attached a type-foundry to the University Press in 1676; this was run first by a Dutchman and then by a German, Peter de Walpergen, who cut the very fine music types that were eventually to give such distinction to the Yattendon Hymnal (Oxford, 1899). With the publication of the first Oxford university *Almanack* and Anthony Wood's *Historia et Antiquitates Universitatis Oxoniensis* (both 1674), Oxford University Press was set on its career as a prime promoter of fine and scholarly printing.

Even under the absolutism of the Stuarts the two university presses enjoyed a certain degree of latitude. Restrictions fell hardest upon the London printers who worked immediately under the eyes of the royal censor, the Star Chamber, and the Stationers' Company. Their number was fixed at 25 in 1586 and at 23 (with 4 foundries) in 1637 and reduced to 20 in 1662; it remained at this figure until 1695. In 1662 York was admitted as the fourth town of the kingdom where printers were allowed to exercise their craft.

The lapse of the Licensing Act in 1695 at last removed the anomalous restriction to the four cities and thus made possible the extension of the printing trade to the provinces. The foundries of John Baskerville in Birmingham, Fry and Moore in Bristol were among the leading firms in the middle of the eighteenth century. But Baskerville's equipment went to France after his death, and the firms of Fry and Moore soon moved to London. The contribution to English letters of provincial publishers was even more modest. Oliver Goldsmith's *Vicar of Wakefield*, it is true, came out in Salisbury in 1766. But Joseph Cottle of Bristol (1770–1853) is the only English publisher outside London whose name looms in the annals of English letters. The accoucheur of the Romantic movement, he ventured his slender means in the publication of Coleridge's *Poems* (1796), Southey's *Joan of Arc* (1796), and Wordsworth and Coleridge's *Lyrical Ballads* (1798). All three, however, placed their subsequent writings with London publishers. The tradition and the lure of the metropolis proved irresistible.

SCOTLAND. In the eighteenth century Scotland, too, obtained at last an honourable place in the annals of printing. Scotland had been almost the last of the civilized countries to see a printing press established within its frontiers; but, as it happened with Caxton in England, her first printers were natives. In 1508 Walter Chepman and Andrew Myllar set up a press in Edinburgh, and James IV at once granted them a protectionist tariff against English competitors. However, for two centuries Scottish printers were never serious rivals of either English or foreign craftsmen. Thomas Bassendyne (d. 1577), who published an edition of David Lyndsay and the first New Testament printed in Scotland, is an honourable exception; he used French and Dutch types.

Robert Waldegrave became the King's Printer in 1591 after he had been forced to leave England for publishing anti-episcopal writings, including the Marprelate tracts. He printed James VI's *Poeticall Exercises* (1591) and *Basilicon Doron*, the first edition of which was limited to seven copies for private distribution (1599). The first public issue, heavily revised, was published early in 1603, and after James VI had become James I of Great Britain a London syndicate reprinted the book four times in the same year. Although the holograph is written in Scots – James never acquired a full command of English – Waldegrave printed it in English. Thus it came about that the *Basilicon Doron* was the first original English book to be translated into modern languages. The first French edition (1603, twice reprinted in 1604) was authorized by Robert Cecil and the English ambassador in Paris; though it seems that James never paid the fee he had promised to the translator. Three pirated editions appeared in the same years. There were also Dutch (two, 1603), German (1604), Swedish (1606) and, of course, Latin (London and Hanau (two), 1604) translations. A Welsh version (London, 1604) was interrupted by the outbreak of the plague; the Welsh publisher, Thomas Salisbury, fled from London and abandoned the work. For reasons difficult to explain, interest in the *Basilicon Doron* revived about 1680: the English edition was reprinted in 1682 (London) and the Latin version in 1679 and 1682 (both in Frankfurt-on-the-Oder).

Scotland came into her own only after the Union with England. In 1713 there was published in Edinburgh a *History of the Art of Printing*, the first history of typography in the English language, though actually for the greater part it is translated from the Frenchman Jean de la Caille's *Histoire de l'imprimerie* (Paris, 1689). The author was James Watson (d. 1722), the publisher of the *Edinburgh Gazette* and the *Edinburgh Courant* and of a collection of *Comic and Serious Scottish Poems* (1706–11). Watson

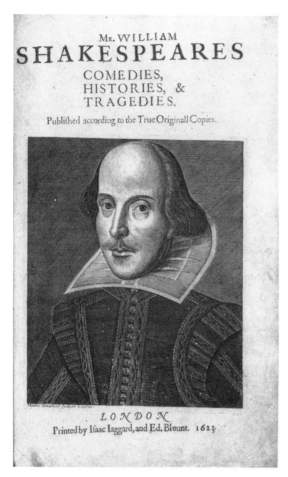

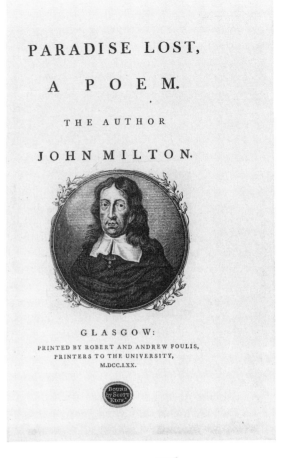

William Shakespeare, *Comedies, Histories, & Tragedies*, the First Folio. Portrait engraving by Martin Droeshout. Jaggard & Blount, London, 1623. [G.11631]

John Milton, *Paradise Lost*. Robert & Andrew Foulis, Printers to the University, Glasgow, 1770. [C.7.d.3]

advocated the importation of Dutch pressmen to improve Scottish printing, and he completely ignored English printing past and present, as he opined that the southern kingdom's 'own writers are very capable to do themselves justice'.

It was, however, Glasgow and not Edinburgh which, from 1740 to 1775, assumed the rank of the printing metropolis of Scotland. Here the brothers Robert (1707–76) and Andrew (1712–75) Foulis (originally spelt Faulls and always pronounced 'fowls') occupied a position as booksellers, printers, publishers and editors not dissimilar to that of Aldus, Amerbach, Froben and Estienne of an earlier age. Apart from theological tracts, the brothers specialized in philosophy and classical, mostly Greek, authors in their original languages and in translations. Their scholarly ambition is evident in the care devoted to proof-reading; every sheet was scrutinized six times, thrice in the office and thrice by the two university professors whom the brothers employed as editors. While their presswork in general equalled the standards of the better English, French and Dutch presses of the time, the Foulises' special claim to fame rests upon their influence upon the development of title-page layout which, so their historian says, 'can scarcely be overestimated'. The Foulis title-page, with 'no lower case, nor italics, nor two sizes of capitals in the same line', constituted a veri-

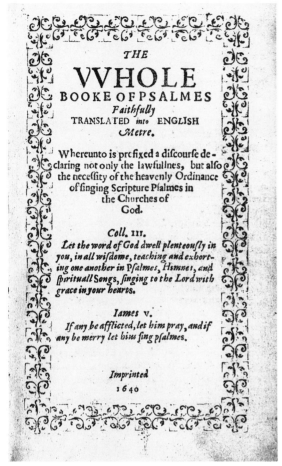

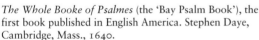

The Whole Booke of Psalmes (the 'Bay Psalm Book'), the first book published in English America. Stephen Daye, Cambridge, Mass., 1640.

[John Eliot], *The Holy Bible ... translated into the Indian Language*. Samuel Green & Marmaduke Johnson, Cambridge, Mass.; the New Testament was first published in 1651, the complete Bible in 1663. [C.10.a.1]

table 'revolution'. By 1795, when Andrew the younger, Robert's son, closed the business, the firm had published some 700 books and pamphlets. Of these, the *Homer* of 1756–8 and *Paradise Lost* of 1770 'are two of the best examples of the dignified simplicity of eighteenth-century printing'.

Part of the excellence of the Foulis Press is due to its founts, which were cut and cast by Alexander Wilson of St Andrews (1714–86). (Giovanni Mardersteig's 'Fontana' type, designed for the publishers and printers Collins, is based on one of Wilson's founts.) His roman and italic types closely followed Caslon, while his Greek founts imitated Garamond's *grecs du roi*.

AMERICA. It was not until 1638 that printing was to reach the New England colonies. In that year Joseph Glover imported a press and three printers from Cambridge, England, to Cambridge, Massachusetts. Glover himself died on the voyage, but Stephen Daye and his sons Stephen and Matthew set up their press under the auspices of Harvard College. Their first print was, fittingly, the form of an 'Oath of Allegiance to the King' (1639); the first book came out a year later as *The Whole Booke of Psalmes*, commonly known as the Bay Psalm Book. Twenty years later a second press was imported from England, again to Harvard College which had secured for

Cambridge, Massachusetts, the sole privilege of printing. In 1663 John Eliot, a graduate from Jesus College, Cambridge (1604–90), had his translation of the Bible into
the Indian language printed by Marmaduke Johnson, the first professional master-
printer in the Americas: this was, says James M. Wells, 'a significant scholarly achievement' and 'a remarkable technical accomplishment'. Johnson also broke the privilege
of Cambridge and in 1674 moved his press to Boston. His example was followed by
the London Quaker, William Bradford, who in 1685 set up the first press in Philadelphia and in 1693 in New York. But it took another 70 years before Georgia, as the
last of the Thirteen Colonies, acquired a press in 1763.

One of Caslon's and Baskerville's early admirers was Benjamin Franklin (1706–
90), the first north American printer of note. He was apprenticed in London, returned
to Philadelphia in 1727, and so prospered that 20 years later he could afford virtually to retire from printing and devote himself to other interests (such as becoming a
Fellow of the Royal Society, U.S. minister in Paris and President of the state of Penn-
sylvania). 'His best pages are competent, rarely more,' says Wells, although he did
produce one typographical masterpiece, an edition of Cicero's *Cato Major* (Philadelphia, 1744). Commercial successes included *Poor Richard's Almanack* (1732–64),
which sold altogether more than 100,000 copies, and *Poor Richard Improved*, 10,000
per year.

The first book in folio to be produced in New England, Samuel Willard's *Compleat
Body of Divinity* (1726), was perforce published on subscription, this being the only
way the printers, Daniel Henchman and Benjamin Eliot, could be sure not to lose
money on it. Henchman showed even more daring in about 1752, when he secretly
printed a Bible and a New Testament in English. What is more surprising even than
his taking the risks attached to defying the jealous restrictions of the Bible patent is
why he did it, given that he was almost certainly using inadequate equipment and
struggling with a limited supply of type and could have imported printed Bibles more
cheaply from high-volume English printers. At that time the Massachusetts government was in the habit of ordering house-to-house searches designed to ensure that
every household possessed a Bible, so well-used importation channels existed.

The Rev. Isaiah Thomas (1749–1831), already a printer (which he remained, later
building his own paper-mill and bindery), assumed also 'the functions and enterprise
of the publisher' when he established in 1770 in Boston *The Massachusetts Spy* (which
continued publication until 1904). Forced to leave Boston by the British on account
of his forthright championship of the cause of American independence, he removed
in 1775 to Worcester, Mass., where he prospered, publishing over 400 books, including the first of several Bibles, the pages for which were set in type by Fry's of London and shipped to Worcester, and in 1785 the first American dictionary, William
Perry's. A 'plain, careful' printer who imported most of his types from Caslon, he
wrote an admirable *History of Printing in America* and established the American Antiquarian Society.

The Revolution played a dual role in creating a wider, and wider-read, public, both
by generating news (and what news!), and by requiring that citizens be well informed.
Before then printing had been a local activity, and printers produced as many copies
of a book as the town booksellers cared to order. By the end of the century Thomas
and others were leading the way towards the decentralization of the American book
trade.

THE
CATO MAJOR

Of *M. Tullius Cicero,*

OR

HIS DISCOURSE OF
OLD-AGE,

ADDRESSED TO

(1) TITUS POMPONIUS ATTICUS.

CHAP. I.

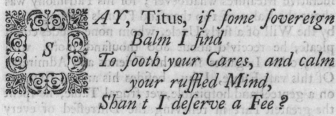

S AY, Titus, *if some sovereign*
Balm I find
To sooth your Cares, and calm
your ruffled Mind,
Shan't I deserve a Fee?

A   For

NOTES.

(1) *Titus Pomponius Atticus,* to whom this Discourse
is address'd, was of an ancient Family of *Rome,* of the
Equestrian Order, the second in Dignity amongst the
Romans. Of all *Cicero's* Friends He appears to have
                                                    been

Cicero, *Cato Major*. Benjamin Franklin, Philadelphia, 1744. [C.20.c.13]

CANADA. By this time printing had spread also to Canada. The first press was established at Halifax, Nova Scotia, by Bartholomew Green Jr of Boston; but owing to his premature death it fell to his partner, John Bushell, to start the first Canadian newspaper, the *Halifax Gazette*, in 1752; it was suppressed in 1766 for the outspoken opposition of its printer, the young Isaiah Thomas, to the Stamp Act. Most early newspapers in the Maritime Provinces and Upper Canada were short-lived, but the two oldest journals of Lower Canada have survived to this day. The *Quebec Gazette*, founded in 1764 by William Brown and Thomas Gilmore and now incorporated in the *Quebec Chronicle-Telegraph*, can boast of being the oldest newspaper in the Americas; the runner-up is the *Montreal Gazette*, first published in 1778 as *La Gazette du Commerce et Littéraire*. Its founder, Fleury Mesplet (1734–94), had learned the printing trade in his native Lyon; found himself in trouble in Paris over his republican and anti-clerical sentiments; set up shop in London in 1773; and in the following year let himself be persuaded by Franklin to emigrate to Philadelphia. In 1776 he moved to Montreal, which the rebels expected to join the United States, but his revolutionary zeal landed him in jail. His enterprising vigour, however, was unbroken. Beside the *Montreal Gazette* he printed some 70 books in Latin, French, English and the Iroquois language.

AUSTRALIA. The first printing press was taken to Sydney by Governor Phillip in 1788, but unfortunately the necessity for including a printer among those sent out with the avowed intention of founding a colony was overlooked, and it was not until the arrival of Governor Hunter in 1795 that in one George Hughes a suitable person was found to start a printing office. The first extant example of his work is a playbill, *The Recruiting Officer*, dated 1800, in which the name of G. Hughes appears as a performer. Printing proper started with the arrival of a creole from the West Indies, George Howe. Howe worked from a room at Government House, his plant being used solely for printing government edicts until 1803, when he obtained permission from Governor King to publish the first Australian newspaper, the *Sydney Gazette and New South Wales Advertiser*; the paper continued until 1842 when a period of industrial depression killed it.

SOUTH AFRICA. For more than a century the sparse population of the Cape were content with reading matter, chiefly of a religious character, imported from the Netherlands. In 1784 a German bookbinder in the service of the Dutch East India Company, by the name of Christian Ritter, set up a small press in Cape Town. He issued an almanac (1796) and other trifles. The British who wrested the colony from the Batavian Republic began the publication of an official weekly gazette in 1800. It was produced by the merchant firm of Walker & Robertson. A year later the government bought up the press and has since continued to publish the gazette. The first book printed in South Africa was a Dutch translation of a tract by the London Missionary Society (1799). The first literary production was a short poem, *De Maan*, by a Dutch pastor, Borcherds, of Stellenbosch (1802).

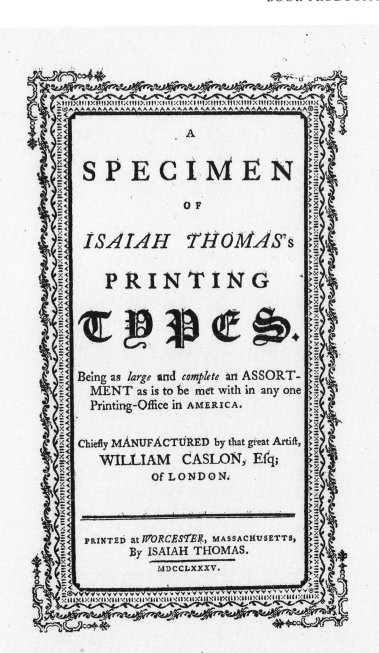

A

SPECIMEN

OF

ISAIAH THOMAS's

PRINTING

𝕿𝖞𝖕𝖊𝖘.

Being as *large* and *complete* an ASSORT-
MENT as is to be met with in any one
Printing-Office in AMERICA.

Chiefly MANUFACTURED by that great Artiſt,
WILLIAM CASLON, Eſq;
Of LONDON.

PRINTED at *WORCESTER*, MASSACHUSETTS,
By ISAIAH THOMAS.
MDCCLXXXV.

Isaiah Thomas, *A Specimen of ... Printing Types*. Thomas, Worcester, Mass., 1785.

Mus & Rana.   I I I.

Du Rat & de la Grenouille.   III.

M Vs bellum ge-
rebat cum Ra-
na. Certabant de re-
gno paludum. Pugna
erat atrox & dubia.
Tandem Mus , fub
herbis latitans , per
infidias hoftem ag-
greditur. Rana viri-
bus corporis & fto-
macho præftabat, pe-
ritiorq; faltandi erat.
Aggrediebatur igi-
tur Murem aperto
Marte. Vterque lan-

L Ɛ Rat faifon guer-
re contre la Gre-
nouille. Ʒeur debat e-
ftoit du royaume des
Marefts. La bataille
eftoit afpre, & douteufe.
Ʒe Rat finalemem fe
cacham deffous les
herbes , affaillit par
trahifon fon enemi. La
Grenouille eftoit la plus
puiffante de corps &
d'eftomac , & mieux
duite à fauter. Ɖarquoy
effe affaillou fe Rat de
pfcine

I 4

AUTUMN.

Crown'd with the fickle and the wheaten fheaf,
While Autumn, nodding o'er the yellow plain,
Comes jovial on; the Doric reed once more,
Well pleas'd, I tune. Whate'er the Wintry froft
Nitrous prepar'd; the various-bloffom'd Spring
Put in white promife forth; and Summer-funs
Concocted ftrong, rufh boundlefs now to view,
Full, perfect all, and fwell my glorious theme.

James Thomson, *The Seasons*, illustrations by William
Hamilton engraved by J. W. Tomkins, 'Engraver to Her
Majesty'. Thomas Bensley, London, 1797. [C.1.e.3]

Esope, *Fables*. Roman and Civilité types; woodcuts by
Bernard Salomon. Jean de Tournes, Geneva, 1607.
[12305.a.31]

3. PUBLISHERS AND PATRONS

The gradual divergence of printer, publisher and bookseller can be traced through
the various forms which the imprint has taken. All three agents still appear until the
end of the seventeenth century in a combination such as: 'Printed by Tho. Cotes, for
Andrew Crook, and are to be sold at the black Bare in Pauls Church-yard' (Thomas
Hobbes's *Briefe of the Art of Rhetorique*, 1637). It can usually be assumed that the
bookshop to which buyers were thus directed was controlled by the publisher. This
is confirmed by the imprint of another book by Hobbes, which runs: 'Printed for
Andrew Crooke, and are to be sold at his shop, at the Sign of the Green-Dragon in
St Paul's Church-yard, 1662.' It is a sign of the growing importance of the publisher
over the printer that the latter's name most easily disappeared from the imprint. Thus
the first edition of Cervantes's *Don Quixote* (1605) refers only to the publisher and
the bookseller: '*En Madrid, por Iuan de la Cuesta. Véndese en casa de Francisco de
Robles, librero del Rey.*' On the other hand, the first Shakespeare folio mentions the
printers only: 'Printed by Isaac Iaggard, and Ed. Blount, 1623.' Rarest is the omission
of the publisher's name in favour of those of the printer and bookseller, as in 'Printed

and Sold by B. Franklin', when it is to be inferred that the publishing risk was also borne by the same man, while W. S. Landor himself paid for the production of his *Poems from the Arabic and Persian*, which came out in 1800 as 'Printed by H. Sharpe, High Street, Warwick, and sold by Messrs Rivingtons, St Paul's Church Yard'. But the phrase 'Printed for William Crook at the Green Dragon without Temple-Bar' is the version which remained most commonly in use until publisher and bookseller, too, parted company. The improved organization of the retail trade made it unnecessary for the publisher to rely on the goodwill of any special retailer. A Leipzig publisher, in 1717, seems to have taken the lead in boldly advertising that his publications are 'available in every bookshop'. Since that time, the fact or fiction that every bookseller of repute has, or at least ought to have, his books in stock has become part and parcel of the modern publisher's publicity.

The occasions when printer and publisher are identical have become increasingly rare. In these cases, whether it is a historic relic or a conscious pride in the art of typography, the imprint almost invariably stresses the fact that the book is published by its printer rather than that the printing has been done by its publisher. '*Typis Johannis Baskerville*', '*Impresso co' caratteri bodoniani*', '*De l'Imprimerie royale*', '*Druck und Verlag von B. G. Teubner*' are typical examples.

In the great English universities the authorities were originally content to let the printer's name stand for the academic publishers. 'Printed by Tho: and John Buck, printers to the University of Cambridge', or 'Cambridge, printed by John Baskerville, Printer to the University', was the usual wording. Thomas Thomas, who in 1583 was appointed the first official printer to the university, emphasized his position by showing the arms of the university on his title-pages, a practice which his successors have continued to the present day.

From the relationship between printer and publisher we turn now to that between publisher and author. Both these professions may be said to have become established in the modern connotation of the terms, so far as Great Britain is concerned, as a result of the Copyright Act of 1709, 'An Act for the encouragement of learning by vesting of the copies of printed books in the authors or purchasers of such copies during the times therein mentioned'. The main beneficiaries of the Act were the authors. For the first time their work was recognized as a valuable commodity for which they could claim the protection of the law and as a property of which they could dispose in the open market to their best advantage. However, the petition for the Copyright Act came from the publishers. They, in fact, profited hardly less than the authors by the security which the law now accorded to the buyer as well as to the seller of intellectual produce. The ensuing disappearance of pirating printers permitted the publisher to fix the prices of his wares at a level which at the same time ensured him a reasonable profit and permitted him to let his author share in it.

These legal changes had far-reaching social results. The old patronage on which authors and printers had to a large extent relied gradually disappeared. The place of the individual patron was taken by the public at large. In order to reach the public, novel ways of publicity had to be developed and older ones to be intensified. Advertisements, prospectuses, stock-lists, general and particularized bibliographies, critical – if possible, favourable – reviews in newspapers and periodicals: all these and other kinds of publicity had henceforth to be adapted to the needs, or supposed needs, of an ever-increasing clientele of ever more varying and unpredictable tastes. The expiration of the original copyright statute in 1731 was probably responsible for the sudden upsurge of serial publications in 1732. Moxon's *Mechanick Exercises*, a teach-yourself series, and Henry Care's *Weekly Pacquet of Advice*, Protestant propaganda pamphlets, both starting in 1678, seem to have been the earliest forerunners of books which could be bought in instalments (what we may now call 'part-works') and this system has remained attractive to publishers and retailers as well as to the thrifty consumer.

The rewards to the successful publisher and the successful author increased correspondingly. The publisher who, through shrewdness or good luck, correctly gauged what the public wanted, or succeeded in making the public want what he had to offer, could now order his printer to strike off copies by thousands instead of hundreds. The author who wrote the right kind of book for the right kind of publisher and got himself established with the public was now able to live on his royalties. No longer had he to pursue his literary work in the time he could spare from his duties as an official, a teacher, a clergyman; nor had he to abase himself before king, prelate, nobleman or city father. That at least is the view accepted since Dr Johnson's day; he defined the individual patron as 'a wretch who supports with insolence and is paid with flattering'.

Until the middle of the eighteenth century it was considered bad manners to write for cash remuneration instead of for reputation. Up to that time only a few writers had ever received a fee from their publishers; and if they received it they were anxious to hide the fact. Erasmus, for instance, was deeply hurt when some Italian colleagues hinted that Aldus Manutius had paid him for a book; and he violently defended himself against similar insinuations on the part of Hutten and others. He was in fact quite shameless in wringing money out of wealthy patrons. His three visits to England were each time prompted, as he coolly stated, by expectations of 'mountains of gold'. He certainly received single gifts and annual pensions amounting to several thousands of present-day pounds sterling from the king, archbishop, bishops, lords and dons. These benefits were surpassed only by Erasmus's self-conceit and ingratitude. Luther never received so much as a farthing for his hundreds of books and pamphlets. Thomas Murner, the Roman Catholic pamphleteer, seems to have been the first to receive a fee, for his *Geuchmatt* in 1514.

The usual way by which an author either solicited favours to come or returned thanks for favours received was the dedication of a work to an individual or a corporation. In fact, these dedications and subsequent rewards were a regular item in the budget of dedicators as well as dedicatees. Thus, in 1502, the humanist poet, Conrad Celtis, received 20 guilders from the city council of Nürnberg for 'the pains' he took over his pamphlet in praise of the imperial city. The Council of Zürich had 38 books dedicated to it between 1670 and 1685; and the expenses of the councillors on this account, like those of others in authority, are not to be distinguished from the sums which are provided for the encouragement of art and literature in the budget of the modern state.

The dedication of the 'unpolished lines' of *Venus and Adonis* to 'so noble a godfather' as the Right Honourable Henry Wriothesley, Earl of Southampton and Baron of Tichfield; of the 'untutored lines' of *The Rape of Lucrece* to the same; and of the Sonnets to their 'onlie begetter', the mysterious 'Mr W.H.', gives a faint idea of the self-abasing adulation which an aspiring author felt obliged to express. Shakespeare's attitude can still be justified by the natural bashfulness of any poet who presents to the world 'the first heir of his invention' as well as on account of the social conventions of the first Elizabethan age. For the patronage extended to men of letters in the six-teenth century was far less a matter of literary connoisseurship than of political propaganda. The Earl of Leicester, who headed the anti-Cecil faction at Elizabeth's court, had up to a hundred books dedicated to him; nearly all of them were practical manuals, historical dissertations, religious tracts – in short, useful books, designed to further the causes in which the patron was engaged. The writers, compilers or trans-lators of these treatises were mostly men who wanted to display their aptitude for certain posts in state or church: and preferment rather than money was in fact their usual reward.

However, the fulsomeness of a dedication usually stands in inverse ratio to the literary merits of the production as well as the literary discrimination of the person to whom it is dedicated. In very few cases can a genuine connection between the dedicatory page and the following text be assumed. On the whole, the dedications are indicative only of the kind of people from whom the author expected some tangible reward. They were, in fact, not infrequently altered from edition to edition, and there are even issues of the same edition with different dedications imprinted.

By the eighteenth century the lack of personal sentiment had led to the fixing of a kind of piece-rate tariff. It ranged normally from five to twenty guineas, with single poems at the bottom and theatrical plays at the top of the scale. More was expected when royalty accepted a dedication: Laurence Echard received £300 from George I for the dedication of his *History of England* (1707) and Benjamin Hoadly £100 from George II for that of his comedy, *The Suspicious Husband* (1747). On the whole, Thomas Gordon (d. 1750) neatly summed up the hollowness of these cash-and-carry dedications when he wrote: 'I have known an author praise an Earl for twenty pages together, though he knew nothing of him but that he had money to spare. He made him wise, just and religious for no reason in the world but in hopes to find him charitable; and gave him a most bountiful heart because he himself had an empty stomach.'

About the middle of the century the dedication for monetary reward died out and was replaced by the genuinely respectful or genuinely affectionate inscription which it has remained. When Henry Fielding dedicated his *Historical Register* (1737) to the public at large, he epitomized the development from 'the great' to 'the multitude' (as Dr Johnson called it) as the author's abiding paymaster and patron.

One of the reasons for the disappearance of individual patronage was its inherent tendency towards confusing literary merit and political expediency. Even the epony-mous patron of all patrons, Maecenas, gently made his Virgil, Horace, Propertius support and glorify the political programme of the Emperor Augustus. In Augustan England patronage was as much a weapon of party politics as a means of furthering literature. Authors as well as their patrons can be distinguished fairly clearly on the party lines of Whig and Tory. Lord Somers, who drafted the Declaration of Rights in 1689 and the treaty of Union with Scotland in 1707, and Charles Montagu, Earl of Halifax, who ruled Exchequer and Treasury under William III and George I, be-friended Addison, Steele, Congreve, Prior, Vertue, Locke and Newton in the Whig interest. Robert Harley, Earl of Oxford, and Henry Saint-John, Viscount Bolingbroke, the Tory leaders under Queen Anne, bestowed their favours on Dryden, Pope and Swift. Whereas these men at least combined their services to a political group with genuine conviction, smaller men did not scruple to sell their pens and their consciences to the highest bidder.

The first tract on *The Case of Authorship by Profession or Trade, stated with regard to Booksellers, the Stage, and the Public* (1758) by the American-born Whig pamphleteer and historian, James Ralph, took, it is true, a dim view of 'the last profession that a liberal mind would choose'. But this opinion was getting obsolete at the very time when it was so forcefully stated by a journalist disappointed in his political and financial expectations. For some of the greatest freelances of all ages, Dr Johnson in England, Voltaire in France, and Lessing in Germany, were now making authorship a full-time, respectable and self-supporting profession.

As a matter of fact, writers could now afford to do without either the occasional or even the regular support of titled patrons. For the professional i.e. the publisher, now outbade the amateur in terms of ready cash. The fees and royalties of authors were rising all the time, since publishers were now able to reap the fruits of the Copyright Act. When considering the sums paid to eighteenth-century writers, the readers should keep in mind that, according to Johnson's estimate – and he knew what he was talking about – the cost of living averaged only some £30 a year. Although the great Doctor cynically stated that he never wrote but for 'want of money which is the only motive of writing I know of', he also admitted that 'the booksellers are generous, liberal minded men'. In fact, he had no reason for complaint about his rewards. He received 10 guineas for *London* (1738), 20 guineas for *The Vanity of Human Wishes*, £125 for *Rasselas* (1759), an additional 100 guineas above the stipulated fees for the *Lives of the Poets*, and £1575 for the *Dictionary* (1755).

In the field of fiction, Henry Fielding probably did better than any other writer. His *Tom Jones* (1749) brought him £700 and *Amelia* (1752) £1000. The two French and one Dutch translation of *Tom Jones* which appeared in the same year, 1750, yielded nothing to the author in the then state of lawlessness of international copyright; but they may have reassured his publisher as to Fielding's hold on the public. When Oliver Goldsmith never got out of debt the fault lay with his extravagance rather than any meanness on the part of his publishers. It is true he received not more than 60 guineas for *The Vicar of Wakefield*; but then it must be remembered that this was a complete loss to the publisher, who, after three editions, was still out of pocket. Goldsmith obtained £250 each for his histories of Rome and Greece, £500 for his English history and 800 guineas for the *History of Animated Nature*. This order may seem deplorable on grounds of literary merit, but it reflects that prevailing interest of the reading public which the publisher's cashier cannot leave out of sight. History, natural history, travels, biographies were in greatest demand. The quack doctor and vitriolic pamphleteer 'Sir' John Hill is said to have made an annual income of £1500 by his compilations on medicine, botany, horticulture, pharmacy, naval history and other subjects for which there was a market during the years of his prolix activities, 1750–75. William Robertson commanded £600 for his *History of Scotland* (1759) and £4500 for his *Charles V* (1769). Out of the *History*, which ran into fourteen editions before Robertson's death in 1793, his publisher, Andrew Millar, made a net profit of £6000; the first American reprint in 1811 is said to have sold 75,000 copies. Millar also rewarded David Hume with £3400 and Tobias Smollett with £2000 for their respective histories of England.

William Strahan, Millar's compatriot and sometime partner, ventured £500 on Adam Smith's *Wealth of Nations* (1776), the bible of free trade. Strahan was also the publisher of Gibbon's *Decline and Fall of the Roman Empire*. The first edition was originally fixed at 750 copies, but had been reduced to 500 when printing began in

WINDSOR-FOREST.

To the Right Honourable

GEORGE Lord LANSDOWN.

THY forefts, Windfor! and thy green retreats,
At once the Monarch's and the Mufe's feats,
Invite my lays. Be prefent, fylvan maids!
Unlock your fprings, and open all your fhades.
GRANVILLE commands; your aid, O Mufes, bring!
What Mufe for GRANVILLE can refufe to fing?

VARIATIONS.
VER. 3, etc. originally thus,
        Chafte Goddefs of the woods,
Nymphs of the vales, and Naiads of the floods,
Lead me thro' arching bow'rs, and glimm'ring glades.
Unlock your fprings —   P.

REMARKS.
This Poem was written at two different times: the firft part
of it, which relates to the country, in the year 1704, at the fame
time with the Paftorals: the latter part was not added till the
year 1713, in which it was publifhed. P.

IMITATIONS.
VER. 6.   neget quis carmina Gallo? Virg.

My humble Muse, in unambitious Strains
Paints the green Forefts & the flow'ry Plains.
                                   Windsor-Forest.

Alexander Pope, *Works*, illustrations by S. Wale engraved by T. S. Müller. J. & P. Knapton, London, 1751. [685.e.1]

June 1775. It then happened that Strahan began to read the manuscript – and immediately raised the printing order to 1000. The first volume came out on 17 February 1776 at the price of a guinea and sold within a fortnight. Out of the six volumes, the last three of which were published on 8 May 1788, Gibbon netted about £9000.

The migration to London of Scottish publishers was partly the result of the attitude of the London trade, which sometimes approached a boycott of Scottish books. Hume's *History*, for instance, hung heavily on the hands of its first Edinburgh publisher, who sold fewer than fifty copies in London within a twelvemonth. Its signal success began when the expatriate Scotsman, Millar, took over the book.

The flowering of English eighteenth-century literature is closely related to the growing personal interest publishers began to take in 'their' authors. All the prominent publishers were large copyright owners. The first publisher to give his firm a profile of its own, Jacob Tonson (1656–1736), was originally a bookseller in Chancery Lane. He acquired the copyright of Milton's *Paradise Lost* and his edition of 1688 put the greatest epic in the English language in circulation: the original publisher, Peter Parker, had sold the 1300 copies of the first edition between August 1667 and April 1669 but waited until 1674 before bringing out a new edition. Tonson became the publisher of Dryden, Otway, Addison, Steele, Pope and Rowe, and through their works and his own famous *Miscellany* did as much for the Augustan age as did Cotta for German classicism a century later. Barnaby Bernard Lintot (1675–1736) took up the same line and, sometimes in partnership with Tonson, brought out Pope, Gay, Farquhar, Rowe, Parnell and Fenton among others.

Robert Dodsley (1703–64), alone and with his brother James, became the publisher of Pope, Akenside, Anstey, Churchill, Young, Goldsmith, Shenstone, Sterne, Bishop Percy and Johnson. He suggested to the Doctor the idea of an English dictionary, and secured Edmund Burke as the editor of the *Annual Register*. Dodsley had started in life as a footman and made his name as versifier and playwright. Alexander Pope helped him to set up as a publisher, and it is probably due to his own earlier experiences that Dodsley showed himself a generous friend of his authors. He paid Edward Young £220 for *Night Thoughts* (1742), Charles Churchill £450 for *The Duellist* (1763), Bishop Percy £300 for the *Reliques* (1765), and returned to Christopher Anstey the copyright of the extremely successful satire, *New Bath Guide* (1766), in addition to a fee of £200. Like almost every publisher, Dodsley once slipped up. He refused to accept *Tristram Shandy* for the modest fee of £50; but he atoned for this blunder by taking the whole work for £650 after Sterne, with the help of a loan, had got the first two books into print at a jobbing press in York (1760). Dodsley's anthologies of plays and poems by 'old authors' did much to revive interest in Elizabethan literature besides Shakespeare.

A peculiarity of seventeenth- and eighteenth-century publishing was the co-operative association. Partnerships had been a characteristic of the trade from the very beginning. Originally, as with Gutenberg and Fust, this was no doubt due to lack of capital on the part of the printer-publisher, but later it was probably caused chiefly by the wish to spread the risk of any publishing venture of uncertain prospects. Here, France led the way in the early seventeenth century when syndicates were as easily founded for a particular enterprise as they were quickly dissolved after its achievement. The first folio edition of Shakespeare's plays in 1623 was such a joint enterprise of the four London publishers William Jaggard, Edward Blount, John Smithweeke and William Apsley. It seems that the driving force behind the great venture was William Jaggard's son, Isaac (born 1595), who had just published the first English translation of Boccaccio's *Decameron* (1620, reprint 1625). The publishers may have entered on the enterprise with some misgivings, for the only previous folio edition of plays was by no means a success: Ben Jonson's *Workes*, thus published in 1616, had to wait until 1640 before a second edition was deemed saleable. But the Jaggards and their partners proved justified.

Characteristic of the English partnerships or 'congers' of the eighteenth century is their business-like organization, including the restriction of membership to genuine publishers who freely bought and sold shares. Johnson's *Lives of the Poets* was thus sponsored by 36 booksellers, his *Dictionary* by a conger of 7; but in 1805 a 160th share of the latter book was sold. This is an extreme case, but shares of $\frac{1}{24}$th were quite common. Thomas Longman, the founder of the firm of Longmans, Green & Co., was an adept at manipulating these congers; John Rivington and John Murray are others who started the subsequent fortunes of their firms this way.

When the Licensing Act expired in 1695, copyright protection in Britain lapsed with it. The Copyright Act of 1709 specified only very limited terms of copyright in place of the perpetual copyright enjoyed before 1695, while failing to set up an effective system to prevent and punish infringement. Not surprisingly the booksellers got together to try to re-establish perpetual copyright *de facto*, and they were frustrated in this in 1774 by a decision of the House of Lords that it had no basis in common law. The congers eventually disappeared because the increasing wealth of individual publishers made them face the inevitable risks of their trade with less apprehension, and chiefly because by the end of the century the spirit of co-operation had given way to the fierce tenets of unrestricted competition.

The eighteenth century, however, did not close before it had produced what, but for the genius of the man, would have been an incomprehensible anachronism. John Bell (1745–1831) deserves a niche of his own in the history of letter-founding, inking, printing, publishing and binding no less than in the history of journalism (newspapers as well as periodicals), bookselling and popular education. Not only did the man try his hand in every one of these professions – which by this time had become each an almost self-contained craft of its own – but he gained for himself a lasting reputation in more than one of them. It is to Bell, the zealous educationist, enterprising publisher and adept editor, that we owe *The British Theatre* (21 vols, published in weekly issues from 1776), the *Poets of Great Britain from Chaucer to Churchill* (109 vols, 1777–92) and the *Constitutional Classics* (1813; including a complete Blackstone) – three series which even after more than 150 years have not been entirely superseded.

To Bell the letter-founder we owe the 'Bell type' which Richard Austin designed for him in 1788 and which, after having fallen out of favour with the English public, gained an immense popularity in America, whence it eventually made a return to England. 'Bell carried farther the implication of Baskerville's types, fused it with that of the new Didot types of 1783–4, and so initiated in England the type-founding style known as "modern" face' – Morison.

But the 'Bell type' was only a side-issue of Bell's indefatigable activities in the world of books and newspapers. He revolutionized the whole typography and display of the English newspaper. He was the co-founder or sole founder of half a dozen morning, evening and Sunday papers. He quarrelled with every associate, but not before he had made them accept his reforms. One of his foundations was *The Morning Post* (1772), which survived until 1937 as one of three London papers of distinction. His *English Chronicle* in 1786 and his *The World* in 1787 banned from the newspaper world the long 'ſ' which Bell had first dispensed with in his *Shakespere* edition of 1785. Bell was the first printer to realize that a newspaper is read at a speed and for purposes different from the reading of a book; and he drew the typographical conclusions. His newspapers broke up the solid setting of the book-page and gave prominence to the paragraph as the unit on which the newspaper-reader's interest is centred. No higher tribute can be paid to Bell, the printer-journalist, than that *The Daily Universal Register* immediately in 1787 copied every feature of typography and layout of *The World* and became dependent on it even more (if that was possible) when on 1 January 1788 it changed its name to *The Times*. The only item *The Times* did not take over until fifteen years later was Bell's most sensible exclusion of the long 'ſ'. Thus John Bell may well be described as the godfather, however unwilling, of what was to become the greatest newspaper in the world.

The profit-motive, which has openly or surreptitiously animated printers and publishers from Gutenberg's time to the present, can more accurately be described as a hopeful expectation of balancing the dubious prospects of uncertain gain and far more certain loss through investing capital in presses, paper and publications. Long before unprofitable political theorists declared the profit-motive the eighth deadly sin, attempts had been made to run the book trade on a non-profit-making basis.

In some cases the promoters of such enterprises actually intended to break into the regular trade, to overthrow its monopoly, to force down prices, and in general to benefit a public which they regarded as insufficiently cared for by the ordinary publishing firm. Such was the case, for instance, with the Society for the Encouragement of Learning which was founded in 1736 but succumbed to the united opposition of the trade after twelve years. Dr John Trusler, an indefatigable projector in the fields of theology, medicine, journalism and typography (in which he can be credited with the design of a script type), also tried his hand at revolutionizing the book trade. In 1765 he established the Literary Society which 'was to print works of reputation at their own risk and give the authors all profits arising from the same'. The fanciful notion that either the public or the author or both would be better off without the publisher never loses its attraction to perfectionist reformers. The Society for the Diffusion of Useful Knowledge pursued similar aims, but the tremendous success of its *Penny Magazine* (1832–45) and *Penny Cyclopaedia* (1833–44) was chiefly due to the enthusiasm and business acumen of its publisher, Charles Knight. The modern book clubs are to some extent the heirs of these associations.

Publication by subscription was another method of excluding the publisher as a middleman and of making the profits flow direct into the author's pockets. This seems to have come into use early in the seventeenth century. The London grammarian and lexicographer, John Minsheu, produced his *Guide to* [eleven] *Tongues* (1617) by subscription. His contemporary, John Taylor, the 'water poet', did the same with his poems. The custom reached its widest application in the eighteenth century. Expensive works, the success of which was difficult to forecast, were usually undertaken by subscription. The two translations of Homer which for more than a century determined the conception of heroic poetry in England and Germany were thus offered to the public. Both proved a signal success to their author-publishers. Pope made £5320 out of his English *Iliad* (1720); Voss had 1240 subscribers for the first edition of his German *Odyssey* (1781).

However, the commonest form of publishing outside the trade is by means of official and private presses. Official presses are usually run by governments or public corporations such as universities; private presses mostly by individual enthusiasts or groups of like-minded people. In every case the owners of these presses produce what their political or scholarly requirements and their literary or typographical predilections make them wish to produce. Considerations of profit always play a minor role, although the managers of official presses and the patrons of private presses are known not to be averse to a favourable balance-sheet.

Official presses became firmly established in the second half of the sixteenth century. The first presses of this kind, those installed at the Sorbonne by Heynlin and Fichet in 1470, and in Alcalá university by Cardinal Ximenes in 1508, did not survive the tenure of office of their first patrons and therefore failed to found a tradition. This was brought about by the Roman Curia.

Pius IV called Paul Manutius, Aldus's son, to Rome in 1561 to act as technical adviser to the press which the pope intended to make the fountain-head of Catholic propaganda. Cardinal Reginald Pole's posthumous *De Concilio* was Paul's first publication in Rome (1562). But Paul lacked the business acumen of his father, and the beginnings of the Stamperia Vaticana were by no means promising. It was left to the organizing genius of Sixtus V to put the papal press on sure and enduring foundations. The bull *Immensa aeterni Dei* of 22 January 1587 created the congregations of cardinals which have since carried out the government of the Church of Rome; and one of these departments was expressly charged with the control of the Vatican Press. Aldus Manutius the younger, Paul's son, was put in its charge. The revised *Vulgate* was the first-fruit of the press. Sixtus himself had read the proofs; but he had also rashly tampered with the text, on which a commission of scholars had spent many years. The edition which Sixtus pronounced the only valid and authentic one was therefore scrapped soon after he died. His emendations were perhaps not quite as bad as his enemies asserted, but the experts whom the amateur had offended happened also to be members of the Society of Jesus, which Sixtus, a Franciscan monk, had cordially disliked. Academic vanity and sectional antagonism therefore avenged themselves simultaneously. In 1592 a fresh commission brought out the Clementine Vulgate, which remained the official Roman Catholic Bible until the *Nova Vulgata Bibliorum Sacrorum* was published in 1979.

The Congregation for the Propagation of the Faith, founded in 1622, set up its own printing press in 1626. This 'Tipografia della Congregazione de Propaganda Fide' printed exclusively books for the mission field and therefore needed types in virtually every language. Its first director, Stefano Paolino, was a type-cutter by profession. He threw himself heart and soul into the new venture, and his first specimen book of 1628 already contained the founts of some 20 Asian and African languages, the very names of which were probably unknown to Paolino's fellow-printers elsewhere. By the end of the eighteenth century this number had increased to forty-four. This office gave Giambattista Bodoni his first training as a typographer. The depredations of the French revolutionaries destroyed this unique printing establishment. '*Pour enrichir la France*', punches, matrices, types and other equipment were sequestrated in 1799 and 1812, and handed over to the French Imprimerie Nationale.

The Imprimerie Nationale is in fact the oldest surviving secular government press. It evolved from the king's private press which Louis XIII in 1640 transformed into the Imprimerie Royale. This origin has always been reflected in the Imprimerie's primary concern with fine printing. Its publishing side has been confined to the production of *éditions de luxe* and monumental series which did not interfere with the activities of private firms.

The two English university presses go back to the reign of Elizabeth I, in Cambridge (1584) and Oxford (1585), although these precise dates do not really correspond with the complicated history of these institutions. Cambridge was first led into a publishing experiment by Richard Bentley about 1700, but this proved a costly failure, and it was not until 1872 that the Syndics became publishers in the full sense. Both as printers and as publishers, the Cambridge and Oxford university presses became the pattern on which other university presses (including those in the United States)

'Pietro Soave' [Sarpi], *Historia del Concilio Tridentino*. John Bill, 'Regio Stampatore', London, 1619. [491.i.8]

pore,c poenitentiam faceret. *Formam hortandi ad respiscentiam, piam quidem, nec Scripturis sacris contrariam, tradunt Canones, quos Archiepiscopo Theodoro Cantuariensi adscribunt nonnulli. Sic autem Canon 29. De Confessionibus, verba Saxonica & Latina, utraque quidem per antiqua, viris doctis legenda hic apposuimus.*

[Old English / Anglo-Saxon passage in left column]

Hortatur nos Scriptura, dicens, Revela Domino viam tuam, & spera in eum. *Item dicit*, Confitemini Domino quoniam in seculum misericordia ejus. *Item*, Delictum meum cognitum tibi feci, & justitias meas non abscondi. *Item*; Confitebor adversùm me injustitias meas Domine, & tu remisisti impietatem peccati mei. *Et iterum*, Confitemini alter alteri peccata vestra, & deleantur. *Et alibi*, Qui abscondit scelera sua, non dirigetur; qui autem ea confessus fuerit, salvabit animam suam à morte. *Et Dominus in Euangelio ait*, Agite poenitentiam, adpropinquabit enim regnum coelorum. Necesse est ut dummodo suadente diabolo multa contra voluntatem, & praeceptum Domini commisimus, per veram humilitatem, & confessionem emendemus penitentes; sicut Patres sancti constituerunt. Et deinceps, cùm aliqua cogitatio mala in cor, suadente diabolo, venerit, citò Episcopo* vel Priori confiteamur, ut per veram confessionem & poenitentiam, regnum Dei habere mereamur: Nimis enim improbus est qui ante oculos Dei peccat, & homini confiteri erubescit.

*[margin: * Sax. Presbytero spirituali. Vide pag. 236. 140. & consument. in facto. § 14. 16. de presbytero Ecclesiae.]*

CAP. 16.
Ut plurima Scotorum Ecclesiae, instante Adamnano, Catholicum Pascha susceperit: itque idem librum de locis sanctis scripserit.

[margin: Deest Sax.]

QUo tempore plurima pars Scotorum in Hibernia, & nonnulla etiam de Britonibus in Britannia rationabile & Ecclesiasticum paschalis observantie tempus, Domino donante, suscepit. Siquidem Adamnanus, presbyter & Abbas monachorum qui erant in insula Hiiscùm legationis gratiâ missus à sua gente venisset ad Aldfridum regem Anglorum, & aliquandiu in ea provincia moratus, videret ritus Ecclesiae canonicos: sed à pluribus qui erant eruditiores, esset solerter admonitus, nè contra universalem Ecclesiae morem, vel in observancia Paschali, vel in aliis quibusque decretis, cum suis paucissimis & in extremo mundi angulo positis vivere praesumeret, mutatus mente est: ità ut ea quae
vide-

The Venerable Bede, *Historiae Ecclesiasticae Gentis Anglorum*. Roger Daniel, Printer to the University, Cambridge, 1643. [490.k.2]

modelled themselves. However, the pre-eminence which both presses have enjoyed in respect to their typographical achievements, as well as their list of publications, is of recent growth, dating from the appointments of Bruce Rogers, Walter Lewis and Stanley Morison in Cambridge, and of Horace Hart and John Johnson in Oxford. The fame of Dr Fell, Richard Bentley and John Baskerville obscures the fact that their efforts to raise the standard of the university presses did not set up a lasting precedent. While those men were in charge Oxford and Cambridge were in the van of good printing in England; but during the greater part of the sixteenth to nineteenth centuries neither Oxford nor Cambridge was conspicuous for its design.

The university presses are rivals of the 'profit-making' publishers chiefly in school and university textbooks. The greater part of their publications is of a strictly academic nature and has little 'commercial' attraction. The only books for which the two presses have always commanded a wide market are the Authorized (King James) version of the Bible and the *Book of Common Prayer* of the Church of England, for which the university presses (and the Queen's Printers) have the exclusive copyright in England (the legal position regarding the printing of Bibles in Scotland is quite different and fairly incomprehensible to the Sassenachs). This side was so important in Oxford that a special department, the Bible Press, was in 1688 separated from the general or Learned Press; Horace Hart reunited them in 1906.

A unique feature in the history of Oxford University Press deserves mention. The first Earl of Clarendon (1609–74) left the manuscript of *The True Historical Narrative of the Rebellion and Civil Wars in England* to the University, of which he had been Chancellor in 1660–7. The proceeds of the first two editions were embezzled by the Vice-Chancellor, William Delaune; but the University built the Clarendon Building for the use of the Press from later profits and a contribution from the printer, John Baskett. Clarendon's son, the first Earl of Rochester, saw it through the press in 1702–4 and, after the passage of the Copyright Act, obtained a special Act of Parliament by which this one book was excepted from the liberalization of the copyright and vested perpetually in Oxford University Press. This pious but ill-advised step has ever since excluded from the open market a masterpiece of English historical writing – a warning example of the bad effects of monopolism in the realm of the mind.

The existence of private presses can be traced to three causes: interest in artistic typography, production of works which, for one reason or other, are unsuitable for the ordinary trade channels, and riding a hobby-horse for the fun of it. Dr Desmond Flower (who has thus defined private printing) would also bring under this heading books which have been ordered and paid for by some enthusiast, such as the Emperor Maximilian's *Theuerdank*, printed by Schönsperger in 1517, and Archbishop Parker's *De antiquitate ecclesiae*, printed by John Day in 1572, as well as books sold by subscription. But it seems more appropriate to limit the term to those presses which work exclusively under the orders – and often with the active participation – of one principal who is usually the owner of the establishment. If this definition is accepted, von Löhneysen, the director of the Brunswick mines in the Harz mountains, may have been the first private printer. In 1596 he set up a press of his own in Zellerfeld on which he printed a number of stately tomes on mining and horsemanship. The private press of Louis XIII of France has already been mentioned. In the eighteenth century private presses became a fashion with the aristocracy, and Madame de Pompadour's press at Versailles (where twenty copies of Corneille's *Rodogune* were printed from silver type in 1760) is as inconsequential in the history of printing as was Marie-Antoinette's Arcadian model farm in the development of agriculture.

There were only two noteworthy private presses at this time – both in England. Horace Walpole ran one from 1757 to 1789 at his country seat of Strawberry Hill near Twickenham. It started auspiciously with some odes by Thomas Gray and included Walpole's own bio-bibliographies of *Royal and Noble Authors and Engravers*, the valuable *Anecdotes of Painting in England* and, above all, *The Castle of Otranto* (1764), which started the 'gothic' novel of horror and mystery and which he followed with a play, *The Mysterious Mother*, 'a tragedy too horrible for representation on any stage'. The other was the press operated from 1813 by Sir Egerton Brydges at his home, Lee Priory, where he produced charming volumes of poetry, his own and that of minor Elizabethan poets.

On the other hand, the books which William Blake (1757–1827) produced with his own hand are as unique in their technical execution as in their literary content.

THE

Hiſtory of the Rebellion, &c.

BOOK I.

Deut. IV. 7, 8, 9.

*For what Nation is there ſo great, who hath God ſo nigh unto
them, as the Lord our God is in all things that we call upon
him for?*

*And what Nation is there ſo great that hath Statutes, and
Judgments ſo righteous as all this Law, which I ſet before
you this day?*

*Only take heed to thy ſelf, and keep thy ſoul diligently, leaſt thou
forget the things which thine eyes have ſeen.*

THAT Poſterity may not be Deceived by the *The Preface of*
proſperous Wickedneſs of thoſe times of which *the Author.*
I write, into an Opinion, that nothing leſs than
a general Combination, and univerſal Apoſtacy
in the whole Nation from their Religion, and
Allegiance, could, in ſo ſhort a time, have produced ſuch a total and prodigious Alteration,
and Confuſion over the whole Kingdom; And
that the Memory of thoſe, who, out of Duty
and Conſcience, have oppoſed that Torrent,
which did overwhelm them, may not looſe the recompence due to their
Virtue, but having undergone the injuries and reproaches of this, may
find a vindication in a better age: It will not be unuſeful for the information of the Judgement and Conſcience of men, to preſent to the world
a full and clear Narration of the Grounds, Circumſtances, and Artifices
of this Rebellion; not only from the time ſince the flame hath been viſible in a Civil war, but, looking farther back, from thoſe former paſ-
ſages and accidents, by which the Seed-plots were made and framed,
from whence thoſe miſcheifs have ſucceſſively grown to the height,
they have ſince arrived at.

AND in this enſuing Hiſtory, though the hand and judgement of God
will be very viſible, in infatuating a People (as ripe and prepared for
Deſtruction) into all the perverſe actions of Folly and Madneſs, making

A 2   the

Lord Clarendon, *History of the Great Rebellion*. Oxford University Press, 1702–4. [629.p.1]

He drew and engraved each page as a whole, text as well as illustrations, very much in the manner of early-fifteenth-century block-books, and he also reverted to colouring by hand. He thus tried to combine the individualism of the medieval scribe with the technical advantages of mechanical reproduction. His typographic achievement is of the highest order, but it is the unique achievement of a solitary genius and is as inimitable as his poetry. And if he had never illustrated a book of his own, says Hodnett, 'he would still be one of the leading illustrators of England. His illustrations of Edward Young's *Night thoughts* (1797), Thomas Gray's *Poems* (1797–8), John Milton's *Paradise lost* (1807–8) and *Paradise regained* (1825) [and others] compose a body of work unsurpassed in range, sensitivity to text, technical variety and artistic distinction.'

5. THE READING PUBLIC

The emergence of the 'good and generous master' of the authors, as Oliver Goldsmith about 1760 called 'the public collectively considered', is a combined result of the Enlightenment and the Industrial Revolution. Rationalism infected the rising middle class, at least in the second generation, with a desire for intellectual improvement. The secular and empiric background of both rationalism and industrialism determined the literary trend of the age. '*Goût*', '*gusto*', '*Geschmack*', 'taste' became the catchwords and criteria by which Europe now judged personal manners as well as literary productions. The elegant discourse replaced the ponderous argument; the novel became the chief vehicle of literary entertainment.

Down to the end of the seventeenth century, both literacy and leisure were virtually confined to scholars and 'gentlemen'; during the eighteenth century, the commercial middle class and especially women acquired a taste for reading; and the introduction in the nineteenth century of compulsory school attendance ever widened the circle of potential readers to whom the Welfare State of the twentieth century has eventually given the social conditions in which to enjoy reading.

The seventeenth century made some decisive moves towards a broadening of general education. The name of the Czech educationist, Amos Comenius (1592–1671), here stands first. He outlined the principles of primary education which have been followed by teachers ever since; and his *Orbis pictus* (1654) was the first picture-book especially designed for children. The petty dukedom of Weimar was the first country to demand compulsory school attendance, at least on principle, in 1619. It was not until a hundred years later that Prussia introduced this principle as the first great power (1717). England did not follow suit until 1870, but this deficiency was compensated for by the endeavour of private individuals and voluntary societies. From the charity schools instituted by the Society for the Promotion of Christian Knowledge (1699), the Sunday schools inaugurated by the printer Robert Raikes at Gloucester (1780), the academies set up by Quakers, Methodists and other dissenting bodies, there came forth an ever-increasing number of potential readers.

In 1791 the London publisher James Lackington made an entry in his diary which neatly expounds the bookseller's point of view: 'The sale of books in general has increased prodigiously within the last twenty years. The poorer sort of farmers, and even the poor country people in general who before that period spent their winter evenings in relating stories of witches, ghosts, hobgoblins etc., now shorten the winter

Lucan, *Pharsalia, cum notis Hugo Grotius et Richard Bentley*. Strawberry-Hill, Middlesex, 1760. [684.i.9]

Francis Davison, *Poetical Rhapsody*. Lee Priory Press, Kent, 1814. [239.l.4]

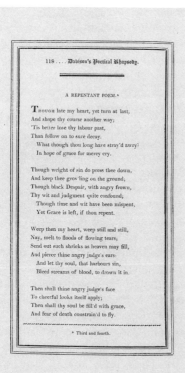

nights by hearing their sons and daughters read tales, romances etc., and on entering their houses you may see *Tom Jones*, *Roderick Random* and other entertaining books, stuck up in their bacon-racks etc. If John goes to town with a load of hay, he is charged to be sure not to forget to bring home *Peregrine Pickle's Adventures*, and when Dolly is sent to market to sell her eggs, she is commissioned to purchase *The History of Joseph Andrews*. In short, all ranks and degrees now read.'

As will be shown in subsequent chapters, the lending library took a prominent place in satisfying this growing demand for reading matter; and a glance at the bestsellers of the time indicates that the novel gave greatest satisfaction to the greatest number of readers.

The new literacy did not draw its nourishment only from novels. From the middle of the seventeenth century onward, a calendar, with some miscellaneous information and a few pious thoughts, began to make its way annually into the houses of people whose literary needs were easily satisfied. The oldest calendar of this type was the 'Miners' Calendar' printed in Goslar from 1650 until after the Second World War. The educationists of the Enlightenment transformed these almanacs into vehicles of popular instruction for the lower classes. Practical advice for home and garden and field spread the advances of human and veterinary medicine and of scientific agriculture and husbandry; philosophical ideas were embodied in homely essays, stories with a moral purpose, and didactic poetry. Some of the miscellanies achieved a huge success. Zachariah Becker's *Noth- und Hilfsbüchlein für Bauersleute* (1788) sold 150,000 copies by 1798 and a million by 1811.

Lackington's proverbial John and Dolly would certainly be charged to buy next year's calendar when they went to the Christmas fair. But during the rest of the year they were as likely as not to be told to bring home from the market town also the latest number of *The Star*, *The Oracle*, *The World* or *The Times*. For by the end of the eighteenth century the periodical press had come to be regarded as a regular accompaniment of everyday life.

6. THE PERIODICAL PRESS

The desire for quick information and for regular entertainment brought into existence the periodical press. The former was catered for by the newspaper, the latter by the magazine or 'periodical' in the narrower sense. Both owed their origins to the business instinct of the printers. They realized that 'the swift currents of the age', of which statesmen and scholars were complaining from the beginning of the sixteenth century, required new channels of expression. They also realized that there was in being a public which was not at all frightened by the rapids but eager to shoot them. And the printers were determined to direct these swift-running waters so as to turn their own mill-wheels.

Hand-written 'news-letters', containing miscellaneous political and economic information, circulated freely between the headquarters and branch offices of the big trading companies of the first half of the sixteenth century. The news-letters of the Augsburg firm of Fugger were even made available to favoured outsiders whom it was thought desirable to make see events and trends as the Fuggers saw them. From the middle of the century onward, speculative printers took the decisive step of transforming these private news-letters into public news-books, which soon developed into news-sheets and eventually newspapers.

The earliest English news-book – or more properly news-pamphlet – is *The Trewe Encountre* of the battle of Flodden Field, printed by Richard Faques in London soon after the event (9 September 1513). The Anglo-Scottish wars of the 1540s produced more pamphlets of this kind, including one of the earliest eye-witness accounts which Richard Grafton published on 30 June 1548. However, all these were *ad hoc* publications concerned only with one topical event of general interest, and without intent of being followed up. Such news-pamphlets became more frequent towards the end of the century when a French correspondent remarked in one of them that 'you in England expect newes with everie happie winde'. Between 1590 and 1610 some 450 English news-books are known to have been issued; over 250 of them still survive in at least one copy.

Very soon, however, the two main characteristics of the newspaper, as we understand the term, established themselves, namely, miscellaneous contents and periodicity of appearance. As early as 1566 there appeared news-sheets in Strasbourg and Basel which were numbered and thus declared themselves as parts of a series.

The editor, publisher and agent (but not printer) of a series of unnumbered news-sheets, which appeared between 1594 and 1615 in Augsburg, deserves mention for an interesting experiment in the field of periodic publications. Samuel Dilbaum, born in Augsburg in 1530, started in January 1597 a monthly under the title of 'Historical Relation or Narrative of the most important and noteworthy actions and events which took place here and there almost in the whole of Europe in the month of —, 1597'. The text was arranged under headings such as Netherlands News, French History, Events in England, Spanish Affairs; and each number comprised from six to twelve leaves. Periodicity was intended, as is shown by 'trailers' advertising the contents of the next issue; it was maintained throughout the year at the end of which a special title-page for all twelve numbers was supplied. However, this remarkable attempt to produce a kind of 'Annual Register' in monthly instalments lapsed after its first year, and only one complete set has survived. The unfortunate choice of the little Swiss town of Rorschach on Lake Constance as the place of printing may have contributed to the failure, and the printer, Leonard Straub (1550–1606), seems to have been more enterprising than prudent – he had learned the trade in the houses of Froschauer in Zürich and Froben in Basel, and became the first printer in St Gall, but never got out of the financial troubles which he brought on himself by the installation of a large paper-mill in 1582.

Newspapers proper made their first appearance with the *Avisa-Relation oder Zeitung*, printed in Wolfenbüttel, and the *Relation* of the Strasbourg printer Johann Carolus, both of which started publication in January 1609. The Wolfenbüttel *Avisa* was founded, directed and (at least partly) written by Duke Heinrich Julius in furtherance of his policy of reconciling the Protestant and Catholic factions; edited in Prague, where the duke spent his last years (d. 1613) as the emperor's councillor, it contains much first-hand political intelligence. The third-oldest newspaper now known is the *Gedenckwürdige Zeitung* which came out from May 1610 in or near Cologne.

A decade later, 'corantos' (as they were usually called) began to spread. Dutch printers were the first in the field; and *Krant* is still the common Dutch term for newspaper. They turned to good account the well-organized network of foreign correspondents who supplied the Dutch East India Company and the States General of the United Provinces with commercial and political intelligence. From 1618 the *Courante uyt Italien, Duytslandt, etc.* and a year later its rival, the *Tijdinghen uyt verscheyde*

Quartieren, came out once or twice weekly. In 1620 Amsterdam printers also brought out corantos in French and English. It was only in 1631 that the first French news-book, *Nouvelles ordinaires de diuers endroits*, was printed in Paris by the booksellers Louys Vendosme and Jean Martin. Their sheet was however speedily killed by Théophraste Renaudot's *Gazette* which was supported by Cardinal Richelieu.

English printers did not wait for official encouragement. Some months after the Dutch map-engraver and printer Pieter de Keere had started the first English-language news-book (of which sixteen issues have survived), the London stationer Thomas Archer printed English corantos in London. The first number seems to have come out in the summer of 1621, but since Archer's corantos are known to us only from references in contemporary letters it is Nathaniel Butter who must be regarded as the *de facto* father of English journalism. His father and his widowed mother had occasionally brought out some 'reports' on topical events, and nearly half of the 200 items Butter published from 1602 under his own imprint – they include the first edition of *King Lear* (1608) and Chapman's *Homer* (1616) – are news-tracts relating to happenings in India, Russia, Persia, Sweden, at sea and at home. His first 'Corante, or, newes from Italy, Germany, Hungarie, Spaine and France' came out on 24 September 1621. He continued for 20 years to publish Corantos, Avisos, Passages, Newes, Relations, etc., 'at the sign of the Pied Bull at St Austin's Gate'. They included the first English series of news-books to be numbered and dated: 50 issues running from 15 October 1622 to 2 October 1623, printed mostly by Bartholomew Downes for a syndicate of which, beside Butter, Nicholas Bourne and Thomas Archer were the most permanent members, as is the case with the greater part of Butter's periodical publications.

English news-writers and news-printers (in the words of the Swedish scholar Folke Dahl) 'were miles ahead of almost all of their continental colleagues'. There are especially two features which have remained a distinguishing mark of English news-sheets. There are the easy and friendly terms prevailing between editors and readers, which started in the 1620s by editors taking the readers into their confidence and led to the readers putting their confidence into 'letters to the editor'; and there is the skilful layout of the news-sheets, which 'gave evidence of a truly journalistic inventive genius' in compelling the prospective reader's attention. For instance, number 44 of 21 August 1623 of Butter's series displays the following items of 'Our last weekly Newes':

What hath last hapned in the Empire betweene the Emperor and the Princes. The state of Tillies and Brunswicks Armies since the last encounter. The King of Denmarks Preparations. Count Mansfields fastnesse. Together with other businesse of the Low Countries and the Grisons. The Election of the new Pope. The Turkish Pyracies. And certaine prodigies seene in the Empire.

This sweeping survey of the various European theatres of war, the recognition of the news value of a papal election and of marvels transcending the course of nature, as well as the reference to the danger to trade and shipping in the Mediterranean – the selection of these headlines would not be unworthy of our leading national newspaper.

The undisguised enthusiasm of Butter and his colleagues for the success of the anti-Habsburg powers was their undoing. The Spanish and Austrian agents in London, 'vext at the soule', launched official complaints and Charles I, himself mortified by the indirect criticism of his policy of appeasement at any price, had all news-books suppressed by Star Chamber decree (17 October 1632). The ban was lifted only on 20 December 1638, and on the same day Butter and Bourne brought out a 96-page issue.

Beginning with the battle-scene which adorned Faques's *Trewe Encountre* (1513), illustrations are frequently to be found in news-books and news-sheets. A Belgian printer, Abraham Verhoeven of Antwerp, was the first to introduce them regularly in his *Nieuwe Tijdinghen*, which had the page of contents adorned with simple wood-cuts meant to whet the onlooker's appetite by display as well as innuendo. The first illustrations inserted in English newspapers were of a decidedly political design: the Commons assembled in Parliament, portraits of the King and Queen and Prince Rupert were among the inducements that might tempt Englishmen in 1643 to buy a copy of *A Perfect Diurnall of the Passages in Parliament*, of which the picture was a kind of nascent 'masthead'. The *Mercurius Civicus* went further: it changed its blocks frequently and brought them into real relationship with its news items. However, for another 150 years illustrations in newspapers were few and far between. It was only from the beginning of the nineteenth century that illustrations became a regular feature of the periodical press.

After the middle of the seventeenth century the news-book was superseded by the news-sheet. The *Leipziger Zeitung*, which began publication in 1660 and continued until 1921, and the *London Gazette* (founded 1665), were among the first thus to take into account the taste of a new class of readers. The change of format and make-up was not a matter of typographical convenience; on the contrary, the production of sheets of an uncommon size must have posed some awkward technical problems. It was rather an outward sign of change which the reading public was undergoing at this period. The scholar ceased to be the main representative of the literate and literary public: the man of the world, the *homme de bon ton*, became the client to whose taste the discerning publisher adapted himself. The politician, businessman or man about town who frequented the fashionable coffee-houses in London, Paris, Leipzig and Hamburg had neither the leisure nor the inclination to obtain the latest intelligence from books; he preferred the sheet which, being really only a sheet, showed him more or less at a glance what news the *Pegasus* or the *Post Boy* had to relate.

The same need for easier access to information which had changed the compact news-book to the volatile news-sheet was instrumental in creating the periodical magazine. Philosophy and learning were the main subjects that filled the pages of the first periodicals. They sprang up almost simultaneously throughout Europe. In Germany the Hamburg theologian and poet Johann Rist started his *Monatsgespräche* in 1663; in France Denis de Sallo, a member of the Paris Parlement, launched the *Journal des sçavans* in 1665; in England the *Philosophical Transactions* came out in the same year under the auspices of the Royal Society; and in Italy Francesco Nazzari issued the Roman *Giornale de' letterati* in 1668.

Soon, however, the *Mercure galant* (1672; renamed *Mercure de France* in 1714) led the way into wider fields, including among its features court and society news, literary criticism, and original poetry. The *Athenian Mercury* (1691) and the *Gentleman's Journal* (1692) were its first English counterparts. Christian Thomasius, the leading German rationalist, in 1688 edited in Leipzig a periodical, the long-winded title of which indicates its outlook and purpose as well as those of many of its successors: 'Entertaining and serious, rational and unsophisticated ideas on all kinds of agreeable and useful books and subjects.' Thomasius expressly welcomed women among its readers, and it did not take long to bring into existence periodicals which addressed themselves exclusively to them, such as the *Ladies' Mercury* (1693), the *Female Tatler*, a companion piece of Steele and Addison's journal, and Gottsched's *Die Vernünftigen Tadlerinnen* ('The Rational Woman-Critics', 1725).

By the early years of the eighteenth century the periodical press, newspapers as well as magazines, had become an established institution, and from decade to decade gained new strength. The provinces, too, were beginning to have their own local papers, mostly bi-weekly at first. The *Norwich Post* (1701–12), the *Bristol Post-Boy* (1702–12), *Sam Farley's Exeter Post-Man* (1704–25) and the *Worcester Post-Man* (1709; still continuing as the *Worcester Journal*) were the earliest.

After the setting up of a daily postal service between Dover and London in 1691, which secured the regular transmission of foreign news to the capital, the daily newspaper became practicable and eventually ousted the twice-weekly or thrice-weekly organs. The *Daily Courant* (1702), the *Daily Post* (1719), the *Daily Journal* (1720), and the *Daily Advertiser* (1730) were the first London papers to emphasize in their very titles their regularity and frequency.

Because of the rigidity of French censorship it was only in 1777 that France received its first daily newspaper, the *Journal de Paris*. When the Revolution proclaimed the freedom of the press, the number of Paris papers immediately soared to 350; it shrunk, however, to thirteen in the bleak climate of the Consulate and to four in the even more rigorous conditions of the Empire.

The English morning paper quickly acquired as its companion the evening paper. The first in the field were Dawks's *Newsletter* (1696), the *Evening Post* (1706), the *Evening Courant* and the *Night Post* (both 1711). All of them were thrice-weekly papers, but it was they and not the daily papers which first carried punctuality as far as the hour of publication. In order to catch the mail to the provinces which left London on Tuesday, Thursday and Saturday nights, the *Evening Post*, for example, was made available to the couriers 'every post night at six a clock'.

No such minute accuracy was, or is, required from the printer of a periodical; but in this field, too, the eighteenth century brought about a progressive standardization. While the newspaper world came to accept daily appearance as the norm, a weekly issue established itself as the most acceptable interval for the publication of the lighter kind of periodicals, with monthly and quarterly reviews providing the heavier pabulum.

Richard Steele (1672–1729) and Joseph Addison (1672–1719) determined more than any other editor the style of the general periodical which, soon imitated in every civilized country, was to become the guide and friend, entertainer and instructor of millions of readers throughout the eighteenth century. The *Tatler* (1709–11) and the *Spectator* (1711–14) are the most famous papers which they edited and to which they contributed 'observations on life and manner'. They provided their readers with moral instruction, comments on literary and artistic subjects, straight news and pleasant entertainment: the *obiter dicta* of Sir Roger de Coverley, Addison's most enduring creation, gave a good idea of the wide range and polished treatment of these topics. The *Spectator* probably had an average of 3000 subscribers; the first edition of its collected essays in book form (1712) ran to 9000 and was reissued ten times within 20 years. The influence these two papers exerted on Europe and America was prodigious. The number of journals which cultivated 'wit' and 'taste' on the model of the *Tatler* and the *Spectator* approached 800 during the eighteenth century. The

Gentleman's Magazine (1731–1907) lived longest, and reached an annual circulation of 10,000 in 1739 and of 15,000 in 1745; and the liberal show of illustrations in woodcut and copper-engraving contributed to its quick success. It was due to the wide appeal of the *Gentleman's Magazine* that the term 'magazine' soon became a generic term for this kind of journal. The *London Magazine* (1732–84) and the *Scots Magazine* (1739–1817, continued as the *Edinburgh Magazine* until 1826) were among its earliest adopters.

A novel feature of these journals was the reviewing of new books. Some periodicals even made literary criticism their main concern. Robert Dodsley's short-lived fortnightly *Museum* (1746–7), the *Monthly Review*, started in 1749 by Ralph Griffiths and continued by his son George Edward until 1825, and the *Critical Review* (1756–1817), of which Smollett was the first editor, exercized a considerable influence in acquainting the gentry and middle class with current literature, foreign as well as English. Although these book reviews were usually of considerable length, actual criticism was hardly voiced, and the general tone was rather that of a modern blurb or publisher's prospectus. The 'Scotch Reviewers' of the *Edinburgh Review* (1802), who made a sport of censuring 'English Bards', changed all that. They introduced partisanship and personalities and bestowed on the reviewer a nimbus of superiority which has persisted, and all too often tempts the contemporary reviewer to use a book which he is incompetent to judge as a mere pretext for exhibiting his cleverness.

7. LIBRARIES

When Antonio Panizzi once called the British Museum 'an institution for the diffusion of culture', he incidentally paid the highest tribute to the library as a factor of the promotion of civilization. There were large and well-organized libraries of manuscripts long before the invention of printing. Julius Caesar was the first statesman to include the endowment of a public library among the amenities which a well-run administration should provide for its citizens. This plan was taken up after his death by C. Asinius Pollio, a patron of Virgil and Horace, who built in 39 B.C. the first public library in Rome. Eventually imperial Rome had 28 public libraries; but with its destruction the idea of libraries open to the general public was buried for a thousand years.

The libraries of the Middle Ages were monastic, episcopal or academic. The library as a storehouse of intellectual treasures of the whole civilized world, as a spiritual pleasure-ground for the humblest workman and as the last refuge of the citizens of the Republic of Letters has been made possible only by the printer's craft. In the Renaissance, princes and nobles, merchants and scholars began to build up collections of books. Federigo, Duke of Urbino, it is true, strictly excluded any printed book from his precious library; but his attitude was exceptional and based only on egoism. Hardly any printed books detracted from the splendour of the library which King Matthias Corvinus assembled in Budapest – perhaps the most precious collection of Renaissance manuscripts and bindings, scattered to the four winds after the king's death in 1490. Others thought otherwise: the library of the Nürnberg humanist Hartmann Schedel consisted of about 200 printed and 400 written books; his younger contemporary, Willibald Pirckheimer, owned only 170 manuscripts among some 2100 books (which the second earl of Arundel acquired in 1636).

Several of these private libraries became the nuclei of national libraries. The

Bibliothèque Nationale has evolved from the library of Charles V; the Mediceo-Laurenziana combined those of Cosimo and Lorenzo de' Medici; the Prussian State Library grew out of the library of Frederick William, the Great Elector; the British Museum had as its chief component the library of Sir Robert Cotton. The University of Oxford owes its library to the diplomatist and scholar Sir Thomas Bodley. It was opened in 1602, and Bodley secured for it a special bounty: he persuaded the Stationers' Company to assign to his foundation a free copy of every book printed in the realm of England. This conception of a 'copyright library' was legally embodied in the Licensing Act of 1663 which stipulated the presentation of three free copies of every publication; the number was gradually increased to eleven but eventually limited to six (British Library, National Libraries of Scotland and Wales, the Bodleian, Cambridge University Library and Trinity College, Dublin). Other nations have taken over this principle. It greatly benefits every class and individual professionally interested in books – publishers and booksellers as well as librarians and scholars – as the copyright libraries are the centres where bibliographical inquiries can be answered accurately and bibliographical studies pursued comprehensively.

The first big libraries which were made accessible to the public were the Ambrosiana in Milan, opened by Cardinal Federigo Borromeo in 1609, and the library brought together for Cardinal Mazarin by Gabriel Naudé in 1645. Naudé also wrote the first modern treatise on collecting, storing and cataloguing books, *Advis pour dresser une bibliothèque* (1627); John Evelyn made it available to English bookmen in 1661. Its most remarkable medieval predecessor was the *Philobiblon* of Richard de Bury, bishop of Durham (d. 1345); it was printed as early as 1473 (in Cologne), has been reprinted regularly and is still worth reading as a charming tribute to the *amor ecstaticus* Richard felt for books.

Most of the great national libraries were founded in the seventeenth and eighteenth centuries; they were in fact a symbol, in the intellectual sphere, of the centralizing tendencies of the absolutist monarchy. The Prussian State Library in Berlin (1659), the Kongelige Bibliotek in Copenhagen (1661), the National Library of Scotland (1682), the Biblioteca Nacional in Madrid (1712), the Biblioteca Nazionale Centrale in Florence (1747), the British Museum Library (1753) and the Library of Congress (1800) are some of these foundations that have justified the ambitions of their founders to serve the highest national interests of their countries.

Descriptive bibliography, which has become an intrinsic part of the functions of the national libraries all over the world, has its origin in the catalogues which were issued to serve the interests of the bookseller. The first comprehensive and regular compilations were the half-annual lists of new publications which the Augsburg wholesale bookseller, Georg Willer (1515–94) published from 1564 to 1627. These catalogues comprised the books displayed at the Frankfurt book fairs which, by this time, had become the principal meeting-place of publishers and booksellers, printers and type-founders from all over Europe. In 1565 Willer lists 318 titles published by German and 226 by non-German publishers. From 1598 the town council of Frankfurt produced an official catalogue which eventually superseded the private ventures of the firm of Willer and others. From 1617 to 1628 the London stationer John Bill published an English edition of the Frankfurt catalogue. With the decline of the Frankfurt fairs the catalogues of its rival, Leipzig, became of greater importance. They began in 1594 and have survived in various forms to the present day, whereas the Frankfurt catalogues lapsed with the Frankfurt fair in 1750. In 1948 the Frankfurt book fair was revived, however, and it has established itself as the principal international meeting-place of the whole book trade, though other fairs have succeeded at Bologna and London and in many other cities.

These fair-catalogues are the precursors of the national bibliographies of current literature, which are now usually in the care of the national libraries of their respective countries. Of these indispensable hand-lists, the oldest is the *Bibliographie de la France* (since 1811), while the U.S. *Cumulative Book Index* (since 1898) is the most comprehensive. In Germany, the *Deutsche Nationalbibliographie* took over the original Leipzig book fair catalogues in 1931. The latest-comer in this field is the *British National Bibliography* (since 1950). Although the principles of arrangement and presentations vary, all these national bibliographies have in common a very high degree of accuracy and completeness.

Far into the nineteenth century, even the 'public' libraries were anything but easily accessible to the public. The way in which librarians everywhere looked at customers is superbly indicated in the regulations issued by the librarian of Gotha in 1774. 'In order to check the previous excessive concourse in the best manner possible', it was decreed that 'anybody who wants to inspect a book has to apply to the librarian who then will show and, if need be, even allow him to read it.'

In fact, the big state, municipal and college libraries were ill adapted to serve the needs of the non-academic and non-professional classes which were increasingly forming the vast majority of the book-reading public. This new intelligentsia set about to help themselves and created two new types of libraries, the 'public library' in the modern connotation of the term and the lending library. Both are children of the eighteenth century, and both originated in the English-speaking world.

The Commonwealth of Massachusetts was a pioneer of the public library movement: Boston was the first town in the New World to provide a public library as early as 1653, and in 1798 Massachusetts took a lead in consolidating its public libraries by an act of the State Legislature. The honour of first allocating a specific annual tax to a free public library must perhaps go to the enlightened citizens of the little town of Peterborough in New Hampshire, who took this step in 1833.

The lending library, that remarkable mixture of commercial enterprise and care for mental improvement, was aptly launched by a Scotsman. Allan Ramsay, poet, wig-maker and bookseller (and father of the great portrait-painter of the same name), attached the first lending library to his bookshop in Edinburgh in 1726. A few years later, in 1731, Benjamin Franklin, at the threshold of his amazing career as printer, publisher and diplomatist, opened a 'Subscription Library' at Philadelphia. The Rev. Samuel Fancourt, a dissenting minister, founded the first lending library in London in the 1730s, but neither this nor his second venture in 1746, 'The Gentlemen and Ladies' Growing and Circulating Library', was a lasting success. This fell to the 'British Library', established by George Bathoe in the Strand, when it was taken over by the consummate maker and promoter of books, John Bell.

By the end of the eighteenth century lending libraries had become a common feature of every town of western Europe. In small places where they could not possibly be run with profit, reading clubs and literary societies took over the function to provide their members with the latest productions of the book market. They may as well be classified among the precursors of local and municipal libraries. Their sudden growth astonished contemporary observers. One critic remarked in 1795 that 'people are used to reading nowadays in places where twenty years since a book was hardly avail-

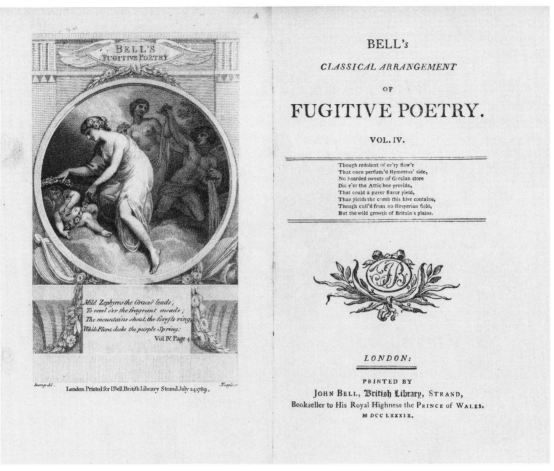

BELL's

CLASSICAL ARRANGEMENT

OF

FUGITIVE POETRY.

VOL. IV.

Though redolent of ev'ry flow'r
That once perfum'd Hymettus' side,
No hoarded sweets of Grecian store
Did e'er the Attic bee provide,
That could a purer flavor yield,
Than yields the comb this hive contains,
Though cull'd from no Hesperian field,
But the wild growth of Britain's plains.

LONDON:

PRINTED BY
JOHN BELL, British Library, STRAND,
Bookseller to His Royal Highness the PRINCE of WALES.
M DCC LXXXIX.

Bell's Classical Arrangement of Fugitive Poetry. John Bell, London, 1789. [1607/4823]

able'. A few years later we hear that 'a passion for reading becomes commoner from day to day and spreads among all classes'. In 1804 the three biggest lending libraries of Dresden had a combined stock of 60,000 volumes, that is to say, one volume per head of the population.

The effect of the lending libraries on the book market was aptly summed up by the London bookseller James Lackington (1746–1815): 'When circulating libraries were first opened,' he says in his memoirs, 'the booksellers were much alarmed, and their rapid increase, added to their fears, had led them to think that the sale of books would be much diminished by such libraries. But experience has proved that the sale of books, so far from being diminished by them, has been greatly promoted, as from those repositories many thousand families have been cheaply supplied with books, by which the taste of reading has become much more general, and thousands of books are purchased every year by such as have first borrowed them at those libraries, and after reading, approving of them, become purchasers.'

HUDIBRAS.

The ARGUMENT of
The FIRST CANTO.

Sir Hudibras *his paſſing Wirth,*
The Manner how he ſally'd forth;
His Arms and Equipage are ſhown;
His Horſe's Virtues, and his own.
Th' Adventure of the Bear and Fiddle
Is ſung, but breaks off in the Middle.

CANTO I.

---

1   WHEN *civil Dudgeon* firſt grew high,
     And Men fell out they knew not why;
     When hard Words, *Jealouſies* and *Fears,*
Set Folks together by the Ears,

1 *When* civil Dudgeon, *&c.*] *Dudgeon.* Who made the Alterations in the laſt Edition of this Poem, I know not, but they
are certainly ſometimes for the worſe; and I cannot believe the
Author would have changed a Word ſo proper in that Place, as
Dudgeon is, for that of *Fury,* as it is in the laſt Editions: *To take*
in Dudgeon, is inwardly to reſent ſome Injury or Affront, a ſort
of Grumbling in the Gizzard, and what is previous to actual Fury.
                                              And

Samuel Butler, *Hudibras*, illustrated by William Hogarth. D. Browne, London, 1726. [1078.f.8]

8. CENSORSHIP

A century after Gutenberg's invention, censorship of the printed word had become
the universal practice of the lay and church authorities throughout Europe. By the
end of the eighteenth century it had been abolished in England, France, Sweden,
Denmark and the United States, and was being challenged everywhere else.

Mainz, the cradle of the art of printing, is also the birthplace of the censorship of
printed books. Archbishop Berthold von Henneberg asked the town council of Frankfurt to examine carefully the printed books to be exhibited at the Lenten Fair in 1485
and to collaborate with the ecclesiastical authorities in suppressing dangerous publications. In response to this, the electorate of Mainz and the imperial city of Frankfurt in 1486 jointly set up the first secular censorship office.

The ecclesiastical authorities, in the later Middle Ages particularly the universities, had always exercized a censorship of the written word. As late as 1479 the University of Cologne, a stronghold of the schoolmen, obtained a papal privilege which expressly extended their censorship to printed books. However, church censorship had been, and was for a long time to be, interested almost exclusively in combating and suppressing heretical writings, and showed a broad tolerance towards sexual immorality and obscenity. Thus the first edict concerning printed books, issued by the Frankfurt censor, was aimed at the suppression of Bible translations into the vernacular; and the first steps taken by the Roman Curia were chiefly directed against heretical and schismatical publications.

Pope Innocent VIII, in 1488, and Pope Alexander VI, in 1501, tried to make censorship uniform throughout Christendom, imposed censorship as a duty on all in authority, introduced preventive censorship, and subjected non-theological books to ecclesiastical supervision. It is to the credit of the Cologne printers that they at once protested against the papal attempts to extend clerical authority beyond the control of heretical works. Their courageous action, however, was of no avail. The Roman church, shaken to its foundations by the Protestant Reformation, and alarmed at the increasing power which the secular state arrogated to itself, pursued the policy laid down in two bulls issued by Pope Leo X in 1515 and 1520. Cardinal Caraffa, the restorer of the Inquisition, decreed in 1543 that henceforth no book, old or new, regardless of its contents should be printed or sold without the permission of the Inquisition. The first list of banned books, printed in Venice, comprised 70 titles.

In 1559 Caraffa, now Pope Paul IV, promulgated the first general *Index librorum prohibitorum*, which banned among other books the writings of several cardinals, the poems of della Casa, and an anonymous book *On the Benefit of Christ*. Of this work one copy only has miraculously survived: it defends the Lutheran doctrine of justification by faith, and was sponsored by cardinals Pole and Contarini. The *Index* remained until 1966 the authoritative guide by which practising Roman Catholics had to regulate their reading. (Perhaps by then the authorities had taken seriously the Jesuit joke, '*Notabitur Romae, legetur ergo*' – once they have taken note of a book people read it.)

Individual books were suppressed for political reasons by various German princes and German and Italian city fathers. Henry VIII of England was the first monarch to issue a list of banned books (1529); in 1538 he forbade the importation of books printed abroad in the English language. Taken in conjunction with the tenor of his privilege granted in 1543 to Grafton and Whitchurch, these royal ordinances display that mixture of religious, political and economic motives which characterizes the theory and practice of all European statesmen of the sixteenth century.

The history of the Frankfurt book fairs exemplifies the deadening effect of state interference on the intellectual as well as the commercial plane. From the end of the fifteenth century Frankfurt was the centre of the German book-trade and even attracted a large number of foreign publishers and booksellers; agents of Aldus Manutius are known to have traded there. In 1579 the Frankfurt book market was placed under the supervision of the imperial censorship commission, since Frankfurt was a Free Imperial City; and the narrow-mindedness and chicanery of the commissioners, ruled by the Jesuits, first stifled and eventually ruined its flourishing book trade. By the middle of the eighteenth century the Frankfurt book market was dead. The last fair-catalogue which appeared in 1750 contained but 42 German, 23 Latin, and 7 French books – and that at a time when the yearly output of books in Germany alone amounted to about 1350 items.

At the same time the Dutch Republic demonstrated the favourable results flowing from the application of a nominal censorship in a liberal spirit. The merchant aristocracy of the Dutch towns, broad-minded and far-sighted, offered a haven of refuge to the persecuted Jews of Spain and Portugal, the Huguenots of France, the Calvinists of Germany and the Socinians of Poland. The conflux of skilled craftsmen and versatile businessmen secured the economic predominance of the Netherlands, while the liberality of her universities and the freedom accorded to the printing press made her the centre of learning and journalism in seventeenth-century Europe. Dutch publishers, above all the printing dynasty of the Elzevirs, issued books in Latin, French, English, German and Dutch, and thus reflected the fact that Holland was in truth the focus of European literacy.

Evading the censor developed into a fine art. The commonest subterfuge was the faked imprint. This might be wholly fictitious, consist in the 'accommodation address' of a foreign publisher, or dispense altogether with naming the printer or place of publication. Dutch printers of Protestant tracts in the 1520s sometimes concealed the place of publication under the name of 'Utopia', thus incidentally showing the popularity of Thomas More's book which had been printed in Louvain in 1516. Others put on the title-page either towns such as Wittenberg, Marburg or Strasbourg from which these Lutheran writings might well have emanated, or conversely the most unlikely 'Rome, at St Peter's court'. They sometimes combined the name of a real printer with a wrong place, e.g. Hans Lufft (of Wittenberg) in Marburg (in fact, Johann Hoochstraten of Antwerp, the printer of Tyndale's Pentateuch, 1530). Whereas a number of Dutch printers went to the stake for publishing Protestant books, none who used feigned imprints was found out.

The Elzevirs seem to have resorted to this deception in order to mislead foreign censors rather than from fear of trouble at home. For, in view of the known tolerance of Dutch censorship, controversial books printed in the Netherlands were, by that very fact, suspect abroad. Thus, Pietro Aretino's *Capriciosi e piacevoli ragionamenti* (1660), published at 'Cosmopoli' without a printer's name, and Pascal's *Provinciales*, with the imprint 'Cologne chez Pierre de Vallée' (1657), were certainly, and Hobbes's *Leviathan*, 'London for Andrew Crooke' (1651), may have been, issued by the Elzevirs in Amsterdam.

Nearly all the great works by which French eighteenth-century creative literature is remembered had to be printed either outside France or under a feigned imprint. Montesquieu's *Lettres persanes* (1721) were published in Holland with the imprint 'Cologne chez Pierre Marteau'. This 'accommodation address', perhaps invented by the Elzevirs who used it first in 1660, covered a variety of books and publishers anxious to avoid censorship and appeared on the title-pages of religious as well as pornographic writings. The same name, in its German form 'bei Peter Hammer in Köln', was at the beginning of the nineteenth century adopted by F. A. Brockhaus for such military and political publications as were likely to drawn down the wrath of the powerful Prussian censorship on the publisher.

Montesquieu's *Considérations sur la cause de la grandeur des Romains et de leur décadence* (1724) appeared in Amsterdam, his *Esprit des lois* (1748) in Geneva. Rousseau's revolutionary books were published in Holland: *La Nouvelle Héloïse* (1761) and *Du Contrat social* (1762) in Amsterdam, *Émile* (1762) at The Hague.

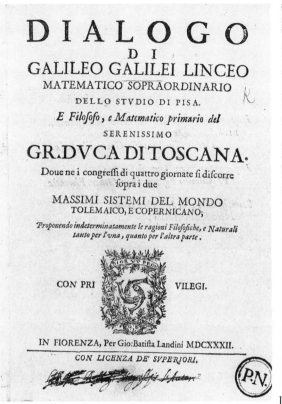

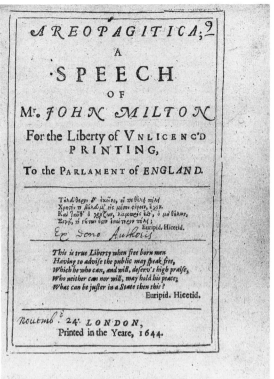

John Milton, *Areopagitica*. London, 1644. [C.55.c.22(9)]

Galileo Galilei, *Dialogo ... del Mondo Tolemaico e Copernicano*. G. B. Landini, Florence, 1632. [C.28.i.4]

Voltaire's *Henriade* was first printed surreptitiously under the title of *La Ligue* at Rouen in 1723, with the fictitious imprint of 'Genève chez Jean Mokpap'. The second edition, now called *La Henriade*, came out in London (1728) with a dedication in English to Queen Caroline, *Le Siècle de Louis XIV* in Berlin (1751).

The first effective blow dealt to restrictive practices in the world of books came from England. An ordinance imposed on printers and booksellers by Parliament in 1643 roused John Milton to write his *Areopagitica*, clad in the form of an address to Parliament and published in 1644. It is the most eloquent advocacy of the 'liberty of unlicensed printing'. Free comment, Milton maintains, is a privilege of citizenship as well as a benefit to the state. 'As good almost kill a man as kill a good book. Who kills a man kills a reasonable creature; but he who destroys a book kills reason itself, the image of God.' He goes on to demolish the argument, ever recurring with the champions of censorship, that a distinction should be made between good and bad books; for 'Truth needs no licensings to make her victorious. Who ever knew truth put to the worse in a free and open encounter?'

By an irony of fate, the abolition of the Licensing Act ('for preventing abuses in printing seditious, treasonable and unlicensed pamphlets, and for regulating of printing and printing presses') was eventually set afoot by an unscrupulous plagiary of Milton's pamphlet and in an unworthy cause. A disreputable Whig scribbler, Charles Blount, attacked in 1693 the Tory licenser in two anonymous tracts, entitled *A Just*

Vindication of Learning and of the Liberty of the Press and *Reasons for the Liberty of Unlicensed Printing*. The text of both was almost entirely stolen from Milton's *Areopagitica*; but the insolent plagiarism was not detected, and even in this disguise Milton's impassioned plea proved its force. Booksellers, bookbinders and printers presented petitions to Parliament. The Licensing Law was renewed for only two years and after the expiration of this period the Commons decided, without a division, to discontinue it. The Lords disagreed, but eventually yielded on 18 April 1695.

Thus, Macaulay says in a famous passage, 'English literature was emancipated, and emancipated for ever, from the control of the government'; and, he sums up, this came to pass by 'a vote, which at the time attracted little attention, which produced no excitement, which has been left unnoticed by voluminous annalists, and of which the history can be but imperfectly traced in the archives of Parliament, but which has done more for liberty and for civilization than the Great Charter or the Bill of Rights'.

A further decisive blow for the freedom of the press was struck by John Wilkes, whose courageous stand against king, government, parliament and magistrates brought about the abolition of 'general warrants' for the arrest of unspecified 'authors, printers and publishers'. Henceforth, prosecution could be instituted only against individuals specifically named and specifically charged.

It is worth noting that the long and detailed list of complaints against the British government which the American colonists embodied in their Declaration of Independence contains no hint of any interference with the liberty of authors, printers and publishers. The great author-printer-publisher, Benjamin Franklin, one of the signers of the Declaration, would no doubt have seen to the insertion of a relevant passage if there had been any reason or pretext for it. Thus it has come about that the Constitution of the United States dispenses with any special safeguards and, as throughout the English-speaking world, leaves the control of the printed word to the normal process of law in the ordinary courts.

It was, however, unfortunate that Congress passed in 1790 a statute which retained one of the worst features of the erstwhile English Licensing Act, namely the restriction of copyright to a privileged class of printers. This statute, it is true, was not limited to a closely circumscribed number of printers and places, but embraced all 'citizens of the United States, or resident therein'. However, it was the decisive step to deny non-American publishers for 160 years the protection which they were subsequently accorded everywhere else in the civilized world. The Congressional Act of 1949 eventually alleviated the strictness, and the signing by the United States of the International Copyright Convention in 1957 removed for good the ill-effects of that survival of Stuart autocracy.

The situation was different in Europe. With the growth of absolutism in the eighteenth century, censorship became more severe as far as political writings were concerned. *Non licet de illis scribere, qui possunt proscribere* was the order of the day. The American and French Revolutions naturally increased the uneasiness of the ruling powers, and books and pamphlets dealing with those revolutionary movements were usually forbidden without discrimination as to the political attitude of the writer. Burke's denunciation of the French Revolution was condemned together with the writings of Helvétius, Montesquieu, Rousseau and Voltaire, who had paved the way for it. Sweden was the first continental country to abolish censorship, in 1766; Denmark followed in 1770. What a liberal application of censorship meant to the printing trade may be gathered from the development of the exportation of books from

Austria: in 1773 its total amounted to 135,000 fl.; twenty years later, in consequence of the thorough-going reforms of the Emperor Joseph II, it had risen to 3,260,000 fl.

The turning-point came with the French Revolution, which embodied Milton's ideas in constitutional acts. On the eve of the French Revolution, Mirabeau issued his pamphlet *Sur la liberté de la presse; imité de l'anglais* (London, 1778), which was in fact a paraphrase of the *Areopagitica*. This publication was instrumental in making the National Assembly declare, on 26 August 1789, in the eleventh clause of the Rights of Man: *La libre communication des pensées et des opinions est un des droits les plus précieux de l'homme; tout citoyen peut donc parler, écrire, imprimer librement.* A clause on these lines has since become obligatory, as it were, in every written constitution; often augmented by a sentence like that appearing first in the Charte of 1830: *La censure ne pourra jamais être rétablie.* Although this principle has been challenged and denounced by reactionaries and dictators again and again, its significance for the printing trade will always remain of particular momentousness.

Three factors tend to militate against the effectiveness of any censorship, even under an autocratic régime: the time-lag between publication and ban, the human qualities of the censors themselves, and the resistance of the public.

Hobbes's *De cive*, published in 1642, was put on the Roman Index in 1654, by which date four editions had been issued; and it was ordered to be burned by Oxford University as late as 1683, when six editions had reached the public.

On the whole the history of censorship offers more examples of mistakes committed through obtuseness than through sensitivity. Censorship for political and moral reasons has probably made itself more obnoxious and ridiculous than censorship for ideological reasons. After all, a trained theologian can without much difficulty decide whether or not certain propositions fall within the teaching of his church. In the field of politics and morals, however, posterity usually finds it very difficult to account for the complete lack of discrimination between good, indifferent and bad writers, even between defenders and opponents of a cause.

Censorship is only one aspect of that hankering after control and uniformity, which is hardly ever absent from government departments. It found an unexpected supporter in G. W. von Leibniz, otherwise one of the most enlightened philosophers and political scientists of his age. He conceived a 'reform' of the German book trade which in effect would have transformed authors, publishers and booksellers into state employees (1668–9). Rules and regulations instead of trial and error, instruction instead of inspiration were to be the guiding principles of literature. 'Nothing must be printed', one of the sections ran, 'without a prefatory statement as to what fresh knowledge the author has contributed to the benefit of the community.' A similar plan was worked out by the Austrian chancellor Metternich, who envisaged a centralized organization of the whole German book trade, under strict government control, in order 'to break the unlimited power of the booksellers who direct German public opinion'.

Metternich's scheme was broached in the year 1819, when the censorship edicts of Karlsbad tried to stifle the liberal movement in Germany by imposing a preventive censorship on all political pamphlets of less than 320 pages. Printers and publishers successfully counteracted this measure by using the smallest possible format, the largest possible types, and every other device which a century-old fight against censorship had taught them.

CHAPTER III

The nineteenth century
1800–1900

The turn of the eighteenth to nineteenth centuries marks a decisive stage in the history of printing. It was not a break but rather a sudden leap forward. It affected the technique of printing, the methods of publication and distribution, and the habit of reading. Compositors and printers, publishers and booksellers, borrowers and buyers of books adopted, or were forced into, new ways of production and consumption. Technical progress, rationalized organization and compulsory education interacted one on another. New inventions lowered the cost of production; mass literacy created further demands, the national and international organization of the trade widened the channels and eased the flow of books from the publishers' stock departments to the retailers' shelves.

The almost complete mechanization of the whole process from letter-founding to bookbinding neither threw out of work the craftsmen nor lowered the quality of their production; nor was the lowering of costs accompanied by diminishing wages or decreasing profits. On the contrary, every section of the trade was nearly all the time expanding in numbers and strengthening its economic security, while the book-buying public was reaping the advantages of greater efficiency, better quality and reduced prices.

The intellectual climate of the age favoured fundamental changes and the printing trade exerted itself to respond to the need. The educational achievements of rationalist thinkers had multiplied the number of literate persons; periodicals, almanacs and newspapers penetrated into classes hitherto altogether lacking contact with literature. The Industrial Revolution had created a new public of great wealth who, in the second generation, were eager to fill the gaps in their intellectual and literary education. The American and French Revolutions mightily stirred interest in controversial matters of politics, economics and society. Locke and Hume, the French Encyclopedists and Kant had taught the public to reason, to question and to discuss the problems and institutions which had hitherto been taken for granted. The rising tide of liberalism and democracy compelled the powers that be, or made it advisable for them, to justify their policies and actions; criticism needed rebutting. In short, public opinion was challenged, and as writers on both sides took up the challenge the printer had to satisfy a demand for publicity unheard-of until that time.

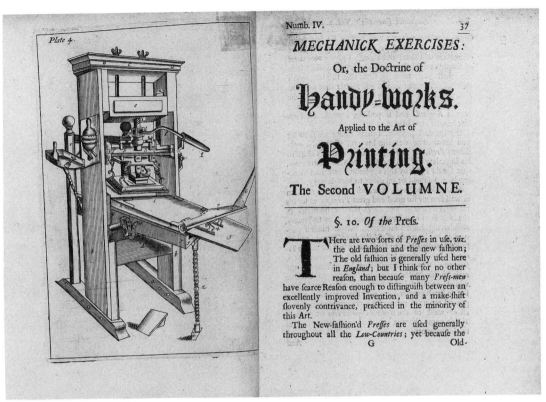

Joseph Moxon, *Mechanick Exercises*. Moxon, London, 1683. [C.113.c.5]

I. TECHNICAL PROGRESS

Three hundred and fifty years elapsed after Gutenberg's invention before any basic change was made in the technique of printing. There was no difference between the humble press on which Gutenberg printed the 42-line Bible and the presses for the accommodation of which John Vanbrugh designed Oxford's spacious Clarendon Building in 1713. Now, within a generation, the printing trade underwent a wholesale alteration. Each and all of these inventions resulted in increasing the output per press and per man-hour beyond the wildest dreams of earlier printers while at the same time reducing the cost of production and the price of the finished product beyond the most extravagant hopes of earlier publishers and book-buyers. Nearly all these inventions had been suggested or even attempted at some earlier date; but inertia and downright hostility to any change had prevented their adoption. As late as 1772 the Basel printers caused the city authorities to ban the use of an improved hand-press because its inventor was not a professional printer. A Jena printer voiced in 1721 the general attitude of the trade when he foamed at 'the damned hellish fiend' who tried to disturb 'the well-established state of repose of the printers' by suggesting all kinds of innovations.

It was an admirer of Dr Fell and van Dyck to whom posterity owes the most comprehensive book on the practice of type-cutting, type-founding, and type-setting before the power press and composing machines were invented – Joseph Moxon (1627–1700). He was a hydrographer by profession and in 1660 was appointed hydrographer to the king; but his interests extended to every kind of applied science and included mathematics, geography, astronomy and architecture (one of his books was dedicated to Sir Christopher Wren) as well as calligraphy and typography. From 1667 to 1679 he published 38 papers for the professional instruction of skilled artisans in the metal and wood-working trades, 24 of which he subsequently republished in book form under the title *Mechanick Exercises, or the Doctrine of Handy-Works* (1683). It was meant as a handbook for every practitioner of book production, which by this time, as Moxon says, 'had found it necessary to divide into the several trades of the master-printer, the letter-cutter, the letter-caster, the letter-dresser, the compositor, the corrector, the press man, the ink-maker, besides several other trades which they take into their assistance, as the smith, the joiner, etc.' It has remained an indispensable mine of information about every aspect of the technical processes of printing as they were practised from Gutenberg to König.

The first revolutionary invention concerned the mechanical manufacture of paper. A machine to supersede the costly and slow production of hand-made paper was invented in 1798 by Nicolas Louis Robert at the Essonnes mill owned by the Didot family, who were engaged in paper-making as well as type-founding, printing and publishing. Robert took his patent to England, and here the first efficient machines were set up in 1803 at Frogmore, Hertfordshire, by the brothers Henry and Sealy Fourdrinier, stationers and paper manufacturers of London, and at St Neots, Huntingdonshire, by John Gamble, a brother-in-law of Pierre and Firmin Didot. The output of paper became ten times as high. Whereas from 60 to 100 lb. could be made daily by hand in one of the old paper-mills, the new paper-machine produced up to 1000 lb. a day. By 1824 the price of some kinds of paper had fallen by a quarter or even a third; by 1843, by almost the half. In 1740 the percentage for paper in the cost of book-production was as high as 20.5 per cent; by 1910 it amounted to 7.1 per cent only. The annual paper production in the United Kingdom was 11,000 tons, all hand-made, in 1800; it rose to 100,000 tons in 1860 when 96,000 tons were machine-made, and to 652,000 tons in 1900 when only 4000 tons were hand-made. At the same dates the price of paper fell from 1s. 6d. to 6½d. and to 1d. per lb.

Almost at the same time an amateur scientist accomplished two inventions which permitted the potential surfeit of machine-made paper to be brought into circulation, as it were. The third Earl Stanhope (1753–1816), perhaps the most brilliant member of a family which for centuries has been producing prominent men in the political, military and intellectual fields succeeded in perfecting two processes which had been tackled but left unfinished by earlier professionals.

William Ged (1690–1749) of Edinburgh – like Gutenberg, a goldsmith by training – took up an idea which Dutch printers had been trying out unsuccessfully in about 1700, namely how to preserve the pages of type for future reprints and thereby avoid resetting the text. Ged took a cast of the type in plaster of paris, and from this mould could produce a fresh metal plate as often as required (1739). The jealousy of the Scots printers, who feared for their livelihood, wrecked the invention. It was revived sixty years later by Firmin Didot, who reversed the process by making the metal cast from sunk faces, thus halving the work of reproduction. Cambridge University bought the secret from Andrew Wilson in 1804, but it was Lord Stanhope who in 1805 made 'stereotyping', as the process came to be called, a commercial proposition at the Clarendon Press in Oxford. The final step was taken in 1829 when, apparently independently, in France, Italy and England, the somewhat clumsy plaster and metal matrices were replaced by papier-mâché which reduced at the same time labour, weight and bulk (although the type-high stereotype plate dates from 1855). The more durable electrotype seems to have been invented simultaneously in 1839 by H. von Jacobi of St Petersburg, Thomas Spencer of Liverpool, C. J. Jordan of London and Thomas F. Adams of New York.

Of even greater importance was Stanhope's improvement of the printing press itself by replacing the wooden press by a much stronger iron structure, and by increasing the bed of, and adapting the lever principle to, the older machines invented by the Dutchman Willem Jansz Blaeu in 1620. Thus it became feasible to print a large forme in one pull, whereas the wooden press required two pulls. John Lewis comments: 'Stanhope's press ... still depended to some extent on the principles that Gutenberg had copied from the Rheingau wine-presses. The first real step forward came with the Albion and Columbian presses, which superseded all other jobbing presses during the first half of the nineteenth century. The Columbian was designed and built by George Clymer of Philadelphia and first introduced into Europe in 1817; the Albion was invented by R. W. Cope around 1820. ... Some of the best ... printing ever done has come off these machines (Morris, for example, used three Albions).' By the mid century the American Croppers had arrived and the Albions and Columbians were out of date, though a surprising number have fortunately survived.

Had he but known it, Stanhope had been anticipated by nearly three centuries by Leonardo da Vinci, who had fully worked out on paper the principles and main features of Stanhope's press of 1804. Its increased multiplying capacity was itself multiplied by Friedrich König's printing machine, which saved the double composition of the inner forme and at the same time allowed far more copies to be pulled per man-hour.

However, it is not these detailed achievements which render König's invention an epoch-making event in the history of printing, but his principle of replacing manpower by steam-power. This was, indeed, as John Walter said in *The Times* of 29 November 1814, 'the greatest improvement connected with printing since the discovery of the art itself', relieving 'the human frame of its most laborious efforts in printing'. The first try-out of the steam-press was a sheet of the *Annual Register* run off in April 1811. Its real importance, however, became clear when it was adopted by *The Times* in 1814. The work done by a hand-press amounted to about 300 sheets in one hour; König's machine raised it to 1100, and brought printing into the Industrial Revolution. The four-cylinder press, invented by Augustus Applegath and Edward Cowper for *The Times* in 1828, allowed 4000 sheets to be pulled per hour. The rotary press invented by the same men for *The Times* in 1848 printed 8000 sheets; and the rotary web-fed press introduced at *The Times* in 1868 raised the rates to over 20,000 sheets per hour. In 1939 *The Times* could be printed at the rate of 40,000 copies an hour of a 32-page paper; today the *Times* presses run over twice as fast. König's invention lowered printing costs by 25 per cent and thus made cheaper and larger editions possible. Before that, large editions were looked at rather unfavourably by printers, who made greater profits from composing than from printing. There were some printers who cared less for the economic advancement of the art than for the art itself. Göschen, the famous Leipzig printer and publisher, to whom König first offered his invention, declined it. 'The machine,' he said, 'will issue many impressions, but nothing beautiful.' It was, however, another Leipzig publisher, F. A. Brockhaus, of Encyclopedia fame, who in 1826 began to apply König's steam-press to the printing of books. By the 1840s Clowes (then in London) had nineteen steam presses, each producing a thousand sheets per hour.

The letter-founding machine which William Church invented in 1822 meant another step forward in the process of cheapening and diffusing the printed word. Until that time, between 3000 and 7000 characters could be cast by hand in a day; the machine raised these figures to between 12,000 and 20,000.

The technical revolution also affected the covering and binding of the printed sheets. Up to the 1820s printed books reached the public in the same state in which handwritten books had left the medieval scriptoria, namely in sheets loose or loosely stitched together; and it was up to the bookseller or the private book-buyer to have these sheets bound into covers made of boards and coated with leather. It was exceptional that a publisher sent forth his products already bound, and this was done only with cheap editions destined for the poorer customers who could not afford to have their books treated by professional bookbinders. Aldus Manutius was the first to sell his popular classics in standard covers; the plain Aldine bindings, much admired today, must have struck his more fastidious contemporaries as shoddy fabrics unworthy of a gentleman's library.

About 1820 leather was gradually being replaced by the cheaper cloth; Pickering's 'Diamond Classics' (1822–32) was the first large-scale venture in publisher's cloth. Towards the end of the century hand-binding was superseded by machine-binding. In fact, the machine-bound book is not 'bound' at all but should properly be described as 'cased', for the printed sheets are not really sunk into the covers (as is done with hand-bound books); the machine merely sticks them on the case, which is prefabricated from cardboard covered with a thin layer of cloth (or, alas, cloth substitute). The mechanically cased book, produced for the publisher, conquered the whole world. The result has been a universal decline of the art of bookbinding. This is compensated for by a remarkable reduction of the cost of the 'bound' book as well as by an increase in the technical and aesthetic perfection of the cases.

An interesting by-product of the publisher's binding is the book-jacket. The earliest English specimens are those wrapped round a *Keepsake* of 1833, an edition of *The Pilgrim's Progress* of 1860 and Dickens's posthumous novel *Edwin Drood* (1870). The jacket became a common feature in the 1890s and has since stimulated the inventiveness of artists as well as typographers. Its usability for advertising purposes was discovered surprisingly late: the first blurb appeared in 1906.

A veritable revolution in the outward appearance and 'feel' as well as in the unlimited availability and cheapness of printing material was brought about by the introduction of wood-pulp into the manufacture of paper, by the side, and sometimes in lieu, of paper made of rags. The great French physicist Réaumur was the first to recommend the manufacture of paper from wood-pulp as early as 1719, but nothing came of this suggestion. Nor did the paper-makers follow up the 'Experiments ... of making paper without any rags' made by the naturalist Jacob Christian Schaeffer, although his book (Regensburg, 1765) ran into a second edition and was translated into Dutch. Schaeffer used various vegetable substances, such as moss, straw and wasps' nests; but distrust of the novelty and, with some justification, its technical feasibility prevented the invention from going beyond the laboratory stage. A Saxon weaver, Friedrich Gottlob Keller, accomplished the feat in 1843, and within a decade the production of wood-pulp paper had spread everywhere. It was to become a leading industry in Canada, Sweden and especially Finland, whose national economy has been described as 'built on paper'.

FABLE XXI.

The RAT-CATCHER *and* CATS.

THE rats by night such mischief did,
 BETTY was ev'ry morning chid.
They undermin'd whole sides of bacon,
Her cheese was sapp'd, her tarts were taken.
Her pasties, fenc'd with thickest paste,
Were all demolish'd, and laid waste.
She curs'd the Cat for want of duty,
Who left her foes a constant booty.
An Engineer, of noted skill,
Engag'd to stop the growing ill.

From room to room he now surveys
Their haunts, their works, their secret ways;
                                        Finds

John Gay, *Fables*, wood-engravings by Thomas Bewick.
T. Saint, Newcastle upon Tyne, 1779. [C.70.b.8]

THE RING OUZEL.

(*Turdus Torquatus*, Lin.—*Le Merle à Plastron Blanc*, Buff.)

THIS bird very much resembles the Blackbird:
Its general colour is of a dull black or dusky hue,
each feather being margined with a greyish ash
colour; the bill is dusky, corners of the mouth
and inside yellow; eyes hazel; its breast is distinguished by a crescent of pure white, which almost surrounds the neck, and from whence it derives its name; its legs are of a dusky brown.
The female differs in having the crescent on the
breast much less conspicuous, and in some birds
wholly wanting, which has occasioned some authors to consider it as a different species, under the
name of the Rock Ouzel.

*History of British Birds, Figures engraved on Wood by
Thomas Bewick*. Sol. Hodgson for Beilby & Bewick,
Newcastle upon Tyne, 1797. [672.g.17]

Commercial printing, such as posters, circulars and sale catalogues, and popular
newspapers and magazines – in brief, all ephemeral reading-matter – were henceforth
universally printed on wood-pulp paper. But inexpensive books were also made economically possible, and the United States became the chief producer and consumer of
non-rag paper.

The inventions which made possible and increased the mass-production of printed
texts were accompanied by three inventions which improved, facilitated or reduced
the cost of printed illustrations. Popular journalism hastened the spread of illustrations as a regular adjunct to printed information: the *Penny Magazine*, printed by
Clowes from 1832, and the *Illustrated London News* (1842) were the pioneers of
educational and entertaining illustration respectively.

The revival and improvement of the technique of wood-engraving (as opposed to
woodcutting) which Thomas Bewick (1753–1828) inaugurated in the last decade
of the eighteenth century benefited fine printing rather than popular printing; but it

was a step in the right direction, in that Bewick restored the sense of typographical harmony which had largely been lost in the era of the uneasy companionship of letter-press and copperplates.

Bewick was not the first to illustrate a book with 'white-line' wood-engravings: a generation earlier, Elisha Kirkall (*c.* 1682–1742) 'was almost certainly the first English artist – perhaps the first European' (Hodnett) to do so. Bewick was however a pioneer in his own time, 'a creative force as a wood-engraver' in working with the burin across the grain of the boxwood. While he was not principally an interpretative illustrator of fiction or belles-lettres, his power to portray the incidental beauties of the countryside in microcosmic tailpieces is one of the glories of English book illustration.

William Bulmer (1757–1830) printed the work of his friend Bewick with some distinction, most notably in William Somerville's *The Chase* (1797, second edition 1804). Bulmer, the exponent of neo-classical fine printing to rival Bodoni and the Didots, was to books what Chippendale was to chairs. He established his Shakspeare Printing Office in 1791 to print the great Boydell Shakespeare, using new types cut by William Martin, and in 1794–6 produced his magnificent two-volume *History of the River Thames*, illustrated with 76 aquatint plates.

The other technical invention at around this time was steel-engraving, which offered to artists brilliant sharpness and a wider spectrum of tone than they could achieve using copper. Mid-century was the heyday of etching on steel.

Further refinements of book illustration were brought about by experiments with halftone blocks (Jacobi, 1847), photogravure (Fox Talbot, 1852) and so on. These came to fruition in the second half of the nineteenth century; first with the success of the printer-publisher Edmund Evans (1826–1905) in the printing of coloured wood-engravings after drawings by, most famously, Walter Crane, Randolph Caldecott and Kate Greenaway, and later with the invention of photographically-made line and halftone process blocks. Experiments and inventions such as these, together with subsidiary improvements, have considerably benefited all the arts and sciences which depend on the visual transmission of their objects to the student; suffice it to mention the two branches of medicine and art history. At the same time, of course, they rendered redundant the amazing skill of the copyist-engravers.

Alois Senefelder (1771–1834) of Munich has the same slightly equivocal claim as Gutenberg to the invention of one of the two principal branches of printing, in Senefelder's case lithography (which he called *Steindruckerei*, 'printing from stone'). It was in fact Simon Schmidt of Miesbach who first printed from stone, in 1787; but whereas he invented a three-dimensional process which came to nothing (etching back the surface of the stone to leave the printing image in relief), Senefelder in 1798 discovered planographic lithography through the use of a greasy ink which adhered to an image drawn on the stone with a wax crayon while simultaneously being repelled by a thin film of water which was itself repelled by the waxy image.

The artist Paul Sandby had first made aquatint fashionable in the 1770s as a medium for topographical illustration; but it was Rudolf Ackermann who some 20 years later achieved the greater success when he published the celebrated aquatint *Microcosm of London* and *Histories* of Oxford and Cambridge, and it was Ackermann who in 1819 published Senefelder's *Complete Course of Lithography*. England had been the first country outside Germany to have a lithographic press (by 1801): Philipp André's *Specimens of Polyautography* was published in 1803 and J. T Smith's

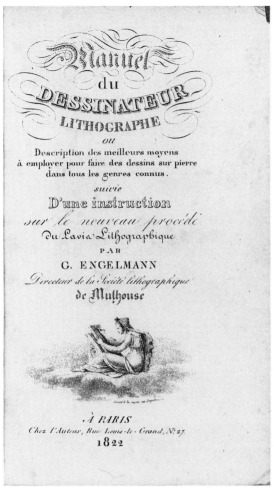

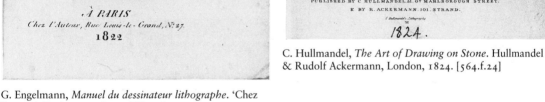

C. Hullmandel, *The Art of Drawing on Stone*. Hullmandel & Rudolf Ackermann, London, 1824. [564.f.24]

G. Engelmann, *Manuel du dessinateur lithographe*. 'Chez l'auteur', Paris, 1822. [7855.bbb.25]

Antiquities of Westminster (1807) contained 'the first known instance of a lithograph … used to illustrate a book' (Twyman).

Lithography spread quickly in Germany, comparatively slowly at first in France. Nevertheless, Marcel de Serres published a full description of the process in 1814, in 1815–16 important and successful presses were established in Paris by Charles de Lasteyrie and Godefroy Engelmann, and in 1822 Engelmann published his *Manuel du dessinateur lithographe*. By then Charles Hullmandel had set up his press in London, where he published *The Art of Drawing on Stone* in 1824.

Although the lithographic draughtsman's work was charged at a far cheaper rate than that of the engraver, and the life of a lithographic stone was potentially far longer than that of a copper-engraving, early lithography was principally in competition with aquatint for the exclusively expensive market in coloured topographical prints and book illustrations. Such books were often published on subscription, in continuation of the eighteenth-century tradition for copperplate and aquatint books. Engelmann's was the leading press in Europe for what was to remain (and to some extent still is) the specialized French taste for artists' prints and *livres d'artiste*. Eugène

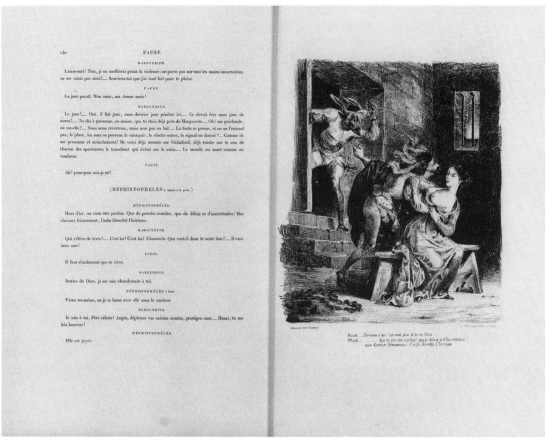

J. W. von Goethe, *Faust*, illustrated by Eugène Delacroix. Motte, Paris, 1828. [1875.b.9]

Delacroix illustrated an edition of Goethe's *Faust* (1828) which created an early precedent for that medium and was a harbinger of the Romantic style in book illustration.

French topographical publishing was overshadowed for 50 years by the over-ambitious *Voyages pittoresques et romantiques dans l'ancienne France*, which started publication in 1818 and after reaching 20 folio volumes and upwards of 3000 lithographic plates had covered only two-thirds of the country. Several lithographic presses – including two in England – printed the plates of over 150 artists (including Ingres, Fragonard, Géricault, Bonington, Boys and Daguerre). The latter name suggests photography, and some plates in later volumes were indeed printed by photolithography (the process of printing a photographic image exposed on a stone or printing-plate). In a parallel development, 1853 saw the publication of six architectural photographs in *Lithographie, ou impressions obtenus sur pierre a l'aide de la photographie*.

Honoré Daumier's satires in *Caricature* (1831–4) and *Charivari* (1833–72), Goya's Bordeaux lithographs and Toulouse-Lautrec's posters and book illustrations are further landmarks of nineteenth-century lithography.

J. C. Le Blon seems to have been (before 1711) the first to apply Newton's tri-chromatic theory to colour printing, making three engraved plates, one for each cardinal colour (red, blue and yellow), which by superimposition of impression should combine to give the true composite result. Even though he later realized that it would be best to add a fourth, black printing, he enjoyed no great success. He was followed later in the eighteenth century by Janinet and Debucourt. The nineteenth century would have been miserable without colour: in 1835 George Baxter was granted a patent for reproducing full-colour subjects by printing tri-chromatic relief blocks on a black key image; a patent for chromolithography was taken out by Gottfried Engelmann in Paris in 1837, and one for chromoxylography (colours to be printed from metal plates, then the line image from wood blocks) by Charles Knight in 1838. In 1839 Hullmandel produced Thomas Shotter Boys's splendid chromo-lithographic *Picturesque Architecture in Paris, Ghent, Antwerp, Rouen, etc.*, and Owen Jones took chromolithography to its utmost in his *Grammar of Ornament* (1856).

Last but not least, in this sketch of the inventions that have expanded the social and economic aspects of printing, come the composing machines. The long list of men who wrestled with this problem begins with the scientist and political economist Johann Joachim Becher in 1682 and includes William Church, who obtained a patent in 1822, and Giuseppe Mazzini, who obtained another in 1843. Before then John Walter of *The Times* had the idea that logotypes (two or more characters cemented together) might speed up composition, but they never caught on. By 1900 more than 1500 patents had been registered in the United States, but only three composing machines have proved of practical value. The first was that invented independently by Robert Hattersley (1866) and Charles Kastenbein (1869). Hattersley's machine was mainly used by provincial newspapers and reached London (the *Daily News*) as late as 1891 when it was on the point of being superseded. Kastenbein's machine was installed at *The Times* office in 1872 and there remained in use until 1908. The main disadvantages of the Hattersley and Kastenbein composing machines were the need for justifying the lines by hand, and afterwards the distribution of type. The latter was so expensive that it could be done economically only by cheap juvenile labour. The opposition of the London Society of Compositors to the employment of unskilled workers explains the restriction of the Hattersley machines to the provinces as well as the exclusive use of the Kastenbein machine by *The Times*, for *The Times* was the only non-union newspaper in London.

Hooker's electric typesetting machine, which William Clowes installed in 1875, worked most satisfactorily for over twenty years but, though supplemented by a distributing machine, does not seem to have been adopted by any other printing firm. The rotary typecaster invented by F. Wicks, patented in 1881, could produce between 35,000 and 70,000 types per hour.

The problem of automatic justification of the lines and of mechanical distribution of the type was finally solved by the Linotype and Monotype machines. Their immediate success, however, was largely due to another invention, that of the punch-cutting machine, made by Linn Boyd Benton, of Milwaukee in 1885. This mechanical engraver made possible the mass-production of punches which was the indispensable prerequisite of mechanical composing.

Although the first Linotype and Monotype machines were commercially installed and successful by 1897, their application to book production characterized the first six decades of the twentieth century, so they will be discussed in chapter IV.

By the beginning of the nineteenth century publishing had firmly established itself as a whole-time profession. It would be justified to call it a vocation, as, even in the increasingly commercialized conditions of modern publishing, idealism has remained an outstanding characteristic of the true publisher.

There have always been numerous booksellers and publishers who placed their business experience and authority at the disposal of the community, especially in the sphere of public and private welfare. A few of them have also played a distinguished part in state affairs, such as Benjamin Franklin, the versatile diplomatist, author, editor, publisher, printer and inventor of the lightning conductor.

The Hamburg publisher Friedrich Christoph Perthes (1772–1843) was instrumental at the Congress of Vienna (1813–15) in securing the re-establishment of the ancient Hanse towns of Bremen, Hamburg and Lübeck as independent republics against the expansionist wishes of Prussia, Denmark and Hanover. The Stuttgart bookseller Georg Friedrich Cotta (1764–1832), Goethe's and Schiller's publisher, was a champion of constitutional democracy in the Württemberg Diet and an untiring advocate of the German Customs Union which took effect a few months after his death. One publisher even exchanged the direction of his firm for the highest office his country has to offer: Harold Macmillan, representing the third generation of his family house, entered the House of Commons in 1920 and, through a series of ministerial appointments including the Foreign Office and the Exchequer, became Prime Minister in 1957.

The stability achieved at the beginning of the nineteenth century can be seen in the large number of firms which have survived to this day. Longman, Constable and Murray have already been mentioned; Chambers, Nelson, Macmillan, Black (1807), Collins (1819) and Cassell (1848) may be added in England and Scotland. In the United States, Harper & Brothers (1817), Little, Brown & Co.; in France Plon (1854) date back over a century. In Germany, the financial collapse of the country after the Kaiser's war and its moral collapse under the Nazi regime and the temporary sovietization of eastern Germany wiped out nearly every firm which throughout the nineteenth century had enjoyed international repute. Vandenhoeck & Ruprecht of Göttingen (1735), C.H. Beck of Munich (1763), Karl Baedeker (1827) of Leipzig (now Munich), F. A. Brockhaus (1805) of Leipzig and Herder of Freiburg (1801) are among the survivors.

The greater power of survival of English publishers compared with their German and French counterparts can partly be explained also by the difference of their publishing policies. By the middle of the nineteenth century a tendency towards severe specialization had become marked in Germany and France, whereas in England and America general publishers were dominant. A change of intellectual movements or literary fashions is bound to affect adversely the fortunes of a firm which has identified itself with a particular group of writers or school of thought.

The cumulative advantages brought about by the stream of technical inventions and improvements were underpinned by the concomitant progress of improved organization and greater legal security on the part of the trade. In the field of organizing the trade, pride of place must be assigned to the Börsenverein der deutschen Buchhändler. Founded in Leipzig in 1825, it soon united within its fold the publishers, wholesalers and retailers of books throughout the German-speaking world. No

VOYAGES

PITTORESQUES ET ROMANTIQUES

DANS L'ANCIENNE FRANCE

Par MM. Ch. NODIER, J. TAYLOR et Alph. DE CAILLEUX.

A PARIS.

DE L'IMPRIMERIE DE A. FIRMIN DIDOT,

IMPRIMEUR DE L'INSTITUT,

RUE JACOB, Nº 24.

M. DCCCXXIX.

C. Nodier, J. Taylor & A. de Cailleux, *Voyages pittoresques et romantiques dans l'ancienne France: Auvergne*, drawing by J. H. Fragonard lithographed by G. Engelmann. Didot, Paris, 1829. [445.i.7–15]

organization of the same comprehensiveness and efficiency has been established in any other country, although associations of publishers and those of booksellers sprang up everywhere during the nineteenth century, leading to such international unions as the International Publishers' Association. Their work has uniformly benefited not only the trade itself but equally so the public and the authors. Among their greatest achievements are the fight against piracy and the establishment of price-maintenance agreements.

The international regulation of copyright has put an end to the century-old twin scandal of privileged and pirated editions – the former enriching publisher and author at the expense of the public, the latter ruining the respectable publisher and author with small benefit to the public. Piracy was as old as the printing trade itself. It was in vain that, as early as 1525, Luther attacked these literary 'highwaymen and thieves', for the sure gain to be extracted from the reprinting of marketable books was stronger than moral scruples. The Signoria of Venice was the first in 1492 to safeguard a printer against unauthorized issues of his books by others. The snag lay in the impotence of every government to make its decrees effective beyond its frontiers and the lack of any inter-governmental understanding. The first effective dam against piracy was erected by the English Copyright Act of 1709; but as it did not apply to Ireland, Irish printers continued to rob English printers and authors, deodorizing their filthy lucre by the sweet perfume of patriotism; in this they were stoutly supported by the Irish authorities, until the Union of 1801 ended this scandal. Thus it came about that three pirated editions of Richardson's *Sir Charles Grandison* (1753) appeared in Dublin prior to the genuine London edition, as disloyal workmen had surreptitiously taken the proofs across St George's Channel.

The United States clung to this outworn creed of the mercantilist era right through the nineteenth century. The firm of Harper & Brothers, of New York, the fastest U.S. printer of the novels of Scott, deserves honourable mention for voluntarily paying fairly substantial royalties to Dickens, Macaulay and other authors unprotected by law. The development of rail transport in the United States brought an end to the colonial pattern of self-sufficient small towns, each with its own bookseller-printer-publisher, and initiated a centralized book trade, first in Boston, then in Philadelphia, which settled for good in the 1840s in New York. There Harpers replaced Lea & Carey as the largest and most efficient printer-publishers: after a disastrous fire in 1853 they built a new plant centred around 28 steam-driven presses. Joel Munsell, publisher and bookseller of Albany, N.Y., 'represents the best American printing of the nineteenth century' – James M. Wells.

The English Copyright Act of 1709 and the French copyright law of 1793 (which provided for a term of two years after the author's death) were the first enactments to secure the right of authors and publishers within large countries. The copyright law of the Grand Duchy of Saxe-Weimar, issued in 1839, was the first of its kind in Germany and the first to embody the 30-year term of protection after the author's death. It took another half-century until at last the Berne Convention of 1886 established the principle of international reciprocity of rights. The Universal Copyright Convention of 1955 eventually provided a system of international copyright protection without impairing the International Copyright Union of Berne, brought up to date last by the Brussels Convention of 1948. All the published works of an author remained in copyright until 50 years after his death – extended to 70 years in 1995.

The abolition of pirated editions exerted a great influence on the calculation of book prices. Hitherto the publishers said, 'Books are expensive because they are pirated, and they are pirated because they are expensive.' Net-price agreements, such as those established by the Börsenverein in 1887 and by the British Publishers' Association in 1899, saved the bookseller from being undercut and forced out of business by unscrupulous profiteers, provided some security for the honest publisher, and also assured the author of his fair share in the proceeds.

On the other hand, it must be admitted that the reading public derived certain advantages from the pirating of books. The cheapness of those pirated editions enticed many to purchase a book, the original edition of which would have been beyond their means. The original edition of the *Œuvres du philosophe de Sans-souci* (i.e. Frederick the Great of Prussia), for instance, cost 27 fl.; a pirated edition published almost simultaneously was to be had at 12 fl. The publishers naturally desired to keep the 'right' to print from the author's 'copy' and to keep it for ever. The public were equally urgent for cheap books. In Britain the question was solved largely as a result of Scottish enterprise. Alexander Donaldson of Edinburgh led the way by breaking a ring of the London booksellers, and John Bell of the 'British Library' followed. The technical innovations in the printing trade made at the turn of the eighteenth–nineteenth centuries, and the spectacular increase of the reading public throughout the nineteenth and twentieth centuries, rendered feasible larger editions at lower prices. This process continued until the outbreak of the First World War, since when taxation, inflation and, in their wake, the rising costs of raw materials and wages have reversed the trend.

The stability and respectability which individual publishers and the publishing trade as a whole achieved during the past 200 years have had their repercussions on the relations between authors and publishers. It has increasingly become the custom for an author to identify himself with a particular firm and for a firm to consider its authors an integral part of the business. There are, it is true, earlier examples of an author preferring one publisher to another – frequently on the basis of personal friendship, as with Erasmus and Froben – or of a publisher helping his author through a lean period. But as a rule there prevailed a latent and sometimes open antagonism between the two, and the relationship of mutual confidence and amity which is now the norm may justly be described as of recent growth. Was Thomas Campbell serious when he once drank a toast to Napoleon because the emperor had ordered a publisher to be court-martialled and shot? In a moment of irritation Goethe once expressed his belief that there must be a special place in hell reserved for publishers. When Byron gave John Murray a Bible with the playful alteration of St John 18: 40, to 'Now Barabbas was a publisher', he made amends (if amends were needed) by addressing to him the lines:

> To thee, with hope and terror dumb,
> The unfledged MS authors come;
> Thou printest all – and sellest some —
> My Murray.

The wayward genius of Walter Savage Landor entrusted his publications to no fewer than 28 different publishers between 1795 and 1863. It is however more frequent to find not only that an author stayed with one publisher but also that a mere business relationship developed into a lasting personal friendship. The histories of every publishing firm are full of examples.

A happy combination of good business instinct and good taste led to a revival of the printer's device in the middle of the nineteenth century. This proprietary mark of quality, proudly introduced by Peter Schöffer, had fallen into desuetude. In England, the Copyright Act of 1709 made the device superfluous, as the Act gave greater security to the property rights of the book-producer than could be obtained by the mere display of a legally unprotected trade-mark. Moreover, the shift of emphasis from the printer to the publisher militated against any special reference to the printer's share in the production. The publishers themselves showed no interest in what they, as children of the Age of Reason, probably considered a pointless survival of less enlightened times: and the congers were too loosely organized to create corporate devices for themselves.

Charles Whittingham the younger, nephew of the founder of the Chiswick Press, is credited with the reintroduction of the printer's device about 1850. The idea was taken up by R. & R. Clark and T. & A. Constable of Edinburgh and William Morris, whose first publication was in fact printed for him at the Chiswick Press in 1889. The reason for this resumption of the old custom was artistic as well as economic. The printer's device was meant to serve typography as well as publicity. Publishers soon adopted devices of their own. The sailing-ship of the Insel-Verlag, La Belle Sauvage of Cassell, the fountain of Collins, the Penguin, Pelican and Puffin of Penguin Books have impressed themselves on the memory of millions of readers. It is somewhat surprising that so many English publishers still refrain from using this simple and memorable means of commercial heraldry and that some of them use their devices only occasionally, whereas most German publishers 'show the flag' on every book.

It is difficult, if not impossible, to obtain a fair estimate of the economic importance of the printing trade as such. Printers proper, compositors, typesetters, origination houses, proof-readers, publishers, designers, booksellers, literary agents, bookbinders and many more professions have become almost independent of each other. One ought to add the vast host of authors, ranging from the indefatigable manufacturer of shockers to the occasional writer of a letter to the editor of a provincial newspaper, the staffs of publicity agencies and many other professions in order to get a somewhat complete survey of all those connected with printer's ink. Among them, remainder merchants and the 'waste-paper' stationers to whom John Dunton, the author of *Religio Bibliopolae* (1728), sold 'many hundred reams of books that my friends had forgot to ask for', must not be left out.

Statistics about the annual output of books are almost valueless, as the basis of computation differs not only from country to country but even within the same country. Thus, the German publishers' association assessed the production in 1937 at 31,761 'units' whereas the national bibliography arrived at 69,002 'units'. And it may be doubted whether the 7839 items claimed for Rumania and the 10,640 calculated for the United States of America in the year 1939 referred to even remotely comparable 'units'.

The number of English master printers was 103 in 1724, i.e. a generation after the lapse of the Licensing Act; of these, 75 were located in London and 28 in the provinces. In 1785 there were 124 printing offices in London, and by 1808 this number had increased to 216. From that time onward further statistics of printing establishments would be misleading. On the one hand, printers began to specialize as they had never done before. The newspaper compositors were the first to set themselves apart from book and jobbing printers: numerous firms applied themselves to

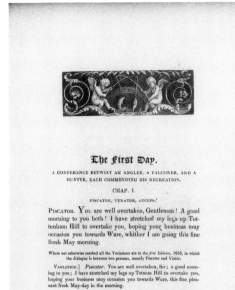

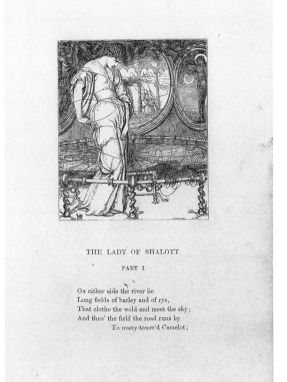

Izaac Walton, *The Compleat Angler*, illustrated by Thomas Stothard. William Pickering, London, 1836. [556.f.10]

Alfred Tennyson, *Poems*, illustrations by John Millais engraved by J. Thompson. E. Moxon, London, 1857. [11647.e.59]

some particular field of printing such as work for the theatres, the railways, colour printing, the printing of law books and so on. Thus, small presses have been able to maintain themselves in some distinct sphere. On the other hand, the vast expansion of the book trade favoured the emergence of big firms which could command the capital needed for the installation of complex machinery, and the master printer of old is now part of the 'managerial' structure of modern economy.

As printers have necessarily always been one of the best educated and most intelligent group of artisans, the influence of their corporations and trade unions has been far in excess of their numerical strength. As early as 1785 London master printers agreed with a compositors' trade union on a negotiated scale of wages for composing work (which incidentally implied the lapse of the control of the trade hitherto exercised by the Stationers' Company), and it was again in the English printing trade that factory inspection was made compulsory as early as 1864. From 1890 onward the various English unions connected with the printing and allied trades moved towards the nation-wide grouping eventually founded in 1902 under the name of the Printing and Kindred Trades Federation. Its original membership was below 50,000 (in 1955 it exceeded 300,000, and comprised virtually the whole trade). The size and influence of the unions declined in later years with the arrival of phototypesetting and offset lithography and the consequent decoupling of composition and printing.

More recently and more powerfully, the growing use of microcomputers and word-processors has completed the process of demystification and with it any exclusive claim to the skills required to produce a book.

3. OFFICIAL AND PRIVATE PRESSES

The governments of Revolutionary and Napoleonic France were the first authorities to use the printing press for large-scale, direct and incessant appeals and orders to the masses. The occasional proclamation or regulation which the paternalistic rulers of the old dispensation addressed to their subjects could be set up and pulled as a casual job by any printer, and the titles of king's printer, *imprimeur du roi*, and so on did not imply any exclusiveness on either part. The spate of commandments to be instantly obeyed and of forms to be forthwith returned, which has ever since been inundating government offices and private dwellings alike, made imperative the establishment of presses under the exclusive control and at the direct bidding of the central administration in every country.

The promulgation of authentic texts of laws and statutes and the prompt issue of forms affecting every aspect of civic life is the main concern of government presses. Thus, the functions of the United States Government Printing Office in Washington, set up by Congress in 1860, were defined as follows: 'All printing for the Congress, the judiciary, the executive departments, independent offices, and establishments of the Government, with specified exceptions, is required to be performed at the Government Printing Office.' The undreamt-of and still increasing expansion of the activities of all branches of the Federal administration has never permitted this press to venture into the field of literary production, even if the Congressional Committee on Printing were to connive at such trespassing on private enterprise.

Most official presses, however, have not been able to refrain from producing more attractive reading-matter. They have usually followed the precedent of the French Imprimerie Nationale and taken special interest either in fine printing with a view to providing national models of the highest standard, or in the publication of expensive works for which there is no commercial market. In this respect, the Österreichische Staatsdruckerei (founded 1804), the Prussian Staatsdruckerei (founded 1851) and the German Reichsdruckerei, in which the former was merged in 1879, have set good examples. In 1900 the Imprimerie Nationale produced a monumental *Histoire de l'imprimerie en France*, composed in large sizes of the Jannon and Grandjean types, profusely illustrated and superbly printed on fine paper.

Less frequently, government presses have directly assumed the function of publishers. In the Swiss canton of Berne the publication of all schoolbooks was a state monopoly from 1599 to 1831. The Austrian state publishing house, which was originally set up in 1772, had a monopoly of all schoolbooks until 1869; after the revolution of November 1918 it was re-endowed with certain privileges, but it was later obliged to compete with other publishers. Only in the Soviet empire was absolute control over all reading-matter exercised by the state through the central administration of printing, publishing and bookselling, Glavpoligrafisdat.

A remarkable development has taken place in the transformation of Her Majesty's Stationery Office into a state publisher. It was founded in 1786 merely to stop the waste of public money that occurred when each Government department bought its own paper, ink, sealing-wax and the like as it pleased. To the general public today,

HMSO is better known as the publisher of official documents, including the daily record of Parliamentary proceedings. This is traditionally known as *Hansard* after the name of the original printer, Thomas Curson Hansard (1776–1833), who from 1803 printed the debates of the two Houses, first for William Cobbett and from 1811 under his own imprint. In addition to the publication of official documents, however, HMSO has gone a long way towards competing with private publishers. Especially since the beginning of the Second World War it has been producing books on topics which stretch the conception of official or government business to its utmost limit. Books and pamphlets on art and archaeology, cooking and husbandry, anthropology and geography, social and martial affairs, historical manuscripts and the English language are represented in its list of publications. Only fiction has not yet appeared in it – although the Opposition of the day may often be inclined to subsume Government White Papers in this category.

It was pleasure in fine printing, or at least in printing according to personal taste, rather than concern with commercial success that made kings and nobles set up private presses in the seventeenth and eighteenth centuries. With the collapse of the aristocratic style of life and the advent of the utilitarian age these private presses disappeared. The ducal press of Parma run by Bodoni was the last of its kind. Lacking the inspiration of connoisseurs and craftsmen of independent minds and means, the standard of printing rapidly declined. Mass-production and mass-literacy further favoured quantitative output at the expense of quality. The chief characteristic of Victorian book production, it has been said, was not so much its bad taste as the absence of any taste at all.

The undisputed sway Britain held in world trade at this time cast an unmerited lustre on British printing. A redeeming feature was undoubtedly the technical perfection of the design, cutting and adjustment of the dreary *Englische Antiqua,* as the 'modern face' types were collectively called in Germany. An ambitious type-cutter such as Johann Christian Bauer (1802–1867), founder of the famous Frankfurt foundry, could do no better than cross the Channel and perfect his skills in the Edinburgh foundry of A. & P. Wilson.

The printer Charles Whittingham the younger (1795–1876) and his frequent customer, the publisher William Pickering (1796–1854), tried in vain to fight the general depravity. Their books are plain, graceful and well printed – signal virtues in the nineteenth century. Pickering in 1830 boldly adopted the dolphin and anchor, and the motto ALDI DISCIP. ANGLUS, as the device for his comprehensive 'Aldine' edition of the English poets. Whittingham in 1844 revived for the celebrated (but fictitious) *Diary of Lady Willoughby* and a folio Book of Common Prayer the 'old face' type of Caslon at the Chiswick Press which he had inherited in 1840 from his uncle Charles Whittingham the elder. Joseph Cundall (1818–1895) designed many attractive popular illustrated books in the 1850s and 1860s, having in the 1840s published the beautiful 'Home Treasury' series of children's books. But theirs were voices crying in the wilderness: there was no time in the late nineteenth century to ponder on principles of typography; the trade was far too busy trying to keep up with both the ever-growing demand for printed matter and the flood of new equipment coming on the market. By chance, however, the Caxton Celebration of 1877 did afford them an opportunity to see the Fell types, which had just been unearthed by Dr Daniel at Oxford.

The private press of the Rev. C. H. O. Daniel, which he ran for almost thirty years at Worcester College, Oxford (until he was elected Provost of the college), was

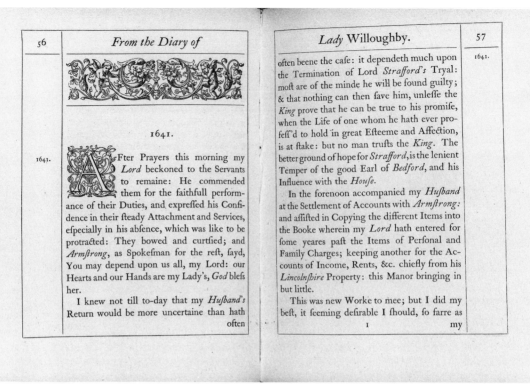

The Diary of Lady Willoughby. Chiswick Press for Longman, Brown, Green & Longman, London, 1844. [C.103.e.22]

remarkable for the tiny size of his editions and for his care in devising agreeable pages, but above all for his revival of the Fell types. These lay scarcely used and largely forgotten at Oxford University Press until in 1877 Daniel spotted them and bought a fount; henceforth he used nothing else. Madan's claim, that 'the use of Fell type … and the celebrated *Garland of Rachel* in 1881 may fairly be regarded as the first genuine signs of the revival of printing in England', seems exalted in light of contemporary distinguished work at the Chiswick Press and the Daniel Press's near-invisibility to the trade at large, yet is true enough.

The appointment of Horace Hart as university printer at Oxford in 1883 now looks to us a more convincing sign of the imminent revival. A totally professional printer, he was a scholar too, and the author of *Notes on a Century of Typography at the University Press, Oxford, 1693–1794* (1900). While modernizing one of the largest book-printing houses in the country (and, in trying to equip it with new types, being obliged to wrestle with the difficulties created by Oxford's unique type-height – which was to remain unique for another hundred years, until the Press ceased to print) he yet made time to study and admire the Fell legacy, though regrettably he was not able to use Fell's types themselves until 1896. In 1899 he completed the printing of *The Yattendon Hymnal*, designed and edited by Robert Bridges and H. Ellis Wooldridge, set in the Fell types with the music types of Peter de Walpergen that had lain unused at the Press since the end of the seventeenth century.

It was at the Chiswick Press that William Morris (1834–96) had the first books printed which unmistakably inaugurated the revival of good printing. Although the

154

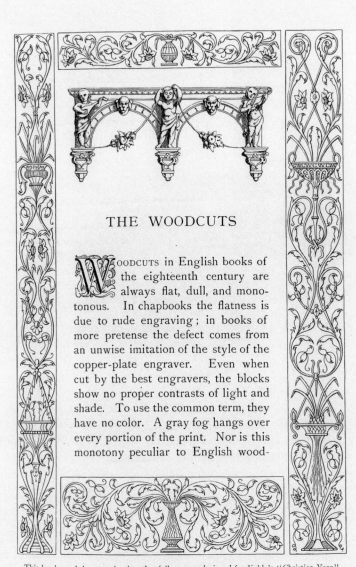

THE WOODCUTS

OODCUTS in English books of the eighteenth century are always flat, dull, and monotonous. In chapbooks the flatness is due to rude engraving; in books of more pretense the defect comes from an unwise imitation of the style of the copper-plate engraver. Even when cut by the best engravers, the blocks show no proper contrasts of light and shade. To use the common term, they have no color. A gray fog hangs over every portion of the print. Nor is this monotony peculiar to English wood-

This border and the seven borders that follow were designed for Keble's "Christian Year" by Charlotte Whittingham and engraved by Mary Byfield.

267

Arthur Warren, *The Charles Whittinghams, Printers.* The border was designed by Charlotte Whittingham and cut by Mary Byfield. De Vinne Press for the Grolier Club, New York, 1896. [Ac.4714/6]

APRIL.

Thenot. Hobbinoll.

Thenot   ELL me, good Hobbinoll,
what garres thee greete?
What? hath some wolfe
thy tender lambes ytorne?
Or is thy bagpype broke,
that soundes so sweete?
Or art thou of thy loved
lasse forlorne?
Or bene thine eyes attem-
pred to the yeare,
Quenching the gasping furrowes thirst with rayne?
Like April shoure so stremes the trickling teares
Adowne thy cheeke, to quenche thy thristye payne.

Hobbin.   Nor thys, nor that, so muche doeth make me mourne,
But for the ladde, whome long I lovd so deare,
Nowe loves a lasse that all his love doth scorne.
He, plongd in payne, his tressed locks dooth teare.

Shepheards delights he dooth them all forsweare;
Hys pleasaunt pipe, whych made us meriment,
He wylfully hath broke, and doth forbeare
His wonted songs, wherein he all outwent.

Thenot   What is he for a ladde you so lament?
Ys love such pinching payne to them that prove?
And hath he skill to make so excellent,
Yet hath so little skill to brydle love?

Hobbin.   Colin thou kenst, the southerne shepheardes boye:

c 3   21

Edmund Spenser, *The Shepheardes Calendar*, illustrated by Edward Burne-Jones. Kelmscott Press, London, 1896. [C.43.c.12]

part he played in the revival cannot be questioned, it should not be forgotten that the actual impetus came from its godfather, Emery Walker (1851–1933). The lecture which he delivered at the Arts and Crafts Exhibition in London in 1888 marks the birth of the new movement, for it was Walker's clarion-call and his friendship with Walker that inspired Morris to put into practice his reforming ideas.

Workers in the Arts and Crafts movement, in self-conscious opposition to the Industrial Revolution, tried to make well-designed things in a craftsmanlike way. Morris applied this principle to the production of books at his Kelmscott Press. Two basic conceptions underlay his work and have since remained fundamental to good printing: the unity of type, ink and paper manifested in imposition as well as impression, and his insistence on the opening (i.e. two facing pages), and not the individual page, as the unit from which the typographic design of a book has to be conceived. Dissatisfied with the paper and vellum on offer, he had them made to his own specification. Dissatisfied with British ink, he imported his own supply from Germany (and when his pressmen complained that it was too stiff he threatened to close the Press down). 'In these important respects he was Baskerville reborn' – Morison.

Three Kelmscott typefaces were designed by Morris and Walker and cut by Edward Prince: the Golden, based on the types of the great Venetian printers of the fifteenth century, notably Jenson and particularly his Pliny of 1476, but tending

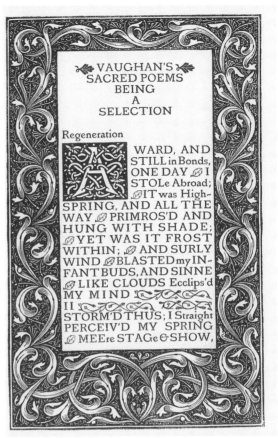

William Morris, *The Defence of Guenevere*. Marginal notes and certain lines of text in red. Kelmscott Press, London, 1892. [C.43.e.5]

Henry Vaughan, *Sacred Poems*, designed, and the decorations engraved, by Charles Ricketts. Ballantyne Press, Edinburgh, for Hacon & Ricketts, London, 1897. [C.99.e.3]

'rather more to the Gothic'. 'After a while,' wrote Morris, 'I felt I must have a Gothic … fount; and herein the task I set myself was to redeem the Gothic character from the charge of unreadableness which is commonly brought against it. The result (which tends to the roman) was seen first in *The Recuyell of the Historyes of Troy* (1893). For the monumental *Works of Geoffrey Chaucer* (1896) a smaller version of the Troy type was required.

Morris certainly put his ideas to the test in the works which he produced at the Kelmscott Press. Fifty-three books with a total of some 18,000 copies issued from it in 1891–8; their impact on every press in every part of the world can hardly be over-stated. This influence, however, was indirect, in that the Kelmscott Press first inspired the creation of a number of other private presses through which it gradually imparted its principles to the mass of printers, though 'Morris set the trade printer a standard which he could never hope to reach, and widened rather than diminished the gap be-tween the ideal book and the book of every day' – A. J. A. Symons.

For Morris himself, ardent socialist though he was, had in mind chiefly the enlight-enment of the few by providing them with choice specimens of what a perfect book should be like. And it must be admitted that in almost every detail his particular preference stood in the way of general application and therefore had to be abandoned

157

William Blake, *Poetical Sketches*, decorations designed and cut on wood by Charles Ricketts. Ballantyne Press, Edinburgh, for the Vale Press, London, 1899. [C.99.e.2]

or modified. Morris's typography was romantic rather than historic (it is no mere coincidence that it was contemporary with the neo-romantic movement in literature), and his delight in gothic type – which posterity has mercilessly classified as pseudo-gothic – ran counter to the whole development of 400 years of western typography. Rightly abhorring the feeble greyishness of contemporary inking, Morris blackened his pages into a graphic pattern which made them all but illegible; disdainful of the cheap and ugly machine-made paper of his day, he employed hand-made paper which was too thick to be practical for everyday handling, as well as too expensive ever to become a business proposition for large-scale editions. The *Chaucer*, Morris's greatest achievement, shows the advantages and disadvantages of his method to the full.

If Morris's roots were in the Middle Ages and the Arts and Crafts movement, Charles Ricketts (1866–1931) was Art Nouveau man; yet they were linked by a scholarly veneration for Renaissance books and an affection for fifteenth-century woodcuts. Ricketts was, says Hodnett, 'the main bridge between the Kelmscott Press and modern fine illustrated book publishing'. He was not a printer, but a designer-publisher, and had his books printed to his designs at the Ballantyne Press. He designed and, with his partner Charles Shannon, illustrated in 1893 an edition of *Daphnis and Chloë*. His Vale Press ran for only seven years, from 1896 to 1903, yet its 48 published works (including as one the 39-volume Shakespeare) are a terrific

HOW SIR TRISTRAM JOUSTED WITH SIR KAY AND SIR SAGRAMORE LE DESIROUS, AND HOW SIR GAWAINE TURNED SIR TRISTRAM FROM MORGAN LE FAY. But anon as the noble knight Sir Launcelot heard of the shield of Cornwall, then wist he well that it was Sir Tristram that fought with his enemies. And then Sir Launcelot praised Sir Tristram, and called him the man of most worship in the world. So there was a knight in that priory that hight Pellinore, and he desired to wit the name of Sir Tristram, but in no wise he could not; and so Sir Tristram departed and left Sir Dinadan in the priory, for he was so weary and so sore bruised that he might not ride. Then this knight Sir Pellinore said to Sir Dinadan, Sithen that ye will not tell me that knight's name, I will ride after him and make him to tell me his name, or he shall die therefor. Beware sir knight, said Sir Dinadan, for an ye follow him ye shall repent it. So that knight Sir Pellinore rode after Sir Tristram and required him of jousts. Then Sir Tristram smote him down and wounded him through the shoulder, and so he passed on his way. And on the next day following Sir Tristram met with pursuivants, and they told him

Thomas Malory, *Le Morte d'Arthur*, illustrated by Aubrey Beardsley. Dent, London, 1893.
[K.T.C.19.a.11]

achievement, not least because Ricketts was not the prisoner of one obsessive or dogmatic design formula but approached each book *de novo*. An eclectic designer, like Whistler, Beardsley and other Art Nouveau designer-artists he was much influenced

THE RAPE OF THE LOCK

CANTO I

WHAT dire Offence from am'rous Causes springs,
What mighty Contests rise from trivial Things,
I sing—This verse to CARYL, Muse! is due:
This, ev'n *Belinda* may vouchsafe to view:

B

I will send you one for 150 guineas." You know
with what brutality—or humour, as we are told it
was—Mr. Whistler replied.

However this may be, one thing is clearly established. In spite of the declarations made in the first
trial, some doubt might have been felt, after reading
Mr. Whistler's letter and the interview, as to whether
he actually took the money. He had the audacity to
state, in a letter to the newspapers, that he had never
used the cheque.* Now the truth is this. The cheque
was given him on February 14, 1894. It was cashed
the next day. The sum in question was never
returned, and never offered to my client. My learned
friend affirms that the money was placed at our
disposal. I am not insisting on a legal offer; Mr.
Whistler cannot be expected to understand the
intricacies of the law. But, as a fact, Mr. Whistler
made no attempt to repay the 100 guineas.* It is
true that Mr. Whistler finally instructed his London
solicitor to offer us the money. But when? On
November 9, 1894.

MAÎTRE BEURDELEY: The day after the summons
had been served.

MAÎTRE BUREAU: Ten months after the payment.

What happened after this scene of February 14?
Mr. Whistler had expressed a wish to add a few

48

Alexander Pope, *The Rape of the Lock*, 'embroidered with
nine drawings by Aubrey Beardsley'. Chiswick Press for
Leonard Smithers, London, 1896. [K.T.C.19.b.9]

James McNeill Whistler, *The Baronet & the Butterfly*.
Whistler's butterflies express a range of emotions. Printed by
Valentine of Paris for R. H. Russell, New York, 1899.
[12331.g.36]

---

by the Japanese style. In his turn his influence, and that of Art Nouveau in general,
can be seen all over modern book design, including the productions of the Nonesuch
Press (which published his passionate *Recollections of Oscar Wilde* in 1932). Although Art Nouveau lasted barely ten years from the publication of the first number
of *The Studio* in 1893, its short life was exciting and its influence pervasive.

The exciting *fin-de-siècle* decade of the Aesthetic Movement opened with the publication of *The Gentle Art of Making Enemies* (1890) by the artist James McNeill
Whistler, whose idiosyncratic book designs, characterized by dangerously balanced
title-pages, are said to have interested Oscar Wilde, and through him Ricketts. Aubrey
Beardsley followed with Malory's *Morte d'Arthur* (1893) – which Morris resented as
a parody of the Kelmscott style – and his notoriously erotic illustrations for Wilde's
Salomé (1894), Pope's *Rape of the Lock* (1894) and Aristophanes' *Lysistrata* (1896).

4. THE READING PUBLIC

The technical and organizational improvements of the nineteenth- and twentieth-
century printing trade were called forth by the growing literacy of ever-widening
classes. In turn, the reading public became larger and larger because it was offered
more and cheaper reading-matter and greater facilities for obtaining it by loan,
purchase or subscription.

Compulsory and free education on the elementary-school level was achieved, at
least on paper, in most civilized countries in the course of the nineteenth century. The

fight against illiteracy has become a growing concern of our own time. At the same time there has become vocal an increasing concern with the results of this increasing literacy.

On the one hand, there is the basic question of the purpose of educating the masses. What use is the knowledge of reading if it is applied to worthless or even debasing trash? The optimists of the nineteenth century had no such qualms. Tolstoy was a voice crying in the wilderness when in 1866 he cursed 'that most powerful engine of ignorance, the diffusion of printed matter' (*War and Peace*, second epilogue). The utilitarians were confident that improved education would result in greater fitness for coping with the economic and technical advances of the time; liberal politicians predicted from it a better preparation for good citizenship and a growth of international understanding. We know the results. 'The penalty of universal literacy', as a writer in *The Times Literary Supplement* put it in 1953, may well be our 'moving into an age when everyone will know how to read but none will turn his knowledge to good purpose'.

On the other hand, there is much doubt about the results of compulsory school attendance, which in Britain was enforced by the Elementary Education Act, 1870. Statistics are invoked to show that semi-literacy or even downright illiteracy is prevalent among the products of our schools. The situation, it is true, has changed from the time, beginning with the invention of script and lasting until the end of the eighteenth century, when the number of people who would read was more or less identical with those who could read. However, these complaints often result from disregarding the general rise of the standard of education as well as some of the principal agencies of modern literacy.

The development of the past 200 years has dethroned the book and the pamphlet as the primary reading-matter. Their place has been taken by the newspaper and the periodical. The transformation of the newspaper into an instrument of mass-information and mass-education, into the voice – often shrill, but always unfettered – of democracy, is the major contribution of the United States of America to the history of the printed word. The American newspaper was perhaps the most influential single factor in converting the millions of immigrants from despotic Russia, authoritarian Germany, lawless Ireland, illiterate Italy into citizens of a democratic republic; in making them throw their national, social, religious differences into the 'melting-pot'; and in teaching them what became known as the American way of life. This process required a simple language, a forthright style and a colourful presentation very different from what European journalists and readers were accustomed to; but it proved to be the medium proper to the spirit of the age of expanding democracy.

Unlike the American press, the English newspapers were, up to the middle of the nineteenth century, severely handicapped by the stamp duty. It was enacted in 1712 and its amount was successively raised from $\frac{1}{2}d.$ to $4d.$ per copy in 1815. This 'tax on knowledge' kept the price of English newspapers artificially high. Moreover, the stamp duty forced the editors to make the utmost use of every square inch of the type area. This need for economy forbade any 'waste' of space through cross-heads, paragraphs, leading and similar devices, and thus required from newspaper readers the closest attention line by line and put a heavy strain on their eyesight. But even the abolition of the stamp duty in 1855 did not greatly influence the make-up of the English newspaper. It was still mainly read by the middle classes, to whom the newspaper was a means of information rather than relaxation.

Change came when American methods, labelled the 'New Journalism', reached England in 1888; that is to say, four years after the Country Franchise Act had nearly doubled the number of voters. It was chiefly these newly enfranchised masses to which the New Journalism addressed itself. Skilfully anglicized by the genius of journalists and businessmen of the calibre of W. T. Stead, Alfred Harmsworth, George Newnes and C. A. Pearson, the New Journalism did away with the solidity and stolidity of the Victorian newspaper. The signal success of the *Daily Mail*, *Daily Express* and *Daily News* in the end forced even the 'high-class' papers, the *Daily Telegraph* and *The Times*, to admit such 'Americanisms' as banner headlines, signed articles, illustrations, crossword puzzles and ready-made advertising displays that had not gone through the hands of the paper's compositors.

If America gave birth to the modern newspaper, Scotland can claim the paternity of the modern periodical. The serious periodical, which addresses itself to the student of politics, literature and the arts, started with the quarterly *Edinburgh Review* (1802–1929); its publisher was Archibald Constable, its first editors Sydney Smith and Francis (Lord) Jeffrey. Its full-blooded Whiggism was counteracted by the Tory *Quarterly Review* (founded 1809), published by John Murray and first edited by William Gifford. Blackwood's monthly *Edinburgh Magazine* (founded 1817) eschewed the fierce partisanship of the two Reviews and put literature before politics. London caught up with the Scots in the 1820s, with the *London Magazine* (1820–9), the *Westminster Review* (1824–1914), the *Spectator* (1828 to date) and the *Athenaeum* (1828–1921). Among the most important later periodicals were the *Saturday Review* (1855–1938), the *Cornhill Magazine* (founded 1860), the *Contemporary Review* (1866 to date) and the *Fortnightly Review* (founded 1865, now incorporated in the *Contemporary Review*). Their success was largely due to the co-operation of notable writers and politicians. Carlyle, Hazlitt and Macaulay wrote for the *Edinburgh Review*; Scott, Canning and Southey for the *Quarterly*; Lockhart, George Eliot and Lord Lytton for *Blackwood's*; De Quincey, Hazlitt and Lamb for the *London Magazine*; and Thackeray was the first editor of the *Cornhill*. Charles Dickens's magazine *Household Words*, in which he serialized *Hard Times*, was launched in 1850 with a circulation of 100,000. The same figure was reached with the fifteenth monthly part of his *Pickwick Papers*, and by the *Cornhill*.

The weekly paper of predominantly political colour has not caught on in any other country. The 'serious' French, German and Italian magazines usually put discussions of literary and artistic affairs in the foreground. The *Revue des deux mondes* (1829–1944), the *Nouvelle Revue de Paris* (founded 1866), the *Nuova Antologia* (1866 to date), *La Cultura* (1881–1935), the *Neue deutsche Rundschau* (founded 1874) have been, or are, the most notable in this field.

F. A. Brockhaus (1772–1823), perhaps the most enterprising German publisher, tried several times to found a periodical which, as he somewhat pathetically said when launching *Hermes* (1819–31), should 'emulate the *Edinburgh Review* in fighting for freedom of thought and against everything which impedes the progress of civilization and the emancipation of the nations that have attained maturity, as far as this is possible in view of the backwardness of political knowledge in Germany'. However, all but one of Brockhaus's ventures foundered on the rock of censorship – Goethe suppressed *Isis* in 1819 – or for lack of interest. His one great success, the *Literarisches Wochenblatt* (1820–98), shows in the very title its specialization; a curious feature of this 'weekly' is its appearance, until 1853, four to six times per week.

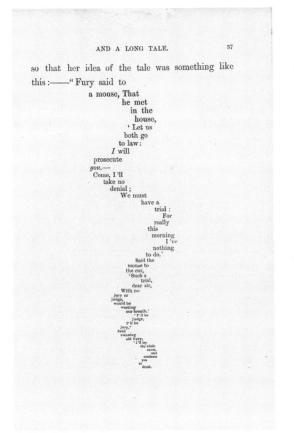
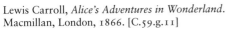

Lewis Carroll, *Alice's Adventures in Wonderland.*
Macmillan, London, 1866. [C.59.g.11]

A. H. Mackmurdo, *Wren's City Churches*. G. Allen,
Orpington, Kent, 1883. [C.102.i.10]

The fierce party struggle between the Whigs and Tories during the Napoleonic wars, accompanied by the equally fierce partisanship of rival schools of literature, gave the impetus to the earliest 'heavy' reviews. A generation later the struggle for parliamentary reform and the enfranchisement of a large new urban population, accompanied by the rising tide of middle-class moralism and scientific realism in philosophy and literature, was responsible for the genesis of the lighter kind of magazine. 'A cheap weekly periodical devoted to wholesome popular instruction, blended with original amusing matter', was the paper Robert and William Chambers wanted to create with their *Edinburgh Journal*; starting in 1832 with 30,000 copies, its circulation rose to 90,000 in 1845 and thus justified the brothers' bold enterprise. After an honourable career of more than 120 years *Chambers's Journal* ceased to appear in 1956, when its circulation stood at about 10,000. In Germany the *Gartenlaube* (1853–1916) tried in a similar vein to combine popular instruction with light entertainment; with 400,000 subscribers in the early 1870s, it can be said to have moulded the literary taste, the secularist philosophy and the pseudo-liberalism of the Protestant *bourgeoisie* of nineteenth-century Germany.

The penny magazines went farthest in bringing regular reading-matter to the masses. They started in the United States in the 1820s, came soon to England, and from England conquered the Continent. The Society for the Diffusion of Useful Knowledge, founded by Charles Knight in 1826, began the publication of the *Penny*

Cyclopaedia in 1833; 75,000 copies were sold at weekly instalments of 1*d*. The first German *Pfennigmagazin* began in 1833 with 35,000 subscribers and soon reached the 100,000. Its editor, the Swiss-born J. J. Weber (1803–80), continued this success with the *Leipziger Illustrierte Zeitung* which, modelled on the *Illustrated London News*, he brought out under his own imprint from 1843. The effect on the readers of these periodicals was described by Charles Knight. 'They took the patronage of men of letters out of the hands of the great and the fashionable, and confided it to the people. They might not create poets and philosophers, but they prevented Kings and Lords pretending to create them.'

The strain of moral improvement and scientific enlightenment has, from the 1880s, gradually disappeared from the general type of 'light' periodicals, and mere entertainment has become their watchword. Even writers on educational features now try to present their subjects 'without tears' – including causeries on the atom bomb or the Budget. At the same time there has taken place an increasing specialization and multiplication of magazines, so that by now there is hardly any activity, interest or hobby that is not being catered for by a weekly or monthly, with cookery and gardening probably leading in appeal to the largest group of readers.

Two classes in particular have swelled the ranks of readers of light magazines since the 1870s – women and children; and the number of magazines specially written for them has been legion. There was a period, lasting roughly from 1870 to 1910, when children's periodicals exerted a great and wholesome influence in supplementing the school curriculum to which the Education Act of 1870 subjected millions of boys and girls. The *Boys' Own Paper* (1879–1966) was the best-known of these often excellent and never harmful magazines; they have been defeated in recent years by comics and television.

While it is undoubtedly true that newspapers and periodicals have obtained a firmer hold on the classes as well as the masses than the book ever had, the relative decline of the book as the principal reading-matter has been paralleled by an absolute increase of book-production and book-circulation. In this respect, the lending library (rental library in American parlance) and the public library must be singled out for their influence on the reading habits as well as the reading-matter of the masses.

The German playwright and short-story writer, Heinrich von Kleist, gave a succinct description of the 'climate' which made the lending libraries prosper. 'Nowhere', he wrote in 1800, 'can the civilization of a town and its prevalent taste be studied more quickly and incidentally more accurately than in its lending libraries.' Books by Wieland, Schiller, Goethe are not in stock, as 'nobody reads them'. – What, then, do you keep? – 'Gothick novels, only Gothick novels: here on the right, those with ghosts, there on the left, those without ghosts: take your choice.'

Wilhelm Hauff, the Swabian novelist, in 1825 wrote a sketch on 'Books and the reading public', which confirms Kleist's experience. The staple diet of the lending libraries consisted of Gothick novels, trashy love stories and – Walter Scott. The immense popularity of Scott's novels needs no explanation; their diffusion all over Europe was accelerated by the fact that, in the days before the Berne Convention on copyright, neither copyright fees nor royalties had to be paid for translations; their place in the lending libraries was assured by the prohibitive price of the original editions. Walter Scott was, if not the inventor, at least the first popularizer of the 'three-decker' which dominated nineteenth-century fiction – the novel published in three volumes at the high, arbitrary and artificial price of 31*s*. 6*d*. This price, more

Christina Rossetti, *Goblin Market*, illustrated by Laurence Houseman. R. & R. Clark, Edinburgh, for Macmillan, London, 1893. [11647.f.33]

than any other factor, explains the dominating position of the circulating library in the English book market between 1820 and 1890.

The man who most profited by this trend and whose name has become almost synonymous with the term 'lending library', was Charles Edward Mudie (1810–90). 'Mudie's Lending Library' was opened in London in 1842; its annual subscription of one guinea guaranteed its success – being the equivalent of the retail price of two parts of one three-decker novel. Within a short time Mudie came near to being the sole arbiter of literary taste in fiction. He certainly exerted a ruthless dictatorship over the authors and publishers of this kind of literature: keeping within the narrow confines of Victorian middle-class respectability was the surest way to find favour with Mudie. Charlotte Yonge, Rhoda Broughton, Ouida, Marie Corelli were the giants among the 'Queens of the Circulating Library': it needs little imagination to picture the level of the average and the pygmies. Anthony Trollope may be ranked among the few survivors of Mudie's deadening patronage. George Meredith's *The Ordeal of Richard Feverel* and George Moore's *A Modern Lover* are typical examples of the kind of literature which Mudie excluded from his shelves as unsuitable for the great English public.

Authors and publishers who conformed to the literary, moral and social standards set up by Mudie enjoyed the security of a steady sale of their products; and when they went on long enough to supply the prescribed fare, they achieved an outwardly impressive popularity. However, their vogue was as artificial and mass-made as their productions. They were successful only as types and cumulatively; no single work of any of them – perhaps with the exception of Yonge's *The Heir of Redclyffe* (1853), which reaped the benefit of coinciding with the high-water mark of the Anglican High Church revival – achieved success on its own merits. But as not a few of these authors wrote up to or over 100 books, they had little difficulty in passing the 100,000 mark or a multiple of it. Mrs Henry Wood, for instance, bagged a total of over 2½ million copies, including the half million of *East Lynne* which two publishers had rejected before Bentley took it on with some misgivings. Mudie's dominion came to an end in the 1890s when the one-volume novel had ousted the three-decker.

It was in the English-speaking countries that public libraries established themselves as an integral part of public instruction and recreation. Only in those countries which are akin to the Anglo-American political and cultural outlook did the public library movement take roots: the Scandinavian countries, the Low Countries and Switzerland. The usefulness of public libraries was recognized earlier in Germany than anywhere else: in 1524 Luther urged the municipal authorities to use the endowments and bequests invalidated by the dissolution of the monasteries for the establishment not only of grammar schools but also of 'good libraries or book-houses'.

The following figures illustrate the success of public libraries in the United States. In 1994 15,273 libraries held 642 million books and circulated 1.5 billion. New York held 11 million and circulated 10 million; Chicago held 11 million and circulated 7 million; Los Angeles held 8 million and circulated 6 million. Comparable British figures are equally impressive. In 1994 4075 libraries held 131 million books and circulated 550 million (a rise of 27 per cent over the 1960 figure of 430 million); London held 7 million and circulated 17 million; Birmingham held 2 million and circulated 6 million; Manchester held 2 million and circulated 3 million. Run as a public utility under the Ewart Bill of 1850, the public libraries have never tried to impose their will on either their customers or their suppliers. Tacitly excluding trash, they have taken their part in the educational system very seriously, in providing for special needs such as children's departments and reference libraries, assisting the student through the publication of select lists on a variety of topics, and generally striking a happy balance between the demands of the low-brow and high-brow sections of the reading world. Their dependence on, and supervision by, democratically elected corporations has tended to even out political and denominational bias, while at the same time exposing the librarians to the fresh wind of public criticism – with the result that all classes of readers are, and know that they are, served well.

5. POPULAR SERIES

'Knowledge is power' – this aphorism of Francis Bacon became, in the nineteenth century, the watchword of the rising middle classes to whom the extension of voluntary and compulsory schooling opened the world of letters. '*Bildung macht frei*' was the motto which Joseph Meyer put on the title-pages of his Groschen-Bibliothek (penny library). It would be easy to mock the education of the half-literate masses of the nineteenth century (and after!) with their belief in 'progress', which only too often meant the blind acceptance of fashionable half-truths; but there was also much serious striving after deeper and wider knowledge. Among the popular institutions which catered for the newly literate – such as evening classes, extension courses, etc. – the popular series of cheap books must rank very high.

As in so many other fields, John Bell was also the pioneer of cheap reprints in uniform editions at a uniform price. He refused to join the conger of London publishers who financed Dr Johnson's *British Poets*, and launched a series, under the same title, of 109 volumes at the price of 6s. (1777–82). Apart from Johnson's prefatory *Lives of the Poets*, which have remained a glory of English literary criticism, his series failed, whereas Bell's succeeded. The reason may be found in the different attitude of the editors: Bell passionately believed in the educational value of his enterprise, whereas Johnson was sceptical about all cheap editions, whose publishers he described as 'no better than Robin Hood who robbed the rich in order to give to the poor'.

The advance on the political scene of a public of less wealth and leisure than heretofore about 1830, and the enforced idleness in comparative comfort which railway travelling afforded from about 1840, were two important stimuli to turn the minds of publishers to the production of cheap literature. Archibald Constable was the first to speak of 'literature for the millions'. Printed on the newly invented machine-made wood-pulp paper, issued in paper boards or inexpensive publishers' cloth, and sold by stationers and railway bookstalls, these books were intended, like modern paperbacks, to be discarded after perusal with little regret on the part of the buyer.

William Pickering's six-shilling classics, Archibald Constable's Miscellany (1827–35), John Murray's Family Library (1829–34), Colburn & Bentley's Novels (1831–54) were the first of these series. They stressed the educational rather than the entertaining side of reading. Constable's series consisted chiefly of writings on travel and history, most of which were specially commissioned for it. Of Colburn & Bentley's series the *Spectator* wrote: 'When classical and highly priced standard works are thus placed within the reach of humble means, assuredly before the lapse of many years there will not be a house which gives the occupier a right to vote that has not also its little library.' Their prices were mostly 6s. per volume, a figure which has to be set against the standard price of 31s. 6d. for a nineteenth-century three-decker novel.

A further advance in mass-production and cheapness was made with the Irish Parlour Library, launched by Simms & McIntyre (1847–63; some 300 vols), and with George Routledge's Railway Library (1848–98; 1300 vols). Both limited themselves to fiction and sold at 1s. each volume. Their instantaneous success was partly due to their display in the railway bookstalls of the firm of W. H. Smith, the first of which was opened in 1848 at Euston Station. Smith also procured for this venture special railway editions of the standard three-decker novels, made up in one volume at the price of 6s.

The first popular series in Europe which made use of the new inventions of cheap mass-production clearly show their indebtedness to English models. The 'Pocket-Novelists' which the Frankfurt publisher Carl Jügel issued in the 1830s show their Englishness by their very title; they were aimed chiefly at the numerous English travellers who visited the romantic Rhine valley and thronged the fashionable spas and casinos of the Taunus mountains. This somewhat ephemeral series was followed by the 'Collection of British [later: and American] Authors' with which the Leipzig printer Christian Bernhard Tauchnitz (1816–95) in 1841 raised his small publishing department to the rank of a house of international fame. With eventually (1939) more than 5400 titles the Tauchnitz series was, for nearly a century, the cherished companion of English-speaking travellers in central Europe and the royal road for foreign students to the treasures of English and American literature. Tauchnitz secured the good will of the English writers and publishers by an unprecedented step. Although not obliged to do so under the then conditions of international copyright, he asked for the 'authority and sanction' of the authors and voluntarily paid them royalties on his reprints; at the same time he pledged himself not to sell these reprints in England and the Empire, while raising no objections to the sale of the original editions in Germany. Macaulay and Thackeray were among the largest beneficiaries of Tauchnitz's liberalism; and when he once apologized for his deficient English, Thackeray replied that Tauchnitz should not worry as 'a letter accompanied by £50 is always in good style'.

William Shakespeare is the author who eventually stabilized the era of popular editions of good literature at bargain prices. Or rather it was 'Unser Shakespeare' who thus became 'a jewel well worth a poor man's taking'. For, preceding Macmillan's *Globe Shakespeare* of 1864 (which, at 3s. 6d., sold 20,000 copies within a few months), the Leipzig publisher Anton Philipp Reclam brought out, in 1858, a 12-volume edition at 1½ taler (4s. 6d.) which, at half the price of the next-cheapest German edition, reached its sixth edition within a year. Moreover, this tremendous success encouraged Reclam to issue in 1865 the 25 individual plays at the equivalent of 3d. each.

By way of parenthesis it may be noted that in those same years the study of textual problems of printed texts also grew out of research work done on Shakespeare. Critical bibliography, as it is now called, was inaugurated in 1855 by Tycho Mommsen, brother of the great historian, and its outstanding achievements – by A. W. Pollard, R. B. McKerrow, Sir W. W. Greg, F. P. Wilson and Fredson Bowers – derive mainly from the scrutiny of texts of the age of Shakespeare.

The signal success of the Shakespeare edition suggested to Reclam the launching of a uniform series of similar booklets of literary quality at the same low price; each volume to be sold separately. Thus was born Reclam's Universal-Bibliothek, the model of popular series all over the world. It began in 1867 with the first part of Goethe's *Faust*; and although plays continued for a long time to be the backbone of the series, the advertisement of the first 40 numbers already contains short stories, poems and essays. The price of 20 pfennigs (2½d.) remained unaltered until 1917. After 75 years, in 1942, it comprised about 8000 numbers, printed in about 275 million copies. After the destruction of its stocks during the Second World War and the subsequent sovietization of the firm, Reclam began its reconstruction in Stuttgart in 1947. By 1967, over 2100 titles had been reissued, totalling over 118 million copies; the list is headed by Schiller's *Tell* with 2,100,000.

Among the most remarkable successes of the Universal-Bibliothek must be counted the Norwegian playwright, Ibsen. Between 1877 and 1942, Reclam sold over 6 million copies of the German translations of nineteen of his works: *Peer Gynt* leads with 719,000 copies, followed by *A Doll's House* (584,000), and even his poems reached the 100,000 mark. Some may consider it even more remarkable that Plato and Kant each achieved a sale of over 930,000 copies, followed by Schopenhauer with 860,000 – of whose first book only 140 copies had been sold in 25 years. Of interest to the English reader is the order of precedence accorded by the German public to British and American writers in this series: Shakespeare (6.4 million copies), Dickens (1.5 million), Mark Twain (776,000), Poe (455,000), Scott (424,000), with

Wilde, Byron, Darwin and Faraday as close runners-up. The postwar series includes translations of *Beowulf*, *Gulliver*, *Robinson Crusoe*, and writings by Conrad, Dickens, Dreiser, Faraday, Faulkner, Forster, Greene, Hemingway, Aldous Huxley, Kipling, T. E. Lawrence, Maugham, Melville, Poe, Priestley, Shaw (*Pygmalion*), Stevenson, Wilde and Thomas Wolfe. Students of literary taste and of national psychology may find food for thought in these lists.

The editor of Cassell's National Library, Henry Morley, had previously edited Morley's Universal Library (which Routledge published and kept in print, at the customary price of 1s., until about 1910). The National Library was started in 1886 and within four years issued 209 volumes in weekly intervals at the price of 3d. each paper-bound and 6d. cloth-bound. Morley wrote an introduction to each volume, and the series covered practically the whole range of English literature. Standard non-copyright fiction was included, but with a strictly moral outlook, and such works as the *Decameron* and *Tom Jones* were carefully eschewed. The Library was a great success, and the average sale of the titles was 30,000 each, amounting to nearly 7 million in all. Later on, in 1907–8, Cassells undertook a similar series, called People's Library; of its 85 titles 900,000 copies were sold at 8d. a title. These were mostly fiction, tempered with Bacon's *Essays*, Marcus Aurelius's *Meditations* and the inevitable Macaulay's *Essays*.

The isolated position of these two Cassell ventures may be ascribed to two factors. One is the high cost of production in Britain owing to the high wages of British compositors and printers, compared with those abroad. The other, the attitude of the Victorian reading public. It seems to have wanted more substantial fare to get its teeth into, at least as regards size; and it therefore asked for larger volumes, which in Reclam's Universal-Bibliothek would occupy three, four or more 'numbers', and these in solid binding, for which Reclam would charge a higher price.

The growth of Reclam's Universal-Bibliothek was greatly facilitated by the expiration, in 1867, of the exclusive copyright privileges which the German Confederation had bestowed on certain authors and publishers. Henceforth, 30 years after the death of an author, his writings became 'free'. This at once released Goethe, Schiller, Lessing, Kleist, E. T. A. Hoffmann, Jean Paul and other classical and romantic writers for inclusion in cheap reprint series.

A similar effect on the English market was produced by the Copyright Act of 1842. This stipulated that copyright should cease seven years after an author's death or 42 years from the publication of a book. The result was that, round about the year 1900, all or most of the writings of Dickens, Thackeray, Disraeli, Lytton, George Eliot, the Brontës, Carlyle, Ruskin – in brief, all the great Victorians – became available.

William Somerville, *The Chase*, wood-engravings by James Scott. Cundee, London, 1804. [11633.d.4]

CHAPTER IV

1900–1955

It is surprising to recall that when the twentieth century dawned the Linotype and Monotype hot-metal composing machines had recently proved themselves, yet most type was still set by hand; William Morris was dead, but five of the great English private presses were well established; Art Nouveau was in the middle of its short life; and, while lithography was a hundred years old, offset lithographic printing was still restricted to tinplate. By 1955, when this book was first published, virtually all commercially produced books were set by Monotype or Linotype and printed from type or relief plates, and the private presses had all but disappeared.

I. LINOTYPE AND MONOTYPE

The first Linotype machine was installed in *The New York Tribune* in 1886. Its inventor, Ottmar Mergenthaler (1854–99), was an immigrant from Württemberg who added his skill as a watchmaker to the restless inventiveness of the Baltimore engineer, James O. Clephane. After ten years' work Mergenthaler produced the Linotype (= line o' type) machine on which almost every newspaper in the world was for many years composed. Mergenthaler's basic innovation was that of circulating matrices, which consist of pieces of brass punched with letters, figures and punctuation marks. On the summons of an operator tapping the keys the pieces of brass are brought together in a line, automatically spaced, for the faces to make a cast impression in type. The matrices are then mechanically returned to the channels of a magazine, whence they may be brought into use over and over again.

The greatest perfection of the composing machine, however, was accomplished by the American Tolbert Lanston (1844–1913), the inventor of the Monotype machine. First produced in 1889 and commercially established in 1897, the Monotype machine is based on principles similar to the Linotype but has the advantage of casting each character and space separately. Whereas a skilled compositor had so far been able to compose about 2000 letters an hour, the average output of the Linotype and Monotype operator is at least 6000 in the same time. There are however important functional differences between the two machines. Whereas the Linotype operator produces 'slugs' (lines of type) single-handed, the punched paper tape produced by the Monotype keyboard operator has to be run on a separate casting machine, which needs its own attendant. Against this may be set the fact that while an alteration in Monotype setting can be corrected by a compositor from a case of type, Linotype alterations necessitate setting up the machine all over again for corrected lines of type to be keyed and run out.

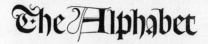

Frederick W. Goudy, *The Alphabet*. W. E. Rudge for Mitchell Kennerley, New York, 1918. [7943.k.61]

D. B. Updike, *Printing Types*. Merrymount Press, Boston, for Harvard University Press, Cambridge, Mass., 1922. [011903.cc.43]

The introduction of these machines attracted snobbish attacks from those such as Bernard Newdigate of the Arden Press who (whatever their motives) believed, or affected to believe, that top-quality work could not be obtained from them. It is true that during the first decades of their existence this belief was given credence by the almost universal dullness of the types cut for them. However, this attitude persisted (indeed, it survives today, in the 'Hand-set in ...' sales pitch) after it had been discredited by some excellent work, particularly from the Monotype Corporation itself, the university presses and Francis Meynell's Nonesuch Press – not to mention the unmistakable economies offered by their use.

In 1922 interest in type design was stimulated by the publication of D. B. Updike's *Printing Types*, and it was probably in that same year that the Monotype Corporation appointed the typographic polymath Stanley Morison (1889–1967) as its adviser on design matters. Morison initiated a programme of recutting for Monotype composition many great designs from the past: Bembo, Poliphilus, Garamond, Ehrhardt, Van Dijck, Baskerville, Fournier, Bell, Walbaum. Additionally during Morison's reign Bruce Rogers's Centaur, Eric Gill's Perpetua, Joanna and Gill Sans and several typefaces designed by Frederick Goudy were made available on the Monotype, and the immensely successful Times New Roman was created. Morison, who added to his Monotype position a similar one with Cambridge University Press, found an ally in the University Printer there, Walter Lewis. The Press was then prominent in fine printing, and Lewis saw advantages in being the first to use the new faces; Morison found it useful that Cambridge were both a ready customer for them and exemplary printers of them. The splendid renaissance of British book production which preceded the Second World War and continued rather palely thereafter was synonymous with Monotype composition.

The Linotype company was far from idle at this time, and produced several distinguished faces including Granjon, W. A. Dwiggins's Caledonia and Electra and Gill's Pilgrim. For the first half of this century, until the arrival of phototypesetting, Linotype composition dominated U.S. book production. While most hot-metal Penguins were set on the Monotype, the vast majority of British paperbacks from other houses were slug-set: the great bulk of these were resettings of successful hardback books, and therefore attracted a very low incidence of authors' alterations.

2. THE LATIN ALPHABET IN SCRIPT AND PRINT

One of the long-term results of Gutenberg's invention was the irretrievable separation of formal book-hand and informal business-hand. The former was absorbed by the printed type while the latter degenerated into the illegibility of every man's hand worse than his neighbour's. This rot was eventually stopped by means which underline the complete ascendency of the type-cutter over the calligrapher. On the one hand the bulk of handwriting has been transferred to the typewriter (and more recently the word-processor and computer), essentially a one-man printing press. On the other hand modern script reformers have drawn their inspiration mainly from the hands of the Florentine and Roman scribes of the Renaissance, which served as models for the cutting of roman and italic founts. This conservative return to the beginnings of modern lettering is equally marked in the typefaces now most commonly used in commercial as well as fine printing.

The nations which thus follow the lead given by the humanists of Italy and France have gained two new adherents in the twentieth century, Turkey and Germany. It was a notable event in the history of civilization when in 1928 Turkey adopted the Latin script and prohibited the publication of books in Arabic characters. The high standard of calligraphy and the resistance of the professional scribes had delayed the introduction of printing in Turkish until 1729 when a Hungarian renegade, who on his conversion to Islam adopted the name of Ibrahim Müteferrika (1674–1745), set up the first Turkish press in Constantinople. After his death the press ceased to exist; it had produced 17 books (in 23 volumes), including an Arabic dictionary and a Turkish-French grammar. The next press was established by Sultan Abdul Hamid I in 1784 as an official press, but it never achieved any distinction.

More gradual was the elimination of Fraktur from the German-speaking world. The first to rebel against the monopoly of gothic were the German scientists, doctors, economists and technicians. The very nature of their studies forced them into international collaboration, and throughout the nineteenth century they printed their books and periodicals in roman, so as to make them reach a non-German public.

The final conversion of German printing to roman type, however, was not achieved

related to me by a cattle man who was engaged in bringing out blooded stock from the East. Among the animals under his charge were two great stallions, one gray and one black, and a fine jackass, not much over half the size of either of the former. The animals were kept in separate pens, but one day both horses got into the same inclosure, next to the jack-pen, and began to fight as only enraged stallions can, striking like boxers

A HARD TRAIL.

with their fore feet, and biting with their teeth. The gray was getting the best of it; but while clinched with his antagonist in one tussle they rolled against the jack-pen, breaking it in. No sooner was the jack at liberty than, with ears laid back and mouth wide open, he made straight for the two horses, who had for the moment separated.

Theodore Roosevelt, *Ranch Life and the Hunting Trail*, illustrated by Frederic Remington. Century, New York, 1902. [10881.g.29]

by the natural growth of popular preference or change of taste as had been the case in western Europe in the fifteenth and sixteenth, in England and America in the seventeenth, and in northern Europe in the nineteenth centuries. It was imposed from above on a reluctant or indifferent people. For some time the Nazis were in two minds. As long as they considered their creed primarily a matter for home consumption, they were inclined to enforce the use of gothic type as the genuine typographic expression of the Nordic soul. When, however, the vistas of the New Order of Europe and of world domination began to fire their minds, Hitler shrewdly realized the advantages that would accrue to them from presenting the case of Nazi Germany in the typographical guise best calculated to be appreciated by the non-German world. Thus on 3 January 1941 it was decreed that 'the so-called gothic type' was a Jewish invention ('*Schwabacher-Judenlettern*') and that therefore Antiqua was henceforth to be the 'normal script' of the German people – despite its nonsensical argumentation, the one good thing Hitler did for German civilization.

This expansion of the Latin alphabet and roman type unfortunately stopped at the frontiers of the former Soviet Union. In the early 1920s Lenin set up a commission to work out a simplified spelling of the Russian language and to make recommendations for its transcription into the Latin alphabet, but the revival and intensification of Russian nationalism under Stalin wrecked this scheme. Far from being abandoned, the Russian alphabet was imposed on the colonial peoples in the Asian parts of the Soviet Union.

In 1958 the Chinese government adopted the *pinyin* 'phonetic spelling' system of 58 symbols, intended to supersede the 30,000 logographs formerly used to print and write Chinese; the government's further aim was to popularize the codified standard Mandarin, now known as *putonghua* ('common language'). The old characters continue in use in Taiwan and (for the moment) Hong Kong.

The advance of the Latin alphabet is all the more remarkable as its characters are in theory by no means suited to the requirements of any modern language. The twenty letters of the original Latin alphabet were meant to reproduce the sounds of an Old Italian dialect; they were not even invented by the Latins but adapted from an altogether different language, colonial Greek; and even this Greek alphabet was originally devised to express the sounds of a Semitic language. Thus it is easily understandable that the characters first designed by the Phoenicians 3000 years ago are most imperfect to reproduce the words uttered by a twentieth-century European.

These inherent difficulties can be clearly shown in the greatly varying attempts of the western nations to find a satisfactory sign for sibilants, in which the Latin alphabet is notoriously deficient. The same sign s has to express (as visible in this sentence) two entirely different sounds, one of which, moreover, may cede its place to c (as in cent) or sc (as in scent), the other to z (as in size). The shooing sound is rendered sh in English, ch in French, sc(i) in Italian, sch in German, sz in Polish, š in Czech; and in transliterating the simple Russian consonant Щ the German compositor has to use seven characters (schtsch), his English colleague four (shch) and even the Czech still two (šč).

Only three later Roman additions – the letters, x, y, z – and three late-medieval inventions – j, v, w – have been preserved in the printed alphabet; and it is to be regretted that William Caxton and his disciples did not save one of the most useful creations of Germanic scribes, namely þ, to denote the dental fricative. Its form had, by the fifteenth century, become almost indistinguishable from that of y; and the early English printers therefore used the latter in printing yᵉ and yᵗ for *the* and *that* – simply in order to save space, not because these words were pronounced ye and yat: 'ye olde English tea-shoppe' is a silly pseudo-archaism.

A small number of ligatures and combinations of existing characters were, however, adopted by printers and thus became naturalized in various national literatures: œ = o+e in French, å = a+o in Scandinavian, ä, ö, ü (sometimes still printed as ȧ, ȯ, u̇) and ß in German. Further attempts to approximate the printed word to its phonetic sound have been restricted to the addition of diacritical marks: here the French led the way when, about 1770, they regulated the use of accents, cedilla, trema, and the like, which has, for instance, made the one letter e fulfil five functions (e, é, è, ê, ë). The Slav and Baltic languages have perhaps gone farthest in thus varying Gutenberg's characters; but it may be thought that the ł, ń, ś, ż, ė, ą, ų, etc., of the Polish and Lithuanian alphabets may have impeded rather than eased the approach to these languages and literatures.

Unfortunately, in 1928 the Turks did not accept any of the western alphabets – although the Czech orthography would have been almost ideal for their purposes – but mixed English, French, German and Rumanian spellings with some inventions of their own. This new Turkish alphabet makes the reading of Turkish texts unnecessarily difficult; e.g. c corresponds to English j, ç to English *ch*, j to French j, ş to English *sh*, and so on; an additional awkwardness is the distinction between dotted i (= French i) and undotted ı (= unaccented French e).

A cognate problem is that of the transliteration into Latin characters of non-Latin alphabets such as Chinese, Russian and Arabic. The present confusion, not only between, say, English, French and German transliterations of the same word but even between different schools of thoughtlessness within the English-speaking orbit has to be encountered to be believed.

3. THE PRIVATE PRESSES

Although the Kelmscott Press closed in 1898, at the turn of the century three years later the extraordinary concentration of the arts and crafts in the English private presses was probably at its most intense. C. R. Ashbee's Essex House Press (1898–1910) had taken over Morris's Albions and several Kelmscott men and continued along Arts and Crafts lines, yet their work unmistakably shows Art Nouveau tendencies. Several fine books were produced, including Erasmus's *In Praise of Folly* (1901), a Prayer Book for the accession of Edward VII (1901) and the *Essex House Psalter* (1902).

The Eragny Press (1894–1914) was the inspiration of the painter and printmaker Lucien Pissarro (son of the French painter Camille). Lucien was a friend of Charles Ricketts and Charles Shannon at the Vale Press, whose type he borrowed before his own was cut. His books have 'an intimacy and charm found in none of the other work of his time' (Fern); his unique mastery of the multi-block colour woodcut technique is evident in the books he illustrated in this way, such as Margaret Rust's *The Queen of the Fishes* (1894) and Judith Gautier's *Poèmes tires du livre de jade* (1911), in which he successfully printed gold as the fourth colour.

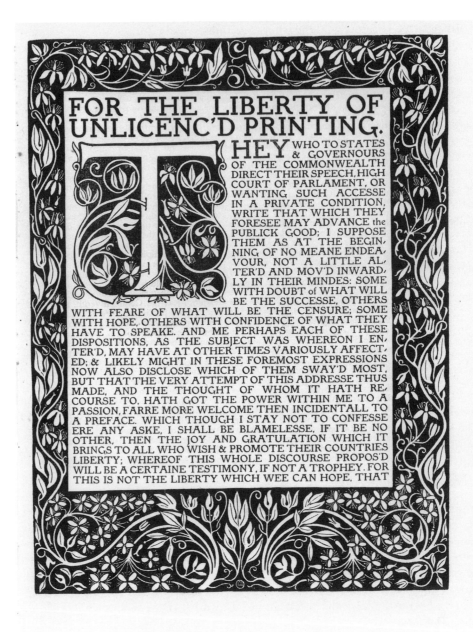

John Milton, *Areopagitica*, borders and initials designed by Lucien Pissarro and engraved on wood by Esther Pissarro. Initials in red. Eragny Press, London, 1903. [C.99.i.1]

Mention must be made here of one of the most important Art Nouveau books, the massive *Also Sprach Zarathustra* (Insel-Verlag, 1908) designed by the architect Henry van de Velde. It resembles a book of the Eragny Press in its type and in the use of gold

The Book of Common Prayer. 'The designs and the type throughout are by C. R. Ashbee; R. Catterson-Smith assisted in the preparation of some of the blocks, which were cut in wood by W. H. Hooper & Clemence Housman.' The Press of the Guild of Handicraft, Essex House, Bow, London, later Chipping Camden, Gloucestershire, 1903. [C.99.l.4]

printing on its ornaments, and shows both Van de Velde's consonance with Morris in the unity of the ideal book, and his profound disagreement in preferring abstract ornament over figurative medievalizing borders.

Although Emery Walker had sensibly declined to be Morris's *de jure* partner in the Kelmscott Press, he agreed to take that part in the Doves Press (1900–17) with T. J. Cobden-Sanderson (1840–1922) – and must have regretted it when they fell out. Their type (Walker's masterpiece, according to Colin Franklin) was directly and judiciously based on that used by Jenson in his *Pliny* (Venice, 1476); they made do with one size of it. Their typography was nearly as austere and majestic as that of Baskerville and Bodoni; none of their books was ever illustrated, their sole embellishments being the coloured calligraphic initial letters drawn by Edward Johnston, such as the famous opening I to the book of Genesis in the Bible (5 volumes, London, 1903–5), which stands in the forefront of English Bibles alongside those of John Baskerville and Bruce Rogers. Doves Press books were characterized by flawless composition and presswork on the finest of papers.

In these respects the only equal of the Doves Press was the Ashendene Press (1894–1935) of C. H. St John Hornby (1863–1946). Like Daniel, early in his printing career Hornby used Fell types from Oxford University Press; but he soon felt the need for a typeface of his own, and called in the ubiquitous Walker. The Subiaco type which resulted from this commission was a recutting of the first roman type of

Sweynheym and Pannartz, used in 1465 for an edition of Cicero's *De Oratore*. As a roman it has – like Morris's Golden type – strong gothic tendencies. It first appeared in the great edition of Dante (1902–9), which Morison called 'a spectacular achievement'. Hornby's later Ptolemy type, seen at its best in his *Thucydides*, was patterned on that used for a *Ptolemy* in 1482 by L. Holle of Ulm. Other fine Ashendene books include the *Ecclesiasticus* and *Morte Darthur*. 'As long as typography is esteemed, the Ashendene books will be given highest rank' – Morison.

The Golden Cockerel Press (1920–61) was unusual among private presses in having three successive owner-managers: Harold Midgeley Taylor, Robert Gibbings and Christopher Sandford. Gibbings reigned from 1926 to 1933, during a period of dull trade-book design, and in that brief time produced no less than 58 very different but always attractive books. His most lasting achievement was, however, to have inspired a great revival of English wood-engraving: as well as illustrating 19 of the books himself he gave early employment to John Buckland-Wright, Blair Hughes-Stanton, Agnes Miller Parker, David Jones and Eric Gill. Gill embellished *Troilus and Criseide* (1927) and *The Canterbury Tales* (1929–31) with borders and initials that work simultaneously as illustrations and as decoration, and Gibbings printed them in Caslon. But every private press seems to have lusted after its own proprietary typeface; the Golden Cockerel was no exception, and Gill designed for Gibbings a hand-

ENTER BARNARDO, AND FRANCISCO,
TWO CENTINELS.

Bar. WHOSE THERE?
Fran. Nay answere me. Stand & vnfolde your selfe.
Bar. Long liue the King.
Fran. Barnardo.
Bar. Hee.
Fran. You come most carefully vpon your houre.
Bar. Tis now strooke twelfe, get thee to bed Francisco.
Fran. For this reliefe much thanks, tis bitter cold,
And I am sick at hart.
Bar. Haue you had quiet guard?
Fran. Not a mouse stirring.
Bar. Well, good night:
If you doe meete Horatio and Marcellus,
The riualls of my watch, bid them make hast.

Enter Horatio, and Marcellus.

Fran. I thinke I heare them, stand ho, who is there?
Hora. Friends to this ground.
Mar. And Leedgemen to the Dane.
Fran. Giue you good night.
Mar. O, farwell honest souldiers, who hath relieu'd you?
Fran. Barnardo hath my place; giue you good night.

Exit Francisco.

Mar. Holla, Barnardo.
Bar. Say, what is Horatio there?

7

William Shakespeare, *Hamlet*, blue initial letter by Edward Johnston. Doves Press, London, 1909.
[C.99.g.30]

Arthur, syre Gawayne and his thre bretheren Agrauayne, Gaherys and sire Mordred sette vpon syre Lamorack in a pryuy place, and there they slewe his hors, and so they fought with hym on foote more than thre houres bothe biforne hym & behynd hym, and sire Mordred gaf hym his dethes wound, behynde hym at his bak, and alle to hewe hym, for one of his squyers told me that sawe hit. Fy vpon treason, said sir Trystram, for hit kylleth my herte to here this tale. So it doth myn, said Gareth, bretheren as they be myn I shall neuer loue them nor drawe in their felaushp for that dede. Now speke we of other dedes, said Palomydes, & lete hym be, for his lyf ye maye not gete ageyne. That is the more pyte, said Dynadan. For sire Gawayne and his bretheren, excepte yow sire Gareth, haten alle the good knyghtes of the round table for the most party, for wel I wote and they myght pryuely, they hate my lord sire Launcelot and al his kynne, & grete pryuy despyte they haue at hym, & that is my lorde syre Launcelot wel ware of, and that causeth hym to haue the good knyghtes of his kyn aboute hym.

⫷CAPITULUM LIX.

How they came to Humberbanke, and how they fonde a shyppe there wherin laye the body of Kyng Hermaunce.

SYRE, SAID PALOMYDES, LETE VS LEVE OF THIS MATERE, and lete vs see how we shalle doo at this turnement. By myn aduyse, said Palomydes, lete vs foure holde to gyders ageynste alle that wyl come. Not by my counceil, said sire Tristram, for I see by their pauelions ther wil be four honderd knyghtes, and doubte ye not, said sir Tristram, but there wil be many good knyghtes, & be a man neuer soo valyaunt nor soo bygge, yet he may be ouermatched. And soo haue I sene knyghtes done many tymes. And whanne they wend best to haue wonne worship they lost hit. For manhode is not worthe, but yf it be medled with wysedome. And as for me, said sir Trystram, hit maye happen I shalle kepe myn owne hede as wel as another. Soo thus they rode vntyl that they came to Humber bank where they herd a crye and a doleful noyse. Thenne were they ware in the wynde where came a ryche vessel hylled ouer with reed sylke, & the vessel londed fast

287

Thomas Malory, *Le Morte Darthur*, illustrations by Margaret Gere cut on wood by W. H. Hooper and J. B. Swain. Headlines and chapter summaries in red, initials in blue. Ashendene Press, London, 1913.
[C.43.i.3]

Canto Quinto.

COSI discesi del cerchio primaio
Giù nel secondo, che men loco cinghia,
E tanto più dolor, che pugne a guaio.
Stavvi Minos orribilmente e ringhia:
Esamina le colpe nell' entrata,
Giudica & manda secondo che avvinghia.
Dico, che quando l'anima mal nata
Li vien dinanzi, tutta si confessa;
E quel conoscitor delle peccata
Vede qual loco d'inferno è da essa:
Cignesi colla coda tante volte
Quantunque gradi vuol che giù sia messa.
Sempre dinanzi a lui ne stanno molte:
Vanno a vicenda ciascuna al giudizio;
Dicono e odono, e poi son giù volte.

30

O tu, che vieni al doloroso ospizio,
Disse Minos a me, quando mi vide,
Lasciando l'atto di cotanto ufizio,
Guarda com' entri, e di cui tu ti fide:
Non t' inganni l'ampiezza dell' entrare!
E il duca mio a lui: Perchè pur gride?
Non impedir lo suo fatale andare:
Vuolsi così colà, dove si puote
Ciò che si vuole, e più non dimandare.
Ora incomincian le dolenti note
A farmisi sentire: or son venuto
Là dove molto pianto mi percote.
Io venni in loco d'ogni luce muto,
Che mugghia come fa mar per tempesta,
Se da contrari venti è combattuto.
La bufera infernal, che mai non resta,
Mena gli spirti con la sua rapina,
Voltando e percotendo li molesta.
Quando giungon davanti alla ruina,
Quivi le strida, il compianto e il lamento,
Bestemmian quivi la virtù divina.

31

Dante Alighieri, *Inferno*, with woodcuts by C. Keates to designs by R. Catterson-Smith based on the original illustrations in the 1491 edition; blue and red initials by Graily Hewitt. Ashendene Press, London, 1902. [C.99.e.11]

some roman reminiscent of his Perpetua, and to accompany it a sloped roman instead of an italic. Gibbings used it for *The Four Gospels* (1931), in which Gill's 'fresh and highly original [engraved] borders and illustrations [are] balanced between the primitive and the modern, ninth-century manuscript illustration distilled into woodcut' – Franklin. The *Gospels* repeated Gill's earlier experimentally dogmatic *Essay on Typography* (1931) in being set unjustified (that is, with standard word-spacing and consequently irregular line-endings), almost unheard of at this period (and still very often looked at askance today). One later Golden Cockerel book demands mention, an edition of Keats's *Endymion* (1947) illustrated with 54 wood-engravings by Buckland-Wright, perhaps the masterpiece of this accomplished artist.

The last of the truly not-for-profit private presses was in Wales, at the Gregynog Press (1922–40) owned by Gwen and Margaret Davies. They inherited great wealth and spent it well, not only in financing their press, but also in the acquisition of the fine collection of French pictures now at Cardiff. Gibbings's revival of wood-engraving found a new home at Gregynog, with important work from Miller Parker (*The Fables of Esope*, 1932) and Hughes-Stanton (*The Revelation of St John the Divine*, 1932, and *The Lamentations of Jeremiah*, 1933). A superb production of Joinville's *History of St Louis* (1937) was embellished with engraved headings, initials and armorial bearings by Reynolds Stone. Although there was talk of 'needing' a proprietary Gregynog typeface, nothing came of it, and the Press's books are exemplars of Monotype composition.

Within the illustration, the printed text reads:

BUT al to litel, weylawey the whyle,
Lasteth swich Ioie, ythonked be fortune,
That semeth trewest whan she wil bygyle
And kan to fooles so hire song entune
That she hem hent and blent, traitour comune!
And whan a wight is from hire whiel ythrowe,
Than laugheth she, and maketh hym a mowe.

From Troilus she gan hire brighte face
Awey to wrythe, and took of hym non heede,
But caste hym clene out of his lady grace,
And on hire whiel she sette vp Diomede;
For which right now myn herte gynneth blede,
And now my penne, allas, with which I write,
Quaketh for drede of that I moste endite.

For how Criseyde Troilus forsook,
Or at the leeste, how that she was vnkynde,
Moot hennesforth ben matere of my book,
As writen folk thorugh which it is in mynde.
Allas! that they sholde euere cause fynde
To speke hire harm; and, if they on hire lye,
I wis, hem self sholde han the vilanye!

O ye herynes, nyghtes doughtren thre,
That endeles compleynen euere in peyne,
Megera, Alete, and ek Thesiphone,
Thow cruel Mars ek, fader to Quyryne,
This ilke ferthe book me helpeth fyne,
So that the losse of lyf and loue yfeere
Of Troilus be fully shewed here.

179

Geoffrey Chaucer, *Troilus and Cryseide*, illustrated by Eric Gill. Golden Cockerel Press, Waltham St Lawrence, Berkshire, 1927. [C.98.gg.4]

This they have in common with the productions of Francis Meynell's Nonesuch Press (1923–68, 1981), perhaps because the type-designer and calligrapher Edward Johnston refused commissions from both presses for the design of private typefaces on the grounds that there was already a sufficiency of good types available. Meynell was quick to see that there is no inherent virtue in hand-setting, that a machine-set page could stand comparison with a hand-set one when both were well done ('the machine ... has brought beauty to the cheap book', he said), and that machine-setting was cheaper. As he wrote in 1938, 'What does it matter ... that few "presses" survive. ... They have served their purpose: they have leavened the lump' (for the Nonesuch Press was a publishing house, not a private press, though its productions and its finances would appear to place it in the latter category). By then Meynell, a master of allusive typography and an exacting searcher for the right paper for each job, had published over a hundred elegant well-printed books in an amazing variety of formats, Monotype typefaces and binding styles. The first Nonesuch book, the *Love Poems* of John Donne, was hand-set and printed at Oxford University Press in the

No more will I count over, link by link,
My chain of grief: no longer strive to find
A half-forgetfulness in mountain wind
Blustering about my ears: aye, thou shalt see,
Dearest of sisters, what my life shall be;
What a calm round of hours shall make my days.
There is a paly flame of hope that plays
Where'er I look: but yet, I'll say 'tis naught—
And here I bid it die. Have not I caught,
Already, a more healthy countenance?
By this the sun is setting; we may chance
Meet some of our near-dwellers with my car.'

THIS said, he rose, faint-smiling like a star
Through autumn mists, and took Peona's hand:
They stept into the boat, and launch'd from land.

SOVEREIGN POWER
OF LOVE! O GRIEF! O BALM!

All records, saving thine, come cool, and calm,
And shadowy, through the mist of passed years:
For others, good or bad, hatred and tears
Have become indolent; but touching thine,
One sigh doth echo, one poor sob doth pine,
One kiss brings honey-dew from buried days.
The woes of Troy, towers smothering o'er their blaze,
Stiff-holden shields, far-piercing spears, keen blades,
Struggling, and blood, and shrieks—all dimly fades
Into some backward corner of the brain;
Yet, in our very souls, we feel amain
The close of Troilus and Cressid sweet.
Hence, pageant history! hence, gilded cheat!
Swart planet in the universe of deeds!
Wide sea, that one continuous murmur breeds
Along the pebbled shore of memory!
Many old rotten-timber'd boats there be
Upon thy vaporous bosom, magnified
To goodly vessels; many a sail of pride,

41

John Keats, *Endymion*, wood-engravings by John Buckland-Wright. Chiswick Press for the Golden Cockerel Press, London, 1947. [C.103.i.9]

Fell types. The last, John Dreyfus's *History of the Nonesuch Press* (1981), was printed at Cambridge University Press in Monotype Barbou and Fournier.

The Shakespeare Head Press (1904–42) deserves more space than can be accorded to it here. It was managed by Bernard Newdigate, whose scorn of machine-setting it was that provoked Meynell to prove him wrong, and of whom Bruce Rogers wrote that within the limits he set to his typography 'he produced magnificently printed books that had astonishing variety and perfect fitness to their texts, [which] will always rank among the finest products of the modern revival'. These books included a series of noble quartos, outstanding among them Froissart's *Chronicles* (eight volumes, 1927–8), and a one-volume Shakespeare of which 50,000 had to be printed to bring the desired price of 6s. within reach (it sold out and had to be reprinted).

Outside England and Wales a select few presses deserve mention. In the United States, the Elston Press; F. W. Goudy's Village Press; Porter Garnett's Laboratory Press; the Grabhorn Press; and Joseph Blumenthal's Spiral Press. In the Netherlands, J. F. van Royen's influential Zilverdistel and Kundera Presses.

THE FAIRY BRIDE.

THERE WAS A BIG CASTLE and a lord and lady and the two eldest sons hated their youngest brother. So the boy did not have his meals with them: he had his meals with the maids. He never got any new clothes: he got nothing except the old clothes which his two elder brothers used to give him. He was filthy. ℭ Now the old lady was heart-broken about her youngest son. "I know not what we shall do with the boy." "I will tell thee," said the old lord to his lady. "I will take out the three boys for a test to-morrow morning." ℭ Morning broke. The old lord summoned his

95

John Sampson, ed., *XXI Welsh Tales*, wood-engravings by Agnes Miller Parker. Gregynog Press, Montgomeryshire, 1933. [C.102.f.11]

Hence vain deluding joyes,
　　The brood of folly without father bred,
How little you bested,
　　Or fill the fixed mind with all your toyes;
Dwell in som idle brain,
　　And fancies fond with gaudy shapes possess,
As thick and numberless
　　As the gay motes that people the Sun Beams,
Or likest hovering dreams
　　The fickle Pensioners of *Morpheus* train.
But hail thou Goddes, sage and holy,
Hail divinest Melancholy,
Whose Saintly visage is too bright
To hit the Sense of human sight;
And therfore to our weaker view,
Ore laid with black staid Wisdoms hue.
Black, but such as in esteem,
Prince *Memnons* sister might beseem,
Or that Starr'd *Ethiope* Queen that strove
To set her beauties praise above
The Sea Nymphs, and their powers offended.
Yet thou art higher far descended,
Thee bright-hair'd *Vesta* long of yore,
To solitary *Saturn* bore;
His daughter she (in *Saturns* raign,
Such mixture was not held a stain)
Oft in glimmering Bowres, and glades
He met her, and in secret shades
Of woody *Ida's* inmost grove, .
While yet there was no fear of *Jove*.

12   13

John Milton, *Four Poems*, wood-engravings by Blair Hughes-Stanton. Gregynog Press, Montgomeryshire, 1933. [C.102.e.13]

Thomas Beedome, *Select Poems Divine and Humane*. Printed at the Nonesuch Press, London, 1928. [C.99.c.42]

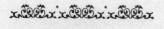

DIVINE
POEMS

The Royall Navy.

What's breath? a vapor: glory? a vaine chat:
What's man? a span: what's life? shorter than that:
What's death? a key: for what? to ope heavens dore:
Who keepes it? time: for whom? both rich and poore:
What's heaven? a haven: what's ships anchor there?
Hope, faith, and love, with one small pinnace feare.
What are those? men of warre: how fraught? with armes:
What burthen? weighty, missing their alarum.
Whose ships? the Kings: what colours? the red crosse:
What ensignes? bloody from their Princes losse:
And whither bound? to earth: Oh! what's their strife?
To conquer breath, and glory, man and life.
Oh! I foresee the storme, Lord I confesse,
Than vapour, or vaine chat, or span I'm lesse.
Save a relenting foe; thy glories are
More excellent in peace, than death and warre;
For to that time, that time his key shall lend,
And to thy tent my yeelding spirit send:
I will strike saile to these, and strive to prove
Thy Captive, in my hope, faith, feare and love.

38

Divine Poems

The Petition.

Heare mee my God, and heare mee soone,
Because my morning toucheth noone,
Nor can I looke for their delight,
Because my noone layes hold on night:
I am all circle, my morne, night, and noone,
Are individable, then heare mee soone.

Thou art all time my God, and I
Am part of that eternity:
Yet being made, I want that might
To be as thou art, Infinite:
As in thy flesh, so be thou Lord to mee,
That is, both infinite, and eternity.

But I am dust, at most, but man,
That dust extended to a span:
A span indeed, for in thy hand,
Stretcht or contracted, Lord, I stand,
Contract and stretch mee too, that I may be
Straightned on earth, to be enlarg'd to thee.

But I am nothing, then how can
I call my selfe, or dust, or man?
Yet thou from nothing all didst frame,
That all things might exalt thy name,
Make mee but something, then, my God to thee;
Then shall thy praise be all in all to mee.

39

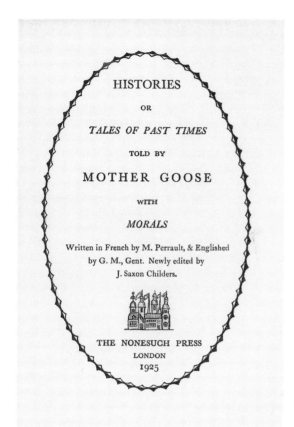

HISTORIES

OR

TALES OF PAST TIMES

TOLD BY

MOTHER GOOSE

WITH

MORALS

Written in French by M. Perrault, & Englished
by G. M., Gent. Newly edited by
J. Saxon Childers.

THE NONESUCH PRESS
LONDON
1925

ERNEST GIMSON
HIS LIFE & WORK

Stratford-*upon*-Avon *at the* Shakespeare Head Press
London Ernest Benn *Limited* Bouverie Street
Oxford Basil Blackwell m.cm.xxiv

Ernest Gimson, *His Life & Work*. Shakespeare Head Press,
Stratford-upon-Avon, 1924. [7808.v.25]

Charles Perrault, *Histories ... Told by Mother Goose*,
woodcuts by W. M. R. Quick based on the 1719 edition.
R. & R. Clark, Edinburgh, for the Nonesuch Press, London,
1925. [12411.aaa.40]

Leipzig was the home of the Insel-Verlag, which began in 1905 to publish a series of German classics, printed by Carl Ernst Poeschel, in a format designed by Walker with calligraphic title-pages by Johnston and Gill. One of their designers was E. R. Weiss (1875–1942), who as a young man was one of the great hopes of the Jugendstil. The outstanding German book designer of his day, he designed Weiss-Fraktur for the Tempel-Klassiker series and worked for the Berlin publishers S. Fischer (who thrive today in Frankfurt) until his death. Germany was indeed the second home of the private press, from 1907 with the founding of the Januspresse by Poeschel and Walter Tiemann, from 1911 with Willi Wiegand's Bremerpresse, from 1913 with the Rupprecht-Presse of F. H. Ehmcke, and above all with Harry Kessler's Cranachpresse at Weimar (1926–33). John Dreyfus has described Kessler's struggles with Walker, Johnston and the punch-cutter Edward Prince in the production of the Cranach roman and italic for the Press's great books, *The Eclogues of Virgil* (1925) with Mediterranean wood-engravings by Aristide Maillol and *Hamlet* (1930) with melancholy northern wood-engravings by Edward Gordon Craig. Lettering for both books was provided by Eric Gill, who also made wood-engravings for *The Song of Songs* (1931). In 1933 Kessler was obliged to flee Germany at an hour's notice, never to return.

William Shakespeare, *Hamlet*, wood-engravings by Edward Gordon Craig. Cranachpresse, Weimar, 1928. [C.106.k.2]

In Italy the work of Giovanni Mardersteig (1892–1977) at the Officina Bodoni from 1923 was quite outstanding. He had moved his press from Switzerland to Verona to print his splendid edition of the complete works of Gabriele d'Annunzio. He was an accomplished type designer and 'probably the finest pressman the world has ever seen' (Will Carter). His long-standing interest in the Veronese author, printer, poet and antiquary Felice Feliciano, who created the first Renaissance geometric construction of the alphabet (which Dürer later attempted), was crowned by his beautiful *Felice Feliciano Veronese: Alphabetum Romanum* (1960).

French bibliophilic enthusiasm has ignored the private press and preferred the autographic *livre d'artiste* (and *éditions de luxe*, a term of opprobrium in Britain). In 1900 Ambroise Vollard published Verlaine's *Parallèlement*, with lithographic illustrations by Pierre Bonnard, and in 1902 the same artist's *Daphnis et Chloë*; this form of publishing has continued to succeed in France. Picasso, Beckmann, Matisse, Vuillard, Dufy, Braque, Chagall (the magnificent *Chagall*, *Lithographe*) and other leading artists used lithography, woodcuts, linocuts, etchings and *pochoir* (hand-colouring through stencils), often to magical effect.

Stéphane Mallarmé's *Un Coup de dès* (1897) was no *livre d'artiste*, but poetry as typography, in which for the first time the white of the paper was intended as a constituent of the poetry itself, and not a mere substrate.

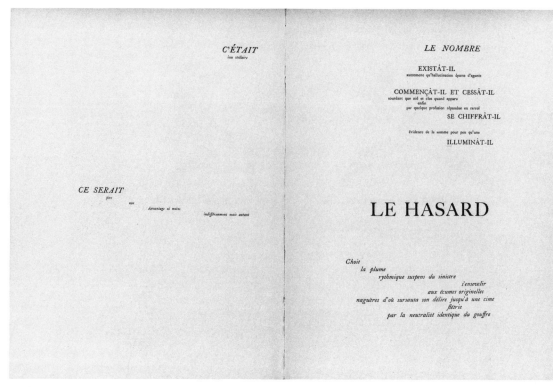

CE SERAIT
pire
non
davantage ni moins
indifféremment mais autant

C'ÉTAIT
issu stellaire

LE NOMBRE

EXISTÂT-IL
autrement qu'hallucination éparse d'agonie

COMMENÇÂT-IL ET CESSÂT-IL
sourdant que nié et clos quand apparu
enfin
par quelque profusion répandue en rareté
SE CHIFFRÂT-IL

évidence de la somme pour peu qu'une
ILLUMINÂT-IL

LE HASARD

Choit
la plume
rythmique suspens du sinistre
s'ensevelir
aux écumes originelles
naguères d'où sursauta son délire jusqu'à une cime
flétrie
par la neutralité identique du gouffre

Stéphane Mallarmé, *Un Coup de dès*. Paris, 1897. [11482.m.10]

4. BOOK PRINTING BEFORE THE SECOND WORLD WAR

The first application of the revival of printing to mass-produced books was made by J. M. Dent. His Everyman's Library, of which the first volumes were issued in 1906, adopted Morris's principles and – at least in its title-pages and endpapers – style.

The combined influence of the private presses was bound to make its mark on commercial printing, but its message was complex and contradictory. That the notion and aim of fine printing was beneficial is undeniable: the proof is there in the interest created among publishers and printers in 1913 by the nine issues of Gerard Meynell's journal *The Imprint*, and in the excellent work produced in the golden half-century which began with the heyday of the Ashendene and Doves presses and coincided with that of Golden Cockerel, Gregynog and Nonesuch. At the same time the Monotype in its pomp was providing not only reliably good machine-setting but also the most astute publicity material in the history of printing, which combined user-friendly technical know-how with an enticing entrée to the scholarly revival of the best historical typefaces. The leading commercial book printers (best defined as those which were not avowedly not-for-profit) installed these faces, sharpened up their presswork and tightened their word-spacing in the best Emery Walker style, and competed for the 'fine' books that many of their customers now wanted.

Walker's name crops up repeatedly, and so does that of Bruce Rogers. They set up the Mall Press together in rather unpropitious circumstances and produced just one book, a handsome edition of Dürer's *On the Just Shaping of Letters* for the Grolier

188

The Table

In Chap. 12 are general directions how and with what baits to fish for the Ruffe or Pope, the Roch, the Dace, and other smal fish, with directions how to keep Ant-flies and Gentles in winter, with some other observations not unfit to be known of Anglers.

In Chap. 13 are observations for the colouring of your Rod and Hair.

These directions the Reader may take as an ease in his search after some particular fish, and the baits proper for them; and he will shew himselfe courteous in mending or passing by some few errors in the Printer, which are not so many but that they may be pardoned.

THE COMPLETE ANGLER

Or, The Contemplative Mans Recreation

PISCATOR ❖ VIATOR

PISCATOR

OU are wel overtaken Sir; a good morning to you; I have stretch'd my legs up Totnam Hil to overtake you, hoping your businesse may occasion you towards Ware, this fine pleasant fresh May day in the morning.

Izaac Walton, *The Compleat* [sic] *Angler*, designed by Bruce Rogers. Riverside Press, Cambridge, Mass., for Houghton Mifflin, New York, 1909. [C.100.h.22]

Club (1916); they collaborated later on what John Dreyfus calls 'the third magnificent book to appear in Centaur' (the typeface designed by Rogers), T. E. Lawrence's translation of the *Odyssey*. Monotype Centaur, which was based on the type used by Jenson in his Eusebius, had made its first appearance in a monumental Bible designed by Rogers and printed in 1935 at Oxford University Press, which can stand comparison with the great folio Bibles of Estienne (1532) and Baskerville (1763). Rogers had already made his reputation as an inventive and accomplished allusive designer with books such as *The Compleat Angler* (Riverside Press, 1909).

In 1917 it became apparent to the Syndics of Cambridge University Press that Horace Hart's use of the Fell types, most recently for two superb Prayer Books, had bestowed on Oxford books a distinction which Cambridge's lacked. Rogers was invited to assess the Cambridge plant and its standards: his detailed and highly critical report is one of the defining documents of twentieth-century typography, comparable to Morris's *Notes on the Founding of the Kelmscott Press*, and opened the door for the appointment a few years later of Walter Lewis as printer to the university and Stanley Morison as typographical adviser.

In the United States the outstanding printers and designers included not only the Riverside Press (where both D. B. Updike, the author of *Printing Types* (1922), and

Rogers worked), but also Updike's Merrymount Press; the De Vinne Press; Copeland & Day; R. R. Donnelley's Lakeside Press; W. E. Rudge at Mount Vernon; C. P. Rollins at Yale University Press; John Henry Nash, Frederic Warde, F. W. Goudy and W. A. Dwiggins. In the Netherlands mention has already been made of the historic firm of Joh. Enschedé & Zonen and its typographer and type-designer Jan van Krimpen. In Britain the Chiswick Press (which had printed for Pickering and Morris); Ballantynes (Ricketts); Newdigate's Arden Press (Burns & Oates, Lee Warner's Florence Press and, for Longmans, Morris's *Collected Works* in 24 volumes); the Curwen Press (Nonesuch); R. & R. Clark (Nonesuch); and the university presses of Oxford and Cambridge led the way. While the princes of the British renaissance (Meynell, Morison, Oliver Simon, Harold Curwen) received their impetus from the work of Morris, St John Hornby and Ricketts, the books they produced are refreshingly miles from the closed rooms of Kelmscott and Vale, though the pure typographical legacy of Cobden-Sanderson and Walker is evident in their plain text pages, if not their arabesque playgrounds.

None of these was asked to print Penguin paperbacks, which started to appear in 1935. Although most of them were set on the Monotype they were typographically undistinguished until Jan Tschichold took charge of their design in 1947. It would be easy, and wrong, to represent the interwar years as the typographical golden age. Some splendid books were produced (one that has not so far been mentioned was the highly original *Nonesuch Century* of 1936), and many competent or better; but also many that were dull indeed, or worse, as at any other time in the history of printing.

No one called Futurism, Constructivism or their adherents dull. In 1914 F. T. Marinetti, with the publication in Milan of his *Zang Tumb Tumb*, backed by French experiments from Apollinaire to Mallarmé, proclaimed in Italy the Futurist experiment in printing directed against 'the so-called typographical harmony of the page, which is contrary to the ebb and flow, the jolts and expositions of the style which moves over the page itself'. The Constructivist urge which surfaced in the Bauhaus, in Russia and in De Stijl in the Netherlands expressed a belief that all problems in design could be solved by rational means and a geometrical approach.

Morison could not have called the Bauhaus or its publications dull, but he did call them 'anti-art'. The Bauhaus stood tradition on its head: its founder, Walter Gropius, taught that all design should be informed by a living sense of purpose, which places function above all other values; Paul Renner, the designer of the sans-serif Futura typeface, believed that type should be a reading-symbol free from any connection with handwriting. Ruari McLean has averred that the Bauhaus 'made little contribution to the advancement of typographic design'. Certainly its attempts to break free from traditional typefaces and its abandonment of capital letters failed to win adherents, yet the *Bauhausbuch* (1923), by flouting the traditional primacy of the text, pointed the way in which the design of the illustrated book would develop in Switzerland and the United States after the Second World War. The Bauhaus published a series of important albums of the 'New European Graphic Art' from 1921 with woodcuts and lithographs by artists including Klee, Kandinsky, Schwitters, Léger and de Chirico.

The Russian El Lissitzky (1890–1941), who had worked with the Futurists, was an intellectual pioneer of modern design, particularly the New Typography, who influenced Lazlo Moholy-Nagy (1895–1946), its first great teacher at the Bauhaus, and worked on *De Stijl*. He collaborated with Hans Arp on *Kunst-ismen* ('art-isms',

Private Baptism

¶ Then shall the Priest say,

SEEING now, dearly beloved brethren, that *this Child is* by Baptism regenerate, and grafted into the body of Christ's Church, let us give thanks unto Almighty God for these benefits; and with one accord make our prayers unto him, that *he* may lead the rest of *his* life according to this beginning.

¶ Then shall the Priest say,

WE yield thee most hearty thanks, most merciful Father, that it hath pleased thee to regenerate *this Infant* with thy holy Spirit, to receive *him* for thine own *Child* by adoption, and to incorporate *him* into thy holy Church. And humbly we beseech thee to grant, that *he* being dead unto sin, and living unto righteousness, and being buried with Christ in his death, may crucify the old man, and utterly abolish the whole body of sin; and that, as *he is* made *partaker* of the death of thy Son, *he* may also be *partaker* of his resurrection; so that finally, with the residue of thy holy Church, *he* may be *an inheritor* of thine everlasting kingdom; through Jesus Christ our Lord. *Amen.*

¶ Then, all standing up, the Minister shall make this Exhortation to the Godfathers and Godmothers.

FORASMUCH as *this Child hath* promised by you *his* sureties to renounce the devil and all his works, to believe in God, and to serve him; ye must remember, that it is your parts and duties to see that *this Infant* be taught, so soon as *he* shall be able to learn, what a solemn vow, promise, and profession *he hath* made by you. And that *he* may know these things the

The Book of Common Prayer, Fell Double Pica Imperial Quarto edition, with initials and rubrics printed in red. Oxford University Press, 1913.

themselves were so choice and valuable they woud magnifie an[d] Illustrate each other. I have taken care in thy Transcription that nothing might be omitted which ought to be incerted. I question not but you will much improve what I here lay before you.

Madam I might well fear lest these my rude and unpolishd lines should offend you but that I hope your goodness will rather smile at the faults commited than censure them.

However I desire your Ladyships pardon for presenting things so unworthy to your View and except the goodwill of him who in all Duty is bound to be

Your Ladyships

Most Humble & most Obe[d]iant

Sarvant

THOMAS NEWINGTON.

Brighthelmstone
May the 20: 1719

To Kill and Roast a Pigg

Take your Pigg and hold the head down a Payle of cold Watter untill strangeled, then hang him up buy the heals and fley him, then open him, then chine him down the back as you doe a porker first cuting of his head, then cut him in fower quarters,

5

Philip James, ed., *A Butler's Recipe Book*, wood-engravings by Reynolds Stone. Cambridge University Press, 1935. [7941.p.1]

Eugen Rentsch, Zürich, 1925). Jan Tschichold (1902–74), while never connected with the Bauhaus, published *Die Neue Typographie* (1928) in which he set out some basic principles of the New Typography – the virtues of asymmetry and sans-serif type – which he later disavowed in favour of a return to the 'immaculate and classic style' (Lewis) he conferred on Penguin books after the War.

5. CENSORSHIP AND OTHER DIFFICULTIES IN THE TRADE

Printers, publishers and booksellers were fortunate enough to escape the strict regulations that bound and often choked the older crafts. Their guilds and associations have always been based on voluntary agreement of the parties concerned and not on compulsory measures of the authorities. There has hardly ever been a limit to either the intensity or the extensiveness of the spreading of the printed word. Work considered dangerous or unprofitable by one printer might be taken on by another without breaking the code of honour of the trade; and any pedlar might sell books and thus bring instruction or pleasure to remote spots never reached by the ordinary bookseller. 'Since the book trade is the territory of the republic of letters, only a free con-

UTOPIA
Written in Latin by Sir Thomas More and done into English by Ralph Robynson

NEW YORK
THE LIMITED EDITIONS CLUB
1934

Thomas More, *Utopia*, designed by Bruce Rogers. The Rudge Press, Mount Vernon, for the Limited Editions Club, New York, 1934. [C.104.f.11]

Herbert Bayer, Walter Gropius & Ise Gropius, eds, *Bauhaus 1919–1928*. Museum of Modern Art, New York, 1938. [07822.ff.26]

Jan Tschichold, *Die neue Typographie*. Deutsche Bücher, Berlin, 1928. [11911.aa.23]

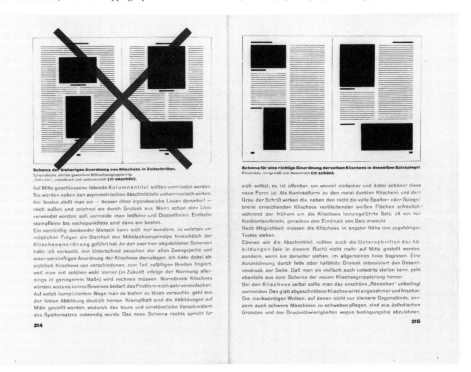

stitution is suitable to the book-trading profession', declared the founders of the Börsenverein of the German booksellers in 1825.

The liberal outlook of the trade received great encouragement throughout the nineteenth century by the gradual disappearance of book and press censorship. Its abolition in Germany (in 1848) and France (definitely in 1872) was of particular importance in view of the high status these countries enjoyed in the republic of letters. However, 'fundamental rights' written into constitutions have always been expressive of the lofty ideals of constitution-makers rather than of administrative practice. With the help of emergency decrees and special laws, governments have continuously and usually successfully tried to introduce some kind of censorship while shamefacedly avoiding the odious name.

The fight against heresy had by the nineteenth century seemed to be relegated to the efforts of the Roman Index, which moreover had become almost disregarded by the laity; but it was unexpectedly revived in the twentieth century in the guise of political censorship on ideological grounds. The Germans started in 1933 with the symbolic burning of thousands of books by Jewish, Marxist, pacifist and other 'decadent' authors, whose works were also eliminated from libraries and bookshops. Authors, publishers and booksellers were dragooned into organizations rigidly controlled by state and party, with the inevitable result that, for the duration of the 'Thousand-year Reich', universal darkness buried German literature and learning.

The harsh censorship the Germans imposed on the conquered countries from 1940 to 1945 led to a revival of the dodges in which earlier generations of printers had found solace and delight. René Billoux, in his *Encyclopédie chronologique des arts graphiques* (Paris, 1943), reprinted on the back of the title-page the privilege granted in 1582 by Henri III to a Paris publisher and saluted the German censor for resuming a tradition hallowed by the '*bon vieux temps*'. The gallant Dutch publisher G. J. van der Woude (d. 1958) brought out an innocent *Boekje over het maken van boeken* (Utrecht, 1941), in which he explained the preparation of copy for the compositor by means of a text on 'Holland, land of our heart' including a stirring patriotic poem; showed, as an example of an effective combination of woodcut and letterpress, a drawing of seventeenth-century *Geusen* with the (strictly banned) national anthem 'Wilhelmus van Nassouwe' beside it; reproduced a magnificent Jewish rabbi of Rembrandt's as a specimen of line-block printing; and used the instructions on proof-marking for some more quiet fun at the expense of the German and Dutch Nazis.

But the Fascists, Nazis and Falangists at least refrained from directly taking over publishing and printing firms; even the Franz Eher Verlag in Munich, which was Hitler's private property, never attempted to obtain a monopoly even of Nazi writings. On the other hand, the Soviet Union and her satellites imposed on the printed word a uniformity more comprehensive and thorough-going than anything ever experienced in a more or less literate society. As the Soviet governments rigidly controlled every means of production and distribution, no private printing presses were allowed and only government-approved books could be printed, published, imported, sold and read – the very antithesis of what printers and writers have been hoping to achieve for centuries.

There is at least one authenticated case in which political censorship has resorted to forgery rather than suppression. The 'definite' edition of Chekhov, published under the auspices of the Soviet Academy, purported to print the poet's writings as he wrote them. In reality, the text had been tampered with by the editors, and whole sections

Ведь я горящій булыжник дум ем

Сегодня в вашем *кричащем* тосте

Я овенчаюсь моим безуміе**М**

*Сцена постепен-
но наполняется
Человек без уха
Человек без го-
ловы и др Тупые
Стали безпо-
рядком едят
дальше*

В Маяковскій

Граненых строчек **босой** алмазник

Взметя **перины** в чужих жили-
щах

Зажгу **сегодня** всемірный празд-
ник

Таких богатых и пестрых нищих

*Старик с кош-
ками*

Оставь

Зачѣм мудрецам погремушек потеха

— 10 —

V. Mayakovsky, *A Tragedy*, illustrated by D. D. Burlyuk. Moscow, 1914. [C.114.mm.4]

Il'ya Zdanevich, *Le-Dantyu as a Beacon*. Moscow, 1923. [C.145.b.15]

omitted altogether, such as his correspondence with revolutionaries who, or whose shades, were no longer acceptable to the rulers in the Kremlin. All Chekhov's occasional references – made, be it remembered, before 1904, the year of his death – to the superiority of European, especially British, institutions, standards or habits were ruthlessly excised. Not the slightest indication revealed this transmogrification of a progressive Russian patriot into a herald of Soviet jingoism.

On the other hand, there are examples of censorship from below as dense and intolerant as censorship from above. Gerhart Hauptmann's fight against the banning of almost every one of his plays from 1889 to 1913 provides documentary evidence of this fact. The licensing authorities in Germany, France, Austria, Hungary, Italy, Russia and the United States were mostly forced to intervene by private pressure groups which rushed to the defence of morality, teetotalism, militarism, religion, child-welfare, nationalism and established authorities down to the village constable.

The non-theological sections of the Index of the Church of Rome used to puzzle Roman Catholic no less than non-Catholic students of literature. Its last edition in 1948 (which a decree of the Second Vatican Council in June 1966 made the last ever to appear) removed, it is true, Boccaccio and Rabelais, but the list of banned authors still included Francis Bacon, Sir Thomas Browne, Richardson, Gibbon, Locke, Hobbes, J. S. Mill and Lord Acton among Englishmen; and Montaigne, Pascal, Stendhal, Balzac, Dumas and Victor Hugo among Frenchmen.

Present-day conditions in Britain are probably as puzzling to an outside observer as are British institutions in general. In theory, political censorship can hardly be more comprehensive than that provided for by the laws protecting the royal family, the Houses of Parliament, the government and constitution of the United Kingdom, or those forbidding to raise discontent among Her Majesty's subjects or to promote ill-will between different sections of the community, through, among other things, 'any printing or writing'. In actual fact, however, most Englishmen are not only totally unaware of these restrictions – even to the extent that it is commonly held that there is no such thing as political censorship – but they are perfectly assured, and rightly, that every judge, jury, magistrate or police officer will in practice protect the liberty of the subject whatever the theoretical powers of the authorities may be.

Where it is agreed among all peoples of the free world that political censorship, except in times of a national emergency, is bad in itself, opinions vary greatly as regards moral censorship – a term mainly applied to countering obscene publications. The main problem here arises from the fact that (to quote Kenneth Ewart) 'the danger is so difficult to assess, and its assessment is itself constantly changing as the so-called "moral code" is itself subject to change'. There is the undisputed need to protect children against exploitation by unscrupulous traffickers in moral corruption, and this aspect is fully covered by the classic definition of 'obscenity' by Chief Justice Cockburn in Regina v. Hicklin (1868): 'The test of obscenity is this, whether the tendency of the matter charged as obscenity is to deprave and corrupt those whose minds are open to such immoral influences, and into whose hands a publication of this sort may fall.' The Obscene Publications Act, 1959, modified this test by providing that the tendency to deprave and corrupt must be considered 'as a whole', that 'the interests of science, literature, art or learning' may be adduced in defence, and that 'expert opinion' can be called in evidence. It is hard to imagine how any legal code can cope more satisfactorily with a subject that by its very nature defies any hard-and-fast definition. The test case of the new Act, Regina v. Penguin Books Ltd

im heldenhaften Kommandanten Bravida symbolisch sein
geliebtes Tarascon.
Dann stürmte er in den Zug, geriet in ein Coupé, das ganz
von Pariser Dämchen besetzt war, die einen Todesschreck be-
kamen, als dieser sonderbare Kerl mit seinen Karabinern
und Revolvern bei ihnen einstieg.

Vierzehntes Kapitel.
Der Hafen von Marseille. Lichtet die Segel!

Am 1. Dezember 186.. Punkt 12 Uhr wandelte
vergoldet von der Sonne eines provenza-
lischen Wintertages ein Türke auf der Cane-
bière, o Gott, was für ein Türke! der die
Marseiller nicht wenig in Aufregung versetzte. So
einen Türken hatten sie, weiß der Himmel, noch
nicht gesehen, und man sieht doch alle Augenblicke einen
Türken in Marseille.
Der fragliche Türke war, das braucht man wohl nicht be-
sonders zu betonen, Tartarin, der große Tartarin von Tarascon.
Er stampfte den Quai entlang, und ihm nach schleifte man
seine Waffenkisten, seine Apotheke, seine Konserven zum
Landungsplatz der Dampfschiffsgesellschaft Touache, wo der
»Zuave«, ein ansehnliches Paketboot, zur Abfahrt bereit lag.
Er hatte noch Ohrensausen von dem Applaus und den
Akklamationen, die seine Abreise aus Tarascon begleiteten.
Nun versetzten ihn der leuchtende Himmel, das blaue Meer
in einen wahren Rausch. Tartarin selbst strahlte wie der
Himmel, martialisch marschierte er daher, das Gewehr ge-
schultert, den Kopf hoch oben in der Luft, und verschlang
mit seinen Augen das Bild, das sich ihm bot: die wunder-
volle Hafenbucht von Marseille, die er zum ersten Male
sah und die ihn entzückte.
58

Alphonse Daudet, *Die Abenteuer des Herrn Tartarin aus Tarascon*, illustrated by George Grosz,
designed by John Heartfield. Otto von Holten & Hermann Birkholz, Berlin, 1921. [Cup.408.ww.33]

William Shakespeare, *Vénus et Adonis*, woodcuts by Roger Grillon. L. Picon, Paris, 1921. [C.97.c.9]

prêtes pour quelque nouveau meurtre. Sur son
échine courbe, il porte des soies hérissées comme
la pique des bataillons, dont il menace perpétuel-
lement ses ennemis; ses yeux de feu étincellent
quand il entre en fureur; de son boutoir, il creuse
des tombes partout où il passe; quand il est irrité,
il renverse tout ce qu'il rencontre dans son
chemin, et quiconque il renverse, il le meurtrit de
ses défenses cruelles. Ses flancs musculeux et
hirsutes sont à l'épreuve du fer de ton javelot; son
cou ramassé n'est point aisément vulnérable;
quand il est furieux il se jetterait sur le lion : les
fourrés de ronces et les épaisses broussailles, au
travers desquels il s'élance, comme effrayés,
s'écartent devant lui.

« Hélas! il n'a point souci de ce tien visage que
chérit l'Amour, ni de ta douce main, ni de tes
lèvres exquises, ni de tes beaux yeux, étonnement
de l'univers; mais si tu tombais en son pouvoir
(ô terreur!) il ravagerait ces beautés comme
l'herbe des champs.

« Ah! laisse-le à sa bauge immonde; la beauté
n'a point affaire avec de tels monstres; ne te mets
pas volontairement à portée de ses atteintes :
ceux qui prennent conseil de leurs amis s'en
trouvent bien. Quand tu as parlé du sanglier, à
ne te point mentir, j'ai tremblé pour ta vie et me
suis sentie défaillir. N'as-tu point vu mon visage,

ma pâleur? N'as-tu pas aperçu dans mes yeux des
signes d'épouvante? Mes genoux ne se sont-ils
point dérobés sous moi, et ne suis-je pas tombée
à la renverse, dans l'herbe? La Crainte agite mon
cœur d'un pressentiment funeste : elle représente
à ma vue un affreux sanglier sous les défenses
duquel je te vois gisant, déchiré; et ton sang
répandu sur les fleurs nouvelles leur fait triste-
ment pencher la tête. Que deviendrais-je, te
voyant ainsi vraiment, moi que cette seule imagination fait trembler? A cette pensée, je sens mon
cœur qui saigne; la crainte me découvre l'avenir :
je prédis ta mort, qui sera ma douleur éternelle,
si demain tu affrontes le sanglier. Que si, à toute
force, tu veux chasser, prends conseil de moi :
cours le lièvre craintif, ou le renard qui vit de
ruses, ou la biche qui n'affronte pas le veneur;
poursuis, à travers la plaine, ces animaux timides,
et que ton cheval infatigable talonne tes lévriers.

« Et quand tu auras lancé le lièvre à la vue

(1960) – the case of *Lady Chatterley's Lover* – fully vindicated the public's confidence in trial by jury.

Few and far between are the cases in which publishers have arrogated to themselves the combined role of prosecutor, judge and executor in determining what the public should, or rather should not, read. The burning of Byron's memoirs which John Murray considered scandalous and libellous is perhaps the worst outrage of this kind, as it entailed an irrevocable loss to literature. On the other hand, the firm of Cotta performed a service to historical scholarship and political science when they went back on their undertaking not to publish the third volume of Bismarck's memoirs during the lifetime of William II. Its publication in 1919 was amply justified by the Emperor's inglorious retirement from the political stage, which Bismarck's penetrating character sketch of the youthful monarch did much to explain to the world.

Price competition in the British book trade in the 1890s reached such a cut-throat level that some publishers felt obliged to take action to save a great many booksellers from falling into bankruptcy. Macmillans led the way by declaring the prices of some of their books to be 'net', i.e. not to be discounted, and on 1 January 1900 the recently-formed Publishers Association promulgated the Net Book Agreement. This provided for joint action by the Association and its member houses to prevent the discounting of books published by its members at net prices. The Agreement collapsed in 1995, having undergone much official scrutiny and many attempts by opponents of retail price maintenance to kill it off. British books are unusual also in having survived many attempts during and since the Second World War to tax them.

Heavy reciprocal damage of a physical nature was suffered during the War by the British and German book trades. Publishing in Britain was then even more concentrated in London than it is today: when almost all the publishing houses in and around Paternoster Row (near the historic Stationers' Hall, which was severely damaged) were destroyed, with them went over 20 million books. Cassells alone lost two million books. Hitler having thus sown the wind, the German book trade reaped the whirlwind. A few Allied bombing raids on Leipzig laid in ruins the whole centre of the German book trade and the subsequent inclusion of Leipzig in the Soviet zone of occupation forced the old publishing houses to rebuild from scratch in the diaspora of Western Germany.

The wartime demand for reading-matter exceeded all previous records. The boredom of the long hours of waiting and inactivity between battles, on the high seas, in air-raid shelters and hospitals intensified the value of the book as a never-failing friend to millions of readers and inculcated the habit of reading to millions of newcomers. Thus the ordeal which, according to the Nazi press, should have extinguished the British book trade, in fact filled it with new buoyancy. (Even 'the stringent terms of the Book Production War Economy Agreement, which prescribed the permissible size of type, width of margins, words per square inch, weight of paper [and so on]' (Unwin), had a radical and purifying effect on book design and production whose influence showed clearly in, for example, Jan Tschichold's work for Penguin Books from 1947.) 'Anything printed, even if upside down and/or in Sanskrit, was saleable' (Flower), but this very success on top of paper-rationing and air-raid damage decimated publishers' back-lists.

There have been bestsellers from the beginning of the history of printing, and we have frequently had occasion to refer to them. But the general increase of literacy in conjunction with the hold on the literate public of lending libraries, public libraries and book clubs has considerably changed the meaning of the word during the past two hundred years. An initial sale of 10,000 copies constituted a bestseller in 1800; an advance order of 100,000 would be the equivalent today. The disposal of 50,000 copies within a year was regarded as a tremendous success throughout the nineteenth century; not a few books top the 500,000 mark each year at the end of the twentieth century.

This may therefore be the proper place for some general observations on the problem of bestsellers. Its peculiar fascination for the historian derives from two facts. On the one hand, it touches on literature, psychology (individual and national), education, taste, as well as the business acumen of publishers and their publicity agents, so that it can be approached from the most diverse angles. On the other hand, it has never been possible to explain the phenomenon to such an extent as to give reliable guidance to authors, publishers or the reading public.

It is, for instance, often maintained that bestsellers are usually second-rate (if not lower) from the literary and aesthetic point of view. Richard Monckton Milnes, a genuine lover and promoter of good books, thought that the 'enormous' success of Macaulay's *History* was in itself enough 'to convince one his book cannot be good', and it was said in the 1930s that 'bestseller is an almost entirely derogatory epithet among the cultivated'. Undoubtedly this holds good for perhaps the greater part of fiction bestsellers, from the *Amadís* romances (which were killed only by *Don Quixote*), through Richardson's *Pamela* (which Fielding's *Joseph Andrews* emphatically did not oust), down to Margaret Mitchell's *Gone with the Wind*, and in our own time such popular novelists as Catherine Cookson, Ian Fleming, Agatha Christie, Jeffrey Archer, Graham Greene and John Updike. Against these may be set Ariosto's *Orlando furioso*, Bunyan's *Pilgrim's Progress* and Goethe's *Werther*, which were bestsellers as well as great literature.

The very definition of the term 'bestseller' is fraught with perplexity. Is the Bible to be counted a bestseller? Undoubtedly, if one goes by the criterion of an undiminished, hardly fluctuating sale over long periods. But this kind of book is hardly meant when one speaks of a bestseller in the technical sense. Rather than diluting the term 'bestseller', one might describe this category as 'steady sellers', for their main characteristic is a steady demand which is, to an astonishing degree, independent of the vagaries of literary movements and styles, and easily transcends linguistic and national barriers – the backbone of series such as Everyman's Library and the Penguin Classics (see below). From the days of the 42-line and 36-line Bibles onward, the Bible has proved the bestselling book in the world – whether published as a whole or in parts, 'designed to be read as literature' or in scholarly editions, in the languages of the originals or in any of the thousand translations, as an 'authorized version' or as the product of private devotion to a never-ending and ever-rewarding task. But it is above all the Bible in the vernacular which has, from Gutenberg's time onward, remained the most saleable steady seller, and this despite (or perhaps because of) the fact that it is usually produced and sold without regard to the profit motive. The Bible Society which Baron von Canstein founded at Halle in 1711 was the first press to

The Holy Bible, designed by Bruce Rogers. Oxford University Press, 1935. [Cup.1247.h.1]

organize and carry out a mass production of cheap editions: within the first thirty years of its activity it printed 340,000 copies of the New Testament at the low price of two groschen apiece and 480,000 copies of the whole Scriptures at nine groschen apiece. The numbers of Bibles since printed, especially after the foundation in London of the British and Foreign Bible Society in 1804, amount to astronomical figures. Of the Revised New Testament, published in 1881, Oxford University Press alone sold a million copies on the day of issue; two American newspapers had the whole text wired to them and gave away the volume as a supplement to their ordinary daily editions. The Oxford and Cambridge presses estimated the demand for the new translation of the New Testament to be possibly one million in the first year after publication in 1961 – it turned out to be nearly four million. In 1994 the 115 United Bible Societies distributed 18 million complete Bibles and a further 600 million portions of the Bible in over 2000 languages.

These cheap editions, however, have at no time impeded the sale of expensive Bible editions of either a purely scholarly or an *édition de luxe* character. The eight volumes of the famous Polyglot Bible which Plantin published in 1568–73 could be printed in 1200 copies, although its price varied from 70 to 200 fl. (£70 to £200). The Oxford Lectern Bible, designed by Bruce Rogers in 1929 and issued in 1935 at £52.10s., was expected to last for some 50 years: by 1955 the stock was exhausted.

Next to the Bible the outstanding examples of steady sellers are Homer and Horace among the ancients, Dante's *Divina Commedia* and Thomas à Kempis's *Imitation of*

Christ among medieval books, Shakespeare's plays and Cervantes's *Don Quixote* among the writers of the European baroque.

The greatest single author to spin money for publishers, booksellers and other authors all over the world has been Shakespeare. The four folio editions of 1623, 1632, 1664 and 1685 testify to his continuous appreciation by the Caroline and Restoration gentry (who alone could afford the pretty stiff price). The 20-odd editions which appeared between 1709 and 1790 prove that he had obtained a sure hold among the educated classes. At the end of the eighteenth century John Bell's editions (1774 and 1785) introduced him to a broader, if less critical, public. In the nineteenth century he reached virtually every home – and every schoolroom. Macmillan's one-volume *Globe Shakespeare* of 1864 may be counted among the most imaginative strokes of a publisher's genius; Reclam's successful venture in popularizing 'Unser Shakespeare' is told of elsewhere in this book; but J. M. Dent's *Temple Shakespeare*, published in 40 volumes between 1894 and 1896, has probably beaten all editions: by 1934, when it was replaced by the *New Temple Shakespeare*, over five million volumes had lifted up or depressed as many schoolchildren.

With more recent authors, it seems that national barriers have prevented a similar unfettered popularity. Molière, Scott, Dickens, Ibsen, Dostoyevsky and Tolstoy are perhaps the only writers who, since the eighteenth century, have become the common property of the whole world. Other writers, whom the English, French, Germans, Italians and so forth regard as stars of the first magnitude in their respective national literatures, seldom penetrate deeply elsewhere. We believe that to Wordsworth and Tennyson, Balzac and Hugo, Goethe and Schiller, Alfieri and Manzoni, Lermontov and Pushkin, Calderón and Camões little more than lip-service is paid outside their national orbits.

An exception is to be found in the happy realm of children's books. The internationality which has so largely disappeared from the bookshelves of the grown-up has been fully preserved in the nursery. The Frenchmen Perrault and Hergé, the German Grimm brothers, the Dane Andersen, the American Mark Twain, the Italian Collodi, the Swiss Johanna Spyri, the English Lewis Carroll and Enid Blyton have become the common property of children all over the world.

A genuine bestseller may be defined as a book which immediately on, or shortly after, its first publication far outruns the demand of what at the time are considered good or even large sales; which thereafter sometimes lapses into obscurity, making people wonder why it ever came to the front; but which sometimes graduates into the ranks of steady sellers. Such a book was Thor Heyerdahl's *Kon-Tiki Expedition* (1949).

The steady spread of literacy and the extension of leisure for cultural pursuits could not fail to affect the size of an average edition as well as modify the concept of what constituted a bestseller. In 1587 the Stationers' Company fixed an edition at 1250 or 1500 copies. Schoolbooks, prayer-books and catechisms were allowed four impressions of 2500 or 3000 each annually; statutes, proclamations, calendars and almanacs were altogether free from these restrictions. In 1635 the number of copies was raised to '1500 or 2000 at the most', unless 'upon good reason shewed' special permission might be granted for 3000. Although these regulations were meant to protect workmen against exploitation and to prevent cut-throat competition among publishers, they probably gauged accurately the normal demand. As late as 1786 the semi-official *Relation* of the Leipzig book fair stated that an edition of 600 copies was considered the saleable maximum of non-fiction.

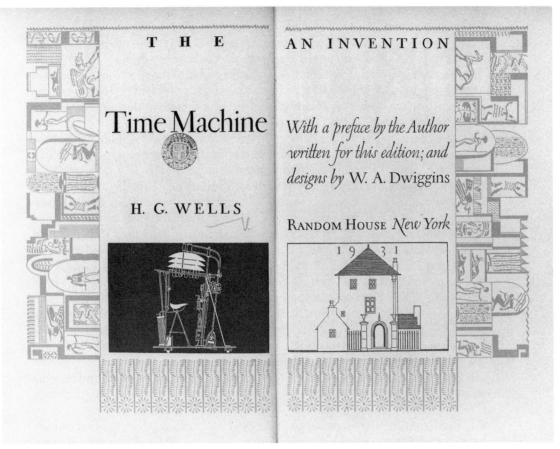

THE

Time Machine

H. G. WELLS

AN INVENTION

With a preface by the Author
written for this edition; and
designs by W. A. Dwiggins

RANDOM HOUSE *New York*

1931

H. G. Wells, *The Time Machine*, designed and illustrated by W. A. Dwiggins. Random House, New York, 1931.
[Cup.503.e.19]

But it was fiction, and popular instruction presented in entertaining shape, that from the seventeenth century onward took pride of place. In this field the first European bestseller was John Bunyan's *Pilgrim's Progress*. The first edition appeared in February 1678 in the normal size of 2000 copies; by the end of the year 10,000 copies had been printed, 4000 of them by a pirating rival. When the lawful publisher, Nathaniel Ponder, brought out his fourth edition in February 1680, he knew already of six pirated editions. The first American edition was published in the following year by Samuel Green of Boston. At the time of Bunyan's death, ten years after the first publication (1688), eleven editions – each probably numbering 4000 copies – had left Ponder's press. Bunyan, however, would have felt uneasy in his conscience had he realized that the mundane aspect of his guide 'from this world to that which is to come' is probably the main motive for its continuing popularity. If *Pilgrim's Progress* is read today chiefly as a gripping novel full of dramatic incidents, it is only following the general trend. From the early eighteenth century onward, the vast majority of bestsellers has been in the realm of purely secular fiction.

This wave started with Defoe's *Robinson Crusoe*, which came out in April 1719 (and the author received £10 for it); the second edition appeared in May, the third in June, and the fourth in August, by which time at least two pirated editions had also been issued. In the following year it was translated into French, Dutch and German;

and when at the suggestion of Jean-Jacques Rousseau (1758) it was adapted to youthful readers, its popularity increased everywhere. The number of more or less good imitations produced all over the continent must be added to the success of the original *Robinson*. Before 1800 about a hundred imitations were published in Germany alone; there appeared Swiss, Russian and Silesian 'Robinsons' and various professions had their Robinsons as well, among them a *Bookseller Robinson*.

The first edition of Swift's *Gulliver's Travels* (1726) was sold within a week, the third two months later, the three together comprising 10,000 copies. The biting political satire directed against the Whig administration and society, the savage fun poked at scientific quacks, and the pessimistic view taken of the human race as a whole were, one suspects, less powerful incitements to the public than the never-fading interest in travellers' tales and the brilliant rationalization of the primeval beliefs in dwarfs and giants. This is certainly the case today, when most of the personal and political insinuations have become devoid of interest if not incomprehensible.

Richardson's *Pamela* (1740), Voltaire's *Candide* (1759), Walpole's *The Castle of Otranto* (1764), Goldsmith's *The Vicar of Wakefield* (1766) and Goethe's *Werther* (1774) were the next books to capture Europe almost on the day of publication. Each of them reflected (and subsequently intensified) a particular facet of contemporary thought and feeling. The reward of virtue and the punishment of vice, the subtle analysis of the human heart and mind, belief and disbelief in 'the best of all possible worlds', the earthiness of utilitarian rationalism contrasted with the irrationalism of the subconscious and supernatural, the combination of moral instruction and exciting plots – all these aspects secured for these novels an immediate response in every class of society, from the sophisticated *salon* to the servants' hall.

The Castle of Otranto heads the unending list of shockers which flooded Europe in the next two generations. They were the *pièces de résistance* of the lending libraries which at that time came into vogue, and successfully displaced better authors in the public favour. Ann Radcliffe's novels, of which *The Mysteries of Udolpho* (1794) gained the widest circulation (and still makes surprisingly good reading), led up to a rational explanation of the piled-up improbabilities and thus satisfied curiosity by means similar to those which were to be exploited by the later writers of detective stories and thrillers.

Goethe's *Werther*, published in 1774, presents a nice bibliographical problem in so far as the unauthorized editions and translations by far outnumber the genuine ones. Their bibliographical details are almost impossible to unravel. Within two years at least sixteen German editions came out, and within twenty years at least fifteen French translations, twelve English, three Italian, and one each in Spanish, Dutch, Swedish, Danish, Russian, Polish, Portuguese and Magyar had flooded Europe. Napoleon, when he met Goethe in 1808, told him that he had read *Werther* seven times.

After the success of his *Werther* Goethe never again touched the bestseller level; Scott and Byron, his younger contemporaries and admirers, never fell below it. Their position is unique in that they are the only bestselling authors who reached this status through the unpropitious medium of verse. Of Scott's *Lay of the Last Minstrel* (1805), Constable and Longman, who shared the copyright, sold 44,000 copies within 25 years. His *Lady of the Lake* (1810) made the fortune – transient, alas! – of Constable, Ballantyne (its printer) and Scott, and enriched the catering trade on the shores of Loch Katrine. It seems surprising to us that Byron's publisher, John Murray, ventured

CHAPTER CXX   THE DECK TOWARDS
THE END OF THE
FIRST NIGHT WATCH

[*Ahab standing by the helm. Starbuck approaching him.*]

"WE must send down the main-top-sail yard, Sir. The band is working loose, and the lee lift is half-stranded. Shall I strike it, Sir?"

"Strike nothing; lash it. If I had sky-sail poles, I'd sway them up now."

"Sir?—in God's name!—Sir?"

"Well."

"The anchors are working, Sir. Shall I get them inboard?"

"Strike nothing, and stir nothing, but lash everything. The wind rises, but it has not got up to my table-lands yet. Quick, and see to it.—By masts and keels! he takes me for the hunch-backed skipper of some coasting smack. Send down my main-top-sail yard! Ho, gluepots! Loftiest trucks were made for wildest winds, and this brain-truck of mine now sails amid the cloud-scud. Shall I strike that? Oh, none but cowards send down their brain-trucks in tempest time. What a hooroosh aloft there! I would e'en take it for sublime, did I not know that the colic is a noisy malady. Oh, take medicine, take medicine!"

← 728 →

Roman Numerals Typographic Leaves and Pointing Hands

☞ Some Notes on their Origin, History and Contemporary Use

by Paul McPharlin

The Typophiles: New York: Mcmxlii

Herman Melville, *Moby Dick*, illustrated by Rockwell Kent. Random House, New York, 1930. [012614.b.40]

Paul McPharlin, *Roman Numerals, Typographic Leaves and Pointing Hands*. Southworth-Anthoesen Press, Portland, Maine, for The Typophiles, New York, 1942. [11914.f.29]

only the 500 copies usual with a book of poetry when he brought out the first two cantos of *Childe Harold* in 1812; they were sold within three days, and four large reprints were issued during the next nine months. *The Corsair* was therefore printed in a first edition of 10,000, and this was sold on the very day of publication in 1814.

These figures are the more remarkable as poetry has always commanded a small market. When in 1800 Longman bought up the stocks of Joseph Cottle, Wordsworth and Coleridge's *Lyrical Ballads* were valued at nil. The Longman ledgers hold much information on the attitude of the publisher and the public towards the poet's production between the years 1800 and 1835. *The Lyrical Ballads* were reprinted in 1800, 1802 and 1805, and the sale of the (together) 1750 and 2000 copies of the two volumes respectively must have seemed satisfactory to Longman, as he ventured to issue Wordsworth's *Poems* of 1807 in 1000 copies: misplaced optimism, for after seven years 230 copies were still unsold. Until 1827 Longman therefore stuck to the usual size of poetry editions, namely 500. Even thus, neither the publisher nor the poet made much profit – for instance, of the *Thanksgiving Ode* (1816) 220 copies were still in stock in 1834; and of the *Ecclesiastical Sketches* (1822) 203 were unsold in 1833. The only poem which had a steady sale was *The Excursion* (1814), and the exceptionally large edition of 1500 of *Yarrow Revisited* (1835) sold out in the year of publication. With the five-volume edition of the *Poetical Works* in 1827, Long-man's confidence in his author began to bear fruit; its 750 copies were exhausted in 1832 and Longman printed a four-volume edition of 2000 copies which was sold by 1836. In both these editions, the 'Excursion' volume was larger by 250 and 500 copies respectively.

One of the reasons for the sales resistance on the part of the reading public must have been the price of these books: the first edition of *The Excursion* cost 42s.; the second (1820), 14s.; the ones included in the *Poetical Works* 10s. 6d. (1827) and 7s. (1832). The few pages of the *Thanksgiving Ode* cost 4s.; of *The Waggoner*, 4s. 6d.; of *The River Duddon*, 12s. This, of course, bears on the publisher's age-old dilemma of a high price restricting the edition and a small edition requiring a high price.

Robert Burns was certainly more successful. His *Poems chiefly in the Scottish Dialect* were published in an edition of 600 in 1786 and reprinted three times during the next seven years, not counting two American editions, published in Philadelphia and New York in 1788 and allegedly exceeding 25,000 copies. But more common is the fate of William Johnson (Cory)'s *Ionica*; the publisher ventured the usual 500 in 1858, and of these 138 were still on his hands in 1872.

In our own century John Betjeman and T. S. Eliot have been bestsellers – Eliot on account of *The Waste Land* and *Old Possum's Book of Practical Cats*, the 'book' of the successful musical 'Cats'. Most recently the popularity of the film 'Four Weddings and a Funeral' propelled W. H. Auden's poem 'Funeral Blues' to fame and his collec-tion *Tell me the Truth about Love* to bestseller status.

On the other side of the Atlantic, Longfellow's *Hiawatha* was, and has remained, the greatest hit in the field of poetry. Of the 5000 copies Ticknor & Fields printed, 4000 had been ordered in advance of publication in November 1855. In December the eleventh edition went to press; eighteen months later 50,000 copies had been sold in the United States and about half that figure in England, not counting German, Swedish, Danish, French, Italian, Polish and Latin translations. But the poets who achieved outward and visible success during their lifetime can be counted on the fingers of one hand.

Scott's signal success as the creator of the historical novel surpassed even that of his verse romances. From the day the first volume of *Waverley* was on sale in 1814 the presses were kept busy turning out one reprint after another. Even a minor story, such as *Rob Roy* (1818), sold 12,000 copies within a month. Robert Cadell, Constable's son-in-law, bought the copyright of the Waverley novels in 1827; by the time of his death in 1849 he had sold 78,270 complete sets of the series. But the sales in England and Scotland were nothing compared with those in Ireland and the United States, where pirates unscrupulously exploited the lack of copyright protection. Pub-lishers in New York, Boston and Philadelphia kept their compositors on the alert when a ship from England sailed in, with the copy – preferably advance sheets – of a new Scott novel on board. In 1822, *The Fortunes of Nigel* was received on a Thurs-day in the printing shop and was with the booksellers on the Saturday following; *Peveril of the Peak* was set, printed and bound within twenty-one hours, *Quentin Durward* (1823) within twenty-eight. Three days' undisputed sales of a 3000-copy printing was the best the first pirate could hope for before others rushed into the racket. By 1830 about 20 American firms were pouring out the Waverley novels.

The same happened in Europe where, again owing to the absence of any legal safe-guards, translators and publishers tried to crowd each other out. All these editions

strokes, thin strokes, and gradations from thick to thin. The engraving is facsimile, & is given to show not good forms or bad, good letters or bad, but simply the forms characteristic of the brush & the pen.)

Figure 2

31

¶ Thus in the letter A (see figure 2), to make three separate strokes of the pen was too much for a man in a hurry, and two-stroke A's became familiar.

(Figure 2, reading in the customary order, shows (1) the essential form of A, (2) the same with the customary thick and thin strokes & serifs as made with a brush, (3) the same as incised with a chisel, (4) the same made with a broad pen, three strokes, (4–7) the two-stroke A, as developed between the fourth & fifteenth centuries, (8–10) sixteenth century writing, (11–13) modern forms of the same, suitable for type.)

By the seventh century this form was well established, and was as much recognizable as A as the original three-stroke Roman form. ¶ In the same way, the form of serif which was easy to make in stone (which is, in fact, the natural way to finish an incised line neatly) was less natural & less easy with a pen. Penmen took naturally to leaving them out whenever their presence seemed unnecessary. ¶ The influence of the tool is perhaps less obvious in stone inscriptions. Inscription cutting is a slow job anyway. But certain forms are more difficult to cut than others, e.g. a thick line meeting another at an angle, as in the K. The letter-cutter naturally avoids such things. ¶ Again, take the letter G. The evolution of our modern small g is seen to be chiefly

Eric Gill, *An Essay on Typography*. Hague & Gill, Pigotts, Buckinghamshire, for Sheed & Ward, London, 1931. [C.100.e.6]

were cheap in every sense of the word – abominable translations, nasty press-work, undercut prices. One German publisher issued two complete editions of about 80 volumes each in one year (1825), the one series at 8 groschen (9d.) the other at 4 groschen per volume; in the same year another German firm sold 30,000 copies of their edition, and two more editions went to press at the same time.

Once again, as in the days of Richardson and Goldsmith, the English novel set a literary fashion to the western world, and the canons of the historical novel established by Walter Scott have since guided his followers everywhere. A considerable number of historical novels after Scott have themselves turned out bestsellers of national and even international fame: Fenimore Cooper's *The Last of the Mohicans* (1826), Alessandro Manzoni's *I Promessi Sposi* (1827), Victor Hugo's *Notre-Dame de Paris* (1831), Alexandre Dumas's *Les Trois Mousquetaires* (1844), W. M. Thackeray's *Henry Esmond* (1852), L. N. Tolstoy's *War and Peace* (1862–9) are some of the best-known examples of this genre in the literatures of the United States, Italy, France, England and Russia.

Throughout the nineteenth century a sale of 10,000 copies within a year seems to have been considered an outstanding success, and anything above that figure constituted a bestseller. The year 1859 was a veritable vintage-year of bestsellers, with Tennyson's *Idylls of the King*, Samuel Smiles's *Self-Help*, Mrs Beeton's *Book of*

Household Management and George Eliot's *Adam Bede* all reaching 20,000 or so within a twelvemonth, yet Fitzgerald's *Rubáiyát of Omar Khayyám*, which was to become the best steady seller of that year's publications, was a complete failure to begin with.

The adventurous side of publishing is exhibited most often in conspicuous failures to recognize a prospective successful author or book. Conan Doyle's *A Study in Scarlet* returned three times to its author before a fourth publisher somewhat reluctantly accepted it; G. B. Shaw's early work was refused the imprint of Macmillan (four times!), Murray, Chatto, Bentley and half a dozen almost equally well-known firms. Not a literary but a political miscalculation made John Murray, in 1831, decline the publication of Disraeli's *The Young Duke*; the passing of the Reform Bill, which accidentally coincided with a transitory depression of the book-trade, presaged to that stout Tory the complete ruin of this country, in which there would be no more place for publishing ventures.

Macmillans (who can afford to let their historian, Charles Morgan, tell some good stories against themselves) were able to make a bestseller of J. H. Shorthouse's *John Inglesant* (1880) because their printers, R. & R. Clark of Edinburgh, had printed at their own risk 9000 copies, vastly in excess of their order, having greater confidence in the success of the novel than the publishers. Macmillan also transferred H. G. Wells's *Kipps*, of which they had sold 180 copies within two years, to Nelson who, within a few months, sold 43,000 copies. Most amazing, Macmillans were so cautious as to limit the first English edition of Margaret Mitchell's *Gone with the Wind* to 3000 copies (1936), although the novel had already proved a bestseller on the other side of the Atlantic with over 100,000 copies ordered before publication. *Gone with the Wind* was, in fact, since Harriet Beecher Stowe's *Uncle Tom's Cabin* (1852) the first American book to make an equal sensation in both the United States and Britain. Even after the story had begun to appear in a Washington weekly, a Boston publisher turned down its publication in book form, and the publisher of the magazine had serious misgivings when he saw the short story for which he had bargained grow into a two-volume novel. Within six months after publication day in March 1852, over 100,000 sets at $1.50 were sold, and a cheap one-volume edition at 37½ cents reached 200,000 before Christmas. As in 1852 American books were not protected by copyright in Britain, about 40 different English reprints came out in the same year. Their prices ranged from 6d. to 15s. Routledge seems to have been the most successful of the English pirates; he frequently dispatched as many as 10,000 copies per day to the booksellers, and all in all sold over half a million out of the million and a half produced by the English trade. In the same year 1852 *Uncle Tom's Cabin* was translated into French, Italian, Danish, Dutch, German, Magyar, Polish and Swedish, to which later on came translations into some 30 more languages.

Such figures have, of course, to be judged by those of the average turnover. The concept of a bestseller therefore varies greatly from country to country. Italian publishers in 1955, for instance, regarded as a bestseller a novel selling 5000 copies or more, whereas their American colleagues would consider 500,000 a proper yardstick. On the other hand, some of the mammoth figures beloved by U.S. publishers and authors are open to reasonable doubt. The Congregational Minister Charles M. Sheldon let himself be persuaded – not unwillingly, one supposes – by an Australian bookseller that his missionary story *In His Steps* (1897) had sold 150,000 copies in this one shop and 'at least a million' throughout Australia. Sampling such encouraging figures, the Reverend finally credited himself with total sales of some twenty million.

Considering the range of potential appeal, non-fiction can hardly be expected to compete with fiction in the realm of bestsellers. But those critics who are inclined to equate bestsellers and light reading greatly underrate the public's taste, curiosity, assiduity or whatever may create a bestseller. Macaulay's *History of England* was meant by its author to outsell the bestselling novel of the day. It did so. The first two volumes which appeared in 1849 sold 40,000 copies in England and 125,000 pirated copies in the United States before the third and fourth volumes came out. Of these, 25,000 were sold on publication day in 1855, leaving 11,000 more applicants un-satisfied, and within a month 150,000 copies had been disposed of, including un-authorized sales of 73,000 in New York and 25,000 in Philadelphia. William Howard Russell expected that the publication in book form of his celebrated dispatches to *The Times* from the Crimean War theatre might sell 5000 copies; his publisher, Routledge, was hoping for more. Neither of them foresaw that 200,000 copies would be sold in 1855–6.

Turning from history proper to the philosophy of history, Oswald Spengler's *Untergang des Abendlandes* and Count Keyserling's *Reisetagebuch eines Philosophen* went into the hundred thousands in the Germany of the 1920s; just as did, after the Second World War, A. J. Toynbee's *A Study of History* in Britain, the United States and (in translation) in Germany. Among biographies John Morley's *Life of Gladstone* was at the time an unheard-of success. Of its three volumes, 25,000 sets were sold in the year of publication (1903), and the first cheap edition (at 5s.) sold 50,000 copies in 1908–9 – an interesting reflection on the hold the Liberal Party had in those days on the mind of the English public, for 50 years later the book strikes anyone incau-tious enough to open it as singularly dull.

Easier to explain is the signal success of Sir Winston Churchill's *The Second World War*. Its six volumes appeared from 1948 to 1954, and each subsequent volume had to be printed in larger editions than the preceding one, necessitating constant reprints of the earlier volumes, so that the whole work presents a complicated bibliographical puzzle. The reason for this is, of course, given in the unique fact that here the greatest single story in the history of mankind is being told by the greatest single participant in that story who, at the same time, happened to be a considerable writer of the English language, a recipient of the Nobel Prize for Literature.

Science, too, is represented among bestsellers. In the middle of the nineteenth century the Rev. John George Wood achieved tremendous successes with his popu-larizing books on natural history; of his *Common Objects of the Country* (1858) the first edition of 100,000 copies sold within a week. In our century Maeterlinck's *La Vie des abeilles* (1901), Sir James Jeans's *The Universe around Us* (1929), Rachel Carson's *The Sea around Us* (1951), Richard Dawkins's *The Selfish Gene* (1976), David Attenborough's *Life on Earth* (1979) and Stephen Hawkings's *A Brief History of Time* (1988) have been outstanding. The printing order by the American mail-order concern of Sears, Roebuck of one million copies of Lew Wallace's *Ben Hur*, in 1913, has so far remained a unique feature of book production.

Bestsellers and steady sellers have a cultural function which is quite independent of their own literary merits. From the publisher's point of view, Dr Desmond Flower has neatly described the latter as 'money-spinners'. This financial aspect, which, of course, applies also to bestsellers, frequently causes the erroneous impression that a lot of people – chiefly publishers, but also printers, authors and booksellers – are making fortunes out of them. As a matter of fact, the gains from bestsellers and steady sellers, as far as they don't go straight to the taxman, are normally ploughed back into business. The greatest gain the general public derives from the very small number of bestsellers and the very small (though fairly assured) profits from steady sellers consists in the fact that they allow a few authors to go on writing without distraction, and a few publishers to take risks on works of scholarship or of unrecognized literary promise and other unprofitable books that otherwise would not see the light of day.

A bestseller does however create problems throughout the trade. Keeping it available can cause difficulties alike for publisher and booksellers, but these are happy difficulties. Then there is the question which attends every new publication and every reprint (only in this case there is scope for an unusually large and expensive error) – How many? and the question peculiar to reprints, When? Just as every publisher has turned down a bestseller, so he has books in his warehouse which he reprinted once too often, when fickle public taste was preparing to say, Enough! Then there is the publisher's problem of paying the printer to reprint the book before the bookshops have paid for their replenishment stock, a problem which has sunk a small publisher before now. Finally, an author fortunate enough to write a bestseller is likely to face not only a commensurately large tax bill but also an expectation on the part of the tax authorities of continuing mega-earnings.

If it were possible to separate the various components whose interplay produces a bestseller, it would appear that the general climate of opinion is the principal factor. The rising tide of abolitionism floated *Uncle Tom's Cabin*, the anti-Republican sentiment of the New Deal era responded to *Gone with the Wind*. On the other hand, an author's previous reputation has apparently no effect on turning a book into a bestseller. Byron's remark, 'I awoke one morning and found myself famous', fairly reflects the experience of most writers of bestsellers. Neither did the failure of Byron's *Hours of Idleness* (1807) prevent the immediate success of *Childe Harold* (to which the above words referred); nor did the success of the earlier verse romances of Walter Scott pave the way for the rapturous acclamation of his prose novel *Waverley*, because this appeared anonymously. In fact, most bestsellers have been written by people 'without a name', i.e. a name previously known to the public; and not a few by people who, like Harriet Beecher Stowe and Margaret Mitchell, have remained one-book authors.

A particular case both of the bestseller and also of publishing on subscription is the book club. As an example, the reader may commit himself to buying say four books per year, selected from twelve new titles and a backlist. The publisher thus knows how many to print to cover the initial orders, and limits his gamble to the additional quantity required for backlist stock, and to announcing the price beforehand.

The idea of book clubs seems to have originated in about 1900 with the Swiss co-operative movement, which supplied its members with books on a non-profit-making or profit-sharing basis. The largest European book club, Büchergilde Gutenberg, was founded in 1924 by the educational section of the German printers' trade union with 5000 members. The first book offered to the members was a volume of Mark Twain's short stories. Despite its trade-union background, the Büchergilde Gutenberg steered clear of politics in the selection of its books, contrary to the Left

over his shoulder. Something sang like an arrow through the air: I felt a blow and then a sharp pang, and there I was pinned by the shoulder to the mast. In the horrid pain and surprise of the moment —I scarce can say it was by my own volition, and I am sure it was without a conscious aim—both my pistols went off, and both escaped out of my hands. They did not fall alone; with a choked cry, the coxswain loosed his grasp upon the shrouds, and plunged head first into the water.

Chapter XXVII

"Pieces of eight"

Owing to the cant of the vessel, the masts hung far out over the water, and from my perch on the cross-trees I had nothing below me but the surface of the bay. Hands, who was not so far up, was, in consequence, nearer to the ship, and fell between me and the bulwarks. He rose once to the surface in a lather of foam and blood, and then sank again for good. As the water settled, I could see him lying huddled together on the clean, bright sand in the shadow of the vessel's sides. A fish or two whipped past his body. Sometimes, by the quivering of the water, he appeared to move a little, as if he were trying to rise. But he was dead enough, for all that, being both shot and drowned, and was food for fish in the very place where he had designed my slaughter.

I was no sooner certain of this than I began to feel sick, faint, and terrified. The hot blood was running over my back and chest. The dirk, where it had pinned my shoulder to the mast, seemed to burn like a hot iron; yet it was not so much these real sufferings that distressed me, for these, it seemed to me, I could bear without a murmur; it was the horror I had upon my mind of falling from the cross-trees into that still green water, beside the body of the coxswain.

I clung with both hands till my nails ached, and I shut my eyes as if to cover up the peril. Gradually my mind came back again, my pulses quieted down to a more natural time, and I was once more in possession of myself.

It was my first thought to pluck forth the dirk; but either it stuck too hard or my nerve failed me; and I desisted with a violent shudder. Oddly enough, that very shudder did the business. The knife, in fact, had come the nearest in the world to missing me altogether; it held me by a mere pinch of skin, and this the shudder tore away. The blood ran down the faster, to be sure; but I was my own master again, and only tacked to the mast by my coat and shirt.

These last I broke through with a sudden jerk, and then regained the deck by the starboard shrouds. For nothing in the world would I have again ventured, shaken as I was, upon the overhanging port shrouds, from which Israel had so lately fallen.

167

R. L. Stevenson, *Treasure Island*, illustrated by John Minton. Paul Elek, London, 1947. [WP.3925/3]

Book Club and Right Book Club in Britain, both of which foundered after a short career.

The Grolier Club was founded in the United States in the 1880s, the Limited Editions Club in the United States in 1929 and the Folio Society in London in 1947. Although their aims have not been identical – in brief, respectively bibliophilic, illustrated-de-luxe and good-commercial-illustrated – all have produced some very fine books, exemplars of modern typography, and prompted the creation of some of the best interpretative illustration of the century.

Popular mass-market clubs have included the Book of the Month Club, the Literary Guild (both founded in 1926), the Book Society, Readers' Union and those owned under the BCA umbrella by the German publishing giant Bertelsmann. Book clubs have now spread virtually over the whole world and done valuable service by bringing books into households which, for some reason or other – such as distance from bookshops – had never troubled to build up a private library of their own. On the other hand, there is the obvious danger – as with the patronage of Mudie's Library – of guiding public taste into more or less narrow channels and of puffing non-controversial mediocrity at the expense of provocative genius.

Oddly enough, the publication of books at reduced prices to the tens of thousands of book-club members not only has no adverse influence on the sales of the original publisher's stock, but rather stimulates them. The result is that reputable publishers gladly co-operate with the book clubs and thereby help to keep up their average standard. Here, perhaps, may be detected the real service done to literature by book clubs: large new sections of the community become, for the first time, 'book-conscious', and gradually make the reading and ownership of books a habit and natural part of their lives. There is of course some countervailing risk, when a few large clubs each have tens of thousands of members, that public taste may be homogenized, and even that worthwhile books that fail to achieve any club accolade may sink without trace.

7. POPULAR SERIES

It is no accident that all the famous British series of cheap hardback more-or-less classic reprints which survived beyond the mid century originated within a span of a few years: Nelson's New Century Library in 1900, transformed into Nelson's Classics in 1905; the World's Classics started by Grant Richards in 1901 and taken over by Oxford University Press in 1905; Collins's Pocket Classics in 1903; Routledge's New Universal Library, intended to replace Morley's Universal Library, in 1905; and J. M. Dent's Everyman's Library in 1906. These series inevitably had in common a great many features, serving as they did the needs of virtually the same classes and categories of readers as understood and anticipated by publishers and editors of virtually the same commercial and scholarly standing. Collins and Nelson published mainly fiction; the other imprints cast their nets much wider and included poetry and drama, history and biography, theology and philosophy, with a high-minded appeal, as Dent put it, 'to every kind of reader: the worker, the student, the cultured man, the child, the man and the woman'.

The success of the series was immediate and generally lasting. After half a century Collins had sold some 29 million copies of about 300 titles, the World's Classics about 12.5 million of 550 titles and Everyman's Library 43 million of over 1000 titles. Of the fiction titles on these lists, the bestsellers were six novels by Dickens, *Jane Eyre*, *Treasure Island*, *Pride and Prejudice*, Blackmore's *Lorna Doone*, Scott's *Kenilworth*, *Twenty-three Tales* by Tolstoy and two collections of *English Short Stories*. Non-fiction was headed by Palgrave's *Golden Treasury of English Verse*, Boswell, Pepys, Gibbon, *English Essays*, the *Anglo-Saxon Chronicle*, Plato, Marx, Mill, Descartes and the Koran.

Dent has left us some interesting comments on the production of the first batches of Everyman: he had to print 20–30,000 copies of Shakespeare and Dickens and an average of 10,000 of books by other authors to achieve the low cover price he had in mind. Dent, who came of a bookbinding family, had a small bindery when he started Everyman. Such was his success with that series that he very soon faced a hard choice: whether to close his bindery so as to become an influential customer of other, larger binderies, or to expand it to cope with his own work. He characteristically chose not mere expansion but rebuilding; and not in London, but in Letchworth Garden City, in Hertfordshire, on a site which proved to be so uneven that a basement had to be constructed, in which he installed printing presses rather than leave it empty.

The historian of literature may be interested in the choice of the first half-dozen or

Fra Luca de Pacioli

OF THE SERAPHIC ORDER OF
SAINT FRANCIS

❧{ I }❧

UCA, ZUNIPERO and AMBROGIO were the religious names of the sons of Bartolomeo, surnamed Pacioli, or Pacciuoli (apparently the correct, or at least the earliest form of the name), or in Latin Paciolus, of Borgo San Sepolcro. This small, but not undistinguished, town lay within that part of Umbria which earliest came under the influence of St Francis and of his first companions. The Seraphic saint, having preached, was well received by the inhabitants; they gave him the ancient hermitage of Mont Casale nearby, and it was during a sojourn here that there took place the incident in which St Francis commanded Brother Angelo, a noble young follower, who had repelled three famous but out-of-luck brigands, to go after them and, kneeling, to offer them bread and wine. Brother Angelo found the three not far from the Borgo, as recounted in the *Fioretti* (chapter xxvi) by Brother Leo, who also tells of the subsequent conversion of the three. Brother Angelo became Guardian of the Convent of San Casale. Again, the first place to which the saint came, still in an ecstacy, after receiving the stigmata on Mount Alvernia, was the Borgo. Unconsciously and amid cries of "Ecco il Santo" he reached a leper house a mile beyond, and later came back to Mont Casale. All this was in 1224: Francis died in 1226. But the effect on Borgo San Sepolcro remained, and the fame of St Francis was carried through the world by eyewitnesses and

Stanley Morison, *Fra Luca de Pacioli*, designed by Bruce Rogers. Cambridge University Press for the Grolier Club, New York, 1933. [Ac.4714.b.9]

so titles with which these series started. The World's Classics began with *Jane Eyre*, Tennyson's *Poems*, *The Vicar of Wakefield*, Hazlitt's *Table-Talk*, Keats's *Poems*, *Oliver Twist*, Lamb's *Essays of Elia* and *Wuthering Heights*. Everyman essayed first Boswell's *Life of Johnson* (2 vols), Lockhart's *Life of Napoleon*, Andersen's *Fairy Tales* and Hawthorne's *Wonder Book* and *Tanglewood Tales*. Collins started with *David Copperfield*, *Kenilworth*, *Adam Bede*, *Two Years Ago*, *John Halifax Gentleman* and *Westward Ho!*. These titles are a remarkable testimony to the discrimination and taste of the editors of these series. Ernest Rhys (1859–1946), who edited Everyman's Library from its inception to his death, was perhaps the most influential personality among them. Penguin Classics opened in 1946 with the *Odyssey*, *Divine Comedy*, *Candide*, Maupassant's *Boule de Suif*, the *Theban Plays* of Sophocles, Xenophon's *Persian Expedition*, Tacitus *On Britain and Germany*, Virgil's *Pastoral Poems* and Turgenev's *On the Eve*.

It has been suggested that the prodigious sales of these 'classics' series are largely spurious because so many of their titles are among the books more or less frequently set for school examinations. *Force majeure* rather than spontaneous interest in literature would thus account for the popularity of *Pride and Prejudice* or *David Copperfield*. No doubt compulsory reading may stimulate the sales of certain authors; and in one case Collins definitely ascribe to its adoption as a set book the sudden rise of a book to the fifth and later even to the third place of their series: H. G. Wells's *The History of Mr Polly*. But it is difficult to believe that the rise of O. Henry's *Short Stories* into the bestselling group of Collins's New Classics is in any way due to the dictates of the examination boards. Moreover, *David Copperfield* also heads all English prose writers in Reclam's library, though it is seldom read in German schools, whereas Goethe's *Faust I*, which is a German schoolbook, had by 1942 sold 1.89 million copies, *Faust II*, which is not read in schools, had sold 1.46 million copies – a difference of only 400,000 copies over 75 years.

Much less can the signal success of the works of Tolstoy in the World's Classics and Everyman be ascribed to any compulsory reading in schools or colleges. His *War and Peace* had its largest sales during the Second World War, when its subject-matter and the prevailing uncritical admiration of everything Russian may have been contributing factors. But Tolstoy's essays, letters and short stories were popular before the War, and his great compatriots Dostoyevsky, Turgenev, Gogol and Chekhov had found entry in Everyman, which even lists *Crime and Punishment* and *The Brothers Karamazov* among its bestsellers.

The mass production of good cheap reading-matter on the model of Reclam was taken up by more than one German publisher. Georg Müller, for example, founded a publishing house in Munich in 1903 to make it possible for every German household to possess the treasures of the world's literature: it produced 400 titles in its first five years, 287 in 1913 alone.

All these houses were moderately successful, though no German house could achieve the popularity and distinction of their rival Reclam until the Insel-Verlag launched its Insel-Bücherei in 1912. This new venture appealed to a more sophisticated public than that which Reclam chiefly catered for, and was therefore more restricted in the choice of its titles. But it applied to cheap mass-produced books the standards of typography and make-up which the revival of typography had up to then devoted only or mainly to *éditions de luxe*. Considering the somewhat highbrow fare, the success of the Insel-Bücherei must be regarded as a high compliment to the

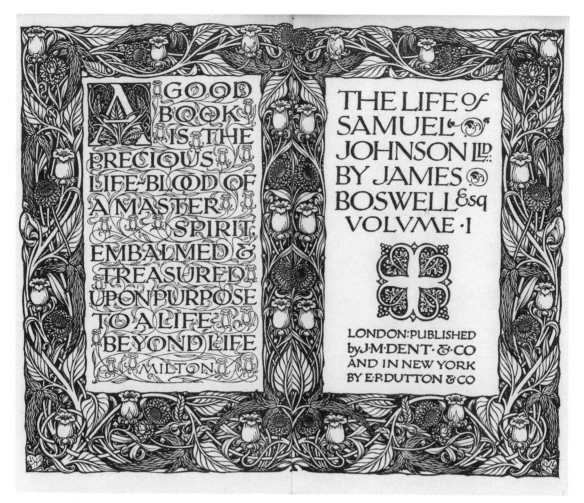

James Boswell, *The Life of Samuel Johnson* (Everyman no. 1). J. M. Dent, London, 1906. [12206.p.1/2]

educated classes in Germany. After 25 years, in 1937, some 500 titles had sold 25 million copies, the three leading books being Rudolf Binding's *Opfergang*, Rilke's *Cornet* (with about 900,000 each) and Stefan Zweig's *Sternstunden* (about 500,000); but even an anthology of Carossa's poems, selected by the poet himself, sold 170,000 copies between 1937 and 1961, in addition to the 50,000 of the large edition. Very soon the Insel-Verlag began to include illustrated volumes containing up to 50 pictures in woodcut, halftone and colour (the precursors of the King Penguins). Here, as with Reclam, the exigencies of the interwar period caused a rise of the original price, without however adversely affecting either production or sales: Rilke's *Cornet* passed the million mark.

Allen Lane did not invent the paperback; indeed, there was no shortage of precedents. Pride of place must go to Tauchnitz, who by 1928 had published Austen, Brontë, Carlyle, Conrad, Dickens, Hardy, Hawthorne, James, Lawrence, Ruskin, Shaw, Trollope, Wells, Wilde and Wodehouse as well as Galsworthy and Mrs Alexander. For a long time the Tauchnitz collection took no notice of the revival of good typography, but in the 1930s Giovanni Mardersteig redesigned the books. Cassell's National Library had been published in paperback at 3*d*. Benn's Sixpenny Library

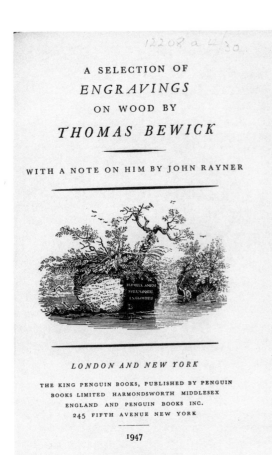

A SELECTION OF
ENGRAVINGS
ON WOOD BY
THOMAS BEWICK

WITH A NOTE ON HIM BY JOHN RAYNER

LONDON AND NEW YORK
THE KING PENGUIN BOOKS, PUBLISHED BY PENGUIN
BOOKS LIMITED HARMONDSWORTH MIDDLESEX
ENGLAND AND PENGUIN BOOKS INC.
245 FIFTH AVENUE NEW YORK

1947

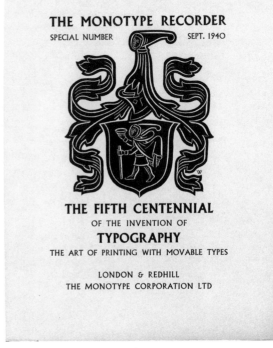

THE MONOTYPE RECORDER
SPECIAL NUMBER   SEPT. 1940

THE FIFTH CENTENNIAL
OF THE INVENTION OF
TYPOGRAPHY
THE ART OF PRINTING WITH MOVABLE TYPES

LONDON & REDHILL
THE MONOTYPE CORPORATION LTD

'The ... gist and promise of this present book' – Beatrice
Warde. The woodcut is by the late Berthold Wolpe.

A Selection of Engravings on Wood by Thomas Bewick.
Edmund Evans, London, for Penguin Books,
Harmondsworth, Middlesex, 1947. [12208.a.4(3)]

of the 1920s and 1930s – short specially-written essays – was still going strong. Albatross, founded in Hamburg in 1932 by J. Holroyd-Reece, aimed higher typographically at the literary level of Aldous Huxley and Sinclair Lewis. Albatross and Tauchnitz (who both published for the Continental market only) merged before the War, and were then obliterated by it. After the War the flood of imported British and American paperbacks forestalled their revival.

When in 1935 Lane planned to publish a series which would, in his own words, supply good literature in attractive form at the price of a packet of cigarettes, the highest authorities of the British book trade were not slow to predict its speedy and inevitable failure. After an anxious start, when the bulk of the first batch of ten titles was taken up not by the trade but by Woolworths, they were quickly proved wrong, and in a short time Lane was keeping his nerve, printing titles in runs of at least 50,000 and dropping titles that failed to sell 700 copies per week; and Penguins were soon not merely reissuing well-known fiction and biographies – the first ten titles had included books by André Maurois, Ernest Hemingway and Mary Webb – but also serious non-fiction, such as Leonard Woolley's *Digging Up the Past* and James Jeans's *The Mysterious Universe*. In 1946, just over ten years after the first Penguin was published, E. V. Rieu's translation of *The Odyssey* – specially commissioned by Lane as

216

the first of a new series of translations of world classics – came out and by 1960 had sold more than a million copies. Of Penguin's sister series, the non-fiction Pelican Books, most of them specially written for this cheap form of publication (the first was G. D. H. Cole's *Practical Economics*, 1937), the sales in some instances reached several hundred thousand copies; even books on fairly limited aspects of archaeology, individual studies of philosophers and psychologists, and history textbooks occasionally sell in similar quantities. After their first 25 years of existence, Penguin Books had published over 3250 titles and sold more than 250 million books. By then (1960) they were selling at a rate of 13 million per year; by 1994 this had increased dramatically, to 45 million per year, and total sales had probably topped one billion.

Penguin have not of course had a monopoly of paperback bestsellers in Britain. The British edition alone of Joseph Heller's *Catch-22* (Arrow), for example, has reprinted every year since 1964 and sold more than three million copies. John Grisham's *The Chamber* (Arrow) sold over one million copies in 1995 and twelve other titles (all novels except Stephen Hawkings's *A Brief History of Time*) over half a million: none were published by Penguin.

Paperbacks have become the backbone of publishing and bookselling, at least in Britain and the United States (where Robert de Graaf and the directors of Simon & Schuster started Pocket Books in 1939 with a daring launch including Brontë, Shakespeare and Samuel Butler as well as popular fiction, and Joseph Myers founded Avon in 1941). The popular appeal of paperbacks has had noteworthy repercussions. Originally they were published by houses which entirely specialized in their production, but from 1945 more and more hard-cover publishers went over to issuing paperbacks as a profitable side-line. At the same time the programme of these series was undergoing a change. All of them started with reprints, and mostly reprints of fiction. Now, entertainment and instruction nearly balance each other: in 1958 there appeared in the United States some 900 fictional and some 800 instructional softcover titles.

Discussion of popular series would not be complete without reference to Reader's Digest's 'Condensed Books', which have introduced hundreds of thousands of readers to a wide range of middlebrow fiction and general non-fiction, presented as three or four condensed texts in one volume.

John Evelyn, *Memoires for my Grand-son.*
Oxford University Press for the Nonesuch
Press, London, 1926. [08407.e.37]

CHAPTER V

The postwar world

1967 saw the death of Stanley Morison and publication of his magnum opus, *John Fell: the University Press and the Fell Types* (Oxford University Press): a book the like of which we shall never see again. A folio of almost 300 pages, some of them in double columns, it was hand-set at the Press in the Fell types (as had been Horace Hart's *Notes on a Century of Typography at the University Press, Oxford* of 1900). Eight pages at a time were set, proofed, printed and the type distributed so that the next eight pages could be set. This is one of the books of the century: no book of comparable beauty has since been produced.

Since 1967 the tools for writing and producing books have changed far more than they did in the preceding 500 years, and printing, publishing and bookselling have become in general – and of necessity – very much more businesslike. During this time there have been all too many pundits prophesying the death of the book and its replacement by electronic media. While it would be foolish, and pointless, to say Never! – and it is true that some reference material has sensibly been transferred to microfiche, CD-ROM and the Internet – in other respects traditional books are still with us, writers continue to write them and publishers and manufacturers to thrive, more or less.

One of the noblest monuments to nineteenth-century devotion to learning is the Oxford English Dictionary, the greatest dictionary of modern times (much of it written or edited by James Murray), which was published in parts between 1884 and 1928. Its complex design was hand-set from type cast at the Press and made over 16,000 pages: some compositors stayed with the Dictionary throughout their working lives. The printed version of the second edition was published in 1989: it took over 100 keyboarders 18 months, expanded the coverage from 400,000 to over 500,000 words and the extent to over 21,000 pages, and was set on a Monophoto Lasercomp. It has since been published as a CD-ROM, in which form (like the *Encyclopedia Britannica*) it is far cheaper than its parent book and – for those who have the facilities to use it – far easier to use.

1. COMPOSITION AND TYPESETTING

When this book was first published in 1955 almost all books were printed by letterpress. Exceptions were some illustrated books and some British editions of American books (or vice versa) photographed from the original setting – in both cases printed by offset lithography – and the occasional illustrated book printed by photogravure or collotype. In the succeeding decades book production (and its implications for publishers) changed radically.

CHAPTER V

THE EFFORTS OF FELL AND HIS FINAL SUCCESS IN CREATING A LEARNED PRESS

§ THE FELL BIBLE, 1672–1675

IT was in 1672 that Fell's Company first set their hands to the great enterprise of a complete edition of the Authorized Version, the bulk of the capital being found by Yate. They knew the risk they were taking in challenging the London 'monopoly', but persisted in their plan in spite of the lesson they had received in the matter of the school-books.[1] The New Testament had been set up in 1672, and the Bible was published in 1675, the year before Fell became Bishop. These were the circumstances.

The University's right to print Bibles asserted.

Fell and Company's Bible was in quarto, a size chosen as being the least likely to attract the disagreeable attentions of the London monopolists who were at the time specializing in octavos and duodecimos. Quarto was an expensive and unpopular size. Moreover, it was a size, like medium folio, mentioned in the compromise reached in 1629 (and effected by an order of the Privy Council) by the Stationers' Company and the King's Printers with Cambridge;[2] and the Cambridge practice had not since been challenged. That is to say the sale of the Quarto Bible printed at Cambridge in 1666 (and other editions) had not been interfered with. In 1673 Hayes, the University Printer at Cambridge, had completed a quarto Bible; although the copperplate title (John Chantry *sculpsit*) is coarse, typographically the book is a handsome piece of work. Printed on excellent paper and rubricated with rules throughout (as it is in the British Museum copy), Hayes's Bible must be ranked as one of the finer English achievements of the period, reaching a level of composition similar to that of the folio printed in Amsterdam in 1672. This was the situation that Fell faced in 1672 when he began at Oxford the composition of his first Bible. He began with the New Testament, which bore the imprint 'OXFORD. At the Theater MDLXXIII.' The Old Testament was completed in 1675, and the whole Bible sold under the same imprint.

The first Oxford Bible.

Typographically the edition does not rise above the commonplace. The design of the copperplate titles (the artist is anonymous) are jejune and the letter-title is badly displayed. The text is composed in the Long Primer of which Fell had bought a fount and the matrices from Holland in 1672. In the same year (1675), unfortunately, Cambridge brought out one more quarto. The Cambridge standards on this occasion are even lower than Oxford's. The copperplates are coarser and the typography is clumsy in the extreme.

---

1 The University's covenant with the Company of Stationers to forbear printing, among other things, certain books commonly used in schools lapsed in 1672, and Fell and his partners printed Lily's Grammar and were beginning to print other books of the kind of which the Stationers were apprehensive (Madan, iii, p. 268). By an agreement of October in that year the Oxford partners undertook to desist for three years from printing privileged books excepting the Bible and the Metrical Psalms bound with it and to hand over what they had printed of

the kind at cost price. In return the Stationers promised £120 annually. Johnson and Gibson, *Print and Privilege*, pp. 64, 69–70.

2 *Acts of the Privy Council of England 1628 July–1629 April* (1958), pp. 403–4. The Privy Council in 1662 confirmed its orders of 1623 and 1629 restricting the formats in which Cambridge might print the Bible to quarto and Median folio and made the restriction applicable to Oxford also: S. C. Roberts, *History of the Cambridge University Press*, p. 68.

818122

G

Stanley Morison, *John Fell*. Oxford University Press, 1967. [NL.4.c]

Before it could oust letterpress as the principal medium for the printing of books, offset litho needed a typesetting system that would provide the text either as film, for direct exposure on the printing plate, or as an image on paper that could be photographed. While 'reproduction pulls' of metal type and line blocks could provide such an image, the cost of make-ready (and of any blocks that might be required), the difficulty of achieving a satisfactory and consistent standard of inking on a proofing-press (or the cost-ineffectiveness of taking the pulls on a relatively high-speed printing-press), and the value of the type-metal tied up – all made this procedure unattractive. Publishers of short-run academic books turned for a time to 'strike-on' typewriter systems (see below) for the production of camera copy; but their limitations (to say nothing of their aesthetic shortcomings) soon made this expedient less attractive.

Although in 1894 Eugen Porzsolt and in 1898 the cinematographic pioneer William Friese-Greene had patented devices for setting typographical characters photographically, nothing had come of this, and it was not until 1925 that the Typary (later to become the Orotype), E. K. Hunter's and J. R. C. August's Thothmic (later to become the August-Hunter) and Edmund Uher's Uhertype were invented and R. J. Smothers experimented successfully with a prototype which led eventually to the Intertype Fotosetter. In 1929 came the American Luminotype. Despite all this experimental activity, commercial manufacture was slow to follow, and no phototype-setting equipment was on display at the 1936 International Printing Exhibition. In that year, however, Edward Rondthaler founded the Photolettering firm in New York to supply display typesetting from photographic masters.

The Monotype Corporation started research work on phototypesetting in 1944, but the pace quickened after the Second World War with the introduction in the United States in 1945 of the Intertype Fotosetter (the first phototypeset publication was set on this machine in the same year, but the first book, Eric Linklater's *Private Angelo*, not until 1957). The first generation of phototypesetters operated in the same way as their parent hot-metal composition systems, type images on transparent carriers replacing metal matrices and a light-source replacing the casting unit and throwing the type image on film or sensitized paper. This was true of the Fotosetter, the Rotofoto (which came into use in 1949) and the first Monophoto (1954). Output speeds were considerably in advance of those offered by hot-metal composition, and further cost savings derived from the elimination of metal type and a 99 per cent reduction in the space required for storing galleys and pages while out on proof and type or plates for reprinting.

Production of the second generation of phototypesetters overlapped with that of the first: indeed, the Photon ('Lumitype' in France, where the early development work took place) was introduced in 1949, the Linofilm in 1958 and the Compugraphic in 1968. Electronic or electro-mechanical devices, the second-generation machines were typographically more flexible than the first by virtue of their ability to mix typefaces and type sizes. On these machines it was possible to vary the 'leading' (which typographers were now learning to call 'line feed' or 'film advance') from line to line, and this escape from the rigid discipline imposed by metal type can now be seen as an essential first step towards modern-day computer-assisted page make-up. Their output was also significantly faster, coping easily with the input of at least three keyboard operators (ten operators by the end of the development cycle of, for example, the Photon). While it has to be said that the output of some of the machines men-

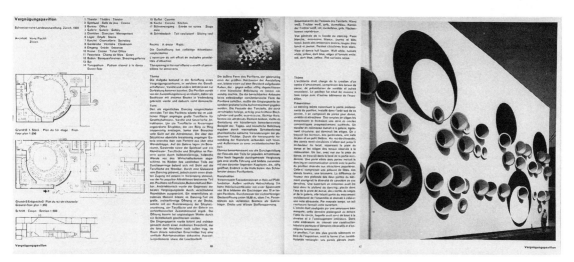

Richard Lohse, *Neue Ausstellungsgestaltung*. Verlag für Architektur, Erlenbach-Zürich, 1953. [Cup.253.df.16]

tioned was (to put it no stronger) typographically undistinguished, the Monophoto retained such fidelity to Monotype-quality letter-forms and letter-fit that late models remained in use in Britain until well into the 1980s.

Another glimpse of the future was seen in 1966 with the Photon 713-20, which incorporated the ability to perform justification and could therefore accept unjustified input tapes. This development went half a stage further in 1968: the Compugraphic came on the market with the additional ability to perform rudimentary line-end word-division. However, publishers (not of course of the same generation as those who witnessed the stressful pioneer days of the Monotype or Linotype) still demanded hot-metal quality, and looked askance at the output of these new machines whenever they could afford to.

The cardinal virtue of the first and second generations of phototypesetters was the perfect sharpness of the type image when exposed direct to film – sharper than metal type or the 'strike-on' image, and sharper than anything that was to follow. (It is something of a paradox in a discussion of phototypesetting that because film is a relatively expensive material; because it is a volatile substance and the density of the image tends to vary from hour to hour and day to day; because it is almost unknown for a first proof to be passed without a call for corrections; and because it was until recently quicker and therefore cheaper to patch in corrections than to re-run the offending passage – for all these reasons most printers avoided outputting on film, preferring to use sensitive paper, photographed only after all the corrections had been made. The ability of the computer to act as a database on which the text could be stored during all the proofing, correction and make-up stages changed all this – see below.)

By the early 1970s the economic decline from the boom years of the 1960s had at last hit the book trade: one factor in this decline was a sharp reduction in the numbers of new universities and tertiary colleges (meaning many fewer new libraries to be stocked), another a marked decline in book-purchase funds in all educational institutions. Academic publishers in particular had to save money wherever they could, and to take advantage of the economies of litho printing they turned for the production of camera copy to 'strike-on' composing machines such as the Varityper and the IBM Selectric and Electronic Composers (the 'golf-ball' machines), really glorified typewriters which when used with one-time ribbons produced an image sharp enough to be photographed ('cold composition'). Their letter-forms were crude compared to those offered by metal type, and lines of text could be justified only by sometimes startling variations in word-spacing from one line to the next; but they could be operated by authors, or more often by trained typists (who were not admitted to printing-craft trade unions, and could be seated in publishers' offices, or even in their own homes). Despite groans of dismay from their designers, publishers were not slow to accept debased typographical standards in return for considerable economies in the cost of composition. That strike-on machines enjoyed only a short period of favour was due to their technical and operational limitations (such as the need to switch 'golf-balls' when changing from roman to italic type) rather than their affronts to traditional typography.

Progress demands faster and faster output, and the output speed of first- and second-generation machines was limited by the operating speed of the flash mechanism and the manoeuvring speed of the film-matrix carrier. Machines of the first part of the third generation, such as the Linotron 303 and 505, overcame these handicaps with a new light-source, replacing the flash with a cathode-ray tube (CRT) in which a fine electron beam (deflected magnetically across the matrix-carrier from one type image to the next, thus obviating the need for the matrix-carrier to move) scans the type image and projects a scanned version of it on film or sensitized paper. The output of all CRT and later digital machines is characterized by the jagged edges on curved and diagonal strokes, and by necessary compromises over the thickness of certain strokes, due to the way in which characters are built up dot by dot. These effects are known to the type-designer, who makes every effort to allow for them, and are invisible to the naked eye (though this was not always so in the early days of CRT machines, and is not so today in the coarse output of the low-resolution laser printers sometimes used for proofing text). CRT machines employ a 'photo-multiplier' to project 'a corresponding though possibly modified pattern of parallel lines which compile the latent image of a character on the output' [i.e. film or paper] (Williamson). This potential to modify the image allows roman type to be sloped (and indeed this was the closest that early models could get to italic), sloped backwards, condensed or expanded by virtually any amount – useful when a long book has to be packed into a short extent (and a heady freedom for some designers, though mercifully the worst excesses proved to be short-lived). The vertical scan of CRT machines, unfortunately, as was the case with the Linotype, more or less precludes true kerning (the overhanging of the extenders of one character over its neighbours – the italic *f*, as in *efe*, in particular); whereas the horizontal scan of the Lasercomp allows kerning, just like its predecessors the Monotype and Monophoto.

Until the arrival of third-generation phototypesetters and the invoking of the power of the computer to assist composition, most keyboard operators were obliged to stop near the end of each line of text in order to decide how to complete the line – whether the next word could be accommodated without spacing the line too tightly or too loosely, or would have to be divided, and if so where – and then to justify the line (i.e. fill the predetermined measure). It had long been recognized that considerable economies could be achieved if only the keyboard operator could be relieved of these tasks, economies which the computer was poised to deliver once it could solve the problems of word-division.

By the heart's still rhetoric, disclosed with eyes)
Deceive me not now, Navarre is infected.
PRINCESS: With what?
BOYET: With that which we lovers entitle affected.
PRINCESS: Your reason.
BOYET: Why all his behaviours do make their retire,
To the court of his eye, peeping thorough desire:
His heart like an agot with your print impressed,
Proud with his form, in his eye pride expressed.
His tongue all impatient to speak and not see,
Did stumble with haste in his eyesight to be,
All senses to that sense did make their repair,
To feel only looking on fairest of fair:
Me thought all his senses were lock'd in his eye,
As jewels in crystal for some Prince to buy
Who tendering their own worth from where they were glass'd,
Did point out to buy them along as you pass'd.
His face's own margent did coat such amazes,
That all eyes saw his eyes enchanted with gazes.
I'll give you Aquitaine, and all that is his,
And you give him for my sake, but one loving kiss.
PRINCESS: Come to our pavilion, Boyet is dispos'd.
BOYET: But to speak that in words, which his eye hath disclos'd.
I only have made a mouth of his eye,
By adding a tongue, which I know will not lie.
ROSALINE: Thou art an old love-monger, and speakest skillfully.
MARIA: He is Cupid's grandfather, and learns news of him.
ROSALINE: Then was Venus like her mother, for her father is but grim.
BOYET: Do you hear my mad wenches?

MARIA: No.
BOYET: What then, do you see?
ROSALINE: Ay, our way to be gone.
BOYET: You are too hard for me.
                          Exeunt.

III. 1

Enter Braggart and Boy.
Song.

BRAGGART: Warble child, make passionate my sense of hearing.
BOY: Concolinel.
BRAGGART: Sweet air, go tenderness of years: take this key, give enlargement to the swain, bring him festinately hither: I must employ him in a letter to my Love.
BOY: Will you win your love with a French brawl?
BRAGGART: How meanest thou, brawling in French?
BOY: No my complete master, but to jig off a tune at the tongue's end, canary to it with the feet, humour it with turning up your eye: sigh a note and sing a note, sometime through the throat: as if you swallow'd love with singing love, sometime through the nose as if you snuff'd up love by smelling love with your hat penthouse-like o'er the shop of your eyes, with your arms cross'd on your thinbelly doublet, like a rabbit on a spit, or your hands in your pocket, like a man after the old painting, and keep not too long in one tune, but a snip and away: these are complements, these are humours, these betray nice wenches that would be betrayed without these, and make them men of note: do you note men that most are affected to these?
BRAGGART: How hast thou purchased this experience?

William Shakespeare, *Love's Labour's Lost*, designed by Jan Tschichold. Penguin, Harmondsworth, 1953. [011768.n.5]

Mathematically speaking, a line of type is justified by subtracting the total width of the characters in the line from the specified length of the line and sharing the result over the spaces separating the words. In hot-metal composition systems the width of every character was immutably fixed (short of deliberately casting it on the 'wrong' body, which was occasionally practised to achieve a special effect), so that it was only by adjusting the word-spaces that each line could be made to fill the measure. Once free of the discipline imposed by the three-dimensional type body, the designers of typesetting equipment realized that although a standard width was assigned to each character, to ensure that it would not touch its neighbours, it was technically simple to allow this ghostly body to vary slightly in size, either at the typographer's request or to assist justification. So-called 'unjustified' setting employs a fixed word-space, and any surplus space falls at the right-hand end of the line in 'ragged-right' setting (or at the left-hand end in ragged-left setting, or evenly distributed to left and right in centred setting). When specifying unjustified setting the typographer may stipulate that no words may be divided, or – to avoid excessive raggedness – that words should be divided 'as if justifying'.

Compositors and hot-metal keyboard operators developed a more or less scholarly knowledge of how to divide words, working from a set of rules ('logic') and a corpus of exceptions to those rules. Thus the 1967 edition of *Hart's Rules for Compositors and Readers at the University Press, Oxford*, instructs the operator setting English to divide (1) 'according to etymology, where this is obvious', (2) where not obvious, 'according to pronunciation' (so that the first half of the word suggests the second), (3) 'between two ... consonants coming together' (but dividing, e.g., fea/ther, (4) 'where there is only one consonant it should normally be taken over' (but dividing, e.g., gener/ally), (5) 'between vowels only when they are sounded separately', and so on. Hart concludes twelve paragraphs of compressed instruction with the daunting rubric that the 'divisions noted as preferable are not free from objection, and should be avoided when it is at all easy to do so'; and elsewhere gives detailed instruction on word-division in other languages. While many other book-printers and publishers were content to 'follow *Hart*', many were not, and printed sometimes quite elaborate booklets detailing their house style. It is possible to find evidence of an attempt to appear more scholarly than the printer next door in some of these efforts.

When 'computer-assisted composition' came in, computer memory was comparatively expensive and manufacturers accordingly tried to rely on the logical rules of word division, and added 'exception dictionaries' of words that do not obey the rules when it became clear that to rely on rules alone spelt disaster. More recently a steady increase in the amount of computer memory available, and a corresponding decrease in its cost, enabled manufacturers to switch to more or less complete dictionaries, with the permissible points of division of each word marked; but this brought its own problems, since certain dictionaries permit so many points of division that it has become a commonplace to see most lines in a book of normal format ending in a hyphen, which produces setting of a commendably even colour but is irritating to read once the frequency of the hyphens has been noticed.

As foreshadowed by the developments already described in the above accounts of the Photon and the Compugraphic, with the arrival of the third-generation machines input keyboards (producing for the most part unjustified tapes, sometimes unkindly called 'idiot' tapes) and 'slave' phototypesetters not only became independent, but were separated from each other by a large cool room containing the computer, ministered to by highly-paid men in white coats (a new phenomenon in the trade). The major bottleneck in pre-press production was now page make-up, still the province of the compositor working with galleys of paper or film just as his father probably had with galleys of metal type. The computer had the power to take over the make-up of all but the most complex pages: thus it could handle text containing broken-off quotations, small type, several grades of sub-heading and run-on chapter headings, and then strip in page heads and page numbers. In other words, with the increasing popularity of third-generation phototypesetters their associated computers took over the make-up of the great majority of unillustrated books.

The conventions governing make-up survived intact from the days of hand-setting, through the hot-metal era and into the era of phototypesetting and computers. To a large extent they are still observed today, thanks to the persistence of those printers and publishers and – particularly those designers – who kept on insisting on their importance despite occasional essays in over-elaboration; economizing attempts at erosion; ignorance on the part of computer engineers of their nature, significance or (so it sometimes seemed) very existence; the inability of third-generation computers to obey them all; and some lack of agreement as to their precise definition. The literal

Joseph Müller-Brockmann, Zürich 1955
Automobil-Club der Schweiz
Unfallverhütung
prevention of accidents
prévention des accidents

Joseph Müller-Brockmann, Zürich 1957
Automobil-Club der Schweiz
Unfallverhütung
prevention of accidents
prévention des accidents

Joseph Müller-Brockmann, Zürich 1958
Automobil-Club der Schweiz
Unfallverhütung
prevention of accidents
prévention des accidents

195 **Das Plakat und die Straße**

Die Straße ist nicht länger der harmlose Spazier-weg der Zeit der Plakate von Chéret und Toulouse-Lautrec. Die Motorisierung beherrscht sie. Sogar das Amt der einstigen Sandwich-Männer wird vom motorisierten, plakatartig aufgemachten Verkehrsmittel, zum Beispiel dem Lieferwagen, übernommen. Die Motorisierung ist jedoch voller Gefahren; es ist fast eine Art von Sühne, daß die Straße ihre Plakatwände für den aufklärenden Hinweis auf diese Gefahren zur Verfügung stellen muß.

The poster and the street

The street is no longer a place for carefree stroll-ing as it was in the days of Chéret and Toulouse-Lautrec. The street is dominated by the auto-mobile. Even the sandwich men have yielded place to motorization and their advertisements now circulate on vehicles such as delivery vans. But motorization is fraught with danger: the fact that the streets must give room on their hoardings to posters warning against traffic dangers is almost a kind of expiation.

L'affiche et la rue

La rue n'est plus l'insouciante promenade qu'elle était au temps des affiches de Chéret et de Toulouse-Lautrec. Elle est dominée par la moto-risation. Même la fonction des anciens hommes-sandwich est aujourd'hui l'affaire de moyens de transport motorisés, par exemple la voiture de livraison, traités comme des panneaux d'affichage. Mais la motorisation est pleine de dangers. Peut-être est-ce pour la rue une sorte d'expiation que de mettre ses murs à notre disposition comme aver-tissement de ces dangers.

Karl Gerstner & Marcus Kutter, eds, *Die neue Graphik*. Niggli, Teuffen, 1959. [7872.pp.21]

framework of these conventions, the chase in which a page of metal type is surrounded by 'furniture' and locked up, dictated the over-riding importance of the basic con-vention that pages should be uniform in depth. In the cheapest of cheap slug-set paper-backs this was just about the only convention that was never broken, since when making up metal type it is fiddly and therefore uneconomic for the type area to vary in size, whether in depth or across the measure, from one page to another.

This convention always made it difficult for typesetters to obey another, which was given almost equal force by designers: the requirement to avoid 'widows', the short last lines of paragraphs falling at the head of the page. Compositors working with hand-set or Monotype-set metal type would often spend hours respacing lines and

225

headings, even to the extent of inserting strips of cigarette paper ('carding' or 'feathering') between the lines of a page which had to be left one line short, to avoid this solecism and to obey other conventions covering the minimum number of lines on a short page and below a sub-heading, the number of consecutive lines ending in a hyphen that could be accepted, and the avoidance of a hyphen at the foot of the page. Unjustified keyboard input and early attempts at computer-driven page make-up put these comfortable conventions at risk, queried and derided by omnipotent computer engineers (or so it seemed to publishers as proof after unacceptable proof came through) and printers who found it intolerably expensive to conform to them. This was a testing time for typography, and it is much to the credit of typesetters, printers and their customers that high standards survived.

'If it ain't broke don't mend it' applies to typography as much as to clocks, and only now did designers of photoset, litho-printed books realize that they had been liberated from the three-dimensional strait-jacket imposed on them by metal type and no longer had to treat a fixed page depth as *sine qua non*. To make it possible for typesetters to advance to the automatic make-up of more complex pages, such as those with footnotes or with integrated illustrations for which spaces could be defined by the keyboard operator, it was imperative to have exact rules for make-up prioritized and codified. By now it was technically possible to advance the film feed by a quarter of a point, rather than the minimum of half a point in metal type, and some printers offered to rerun an awkward page with a quarter of a point deducted from or added to the standard line feed (and one more or less line on the page) in order to avoid widows and other solecisms. It was in response to this tactic, considered in many quarters to be barbaric (although the variation in interlinear space is almost impossible to identify with the naked eye, pages so doctored no longer back up or align with their neighbours), that some designers conceded that they would prefer to allow two facing pages to fall a line short or long.

The third generation of phototypesetters reached its second part with the Linotron 202, in which master characters are stored not as photographable images but digitally: the digitized characters are generated as type images on paper or film via a CRT. This machine gained wide acceptance throughout the book trade. Digital storage is a feature also of the Monotype Lasercomp, the first fourth-generation machine. It differs fundamentally from previous phototypesetters in having no moving parts except for a rotating polygon which deflects the projected image to its position on the line next to the previous character; and in having as its light source a helium-neon laser instead of a CRT. The operation of the Linotronic 300 is similar. The term 'phototypesetter' is now obsolescent; its replacement, 'imagesetter', implies the dual nature of the output of modern machines, both typesetting and illustration.

Computers can now handle the make-up of all but the most complex pages. For many years footnotes posed too many problems for satisfactory automatic make-up to be possible, but they can now be handled satisfactorily; so can tables (except those that are so wide that they have to be turned on their sides). Digitized data defining line and halftone illustrations, both monochrome and colour, that can be scanned (rather than photographed by a process camera) can now be incorporated with the text input, thus permitting the integrated output of an illustrated book on paper or film; or even direct to printing plate.

As a consequence of this advance in computer-assisted line-division and page make-up, first proofs are usually run out economically on a low-resolution laser-printer;

Christopher Smart

A SONG
TO
DAVID

EDITED BY
J. B. BROADBENT
Fellow of King's College, Cambridge

Rampant Lions Press
DISTRIBUTED BY THE BODLEY HEAD

Christopher Smart, *A Song for David*, frontispiece by Lynton Lamb. Printed in black and blue by Will Carter at the Rampant Lions Press, Cambridge, 1960.

although the output is typographically coarse, it is adequate for proof-reading. The final high-resolution output on film or paper is not made until all corrections and author's alterations (a distinction – sometimes a fine one – on which may rest the allocation of the cost of eliminating errors to the typesetter and his customer the publisher, and by the publisher to himself and the author) have been entered on the database, and probably a revised check made to ensure that no errors have survived and no new ones have been introduced. This is still more likely than might be supposed. Single metal characters ('sorts'), metal slugs and correction-lines on film or paper may respectively be spilt ('pied'), misplaced out of sequence and stripped in askance; altering a database may introduce unacceptable word-divisions or new errors.

We saw earlier that when publishers obliged to economize on composition costs began to accept strike-on camera copy this might come from an author's IBM golf-ball typewriter. It was not only typographical purists who disdained the choice offered by that machine, either unjustified setting or justified setting with unacceptably variable word-spacing; but the purists were almost alone (in still saying 'Not good enough') when authors threw out their typewriters and turned to dedicated word-processors and mini-computers running word-processing packages, many of which

227

were capable of more sophisticated word-division. When universities and colleges began to make secretaries redundant and to replace them with this equipment, academic authors and publishers were not slow to use it for the rapid production – which continues today – of camera copy for conference proceedings and other documents whose speed of publication is more important than their adherence to the finer points of design.

An early and continuing use of computers was for the management of large databases such as inventories, parts lists and catalogues, and when printed publications carrying this information were wanted ad hoc arrangements were made for the computer tapes to drive dedicated phototypesetters. It was not, however, this specialized activity which prompted the 'new technology' revolution, so much as the realization among academic authors, particularly those working in departments of computing, that if the input tapes or floppy discs they used in writing books and articles for learned journals were compatible with the typesetter's equipment, there should be no need for the typesetter to re-key the text. At that time there was in fact tantalizingly little chance of that compatibility: manufacturers were falling over themselves to bring out new products while keeping a jealous eye on their competitors, and the industry was not yet mature enough to have begun to think about standards. The interim solution was the 'black box', able to translate data between particular pairs of input devices and phototypesetters. Since most printers used only one make of phototypesetter, bureaux were established to offer black-box services to printers and typesetters and their customers; this was particularly useful in Britain, where their union stamp on work disguised from the then highly suspicious printers' craft unions its 'unauthorized' origin at the hands of the author.

Today 'incompatible' is a word rarely heard in this connection, and most typesetters can accept magnetic tapes or floppy discs from almost any input device. Enormous effort has gone into the creation and continuing development by teams from both sides of the Atlantic of SGML (the Standard Generalized Mark-up Language), which had its origins in IBM; with it has come IBM's dominance of parts of the computer market, the parallel growth of IBM-compatible software, and the establishment of Adobe's PostScript as the new standard of text composition and output. The importance of PostScript cannot be overstated: it has become both the industry-standard page description language and the output language for the most popular DTP (so-called 'desk-top publishing') systems. Adobe's Apple-Macintosh gained dominance in the micro-computer DTP market with PostScript, which enables an author to set text, create images for line illustrations (it is particularly proficient at graphs and other diagrams with a mathematical base), incorporate scanned halftones or define their shapes, and make up the whole document into pages, with the facility to alter the layout, edit the text and re-size the illustrations until each page is satisfactory. The author can then 'print' out the final pages on a low- to medium-resolution laser-printer – and thus, after binding, 'publish' the document from his desk – or forward it on tape or disc, or via a modem over the telephone network, or by electronic mail, to a typesetter for high-resolution output on an imagesetter and litho printing. Virtually all typefaces used for text composition are available in PostScript form, and new designs have to conform to its requirements as well as to those of the imagesetter manufacturer commissioning them.

One other source of text input should be mentioned here: OCR (optical character recognition), the technique whereby the characters in a typed or typeset document

FEBRUARY

A THAW

The snow is gone from cottage tops
The thatch moss glows in brighter green
And eves in quick succession drops
Where grinning icles once hath been
Pit patting wi a pleasant noise
In tubs set by the cottage door
And ducks and geese wi happy joys
Douse in the yard pond brimming oer

22

Here are some odd words, either forgotten or
undiscovered, with which you can bamboozle almost
anyone. They are arranged in Garlands which bring
you always back to the beginning. Once
you have been through them two or
three times, you will be able to use
them whenever you wish.

What is a tingle-airey?

A *tingle-airey* is a hand organ, usually
played on the street by the turning
of a handle, and often decorated
with mother-of-pearl or
piddock shells.

43

Alastair Reid, *Ounce, Dice, Trice*, illustrated by Ben Shahn.
Atlantic Little Brown, Boston, 1960. [12974.dd.12]

John Clare, *The Shepherd's Calendar*, wood-engravings by
David Gentleman. Oxford University Press, 1964.
[X.909/1114]

are machine-read, their outlines matched against a computer memory of the generalized shapes of known characters, identified, and captured in a database which can
then be fed to a typesetting system. Difficulties can arise from a poor-quality or low-
resolution original – and handwritten corrections cannot be machine-read – but this
process is a useful way of converting an established text, particularly the text of an
old book which has to be reset for reissue in a new format.

   Publishers and typesetters attempting to convert an author's keyed text can expect
to encounter two related difficulties: both may be seen as aspects of authorship. The
first is, simply, that it is no easy task to create for publication a text that satisfies the
author and the publisher; it is doubly difficult to do so without error, whether of
spelling or punctuation or consistency or some larger consideration. Second, the publisher's editor will probably call for alterations to the submitted text. All the errors
must be removed and all the alterations made before the text can sensibly be typeset.
By now the author will probably find it irksome to perfect his text down to the
last space and comma, and may have come to realize that in providing cost-free
typesetting he is subsidizing the publisher. To which publishers – particularly those

specialist houses who almost insist on receiving the text in one of the forms here described – may respond that this is now the way of the publishing world, that this is the author's guarantee that the book will appear exactly as he released it, that there is no better way to speed up publication and keep prices down, and even that without this economy in the cost of composition they could not publish the book at all. The author may well suspect special pleading, but has no way to confirm it.

Once a text exists in database form, whether keyed by the author or a typesetter, it can be typeset in different styles for different purposes: most paperbacks, for example, are re-issues of books already published in a larger hardback format, and do not require to be keyed again if access can be gained to the tapes or discs of the original setting; related sections taken from one or more reference books may be repackaged under a different title; an annotated edition of a classic may be published as a plain text with its scholarly apparatus stripped out. The database remains and can be updated as and when a new edition is required. Its contents can be published in a non-print medium such as floppy disc or CD-ROM, or accessed under licence by remote computer through the Internet. Publishers have worried about the long-term future of the book against competition from such other media, and certainly large catalogues and other specialized works of reference can now be kept available and up to date only by transfer to computer. In 1994 Chadwyck-Healey published *The English Poetry Full-text Database*, carrying the works of 1350 poets from AD 600 to 1900 on CD-ROM: all interested academics will want their institutional libraries to acquire this, but the price of £30,000 will be a significant deterrent (so will the cut-off date of 1900, inevitable if the publisher was to avoid treating with numerous copyright holders and paying sometimes very high copyright fees), and ink-on-paper publishers will continue to keep in print at least selections from the works of those classic British poets whose works are still bought – not by any means every one of those 1350 names whose complete works can now be read on screen.

Although the history of printing is the subject of this book, mention might be made here of a potentially enormous difficulty for future textual and bibliographical historians which is still hull-down on the horizon. It is inevitable that technical development and decreasing cost will encourage publishers to widen the scope of the material issued on CD-ROM, the Internet and other non-print media. They will particularly want to take advantage of the virtual absence of any economies of scale in the manufacture of non-print publications, and of the facility which they provide for the rapid and frequent editing of the database, in order to minimize stock-holding and offer constantly up-dated reference material. Librarians will find it increasingly difficult to subscribe to such publications, and almost impossible to identify editions and definitive texts in the manner to which they are accustomed.

2. PRINTING

In 1955, when almost all books were printed by letterpress, the Wharfedale, which dated from 1858, and particularly the quad-demy Miehle, first built in the 1880s, were the standard flat-bed machines (they were still being manufactured as late as 1970). Paperbacks and other longer runs were printed on rotary presses from curved metal or rubber stereotype plates. A few illustrated books were printed by photogravure, and a tiny handful by collotype. Direct lithography was favoured for some artists' books. Offset lithography was in use for some illustrated books (particularly

Fifty Years

¶ Being a Retrospective Collection of
Novels, Novellas, Tales, Drama, Poetry, and
Reportage and Essays *(Whether Literary,
Musical, Contemplative, Historical, Biographical,
Argumentative, or Gastronomical)*
¶ All Drawn from Volumes Issued during
the Last Half-Century by
ALFRED and BLANCHE KNOPF
Over This Sign and Device

¶ *The Whole Selected,
Assembled, and Edited, with an Introduction
and Sundry Commentaries, by*

Clifton Fadiman

NEW YORK: Alfred · A · Knopf
1965

Clifton Fadiman, ed., *Fifty Years*. Title, device, author and date in red. Alfred A. Knopf, New York, 1965. [X.972/56]

those with illustrations integrated into the text, and most particularly those with colour illustrations) and a few cheap reprints and British editions of American books (or vice versa) photographed from the original setting.

By 1960 the picture had begun to change. Flat-bed letterpress machines, notoriously 'studies in inefficiency' (Wallis), were frustratingly slow, make-ready times were inordinately long (taking up on average 50 per cent of press time), and printers wanting to invest in the future looked askance at the value of type metal out on proof or 'awaiting reprint' and the space it occupied. At the same time, illustrated magazines were thriving, with more and more use of colour; far-sighted book publishers, seeing a similarly growing market for illustrated books, were discouraged by the high cost of halftone blocks and the art paper needed to print them. Offset litho promised the most attractive improvements in all these areas: presses were already at least as fast and make-ready times very short, blocks were eliminated, and plates or film, being almost one-dimensional, took up comparatively little storage space. Printers – particularly those catering to the educational and reference publishing markets with their steady reprints, hitherto printed from stereo- and electro-plates – began to install big aluminium-plate litho presses. To some extent this was an act of faith, since photo-typesetting had not yet proved that it would soon relegate metal type to the private presses; to some extent it was the spur needed to encourage the rapid development of phototypesetting described elsewhere.

The story of mainstream book-printing since the 1960s has therefore been the story of the virtual disappearance of flat-bed letterpress (and collotype), the survival of rotary letterpress for printing mass-market paperbacks, the steady improvement of sheet-fed litho and the rise of web-fed litho. However, two attempts to breathe further life into relief printing deserve mention. The first was the sheet-fed rotary press, printing text and halftones from flexible composition plates and typically adaptable enough either to run as a perfector or to print two colours. The Dawson, Payne & Elliott, for example, could at least equal contemporary litho presses for speed, and offered respectable quality (or better in skilled hands) for text and line work; unfortunately, halftones tended to look starved, and once litho could deliver reliably good halftones there was no future for these presses. The second was the web-fed American Cameron belt press, an enormous machine on whose belt are mounted all the relief single-page plates (either rubber plates made by moulding metal type, or plastic Grace plates made by photo-etch from camera copy) needed to print a book (unless of exceptional length), head to tail and usually four-abreast across the belt. The reel of printed paper is folded as it comes off the press and fed straight to an adhesive-binding unit. Several giant book plants, including R. R. Donnelley in Chicago and Collins in Glasgow, installed Camerons in the 1970s, but without achieving satisfactory quality; the Italian printer Mondadori has had greater success, and retains more than one Cameron, each integrated into a dedicated binding line.

The growth of web offset (litho) in the 1950s and 1960s, particularly in the United States, offered immediate economies in production. The web-fed concept, where paper is delivered to the press from a reel and after printing can be split into ribbons if required, folded and delivered to an integrated binding line, is so flexible that numerous machines have been designed expressly to print one title (such as telephone directories and the *Reader's Digest*). For any other than short-to-medium runs and top-quality work, rotary printing from the web is now the dominant technology in letterpress ('flexography', typically used for paperbacks), litho (for books, newspapers and magazines) and gravure (catalogues and magazines). Some prophets have expressed the belief that within the next few years it will be possible to print even the most demanding art books by web offset. Web presses vary greatly in size, from 'mini-webs' to the Book-o-Matic, which uses plates 1500 × 3080 mm (59 × 118 in.) which have to be carried by several men, and in configuration – four- and five-colour presses are commonplace. Not only are some dedicated to certain printing jobs, but the converse also is true: printers can offer cost reductions to customers who will accept a standard product printed on standard paper, such as the mini-web 'Book Plan' offered in Britain by Biddles. The economies offered by web offset's ability to print, fold and deliver large numbers of pages per pass of the press, and by the avoidance of the cost of cutting the reeled paper into sheets, are thus augmented by the economies achieved by standardization. The fixed 'cut-off' (cylinder circumference) restricts the designer's choice of format; pages may be laid down along or across the web width, but in the latter case the grain of the paper runs at right angles to the spine, so that the bound book handles less well. Despite the huge size of some of these presses, the break-even point above which web-fed offset litho printing becomes cheaper than sheet-fed can in some plants be as low as 3000 copies.

Despite the success of web offset in defining a significant share of the market in book printing, most books other than mass-market paperbacks are still printed by sheet-fed rotary litho. Most book printers are equipped exclusively with these presses, which have developed steadily since 1875, when they were devised by Robert Barclay of London for printing on tinplates; since 1904, when the America printer Ira W. Rubel designed the Potter Press to print on paper; and since 1906, when the first British machine was patented by George Mann. A wide variety of press sizes and one-, two- and four-colour configurations exists; some two-colour presses can be used to perfect a single-colour job, though printing one side of the sheet at a time usually ensures higher quality.

When Allen Lane startled the cosy world of the British book trade in 1935 with his first batch of Penguins, sheet-fed letterpress was the only option: printing flat-bed or rotary from stereos or electros, or flat-bed from type. Their almost instant success (three million Penguins sold in the first year, not to mention the imitations which were not slow to appear) put a considerable strain on the printers. The launch of Pocket Books in the United States in 1939 had the same effect – an effect intensified by the insatiable demand for books, any books, during the Second World War. Penguins had sold so well before the War that Lane was able to secure a relatively generous allocation of paper when the war started, and his printers were obliged to dedicate presses and other plant to his requirements.

It was not until the early 1950s that Strachan & Henshaw and Timson began to manufacture the web-fed rotary flexographic presses that still dominate the market. Originally designed to print from rubber plates moulded from metal type, they have since been adapted successively to print from photopolymer relief plates created by photo-etch from film or camera copy, while more recently some printers have been able to convert them to offset litho or dual purpose. Custom-built for the original (and current) 'A' standard format, 178 × 111 mm (7 × 4⅜ in.), these presses fit eight pages head to head and foot to foot across the web – the grain of the paper therefore running at right angles to the direction of the spine – and deliver 64 perfected pages per cylinder impression off each of two cylinders to in-line folders and an integrated adhesive-binding unit. To put their productivity in perspective: the old sheet-fed presses ran at about 1100 sheets per hour; early web machines at about 15,000 impressions per hour; later versions at about 20,000.

The U.S. printer R. R. Donnelley can make printing plates directly from the database. Not only does this eliminate the cost of making and storing film and one stage of manufacture; by working direct from the database it also gives to the publisher the facility to change the format of a book at will and to the printer the ability to reimpose work instantly in the event of press breakdown. At the time of writing one- and two-colour work can be undertaken; four-colour work is expected to follow shortly. Increasingly, printers will be offering this facility.

Collotype – 'one of the most pleasing and interesting of printing processes' (Williamson) – survives if at all only by its fingertips. The reasons why it has to struggle are easy to find: it is a slow and difficult process requiring constant skilled attention (and therefore expensive); a wide range of tonal contrast in the image may cause extra problems; line images and type lose some sharpness; and the life of the printing plate is extremely short. This is a great shame, as its apparent ability to print in continuous tone (in reality a fine irregular grain) would otherwise make it ideal for reproductions of paintings, photographs and particularly drawings. It is a planographic process, based like lithography on the antipathy of water and greasy ink, and employs a continuous-tone negative for the transfer of the image to the plate.

Photogravure is an intaglio process, originally flat-bed but now universally rotary, in which the scanned image is etched into the surface of a metal plate which is then wrapped around a cylinder. Web-fed gravure, widely used for illustrated magazines, mail-order catalogues and postage stamps, may be described as a medium-quality process best suited to the production of very-long-run and thus low-cost colour work. Sheet-fed gravure is capable of producing excellent rich halftones, but type and line images are likely to suffer from a lack of sharpness. Unfortunately the high cost of plate preparation makes it relatively expensive even for medium runs.

Direct lithography has been in continuous use for book illustrations – and complete illustrated books – for the 200 years of its history. The artist may work on a lithographic stone; on a small plate which the printer transfers to his machine plate once the artist is satisfied with it; or on a sheet of grained transparent plastic (such as Plastocowell, which was introduced in Britain in 1948 by the sadly now defunct firm of W. S. Cowell of Ipswich) which is then exposed to light against the machine plate in a printing-down frame. Any autographic method has two disadvantages for the artist: the need to draw each colour separately, and the need to draw, as it were, back to front. The corresponding gain in sharpness and colour fidelity (since direct lithography has no need of the halftone screen or the standard process colours) is more than adequate compensation.

The pursuit of quality in litho – particularly in the reproduction of photographs – has led to numerous experiments in apparently continuous-tone printing. In fact, the plate has a fine but irregular grain, giving a printed result similar to collotype. Although some impressive results have been achieved, none of these experiments has been successful enough to encourage the widespread adoption of this process.

The other processes used to create images – and in some cases printing surfaces – for illustrations are best regarded as exercises in print-making rather than printing. Wood-engravings, wood-cuts, lino-cuts, etchings, aquatint, pochoir, and copper- and steel-engravings all have their own literature.

Can break a spirit already more than bent.
    The miserable one
Turns the mind's poison into food,—
Its medicine is tears,—its evil good.

III

Therefore, if now I see you seldomer,
    Dear friends, dear *friend*! know that I only fly
      Your looks, because they stir
    Griefs that should sleep, and hopes that cannot die:
The very comfort that they minister
      I scarce can bear, yet I,
      So deeply is the arrow gone,
Should quickly perish if it were withdrawn.

IV

When I return to my cold home, you ask
    Why I am not as I have ever been.
      You spoil me for the task
    Of acting a forced part in life's dull scene,—
    Of wearing on my brow the idle mask
      Of author, great or mean,
    In the world's carnival. I sought
Peace thus, and but in you I found it not.

V

Full half an hour, to-day, I tried my lot
    With various flowers, and every one still said,
      'She loves me—loves me not.'
    And if this meant a vision long since fled—
If it meant fortune, fame, or peace of thought—
      If it meant,—but I dread
    To speak what you may know too well:
Still there was truth in the sad oracle.

62

VI

The crane o'er seas and forests seeks her home;
    No bird so wild but has its quiet nest,
      When it no more would roam;
    The sleepless billows on the ocean's breast
Break like a bursting heart, and die in foam,
      And thus at length find rest:
    Doubtless there is a place of peace
Where *my* weak heart and all its throbs will cease.

VII

I asked her, yesterday, if she believed
    That I had resolution. One who *had*
      Would ne'er have thus relieved
    His heart with words,—but what his judgement bade
Would do, and leave the scorner unrelieved.
      These verses are too sad
    To send to you, but that I know,
Happy yourself, you feel another's woe.

63

P. B. Shelley, *Selected Poems*, wood-engravings by Richard Shirley Smith, designed by John Dreyfus. Cambridge University Press for the Limited Editions Club, New York, 1971.

3. PAPER

Almost all the paper used for books, magazines and newspapers over the last quarter-century has been made from wood pulp. Printing papers made from rags, hemp or esparto grass are now so expensive as to be found only between the covers of privately-printed books and other limited editions – and might have disappeared were it not for the post-war discovery of the pleasures of printing by letterpress on a domestic scale.

The invention and commercial success of wood pulp has been described in ch. III. Unfortunately, the lignin in untreated ('mechanical') wood pulp is excessively acidic: paper made from this pulp therefore contains within itself the seeds of its own destruction. Many millions of items printed on it have yellowed and crumbled to dust within decades of their manufacture. Librarians, archivists and curators see their collections disintegrate before their eyes; a surviving early prospectus of the London and North Eastern Railway of about 1923 or an early Macmillan book-list is more fragile, conceivably of greater rarity, than a fifteenth-century poster of Anton

Koberger or a business report of the Fuggers. Original publications in paperback, including some of Penguin Books' distinguished Pelican list, are likely to become very scarce. One important British publishing house's history of itself, published as recently as 1975, is already yellowing. Very large sums of money which librarians could have spent on acquisitions have had to be diverted to the preservation of their decaying stocks.

'If libraries of the twenty-fifth century are to possess books of the twentieth, as today's possess books of the fifteenth, we must seek out and use papers which will survive in store for hundreds of years' (Williamson). Within the last ten years determined pressure by enlightened publishers and trade associations on both sides of the Atlantic has (it is to be hoped) persuaded printers and publishers to insist on acid-free paper made from exclusively chemically treated wood pulp – paradoxically known as 'wood-free' – for all publications not intended to be ephemeral. Before the totally permanent book can become an everyday reality, however, binders also must switch to acid-free endpapers, boards and cover materials. Another contentious issue in north America concerns the addition of sulphur as a whitener. As this practice is legal in the United States but illegal in Canada (nearly half of whose land-mass is covered in forest), some Canadian publishers have taken to importing U.S. paper.

Cartridge, the strongest paper used for commercial book production, may be coated, as indeed may any other paper. The demand for coated – and therefore smoother – stock has increased greatly in parallel with the rapid growth in litho printing, facilitating as it does the publication of books and magazines with integrated halftone illustrations, though publishing conservatism has ensured that books of plain text printed on uncoated stock, with one or more halftone sections on coated stock, are not yet a thing of the past. While a competent litho house can print halftones well enough on uncoated stock, some coating will undoubtedly enhance them; but glossy so-called 'art' paper, heavily loaded with china clay, is used much less than it was when letterpress was dominant. This is fortunate for future generations of readers, since china clay is acidic whereas its modern substitute, calcium carbonate, is alkaline.

4. BINDING

The vast majority of books that are not paperbacks are hardbacks. That is to say, such variants as loose-leaf books, portfolios and educational card-packs have – like non-print media such as floppy discs, microfiche and compact discs – had remarkably little impact on the traditional printed book. The search for economy has however brought significant changes to traditional binding methods.

To start at the beginning: while web-fed rotary presses customarily deliver folded sections to an in-line binding unit, the folding of flat sheets has been greatly improved by the development of air-powered buckle-folders at the expense of knife folders. The greater flexibility of buckle-folders, which are not limited to folding the sheet in half and then in half again (as was the case with knife folders), allows a sheet to carry many more multiples of four pages than was formerly the case, and this has gone a long way towards eliminating 'oddments'. For example, a book of 324 pages can now be printed as nine sheets each of 36 pages, whereas knife-folding would entail printing it as ten 32s (or five 64s), plus the odd four pages; and these four pages would

I mentioned before that I had a great mind to see the whole island, and that I had travelled up the brook, and so on to where I built my bower, and where I had an opening quite to the sea on the other side of the island. I now resolved to travel quite cross to the sea-shore on that side; so taking my gun, a hatchet, and my dog, and a larger quantity of powder and shot than usual, with two bisket cakes and a great bunch of raisins in my pouch for my store, I began my journey.

107

a vague, muffled, inner sound, as of submerged sword-fish rushing hither and thither through shoals of black-fish. Soon, in a reunited band, and joined by the Spanish seamen, the whites came to the surface, irresistibly driving the negroes toward the stern. But a barricade of casks and sacks, from side to side, had been thrown up by the mainmast. Here the negroes faced about, and though scorning peace or truce, yet fain would have had respite. But, without pause, overlapping the barrier, the unflagging sailors again closed. Exhausted, the blacks now fought in despair. Their red tongues lolled, wolf-like, from their black mouths. But the pale sailors' teeth were set; not a word was spoken; and, in five minutes more, the ship was won.

Nearly a score of the negroes were killed. Exclusive of those by the balls, many were mangled; their wounds – mostly inflicted by the long-edged sealing-spears, resembling those shaven ones of the English at Preston Pans, made by the poled scythes of the Highlanders. On the other side, none were killed, though several were wounded; some severely, including the mate. The surviving negroes were temporarily secured, and the ship, towed back into the harbor at midnight, once more lay anchored.

[104]

Daniel Defoe, *Robinson Crusoe*, illustrated by John Lawrence. Folio Society, London, 1972. [X.989/14110]

Herman Melville, *Benito Cereno*, wood-engravings by Garrick Palmer. W. & J. Mackay, Chatham, Kent, for the Imprint Society, Barre, Mass., 1972.

have to be either printed separately on a small press or (in the case of a long run) ganged up on the large sheet – either way incurring extra costs in paper-cutting and separate folding, sometimes by hand. Avoiding oddments was therefore a rather unrewarding duty for designer, estimator, printer and binder alike. Buckle-folders can fold sections up to 64 pages in length; even longer when folding bible and other thin papers.

Traditional thread-sewing has more or less held its own in the face of competition from adhesive binding and other more recent cost-cutting alternatives, to some extent because early experiences with deciduous adhesive-bound books reinforced the conservatism of librarians and publishers' production departments, and also because well-made sewn books still handle better than any others. Like other binding processes it has achieved economies through automation: hand-operated sewing-machines, where they survive at all, are now mostly relegated to a corner of the room.

Slotted ('burst') binding is a process in which small holes are made in the back of the section at the folding stage, and glue is forced through the holes into the middle of the section. The resultant binding is very strong and being somewhat cheaper is likely to supplant thread sewing; it is already widely used for cased books of all types.

Another cheaper substitute for thread sewing is the technique of thread sealing.

Again slots are cut into the backs, but here short lengths of thread are led through the section and glued in position.

The search for manufacturing economies has persuaded many publishers to save on the cost of sewing by specifying larger sections than the pursuit of quality would suggest, for example 32-page sections where 16-page sections would make for a more satisfactory book.

None of the processes described above entails milling the backs of the sections, unlike unsewn adhesive (so-called 'perfect') binding in which about 3 mm is cut off and the leaf edges roughened the better to accept the applications of (cold or hot) glue which alone hold them together. The first patent for this process was taken out by William Hancock in 1836, but regrettably (since the saving in cost facilitated the publication of many cheap books) his rubber adhesive dried out and the books fell to pieces. The Sheridan Perfect Binder, which used glue in place of rubber, dates from 1911, but it was at least 60 more years before paperbacks could be relied on not to shed their leaves. Before then, unfortunately, the search for manufacturing economies had persuaded some publishers to start issuing hardback books in unsewn bindings: the weight of the boards, or the mechanical force of the joints, or both, caused many such books to self-destruct very quickly. However, modern adhesive-binding techniques are vastly superior, although librarians will never love their products, since they cannot be satisfactorily rebound should they survive long enough to need it. A perennial problem besetting adhesive binding is the reluctance of the adhesive to adhere as firmly to coated, or to printed, paper as to unprinted uncoated stock: this has resulted in the loss of sections or leaves printed with halftone illustrations. The life expectancy of the modern paperback has been extended, and its appearance enhanced, by the lamination of a thin sheet of plastic to the printed cover.

Mention may be made at this point of two modern developments which have proved useful for books intended to lie flat when in use: again the backs are trimmed off, but here the leaves are held together with coils of plastic (the 'comb') or wire ('Wire-O'). These are not intended to be loose-leaf arrangements, but neither process recommends itself for books intended for a long life.

Modern binderies feature production lines which, though reminiscent of a fantasy machine designed by the comic artist W. Heath Robinson, carry the sewn book-block swiftly through the gluing, rounding-and-backing, limp-covering, three-knife-trimming and casing-in processes.

The cost-savings achieved through the technical progress described above, while considerable, have not proved sufficient to encourage publishers in the use of superior binding materials. Quite the opposite, in fact: in Britain particularly the splendid range of bookcloths that was available until about 1970 has literally been decimated in the face of publishers' determination to find further savings by the use of paper-based materials embossed to resemble cloth, the best of which are superior to low-grade cloth but inferior to anything better, while the worst will scuff and tear much like simple paper. Attempts have been made to popularize durable plastic covering materials, but since these cost as much as cloth without either looking or feeling like it they have not generally caught on in what still behaves like a conservative trade when it can afford to.

For perhaps half a century an unjacketted hardback was virtually unthinkable except in some corners of medical and scientific publishing, but the hard-up 1980s saw some erosion of this principle among academic publishers. Realizing that the 90 per cent of the copies of some titles which went straight to libraries would immediately be stripped of their jackets, they resorted instead to one of two compromises, either covering the case with a laminated printed design on paper (a style of binding already familiar from children's and educational books) or, if using cloth, stamping the title on the front board as well as the spine. The latter practice created some difficulties when – as was quite often the case with books with some general appeal – a simultaneous paperback edition was issued: literary editors tended to disdain the drab-looking hardback and overlook the paperback, with the result that some important books were scarcely reviewed.

5. DESIGN

The virtual disappearance of hot-metal typesetting and letterpress printing in the face of the comprehensive success of computer-assisted phototypesetting and litho has brought profound changes to typography and typographic design. What was a connected sequence of interdependent activities carried out under one roof has become a set of discrete functions each of which may be performed anywhere in the world.

Metal type was set by the printer; the choice of printer was based on a number of considerations, among which cost and proximity to the principal market were of necessity more important than the range of typefaces and type sizes available there. Each size of each typeface represented a capital cost, each additional face or size an additional cost (which the job it was bought for at the persuasive request of a customer would probably not recover); so it is not surprising that some competent, even moderately distinguished, book printers offered quite restricted ranges.

Typeface, size, body size and measure all had to be selected before keyboarding for hot-metal setting could begin; and once keyboarding was started they could not be altered. In slug setting, additionally, keyboarding fixed the spacing between characters and words irrevocably; whereas single characters set by Monotype could at least be respaced by hand, and this was occasionally done in 'fine' printing to tighten up the word-spacing. Characters could be assembled in only one size and in only one mode: from left to right, horizontally; and they could not be distorted (by design).

The impression of metal type into the paper is an important element in the character of a letterpress book, complementing as it does not only the feel and colour of the paper but also the design of the type. Any designer who has worked with letterpress will regret the loss of this distinctive attribute; litho when not at its best can be a rather lifeless process, and even at the best of times it is of course inherently and literally flat. Additionally, the facility and relative economy of incorporating halftone illustrations in the text has encouraged the growing use of coated and machine-finished papers at the expense of the rougher antique woves that were once so common. For all these reasons, some of the character seems to have drained out of some typefaces.

Phototypesetting now makes it possible to key the text (or to capture it by optical character recognition) before the book has been designed, anywhere; to compose, slant, condense or expand characters of differing sizes (almost infinitely differing, in some systems) selected from a vast range of typefaces, and incorporate illustrations in the text database, anywhere; to print and bind the book, anywhere again; and finally to redesign it for a new edition without the need to rekey it.

Today's book-designer, then, is liberated from the strait-jacket imposed by three-dimensional metal typography and one printer's limited repertoire of types. Almost anything is now possible (and quite often seen). Despite the proliferation of new type-faces since the advent of phototypesetting, however, there are probably less than three dozen faces suited to everyday bookwork – of which only two or three were designed specifically for phototypesetting, the others having been derived from successful Monotype and Linotype hot-metal designs which were themselves copied from or based on the original designs of such masters as Aldus, Garamond, Granjon, Plantin, Baskerville and Caslon. Most typesetting houses will have most – conceivably all – of this range available, in one version or another.

Piracy of typeface designs has always been a problem, but it attracted significant notice only with the advent of phototypesetting, when inferior copies of proprietary designs were marketed by certain new manufacturers of typesetting equipment under thinly-disguised new names. With the adoption of PostScript for computer-assisted composition, the copying of copyright designs has been widely licensed by their own-ers. For technical reasons at least (principally concerned with the number of units from which each character is built up), and very often for aesthetic reasons as well (such as the relation of the height of the lower-case 'x' to the length of the ascenders and descenders in 'h' and 'j'), no typeface looks identically the same when set on dif-ferent makes or kinds of machine. Since it is no longer possible – perhaps it never was – to think of one particular version of a typeface as the platonic ideal of that de-sign, the book-designer is guided by availability, economy in use, and taste in choos-ing which version to use for each job.

It is now commonplace for the designers of newspapers and magazines to make up complete pages on screen, using a pre-defined grid: once the text is captured and the illustrations have been scanned, these elements can be arranged and manipulated, the type-size altered, the illustrations enlarged, reduced or cropped, until a satisfactory result has been achieved. This way of working has spread to the design of heavily-illustrated books and there is every reason to suppose that, as more authors write their books on computers, and to the extent that publishers learn to make increasing use of computers as editorial tools, it will continue to progress.

Despite a steady flow of technical improvements in all branches of typesetting and printing, progress in the typographic arts is less easy to discern. A number of in-disputably fine books are produced every year, but so are many more dull or feeble designs, while some potentially attractive books are spoilt in the execution (frequently because of the use of cheap but inadequate paper). Inevitably, the prime motivation behind the development of new and improved equipment is economic, and certainly printers and publishers will always seek cost savings; but the secondary motivation is often greater refinement, as in, for example, the range of type-sizes and typefaces available on demand, and greater flexibility in letter-fit and spacing. Yet the design of the great majority of contemporary books is no more adventurous, and the use of space no more refined, than was the case when type was cast in hot metal. Al-though the magisterial 'laws' of book design laid down by Stanley Morison in *First Principles of Typography* are so mild, and so few in number, that they cannot still exert any corrective centrist influence on unorthodoxy (if indeed they ever did), ex-cessive respect for tradition, and the regrettable use of standard designs (as if one book were really just like another, on a production line), have tended to shut out experiment.

EUROPEAN DRAWINGS
1375–1825

Catalogue compiled by
CARA D. DENISON & HELEN B. MULES
with the assistance of
JANE V. SHOAF

1981
The Pierpont Morgan Library
Oxford University Press
NEW YORK · OXFORD · TORONTO

Cara D. Denison & Helen B. Mules, *European Drawings 1375–1825*. The Stinehour Press, Lunenburg, Vermont, for the Pierpont Morgan Library, New York, 1981. [L.45/1086]

The
HISTORY
and
POWER
of
WRITING

HENRI-JEAN MARTIN

Translated by Lydia G. Cochrane

THE UNIVERSITY OF CHICAGO PRESS
Chicago and London

H.-J. Martin, *The History and Power of Writing*. Chicago University Press, 1994. [YC.1994.b.6342]

6. PRINTERS AND PUBLISHERS

The replacing of letterpress by litho and of hot-metal composing by successive photo-typesetters, one generation quickly supplanting the previous one; the consequent un-coupling of keyboarding, composition and printing; the arrival of the 'author's disc'; the need to improve productivity in their binderies with modern equipment; all revealed just how under-capitalized and unprepared for major change were most book-printing plants, of whatever size and irrespective of their ownership. At that time the bigger university presses in Britain and the United States had their own plants, as did such major publishers as Harper, Doubleday, Rand McNally, Collins, Heinemann, Blackie, Dent and Hutchinson, and the great Italian firm of Mondadori. It was very difficult for such large publishers to manage their works as efficiently as the independent printers who were competing for the same business: there were just too many temptations to understate costs, to accept sub-standard work which would have been rejected had it come from a different source, and in hard times to feather-bed the works with third-rate publications and unnecessary reprints. The survivors from this distinguished group of publisher/printers (such as Cambridge and Toronto University Presses, Rand McNally, the American Mathematical Society, Mondadori) had to learn – not least from the bitter experiences of those who did not survive – to derive the greatest possible functional benefit from the relationship while operating financially at arm's length.

Book printing ceased at the University Press, Oxford, in 1989 after over 400 years' continuous history. Since the 1950s Oxford, earlier and to a greater extent than Cambridge, had developed high-volume publishing – of schoolbooks, of English-language learning materials for the fast-growing markets of the Third World, and of popular reference books – and had rebuilt its printing works in the centre of Oxford to meet this demand. Unfortunately it failed to meet it competitively, and – on a black day indeed for lovers of good printing – the University's Press Delegates thought they had no option but to close what had been from time to time one of the world's most distinguished printing houses. The postwar rationalization of the trade has also seen the failure of such celebrated British book-printers as R. & R. Clark, W. S. Cowell and the Curwen Press.

The Glasgow factory of William Collins (now HarperCollins since the takeover by News International in 1989) functioned until the late 1960s solely to manufacture letterpress books for publication under that imprint; no work was accepted from outside the firm. A huge array of Monotypes and Linotypes, of flat-bed and rotary paperback presses, kept pace with the demands of one of the world's largest and most successful publishers; very little work went outside to other printers. The management had to change all this, and did so within 20 years: printing there is now by litho, typesetting is bought in by the publishing departments (who are free to buy manufacturing competitively where they will), and HarperCollins prints and binds for many other customers. As this book goes to press there is news that this plant has been sold.

Collins were not alone in giving up typesetting completely; other printers did the same, or hived it off as a separate 'profit-centre'. The fundamental shake-up in book-manufacturing which uncoupled keyboarding, composition and printing also brought in authors' discs, which reduced the amount of copy to be keyed but still needed de- and re-coding and usually a fair amount of correction (it is difficult enough to write a coherent book, without being obliged to type it perfectly as well). The last 20 years have seen the swift rise of free-standing typesetters, equipped both to key texts and to process authors' discs before delivering camera copy or film in page form ready for platemaking.

At a time of growing economic stringency many academic books have been published only because the author was able to supply it on disc (or on tape from a main-frame computer), thus halving (roughly) the cost of composition, the largest single item in the cost-structure of a short-run book. Early problems of technical incompatibility having been resolved – not to mention those caused by authors recognizing in the challenge of putting their books on disc an Everest that had to be climbed – most publishers now welcome authors' discs and some prefer or even demand them. The printed result should be indistinguishable from a book produced in the traditional way, unless – as is technically feasible – the author has been able to devise and impose its typographical design at his keyboard. Because book-publishers have generally been slow to install the equipment and invest in the training needed to enable their staff to key, edit and design texts on screen, the author who delivers his text on disc can if he insists retain much editorial control of it.

Universities, and therefore university libraries and academic publishing, shared the economic boom of the 1960s: as an example, Cambridge University Press (admittedly enjoying the advantage of publishing in English for a worldwide market) was accustomed to print 2500–3000 copies of a scholarly monograph or 10,000 copies of a paperback university textbook. This permitted unstinting editorial care, individual design and a relatively low selling price. Soon after the end of the boom in about 1969 the Press – unable, in common with most other publishers, to adjust quickly enough to dwindling sales and a sudden need for financial savings – found itself encumbered with a warehouseful of beautifully-produced, moderately-priced books for which there was insufficient demand. Shortly thereafter the Press was saved from bankruptcy only by swift and decisive action, so successfully that its growth, as measured by the number of new titles published each year, never faltered. With well over one thousand new titles each year it is now one of the world's largest publishers.

For decades it was common to extol the value to a publishing house, such as Cambridge, of its backlist, those steady sellers which kept on selling and therefore reprinting. While reprints were advantageous to the publisher (so long as he was not tempted into ordering one too many), the possibility of them was a nuisance to the letterpress printer, who had to decide whether to keep the type standing, and if not whether to make stereotype or electrotype plates which might never be needed. Standing type and plates occupied valuable space as well as locking up working capital. Paradoxically, by the time litho – ideally suited technically to facilitating reprints – had replaced letterpress, the backlist had declined in importance, and it was principally by selling new books efficiently that hardback publishers survived the difficult decades since the end of the 1960s boom. The output of British publishers rose relatively slowly before the Second World War, but increasingly fast after it, as is shown by the following table of new books published (which takes no account of new editions of existing books). Book production during the War was of course severely curtailed by the rationing of paper and other factors.

1905	6817	1955	14192
1915	8499	1965	21045
1925	9977	1975	27247
1935	11410	1985	44174
1945	5826	1995	88718

There are about 675,000 books in print in Britain. Most publishers now assert that all other publishers are over-producing; the rest of the trade is quite certain of it.

The point has long since passed when any library or bookseller can stock more than a fraction of the books in print, or when every book which merits reviews receives any. Indeed, so great and so urgent is the flood of publication of scientific papers in learned journals and conference proceedings that many institutional libraries have had to limit their acquisition of books very severely. The decline in library sales occasioned by over-production and the severe cuts in acquisition funds caused by the worldwide recession have forced academic publishers to cut print-runs by as much as two-thirds when compared to the 1960s. Similar cuts in the funding of education have had a similar effect on schoolbook publishing – offset to some extent for British publishers by the dramatic success (not only in the Third World but also in countries such as Spain, Greece and the United States) of English-language-learning books – a branch of publishing which scarcely existed until the 1960s.

Print runs have tended to be cut in general publishing also, in response to both the recession and also, since the mid 1980s, the equipping of books with bar-codes and retail shops with electronic-point-of-sale systems which provide facilities for far tighter stock control than was previously possible. Each shop and wholesaler so equipped now needs to carry much less reserve stock, and is able to respond quickly and efficiently to the pattern of sales discerned by the system. Publishers are glad to receive this advice from their customers and – rather than fill their warehouses with stock which may never be needed – expect their printers to deliver frequent reprints of successful books, particularly mass-market paperbacks.

The paperback side of the book trade has changed profoundly since this book was first published: most importantly, from a 'horizontal' structure in which various independent hardback houses negotiated the sale of rights to various independent paperback houses, to a 'vertical' structure in which hardback and paperback houses are joined by corporate links. In visual terms, of course, paperback covers have changed almost out of recognition, and paperbacks have shared in the general tendency for books to be larger in format than they were a generation ago (so that the American term pocketbook has become something of a misnomer).

Modern publishing is characterized by its being simultaneously cannibalistic and viviparous: while one publishing house is acquiring another, a third is opening for business. One of the most distinguished firms to have been established before the Second World War, the Cresset Press, was sold after the War, on the death of its founder, to Barrie & Jenkins, who had already acquired several other houses. The Barrie group was then taken over by Hutchinson, already the owners of (it was said) more firms than anyone could for certain tell. Shortly thereafter the by now unwieldy Hutchinson group was sold to London Weekend Television, who presumably hoped to repeat the success of the Granada television and book-publishing empire. This was not to be, and Hutchinson was sold again, to the very successful new firm of Century. The powerful Century Hutchinson empire later came – together with the distinguished group comprising Jonathan Cape, Chatto & Windus and the Bodley Head – under the control of the American Random House. The founders of Century then went on to buy the comparatively ancient firm of J. M. Dent and the postwar phenomenon, Weidenfeld & Nicolson, and create Orion.

At the time of writing other prominent groupings include Groupe de la Cité (with the reference-book publishers Larousse, Chambers of Edinburgh and Harrap); the newspaper groups, International Thomson (owners of Nelson and Routledge) and News International (HarperCollins); the media group Pearson (Penguin – which had already acquired Hamish Hamilton, Michael Joseph and Frederick Warne – Addison-Wesley, Longman, Churchill Livingstone and Pitman); and Reed-Elsevier, once a giant in the world of paper production but now a giant in book publishing with Hamlyn, Octopus, Mitchell Beazley, Butterworth, Methuen, Sinclair-Stevenson and the erstwhile Heinemann group (Secker & Warburg, Ginn and Heinemann itself). Many of the firms mentioned are of postwar foundation, as are such confident newcomers as Dorling Kindersley, Headline (merged with Hodder & Stoughton, already the owners of Edward Arnold) and Bloomsbury.

The ownership of publishing has become increasingly international. This is illustrated not only in the British acquisitions made by the Groupe de la Cité, Random House and International Thomson but also in the practices of publishing abroad invented after the Second World War by Oxford University Press who, having opened in New York in 1896, by 1948 had eight, by 1978 twenty-six branches and offices

Binding on Cotswold

Long ago on a summer day,
Soon as the dew had dried away,
We started out in the morning heat
To cut ten acres of dead-ripe wheat.

Captain, Major and trusty Will
Trundled the binder up the hill:
Three more beauties, nibbling clover,
Waited near for a quick turn over.

Soon the sails were swirling round
Cresting over the rising ground,
Canvasses clattering might and main:
'Daaz that bottom un - jammed again!'

Scissoring hiss of the whetted knives,
Rabbits bolting out for their lives,
Jostling villagers think of the pot
And one-eyed Jim is a deadly shot!

17

Jim Turner, *Cotswold Days*, illustrated by Miriam Macgregor. Whittington Press, Andoversford, Gloucestershire, 1977. [Cup.510.dga.9]

abroad (and had closed twelve others). Much of this activity went to creating and satisfying the flourishing postwar market in English language teaching, a market also served by some of the leading British schoolbook publishers. Cambridge has highly successful branches in the United States and Australia, while Yale and Harvard University Presses, McGraw-Hill, Wiley, Little Brown, Harcourt Brace Jovanovich (owners of Academic Press, W. B. Saunders and Holt Rinehart & Winston) and the Dutch giants Elsevier and Kluwer flourish in Britain. The German house of Bertelsmann owns the American firm Bantam Books and Transworld, one of the most successful British publishers of the 1990s; and Holtzbrinck bought Macmillan in 1995.

Internationalization, increased efficiency on the part of British and American publishers in finding and serving worldwide markets for books in English and the growing dominance of English as the world's first or second language have put severe pressure on publishers in other languages, whose (always finite) markets have been so eroded as to reduce the print-runs for some specialized books to the point where they could cease to be viable. Yet, as we have seen, the print-runs of academic books in English are barely one-third of those obtaining for comparable books in the 1960s. This caution is attributable to constant increases in the cost of money; historically, to constant (and occasionally steep) rises in manufacturing costs; and to a generally clearer perception of true costs (of warehousing, distribution and other overheads as well as production), which has led to annual increases in backlist prices and to new-book prices far in excess of three times those of the 1960s. It is not easy to disentangle the spiral of cause and effect here.

Ever since the pioneering Paul Hamlyn escaped the restrictions of paper-rationing and cut costs by manufacturing complete books in eastern Europe in the 1950s, book production has become increasingly international, a development facilitated by the replacement of letterpress by litho and the operational decoupling of typesetting from keyboarding and printing. These fundamental changes, and the rise of book packagers and the international co-edition that followed them, have encouraged publishers to look abroad for typesetting, the origination of halftone illustrations, and printing and binding as ways to minimize the costs of production. There is today nothing extraordinary in the idea of a book keyed and typeset in Hong Kong, originated in Singapore and printed and bound in Italy for sale worldwide by an Anglo-American publisher; or of another keyed by its author in Germany, typeset in London and printed in Japan for a Californian publisher. Litho printing has made it possible for the publishers participating in an illustrated co-edition each to supply to the printer film of the text in their own language; the various editions are then run off in succession. The considerable economies thus achieved – of machine time and platemaking (with simply a set of new black plates to be made for each edition), of scale in the supply of paper, and particularly of the cost of illustration origination – have enabled innovative publishers and packagers to produce some fine reasonably-priced books which would not have been viable in the print-runs thought appropriate for the likely sales in one language only.

Packaging has developed and flourished since the Second World War in a trade avid for attractive new books at attractive prices. The packager offers ideas to publishers in various countries, in the form of specimen pages and jackets supported by quotations for the complete cost (of manufacturing and delivery to the publisher's warehouse, plus fee or royalty payment to the author and, where necessary, translation fee). The authors are often well-known writers with (ideally) a particular interest in

3

THE CHANCERY TYPES OF ITALY AND FRANCE[1]

WRITTEN WITH A. F. JOHNSON

IN THE ARTICLE entitled 'Towards an Ideal Type', which appeared in the second number of *The fleuron*, the briefest incidental reference was made to certain sloping varieties of the neo-caroline script which developed during the early decades of the fifteenth century. It was explained that this hand was adopted during the pontificate of Nicholas V (1447–51) for the exclusive use of that department of the Vatican chancery which was concerned with the engrossing of papal briefs.

Upon the model of this papal script, or as it became known throughout Italy, the *cancelleresca* or *chancery*, a number of printing types were cut; and it is proposed in this article to offer some account of these and of the printers who used them.

Analysis of the chancery type yields a number of interesting characteristics. First: the upper case is upright as becomes a rigid and somewhat static form. Secondly, the more dynamic lower case, though it generally slopes as becomes a cursive character, is also found upright.[2] The terminations to the lower-case ascenders and descenders vary. They occur as either round kerns (see Fig. 8A) or pointed serifs (see Fig. 8B).

A   *b d   h p   l*

B   *b d   h p   l*

8. The chancery type: round kerns (A) and pointed serifs (B)

There are generally two varieties in g, as shown in Fig. 9.

ʃ   g

9. The chancery type: two forms of g

There can be little doubt that for all its beauty the chancery letter, originally at least, was accounted as the poor relation in the family of letters. As script, it was used for correspondence and for documents of lesser importance; and as type, it was first used for the cheapest class of classical text, and that at the lapse of thirty or more years after the introduction of printing into Italy.

Its debut in typography cannot be rated higher than as a partial success. It is much less elegant than serviceable, and its utility is seriously compromised by the presence of an enormous number of ligatures – Updike has counted no fewer than sixty-five tied letters in the Aldine *Virgil*, 1501, and *Dante*, 1502.

But when the author of *Printing Types* proceeds: 'This Aldine character became the model for all subsequent italic types' (Vol. I, p. 129), we think we detect room for qualification. More exactly, per-

[1] [First published in *The fleuron* III (1924). This essay and 'The italic types of Antonio Blado and Lucovico Arrighi' (see below, pp. 104–13) have now been partly superseded by the work of E. Casamassima (see note 3, below) who has identified several more stages in Arrighi's italic and whose numbering of Arrighi's types is at variance with Morison's.]

[2] This is important when it is realised that in England and U.S.A. the tendency is to regard *italic* as essentially a sloping character.

30

Stanley Morison, *Selected Essays on the History of Letter-forms in Manuscript and Print.* Cambridge University Press, 1981. [2708.p.17]

the subject, which has to be of sufficient general interest in sufficient countries (for the economies of scale essential for attractive pricing to be realized) and to lend itself to fresh popularization and generous, unhackneyed illustration. Britain is the home of packaging: an English-language edition is almost essential if the arithmetic is to work, but the domestic American market is so large that publishers there (with the notable exception of those producing large high-quality art books) seldom need to print extra copies to achieve that.

The first packaging firm was Adprint (whose principal business was as advertising agents) which sold the idea of the 'King Penguin' series, modelled on the Insel-Bücherei, to Penguin Books; the first two titles (*A Book of Roses* and *British Birds*) were published in 1939. Adprint then created several series of well-produced popular books, including 'Britain in Pictures' (Collins, from 1941), the 'New Naturalist Library' (Collins, from 1945) and 'New Excursions into English Poetry' (Muller, 1944–7 – seven verse anthologies, each illustrated with sixteen original lithographs by a different artist; an odd feature of this brave series, considering that the illustrations were specially commissioned, is the preponderance of landscape illustrations that force the reader to turn the page). All these books, and the many others produced by Adprint until 1960, were published only in Britain.

Rainbird McLean established themselves as packagers with two fine folios, both published by Collins in the 1950s: *Great Flower Books* and *Great Bird Books*. (Like the first two 'King Penguins', they reproduced plates from classic out-of-copyright colour books.) The firm then developed an original format for quarto illustrated books, of which the most successful was Nancy Mitford's *The Sun King* (1966); these books were bought in large quantities by leading publishers in many countries. After having played a prominent role in the design and production of the postwar illustrated book, Rainbird McLean was eventually absorbed into the Thomson group. By then they had a number of rivals, and by 1994 there were over 50 book-packagers in Britain alone.

7. CONTEMPORARY FINE PRINTING

Letterpress printing on a small or domestic level flourishes despite the all-but complete conversion of commercial printing to litho, the consequent scarcity of Monotype and Linotype matrices and spare parts, and the disappearance of many of the best papers. In Britain one may point to Will and Sebastian Carter's 60-year-old Rampant Lions Press, John and Rosalind Randle's Whittington Press (publishers and printers of the distinguished typographical annual *Matrix*), Simon Lawrence's Fleece Press, Jonathan Stephenson's Rocket Press, Ian Mortimer's I. M. Imprimit and the University of Wales's Gwasg Gregynog (heirs to the Gregynog Press). In the United States Henry Morris's Bird & Bull, Leonard Baskin's Gehenna, Andrew Hoyem's Arion, Harry Duncan's Cummington, Walter Hamady's Perishable, James and Carolyn Robertson's Yolla Bolly Presses and Alan James Robinson's Press of the Sea Turtle deserve especial mention. Somehow the Stinehour Press, while equipped with phototypesetting and delivering litho printing the equal of any (its inheritance from the late Harold Hugo's Meriden Gravure Company), still offers first-class Monotype setting and letterpress printing.

8. CD-ROM AND THE INTERNET

When the Institute for Historical Research recently announced its new online electronic journal, *Reviews of History*, the project director predicted that within the next ten years 'everything' would be available on the Internet to anyone with access to the Internet on his own, his school's, his employer's, his library's or his local café's computer. Although this begs certain questions as to the definition of 'everything', the willingness of users to engage in sustained reading on screen and the resolution of important issues relating to the cost of access and charges for access to copyright material, it nevertheless seems likely that in some contexts the Internet will succeed (to a greater extent than CD-ROM) in capturing a critical mass of both information and readers. While few commentators are yet predicting the general demise of the printed word, specialized vehicles for it such as reference books and academic journals must be vulnerable to the desertion of enough of their traditional readers to render their resultant print-runs uneconomic. This suggests considerable changes in the lives of publishers, booksellers, librarians, café proprietors (who could find their establishments reverting to their earlier role as information exchanges) and above all printers. Those printers who abandoned typesetting to specialize in putting ink on paper may have to redefine their place in the new information chain.

For over five hundred years printers and publishers have published what they have deemed worth publishing, and many thousand manuscripts have failed to achieve immortalization in print. While inevitably the world has been the poorer for the loss of some of them, it is not unreasonable to believe in the value of this process of enlightened selection and rejection. From now on, 'everything' on the Internet will include whatever any author chooses to publish on it.

Antonio de Guevara, *The Praise and
Happinesse of the Countrie-Life*,
wood-engravings by Reynolds Stone.
Gregynog Press, Montgomeryshire, 1938.
[C.108.b.3]

Conclusion

Rivals of the printed word have sprung up in films, broadcasting and television. The printing press made it possible for millions of people to read the same text at the same moment: radio, television and the cinema enable millions of people to hear the same text spoken and to see the same performance acted at the same moment. To what extent are these new means of mass communication going to affect the future of the printed word?

Certainly the number of people who rely on radio and television for entertainment and instruction is steadily increasing. Yet is the number of readers decreasing? Statistics have proved the contrary. When newspapers took up reviewing books, they did not divert the interest of their readers from newspapers to books. An increase in the sale of books was by no means damaging to the circulation of newspapers: both could thrive very well side by side without their respective spheres overlapping. The same forecast may be ventured as regards the competition for the favour of the public between broadcast and book. Publishers, booksellers, teachers and librarians can testify to the fact that a good many people are currently being induced to read books after having listened to literary broadcasts (such as reviews of new publications, recitals from poetry, or serialized adaptations of novels) or after having watched on the screen the filmed version of a play or story.

The peaceful coexistence of print, sound and vision is to a large extent guaranteed by the psycho-physiological make-up of the human race. The basic division into visual, auditory and motorial types means that the primary and strongest impulses are conveyed through the eyes, the ears and the muscles respectively. These types, though of course not clear-cut, are sufficiently differentiated to ensure the permanence, side by side, of three groups of people who derive the deepest impression and greatest satisfaction from either reading words printed, or listening to words spoken, or watching words acted.

Before the days of Edison and Marconi the printer was the sole distributor of the word by means of large and uniform publication. After the loss of this monopoly the printer will have to reconsider his position, which may be said (with a grain of salt) to have remained unchanged since the time of Gutenberg. However, as this open competition will certainly result in further improving the printer's craft it is all to the good. In the long run the general public, the last judge of the printer's endeavours, will benefit by it, and the printer will continue to hold the proud position of a man – as Gutenberg's epitaph puts it – 'well-deserving of all nations and languages'.

SHS

Select bibliography

(Shortage of space precludes the inclusion of anything remotely like a full bibliography. The privilege of selecting carries with it the obligation to reject: I have regretfully omitted many once standard works, many more specialized and suggestive monographs and – since few of us today are tri-lingual, as S. H. Steinberg was – almost all works not printed in English. JT)

HISTORICAL AND BIOGRAPHICAL

Altick, R. D. *The English Common reader.* Chicago, 1957.

Ball, J. *William Caslon 1693–1766.* Kineton, Warwickshire, 1973.

Barker, N. *Stanley Morison.* London, 1972.

Barker, N. *The Oxford University Press and the Spread of Learning 1478–1978.* Oxford, 1978.

Barr, J. *Officia Bodoni.* London, 1978.

Bennett, H. S. *English Books and Readers: 1475–1557.* Cambridge, 1952.

Bennett, H. S. *English Books and Readers: 1558–1603.* Cambridge, 1965.

Bennett, H. S. *English Books and Readers: 1603–1640.* Cambridge, 1970.

Berry, W. T. & H. E. Poole. *Annals of Printing.* London, 1966.

Black, M. H. *Cambridge University Press, 1584–1984.* Cambridge, 1984.

Blagden, C. *The Stationers' Company: a History 1403–1959.* London, 1960.

Brewer. R. *Eric Gill: the Man who Loved Letters.* London, 1973.

Briggs, A., ed. *Essays in the History of Publishing.* London, 1974.

Carter, H. *A History of the Oxford University Press: vol. 1: to the Year 1780.* Oxford, 1975.

Carter, H. *A View of Early Typography up to about 1600.* Oxford, 1969.

Carter, J. & P. H. Muir, eds. *Printing and the Mind of Man.* London, 1967. 2nd edn, Munich, 1983.

Cave, R. *The Private Press.* 2nd edn, New York & London, 1983.

Clair, C. *A Chronology of Printing.* London, 1969.

Clair, C. *A History of European Printing.* London, 1976.

Clair, C. *A History of Printing in Britain.* London, 1965.

Cross, N. *The Common Writer: Life in Nineteenth-Century Grub Street.* Cambridge, 1985.

Crutchley, B. *Two Men* [Lewis and Morison]. Privately issued, Cambridge, 1968.

Darnton, R. *The Business of Enlightenment.* Cambridge, Mass., & London, 1979.

Darton, F. J. H. *Children's Books in England.* 3rd edn, revised by B. Alderson, Cambridge, 1982.

Day, K., ed. *Book Typography 1815–1965.* London, 1966.

Dent, J. M. *Memoirs.* London, 1928.

De Vinne, T. L. *The Practice of Typography.* 4 vols, New York, 1900–4.

Dreyfus, J. *A History of the Nonesuch Press.* London, 1981.

Dreyfus, J. *Into Print.* London, 1994.

Eisenstein, E. L. *The Printing Press as an Agent of Change.* 2 vols. Cambridge, 1979.

Eisenstein, E. L. *The Printing Revolution in Early Modern Europe.* Cambridge, 1984.

Feather, J. *A History of British Publishing.* London, 1988.

Febvre, L. & H.-J. Martin. *The Coming of the Book: the Impact of Printing, 1450–1800.* London, 1976.

Fifty Penguin Years. London, 1985.

Flower, D. *The Paper-Back.* London, 1959.

Foxon, D. *Pope and the Early 18th-Century Book Trade.* Oxford, 1991.

Franklin, C. *Emery Walker.* Privately issued, Cambridge, 1973.

Franklin, C. *The Private Presses.* 2nd edn, Aldershot, Hampshire, 1991.

Goldschmidt, E. P. *Medieval Texts and their First Appearance in Print.* London, 1943.

Handover, P. M. *Printing in London from 1476 to Modern Times.* London, 1960.

Hare, S., ed. *Penguin Portrait*. London, 1995.

Harrop, D. *A History of the Gregynog Press*. Pinner, Middlesex, 1980.

Hart, H. *Notes on a Century of Typography at the University Press, Oxford, 1693–1794*. Oxford, 1900.

Heilbronner, W. L. *Printing and the Book in 15th-Century England*. Charlottesville, Va., 1967.

Hellinga, L. *Caxton in Focus: the Beginning of Printing in England*. London, 1982.

Hind, A. M. *A History of Engraving and Etching*. London & New York, 1908.

Hirsch, R. *Printing, Selling and Reading*. Wiesbaden, 1967.

Hurlimann, B. *Three Centuries of Children's Books in Europe*. London, 1967.

Hutt, A. *Fournier: the Compleat Typographer*. London, 1972.

Jennett, S. *Pioneers in Printing*. London, 1958.

Johnson, A. F. *Selected Essays on Books and Printing*. Amsterdam & London, 1970.

Johnson, J. & S. Gibson. *Print and Privilege at Oxford to the Year 1700*. Oxford, 1946.

Johnston, P. *Edward Johnston*. 2nd edn, London, 1976.

Jones, H. *Stanley Morison Displayed*. London, 1976.

Joyce, W. L. et al., eds. *Printing and Society in Early America*. Worcester, Mass., 1983.

King, A. H. *Four Hundred Years of Music Printing*. London, 1964.

Levarie, N. *The Art and History of Books, 1968*. Reissued New Castle, De., & London, 1995.

Lewis, J. *Anatomy of Printing*. London, 1970.

Lowry, M. *Nicholas Jenson and the Rise of Venetian Publishing in Renaissance Europe*. Oxford, 1991.

Lowry, M. *The World of Aldus Manutius*. Oxford, 1979.

MacCarthy, F. *Eric Gill*. London, 1989.

McKenzie, D. F. *The Cambridge University Press, 1696–1712*. 2 vols, Cambridge, 1966.

McKitterick, D. *A History of the Cambridge University Press: vol. 1: Printing and the Book Trade in Cambridge, 1534–1698*. Cambridge, 1992.

McLean, R. *Jan Tschichold: Typographer*. London, 1975.

McMurtrie, D. C. *The Book*. London & New York, 1943.

Madison, C. A. *Book Publishing in America*. New York, 1966.

Martin, H.-J. & R. Chartier, eds. *Histoire de l'edition française*. Paris, 1982–6.

Mayor, A. H. *Prints and People*. New York, 1971.

Meggs, P. B. *A History of Graphic Design*. New York & London, 1983.

Moran, J. *Stanley Morison*. London, 1971.

Morison, S. *Four Centuries of Fine Printing*. Folio edn, London, 1924; 4th (8vo) edn, London, 1960.

Morison, S. *John Fell: the University Press and the Fell Types*. Oxford, 1967.

Morison, S. & K. Day. *The Typographic Book 1450–1935*. London, 1963.

Morpurgo, J. E. *Allen Lane: King Penguin*. London, 1979.

Muir, P. *English Children's Books 1600–1900*. London, 1954.

Mumby, F. & I. Norrie. *Publishing and Book-selling*. 5th edn, London, 1974.

Murray, K. M. E. *Caught in the Web of Words: James Murray and the Oxford English Dictionary*. New Haven, Conn., & London, 1977.

Needham, J., ed. *Science and Civilization in China: vol.5, pt 1: Paper and Printing*, by Tsien Tsuen-Hsuin. Cambridge, 1985.

Norrie, I. *Mumby's Publishing and Bookselling in the Twentieth Century*. 6th edn of part of Mumby & Norrie, London, 1982.

Owens, L. T. *J. H. Mason, 1875–1951, Scholar-Printer*. London, 1976

Painter, G. D. *William Caxton*. London, 1976.

Pardoe, J. *John Baskerville of Birmingham*. London, 1975.

Peterson, W. S. *The Kelmscott Press*. Oxford, 1991.

Poole, H. E. & D. W. Krummel, 'Printing and Publishing of Music', in S. Sadie, ed., *The New Grove Dictionary of Music and Musicians*, vol. 15. London, 1980.

Raven, J., et al., eds. *The Practice and Representation of Reading in England*. Cambridge, 1996.

Reed, T. B. *A History of the Old English Letter Foundries*. 2nd edn, London, 1952.

Rivers, I., ed. *Books and their Readers in Eighteenth-Century England*. Leicester & New York, 1982.

Rogers, B. *Report on the Typography of the Cambridge University Press* [1917]. Cambridge, 1950, and London, 1968.

Silver, R. G. *The American Printer 1787–1825*. Charlottesville, Va., 1967.

Simon, H. *Song and Words: a History of the Curwen Press*. London, 1973.

Sutcliffe, P. *The Oxford University Press*. Oxford, 1978.

Sutherland, J. *Victorian Novelists and Publishers*. London, 1976.

Sutherland, J. *Victorian Fiction: Writers, Publishers, Readers*. London, 1995.

Thomas, I. *The History of Printing in America*. 2 vols, Worcester, Mass., 1810; 2nd edn, Albany, N.Y., 1874.

Twyman, M. *Lithography 1800–1850*. Oxford, 1970.

Twyman, M. *Printing 1770–1970*. London, 1970.

Unwin, S. *The Truth about Publishing*. London, 1926; 8th edn, London, 1976.

Voet, L. *The Golden Compasses: a History and Evaluation of ... the Officina Plantiniana at Antwerp*. Amsterdam & London, 1969–72.

Wallis, L. W. *A Concise Chronology of Typesetting Development, 1886–1986*. London, 1988.

Weber, W. *A History of Lithography*. London, 1966.

Wells, J. 'Book Typography in the United States of America', in Day (1966).

Winship, M. *American Literary Publishing in the mid Nineteenth Century*. Cambridge, 1995.

Wright, L. B. *Middle Class Culture in Elizabethan England*. Chapel Hill, N.C., 1935.

Wroth, L. C. *The Colonial Printer*. 2nd edn, Portland, 1938.

ILLUSTRATION AND TYPOGRAPHY

Bland, D. *A History of Book Illustration*. 2nd edn, London & Berkeley, Ca., 1969.

Bland, D. *The Illustration of Books*. 3rd edn, London, 1962.

Blumenthal, J. *Art of the Printed Book 1455–1955*. Boston, Mass., & London, 1973.

Bradshaw, C. *Design*. London, 1964.

Carter, S. *Twentieth Century Type Designers*. 2nd edn, London, 1995.

Dowding, G. *Factors in the Choice of Type Faces*. London, 1957.

Dowding, G. *Finer Points in the Spacing and Arrangement of Type*. 3rd edn, London, 1966.

Ede, C. *The Art of the Book*. London, 1951.

Evans, H. *Newspaper Design* (Book 5 of 'Editing and Design'). London, 1973.

Gill, E. *An Essay on Typography*. London, 1931.

Goudy, F. *Typologia: Studies in Type Design and Type Making*. Berkeley, Ca., 1940.

Gray, N. *Nineteenth Century Ornamented Types and Title Pages*. London, 1937; 2nd edn (*Nineteenth Century Ornamented Typefaces*), London, 1976.

Hammelmann, H. *Book Illustrators in Eighteenth-Century England*. New Haven, Conn., & London, 1975.

Harthan, J. *The Illustrated Book: the Western Tradition*. London, 1981.

Hodnett, E. *Five Centuries of English Book Illustration*. Aldershot, Hampshire, 1988.

Hunnisett, B. *Steel-engraved Book Illustration in England*. London, 1980.

Hutchins, M. *Typographics*. London, 1969.

Jaspert, W. P., W. T. Berry & A. F. Johnson. *The Encyclopaedia of Type Faces*. 4th edn, London, 1970.

Johnson, A. F. *Type Designs*. 3rd edn, London, 1966.

Johnston, E. *Writing and Illuminating, and Lettering*. London, 1907.

Kinross, R. *Modern Typography*. London, 1992.

Lewis, J. *The 20th Century Book*. 2nd edn, London & New York, 1984.

Lewis, J. *Typography*. 2nd edn, London, 1967.

Luna, P. *Understanding Type for Desktop Publishing*. London, 1992.

McGrew, M. *American Metal Typefaces of the Twentieth Century*. 2nd edn, New Castle, De., 1993.

McLean, R. *Modern Book Design*. London, 1958.

McLean, R. *The Thames & Hudson Manual of Typography*. London, 1980.

McLean, R. *Victorian Book Design*. 2nd edn, London, 1972.

Meynell, F. & H. Simon, eds. *A Fleuron Anthology*. London, 1973.

Miles, J. *Design for Desk-top Publishing*. London, 1987.

Miscellany of Type, A [at the Whittington Press]. Andoversford, Gloucestershire, 1990.

Morison, S. *A Tally of Types*. 2nd edn, Cambridge, 1973. Reissued Boston, Mass., & London, 1996.

Morison, S. *First Principles of Typography*. Cambridge, 1951.

Morison, S. *Letter Forms*. London, 1968.

Morison, S. *Selected Essays on the History of Letter-Forms in Manuscript and Print*. 2 vols, Cambridge, 1980.

Morison, S. *The Typographic Arts*. London, 1949.

Morris, W. *The Ideal Book*. California, 1982.

Ray, G. N. *The Art of the French Illustrated Book 1700–1914*. New York, 1986.

Ray, G. N. *The Illustrator and the Book in England from 1790 to 1914*. New York, 1991.

Rice, S. *Book Design*. 2 vols, New York, 1978.

Rogers, B. *Paragraphs on Printing*. New York, 1943.

Rosner, C. *The Growth of the Book Jacket*. London, 1954.

Ryder, J. *Flowers and Flourishes* [Settings of printers' flowers]. London, 1976.

Scholderer, V. *Greek Printing Types 1465–1927*. London, 1927. New edn, Thessalonika, 1995.

Simon, O. *Introduction to Typography*. 2nd edn, London, 1963.

Sutton, J. & A. Bartram. *An Atlas of Typeforms*. London, 1968.

Sutton, J. & A. Bartram. *Typefaces for Books*. London, 1990.

Tracy, W. *Letters of Credit: a View of Type Design*. London, 1986.

Trevitt, J. *Book Design*. Cambridge, 1980.

Tschichold, J. *Asymmetric Typography*. London & Toronto, 1967.

Tschichold, J. *The Form of the Book*. London, 1991.

Tschichold, J. *The New Typography*. Los Angeles, Ca., 1995.

Type for Books [Specimen Monotype settings]. London, 1959.

Updike, D. B. *In the Day's Work*. Cambridge, Mass., 1924.

Updike, D. B. *Printing Types*. Cambridge, Mass., & Oxford, 1922; 2nd edn, 1937.

Van Krimpen, J. *On Designing and Devising Type*. New York, 1957.

Wakeman, G. *Victorian Book Illustration*. Newton Abbot, Devon, 1973.

Warde, B. *The Crystal Goblet*. London, 1955.

Western Type Book, The [Specimen Monotype & Linotype settings]. London, 1960.

Williamson, H. *Methods of Book Design*. Oxford, 1956; 3rd edn, New Haven, Conn., & London, 1983.

Williamson, H. *Photocomposition at the Alden Press, Oxford*. London, 1981.

Wilson, A. *The Design of Books*. New York, 1967.

Zapf, H. *Manuale Typographicum*. Cambridge, Mass., & London, 1970.

TECHNICAL

Bann, D. *The Print Production Handbook*. London, 1985.

Butcher, J. *Copy-editing*. 3rd edn, Cambridge, 1992.

Chicago Manual of Style, The. 14th edn, Chicago, 1993.

Hart's Rules for Compositors and Readers at the University Press, Oxford. 39th edn, Oxford, 1983.

Craig, J. *Production for the Graphic Designer*. New York & London, 1974.

Gaskell, P. *A New Introduction to Bibliography*. Oxford, 1972. Reissued New Castle, DE, & Winchester, Hampshire, 1996.

Hunter, D. *Papermaking*. 2nd edn, New York & London, 1948.

Jennett, S. *The Making of Books*. 5th edn, London, 1973.

Lee, M. *Bookmaking*. 2nd edn, New York, 1979.

Legros, L. A. & J. C. Grant. *Typographical Printing Surfaces*. London, 1916.

Lewis, J. & E. Smith. *The Graphic Reproduction and Photography of Works of Art*. London, 1969.

Moran, J., ed. *Printing in the 20th Century: a Penrose Anthology*. London, 1974.

Moran, J. *Printing Presses*. London, 1973.

Moran, J. *The Composition of Reading Matter*. London, 1965.

Moxon, J. *Mechanick Exercises*. London, 1683; 2nd edn, revised by H. Davis & H. Carter, Oxford, 1962.

Oxford Dictionary for Writers and Editors, The. Oxford, 1981.

Peacock, J. *Book Production*. London, 1989.

Ryder, J. *Printing for Pleasure*. 2nd edn, London, 1976.

Southward, J. [Numerous publications, London, 1871–1911.]

PERIODICALS

Alphabet & Image (1946–8)

Bibliographical Society of America, Papers of the (1904–)

Black Art, The (1962–5)

Book Collector, The (1952–)

Book Collector's Quarterly, The (1930–5)

Book Design and Production (1958–64)

Book Handbook, The (1947–52)

Bookways (1991–5)

Colophon, The (1930–40)

Colophon, The New (1948–50)

Fine Print (1975–90)

Fleuron, The (1923–30)

Gutenberg Jahrbuch, Das (articles are published in their original language) (1926–)

Image (1949–52)

Imprint, The (1913)

Library, The (1889–)

Matrix (1981–)

Monotype Recorder, The (1902–70, 1979–90)

Motif (1958–64, 1968)

Penrose Annual, The (1895–1982)

Print Design and Production (1965–7)

Printing and Graphic Arts (1953–65)

Printing Historical Society, Journal (1965–) and *Bulletin* (1980–)

Publishing History (1977–)

Shipcott, G. *Typographical Periodicals between the Wars*. Oxford, 1980.

Signature (2 series, 1933–54)

Studies in Bibliography (1948–)

Typographica (2 series, 1949–67)

Typography (1936–9)

Typos (1980–2)

Index